Coastal Policing in Eighteenth-Century Britain

Joseph Mallord William Turner, *Martello Towers near Bexhill, Sussex* (c.1808). © Tate, reproduced by permission.

Coastal Policing in Eighteenth-Century Britain

The Riddle of the Coast, c.1660–1822

Hannes Ziegler

THE BOYDELL PRESS

Published in association with

© Hannes Ziegler 2025

All Rights Reserved. Except as permitted under current legislation
no part of this work may be photocopied, stored in a retrieval system,
published, performed in public, adapted, broadcast,
transmitted, recorded or reproduced in any form or by any means,
without the prior permission of the copyright owner

The right of Hannes Ziegler to be identified as the author of this work has been asserted
in accordance with sections 77 and 78 of the Copyright, Designs and Patents Act 1988

First published 2025
The Boydell Press, Woodbridge

ISBN 978 1 83765 192 4

The Boydell Press is an imprint of Boydell & Brewer Ltd
PO Box 9, Woodbridge, Suffolk IP12 3DF, UK
and of Boydell & Brewer Inc.
668 Mt Hope Avenue, Rochester, NY 14620-2731, USA
website: www.boydellandbrewer.com

Our Authorised Representative for product safety in the EU is Easy Access
System Europe – Mustamäe tee 50, 10621 Tallinn,
Estonia, *gpsr.requests@easproject.com*

A CIP catalogue record for this book is available
from the British Library

The publisher has no responsibility for the continued existence or accuracy of URLs for
external or third-party internet websites referred to in this book, and does not guarantee that any content on such websites is, or will remain, accurate or appropriate

In memory of the Barnsbury days,
in gratitude to the Bloomsbury people,
in dedication to my wife and children.

Contents

	List of Tables	viii
	Preface	ix
	Acknowledgements	xii
	List of Abbreviations	xiii
	Introduction	1
1.	Jacobitism, Coastal Policing, and Fiscal-Military Reform (1660–1702)	17
2.	Littoral Space and Coastal Mobility	53
3.	Coastal Administration and the Art of Enforcement	98
4.	The Social History of Coastal Policing	155
5.	Reform, State-Building, and the Birth of the Coastguard (1784–1822)	204
	Conclusion	250
	Bibliography	263
	Index	291

Tables

1	Customs Staff Numbers and Costs (England and Wales), 1685–1714	49
2	Preventive Officers on the English Establishment by County, 1702–1802	65
3	Total Customs Staff on the Irish Management, 1702–1782	77
4	Ireland: Preventive Staff relative to Customs Staff Totals by Port and Region, 1690–1782	79
5	Customs Returns and Management Charges (England and Wales), 1778–1782	152
6	Customs Receipts and Seizures Receipts (England and Wales), 1760–1784	152
7	Preventive Establishments in England and Scotland, 1821	240
8	Preventive Establishments in England, Ireland, Scotland, 1820–1844	241

Preface

The pencil sketch on the second page of this book, drawn by Joseph Mallord William Turner in 1808, pictures a sparse coastal scene. A dimly visible line of Martello towers in the background, stark white cliffs, the shoreline, and a tumultuous towering sky. In the foreground the broken hull of a boat, two figures toiling on the road, and two riders rapidly approaching. What is depicted here is in many ways typical of the southern English coastal scenery of the time. It is what Turner could have seen, and probably did see, on the coast near Bexhill not long after 1800. According to Stopford Brooke, one of its interpreters, the scene portrays "the human life and work and sorrow of the sea-shore". The "two swift-riding men" are identified as officers of the Customs and the Martello towers form a vivid reminder of the Napoleonic threats of invasion during the wars that ended in 1815. To the English observer of the nineteenth century such as Brooke, the scene's deeper meaning is clear: "It is", he claimed, in the "guardianship of England that the sentiment of the subject lies, and the central tower, all in light, fixes our feeling on this thought." The storm, moreover, "defends England also, nor is the great chalk cliff without its aspect of defiance".[1] But if that is so, then wherein lies the sorrow of the sea-shore?

The seacoast occupies a near mythical place in English and British national identity. Incidentally, it also points to a profound contradiction at the heart of this identity. From Shakespeare's "rocky shore" that "beats back the envious siege" to Churchill's call to fighting on the beaches, the seacoast is a strong reference to British insularity. Imageries such as the cliffs of Dover and the south coast scenery famously represented in Turner's coastal sketches and paintings become indicative of political liberty, domestic

---

[1] Stopford Brooke, *Notes on the Liber Studiorum of J.M.W. Turner* (London, 1885), pp. 111–112. On Turner's coastal scenes see also Eric Shanes, *Turner's Rivers, Harbours and Coasts* (London, 1981). On the coast and national identity Christiana Payne, 'Our English Coasts: Defence and National Identity in Nineteenth-Century Britain', in Tricia Cusack (ed.), *Art and Identity at the Water's Edge* (Farnham, 2012), pp. 21–36; Christiana Payne, *Where the Sea Meets the Land: Artists on the Coast in Nineteenth Century Britain* (Bristol, 2007); Charles Hemming, *British Painters of the Coast and Sea. A History and a Gazetteer* (London, 1988).

security, and steadfastness in the face of adversity. It is at the shore that "this precious stone set in a silver sea" becomes manifest, where it spreads its physical embrace of national belonging around "this happy breed of men", and where it erects its "moat defensive" to the outside world.[2] And that is not its only meaning. The coast also represents the vantage point for British ventures into the world. In an equally prominent reference to insularity, Britain's "maritime destiny" and imperial success seemed "compelled by nature". In a time when empire was an inherently coastal undertaking, both the mastery of the sea and the command of the seacoasts were, by the English, understood as naturally afforded characteristics bestowed by their geographical condition. Furthermore, this maritime ingredient of Britain's imperial enterprise, reconciled the traditional ideological opposition between empire and liberty and merged it into a British identity both imperial and free.[3] Whether oriented inland or seaward, therefore, this ideology imagines the coast as a symbol and a reminder of British national characteristics.

If this ideology is Janus-faced rather than one-sided, it still tends to disambiguate the ambiguous. British history, especially in the twenty-first century, provides numerous examples of how an ideology that understands itself as both open to the world and at the same time closed to the world runs into contradictions on the level of practical political policies. Either Britain is an island, or it is not. To have it ideologically both ways complicates the resolution of practical problems, and these problems tend to

---

[2] William Shakespeare, *Richard II*, ed. Anthony B. Dawson, Paul Yachnin (Oxford, 2011), pp. 169–170. On identity and insularity Kathleen Wilson, *The Island Race. Englishness, Empire and Gender in the Eighteenth Century* (London, 2003); Linda Colley, *Britons: Forging the Nation, 1707–1837* (New Haven, 1992); Jodie Matthews, Daniel Travers (eds), *Islands and Britishness: A Global Perspective* (Newcastle, 2012); Ken Lunn, Ann Day, 'Britain as Island. National Identity and the Sea', in Helen Brocklehurst, Robert Phillips (eds), *History, Nationhood and the Question of Britain* (Basingstoke, 2004), pp. 126–136; Alex Law, 'Of Navies and Navels: Britain as a Mental Island', *Geografiska Annaler*, 87 (2005), 267–277; David Cressy, *England's Islands in a Sea of Troubles* (Oxford, 2020); Douglas Hamilton, John McAleer (eds), *Islands and the British Empire in the Age of Sail* (Oxford, 2021).

[3] David Armitage, *The Ideological Origins of the British Empire* (Cambridge, 2000), p. 101. On the coastal nature of early modern empire John R. Gillis, *The Human Shore. Seacoasts in History* (Chicago, 2012), pp. 68–98; Jonathan Scott, *When the Waves Ruled Britannia: Geography and Political Identities, 1500–1800* (Cambridge, 2011); Jerry Bentley, Renate Bridenthal, Kären Wigen (eds), *Seascapes: Maritime Histories, Littoral Cultures, and Transoceanic Exchanges* (Honolulu, 2007); Yogesh Sharma (ed.), *Coastal Histories. Society and Ecology in pre-Modern India* (Delhi, 2010); P. J. Marshall, 'Empire and British Identity: The Maritime Dimension', in David Cannadine (ed.), *The Empire, the Sea, and Global History* (New York, 2007), pp. 41–59.

concern the margins. The coast, for instance, is rarely directly the object of political programmes, but it is where their inherent contradictions typically become manifest. Migrant boats, fishing rows, smuggling, and Customs borders in the Irish Sea are the result of political and economic policies that have no direct concern with the coast, but that materially affect this space on an everyday basis. To emphatically lay claim to the coast as a positive symbol of British national identity is to ignore that the coast is an inherently conflictive and contested space. Such a view also risks losing sight of the fact that many such conflicts are direct corollaries of ideologically driven policies. An ideologically inspired view of the coast, in other words, risks losing sight of a considerable part of its contested history. In the dead angle of such a perspective, it becomes impossible to recognize that many of these everyday conflicts are unresolvable unless their original political determinants are called into question.

To appreciate this ambiguity is to be able to read Turner's sketch from a different angle. What is it, for instance, that motivates the urgency of the only physical movement on the scene, namely the racing of the Customs men towards the spectator? What lies there, that warrants such haste? For Brooke, Turner's Customs officers were merely an "element of romance" in the depiction of English identity.[4] In reality, they were the very meeting point of the contradictions that haunted the coast in Turner's time. What they were after – the smugglers, the spies, and the territorial integrity of the kingdom – was always beyond their grasp, just outside the scene. If the sorrow of the seashore has any visible representation in the scene, it is in the futility of the chase that we find its clearest expression.

[4] Brooke, *Notes*, p. 112.

Acknowledgements

The research for this book started in 2016, several months after the Brexit referendum. Political developments in British and European politics between 2016 and 2022, when the manuscript was finished, indubitably rubbed off on its subject matter and focus to some extent. But it is not intended as a political commentary. The research was conducted at the German Historical Institute in London and was financed by the Max Weber Foundation. I am extremely grateful for the unique opportunity to do so, as I am for the assistance, help, and collegiality of the staff at 11 Bloomsbury Square over the years.

Many colleagues and friends have contributed to the project, and it is impossible to name them all. For their comments and their advice, both great and small, I am grateful to Ronald G. Asch, Jonathan Barry, Tobias Becker, Felix Brahm, Arndt Brendecke, Stephan Bruhn, Mirjam Brusius, Annette C. Cremer, Dagmar Freist, Stefanie Freyer, David Scott Gehring, Andreas Gestrich, Paul Grimm, Daniela Hacke, Kilian Harrer, Mark Hengerer, Christina von Hodenberg, Bernhard Hollick, Vitus Huber, Mark Knights, Paola Molino, Markus Mößlang, Franziska Neumann, Felix Römer, Cornelia Linde, Matthias Pohlig, Jenny Pleinen, Rachel Renault, Michael Schaich, Sébastien Schick, Falko Schnicke, Indra Sengupta, Sina Steglich, Roland Wenzlhuemer, Andrea Wiegeshoff, and Peter Wilson. I am especially grateful to María Ángeles Martín Romera, who has encouraged the project throughout. I would also like to thank the anonymous reviewers for their incisive comments on the initial manuscript. Finally, my thanks go to the editors of the series at Boydell & Brewer for welcoming the manuscript and to Elizabeth McDonald for seeing it into press. Any errors or shortcomings remain obviously my own. The book is dedicated to my wife and my children: their regular calling me back to the present was as non-negotiable as it was necessary.

Abbreviations

Add. MS	Additional Manuscripts
Ashworth, *Customs*	Ashworth, William, *Customs and Excise: Trade, Production, and Consumption in England 1640–1845* (Oxford, 2003)
BL	British Library, London
CSPD	Calendar of State Papers Domestic (see bibliography for full details)
CTB	William A. Shaw, F. H. Slingsby (ed.), *Calendar of Treasury Books, 1660–1718*, 32 vols (London, 1904–1962)
CUL Ch(H)	Cambridge University Library, Cholmondeley (Houghton) Papers
Eighteenth Century Documents	Arthur Lyon Cross (ed.), *Eighteenth Century Documents Relating to the Royal Forests, the Sheriffs and Smuggling* (London, 1928)
EHR	*The English Historical Review*
ESRO	East Sussex Record Office
Finch	Historical Manuscripts Commission, *Report on the Manuscripts of the Late Allan George Finch Esq.*, 5 vols (London, 1913–2004)
'First Report'	'First report from the committee, appointed to enquire into the illicit practices used in defrauding the revenue (24 Dec. 1783)'. Repr. in Sheila Lambert (ed.), *House of Commons Sessional Papers of the Eighteenth Century 38* (Wilmington 1975), pp. 215–278
GCA	Glasgow City Archive
HJ	*The Historical Journal*
Hoon, *Organization*	Hoon, Elizabeth, *The Organization of the English Customs System 1696–1786* (Newton Abbot, 1938, repr. 1968)

JBS	*Journal of British Studies*
JHC	Journals of the House of Commons (see bibliography for full details)
NMM	National Maritime Museum, Greenwich
NRS	National Records of Scotland, Edinburgh
'Third Report'	'Third report from the committee, appointed to enquire into the illicit practices used in defrauding the revenue (23 March 1784)'. Reprinted in Sheila Lambert (ed.), *House of Commons Sessional Papers of the Eighteenth Century 38* (Wilmington, 1975), pp. 333–389
SHR	*The Scottish Historical Review*
TNA	The National Archives, Kew
WSRO	West Sussex Record Office

Introduction

This is a study of coastal administration and coastal policing in eighteenth-century Britain. Its argument is twofold: with the rise of the British fiscal-military state during the seventeenth century, the political significance of the coast changed dramatically. Driven by economic and political concerns, the coast became, for the first time, a politically distinct space complete with designated legislation and unique bureaucratic structures. The study shows both why and in response to what circumstances the necessity for coastal enforcement first arose, and how this political interest in coastal policies fluctuated in relation to political events and economic policies across the century. In mapping these fluctuations the book argues, secondly, that satisfactory solutions to the problem of coastal enforcement remained forever elusive. Endless debates could not solve the political riddle that the coast presented, namely that the apparent ineffectiveness of coastal policies was a result, not of bureaucratic failures or the criminal ingenuity of the smuggler, but of the inherent contradictions of the fiscal-military rationale itself. This failure was twofold: an exclusively fiscal focus on coastal enforcement fell forever short of its administrative complexity. And economic policies of protectionism combined with political interventionism in imperial and European affairs ensured both the necessity for stricter coastal policing and rendered its execution more difficult. Taken together, these arguments aim to bring the well-established conceptual findings about the ambiguity of the coast to bear on the domestic setting. By placing the political awareness of the coast and the instruments of coastal administration into the context of the eighteenth-century British state, the study exposes important limitations of the fiscal-military state, ultimately arguing that it was precisely on the domestic coasts that the process of state-building remained, in many ways, inconclusive. These arguments are developed by an in-depth analysis of the British Customs and, in particular, its previously unexplored preventive, that is its coastal branch. The main focus is on England and Wales while also integrating the Irish, the Manx and the Scottish case.

Coastal Histories

The history of coastal administration is deeply embedded in narratives that are not its own. Whether this is the history of fiscal policies and the Customs bureaucracy, criminal history and smuggling, or specific aspects of military, naval, or maritime history, coastal policing is seldom a subject in its own right. Its history, therefore, currently only exists as a series of glimpses and side glances. Fortunately, the historical study of the coast has, of late, developed into a field of its own, both thematically and conceptually. However, political aspects of bureaucracy, surveillance, and control are notable for their almost complete absence in this field. To some extent, this can be explained by the genesis of this "new coastal history".[1]

The seaside and the beach have, for the better part of the twentieth century, remained confined to the margins of academic research. Cultural practices of sea-bathing, the interest in the natural history of the shore expressed via fossil collections, and the British development of the seaside resort from the eighteenth century onwards have mainly received attention in more popular varieties of historical writing as well as some specialised consideration in the fields of leisure history, the history of science, and urban history.[2] These were seen as specific cultural practices in the context of narratives whose interest in the seacoast as a space was coincidental rather than conceptually focused. Another species of coastal themes – fishing and wrecking, smuggling and privateering – have, in the meantime, traditionally been studied in the context of maritime history proper, which, until recently, has not felt the need to consider the coast as a space of its own.[3] Wherever there was a more conceptual interest in the

---

[1] David Worthington (ed.), *The New Coastal History: Cultural and Environmental Perspectives from Scotland and Beyond* (London, 2017). For a recent overview see Hannes Ziegler, 'Cultures of the Edge? The Place of the Coast in Maritime Historiographies of Britain', *German Historical Institute London Bulletin*, 40 (2018), 68–90.

[2] See J. K. Walton, *The English Seaside Resort: A Social History 1750–1914* (Leicester, 1983); Peter Borsay, *A History of Leisure: the British Experience since 1500* (Basingstoke, 2006); Peter Borsay, John K. Walton (eds), *Resorts and Ports. European Seaside Towns since 1700* (Bristol, 2011); John K. Walton, 'Coastal resorts and cultural Exchange in Europe, 1780–1870', in Peter Borsay, Jan Hein Furnée (eds), *Leisure Cultures in Urban Europa, c.1700–1870. A Transnational Perspective* (Manchester, 2016), pp. 260–277; David Gange, *The Frayed Atlantic Edge* (London, 2020).

[3] For instance, Philip Payton, Alston Kennerley, Helen Doe (eds), *The Maritime History of Cornwall* (Exeter, 2014); Cathryn Pearce, *Cornish Wrecking, 1700–1860: Reality and Popular Myth* (Woodbridge, 2010); Stephen Fisher, *Studies in British Privateering, Trading Enterprise and Seamen's Welfare, 1775–1900* (Exeter, 1987); Geoffrey Morley, *The Smuggling War: The Government's Fight against Smuggling in the 18th and 19th Centuries* (Stroud, 1994).

coast as such, this has come rather from the fields of art history and literary studies.[4] In a double sense, therefore, the subtitle of Alain Corbin's monograph, first published in French in 1988, was apt: *The Discovery of the Seaside* was indeed a European cultural process spanning the decades between 1750 and 1840, but it also prompted its discovery in academic fields since the 1990s.[5] Written, as it was, in the eclectic style of the cultural historian, Corbin combined the existing strands of interest in the coast into a single narrative of a gradual process of re-evaluation: from a dark place of danger and fear, the coast gradually emerged as an emphatically positive space in the European mind, as a place of leisure and recreation, and as a playing field for new cultural and social practices.

This cultural historical narrative developed by Corbin was reinforced, in approximately the same period, by three further strands of research that started to develop an interest in coastal themes. Much like its mother disciplines in the natural sciences, environmental history gained an interest in the coast as a space of diversity and a zone of historically shaped ways of interaction between humans and nature not typically found in other habitats. The biological description of the coast as an ecotone, that is, a zone of transition between distinct biological communities, also held true, environmental historians realised, in a social and economic sense, and made the coast worth studying for its own sake.[6] A similar realisation came from the spheres of social and economic history. Gérard Le Bouëdec, in particular, recognised the economic activities of premodern littoral communities as a specifically coastal "pluriactivité", that is a way of life and a form of subsistence inherently tied to the natural and seasonal conditions

---

[4] To name but the most recent examples: Gillian Mary Hanson, *Riverbank and Seashore in Nineteenth and Twentieth Century British Literature* (Jefferson, 2006); Christoph Singer, *Sea Change: The Shore from Shakespeare to Banville* (Leiden, 2014); Nicholas Allen, Nick Groom, Jos Smith (eds), *Coastal Works: Culture of the Atlantic Edge* (Oxford, 2017); Nicholas Allen, *Ireland, Literature and the Coast: Seatangled* (Oxford, 2021); Tricia Cusack (ed.), *Art and Identity at the Water's Edge* (Farnham, 2012); Christiana Payne, *Where the Sea Meets the Land: Artists on the Coast in Nineteenth Century Britain* (Bristol, 2007).

[5] Alain Corbin, *The Lure of the Sea. The Discovery of the Seaside in the Western World, 1750–1840* (Berkeley, 1994).

[6] Eric Soothill, Michael J. Thomas, *The Natural History of Britain's Coasts* (London, 1987); Environment Agency, *The State of the Environment of England and Wales: Coasts* (London, 1999); Heather Viles, Tom Spencer, *Coastal Problems* (London, 1995); Basil B. Cracknell, *Outrageous Waves: Global Warming and Coastal Change in Britain through Two Thousand Years* (Chichester, 2005); John Hassan, *The Seaside, Health and Environment in England and Wales since 1800* (Aldershot, 2003); John Gillis, Franziska Torma (eds), *Fluid Frontiers: New Currents in Marine Environmental History* (Cambridge, 2015).

afforded by coastal life.[7] Finally, the inherently coastal character of early modern imperialism and exploration has also led global and imperial historians and ethnographers to realise that the beach must be considered a space of high symbolic and cultural significance. As a conceptual approach to early exploration, Greg Denning's beaches of encounter have remained influential in global and imperial history ever since.[8] The generally renewed interest in maritime history in recent years, moreover, has helped keep watery topics more broadly at the centre of attention.[9]

Given this background, it is little surprising that the "new coastal history", insofar as it can be considered an established sub-field, remains slanted towards a specific set of questions. Environmental problems and themes combine with questions of global history and the study of cultural practices.[10] Conceptually, however, its outlook is often vague. Whereas its assessment of coastal space as profoundly ambivalent and liminal – in the words of Isaac Land, "messy, intermediate places" – is reminiscent of the conceptual ideas of the more established sub-field of island studies, no set of conceptual assumptions specific to coastal settings has so far been established.[11] In this respect, it is simply not sufficient to claim that scores of historians are undertaking coastal history without their realising they are doing so.[12] Similarly, John Gillis' contention of the existence of historically specific "edge species" is as enticing as it is vague, seeing

---

[7] Gérard Le Bouëdec, 'La pluriactivité dans les sociétés littorales XVIIe–XIXe siècle', Annales de Bretagne et des Pays de l'Ouest, 109 (2002), 61–90.

[8] Greg Dening, 'Writing, Rewriting the Beach: An Essay', Rethinking History, 2 (1998), 143–172. See also Greg Dening, Islands and Beaches: Discourse on a silent land, Marquesas, 1774–1880 (Carlton, 1980); Greg Dening, Beach Crossings: Voyaging Across Times, Cultures and Self (Philadelphia, 2004).

[9] For instance, Maria Fusaro, Amélia Polónia (eds), Maritime History as Global History (St. John's, 2010); Glen O`Hara, '"The Sea is Swinging into View": Modern British Maritime History in a Globalised World', EHR, 124 (2009), 1109–1134; Alison Bashford, 'Terraqueous Histories', HJ, 60 (2017), 253–272.

[10] See the contributions in Worthington, New Coastal History; Sharma, Coastal Histories.

[11] Isaac Land, 'Tidal Waves: The New Coastal History', Journal of Social History, 40 (2007), 731–743. There is considerable overlap between this approach and island studies. "Islands", Sue Farran contends, "are defined by their coasts". Sue Farran, 'The Coastal Zone of Islands: Comparative Reflections from the North and South', Island Studies Journal, 1 (2006), 55–80. For an introduction, see John Gillis, Islands of the Mind: How the Human Imagination Created the Atlantic World (Basingstoke, 2004); Rod Edmond, Vanessa Smith (eds), Islands in History and Representation (London, 2003).

[12] David Worthington, 'Introducing the New Coastal History: Cultural and Environmental Perspectives from Scotland and Beyond', in David Worthington (ed.), The New Coastal History. Cultural and Environmental Perspectives from Scotland and Beyond (London, 2017), pp. 3–30, at p. 5.

that his arguments are, to date, a number of theoretical assertions rather than empirically founded claims.[13] More convincingly, Michael Pearson has spoken of the unique economic and cultural features of "littoral society", but his assertions, too, remain largely unproved.[14] As an empirical study of the socio-economic uniqueness of littoral communities, it is Le Bouëdec's work that still provides the best assumptions about the nature of premodern coastal life.[15] His work also stands for perhaps the most essential of contentions regarding the coast, namely that it warrants specific attention in its own right and that doing so affords new perspectives on established themes and questions. To date, the range of such themes still remains limited. At the same time, the conceptual questions of coastal history are well suited to expanding it.

In this current state of the field, the present study can be understood as an intervention both thematically and conceptually. If one is to understand the ambiguities and dynamics of the British coast in the eighteenth century, both in its own right and as a precursor to contemporary debates, it is not enough to focus on cultural practices alone, illuminating as these are. The discovery of the beach is only part of the story. From at least the last decade of the seventeenth century, the British coasts became an area of intense and increasing state activity in political, economic, and military terms. Coastal surveillance, and the control of coastal mobility, became integral to the eighteenth-century British state. This requires explanation and contextualisation alongside the established narrative of the discovery of the coast as a space of leisure and recreation. In this thematic sense, the present study can be understood as a corrective.

[13] John Gillis, *The Human Shore: Seacoasts in History* (Chicago/London, 2012).
[14] M. N. Pearson, 'Littoral Society: The Case for the Coast', *The Great Circle*, 7 (1985), 1–8; M. N. Pearson, 'Littoral Society: The Concept and the Problems', *Journal of World History*, 17 (2006), 353–373. See also Michael Pearson (ed.), *The World of the Indian Ocean, 1500–1800: Studies in Economic, Social and Cultural History* (Aldershot, 2005).
[15] Gérard Le Bouëdec, *Activités maritimes et sociétés littorales de l'Europe atlantique, 1690–1790* (Paris, 1997); Christophe Cérino, Aliette Geistdoerfer, Gérard Le Bouëdec, François Ploux (eds), *Entre terre et mer: Sociétés littorales et pluriactivités (XVe–XXe siècle)* (Rennes, 2004); Graeme J. Milne, *People, Place and Power on the Nineteenth Century Waterfront* (Basingstoke, 2016); Frédérique Laget, Philippe Josserand, Brice Rabot (eds), *Entre horizons terrestres et marins: Sociétés, campagnes et littoraux de l'Ouest atlantique* (Rennes, 2017); Andrew Lipman, *The Saltwater Frontier: Indians and the Contest for the American Coast* (New Haven, 2015); Christopher L. Pastore, *Between Land and Sea: The Atlantic Coast and the Transformation of New England* (Cambridge, MA, 2014); David Worthington 'Ferries in the Firthlands: Communications, Society and Culture along a Northern Scottish Rural Coast, c. 1600 to c. 1809', *Rural History*, 27 (2016), 129–148.

On a conceptual level, this necessitates an acknowledgement of coastal space as an area of state activity, and of the status of coastal space as political. The key to this, it is argued here, is to extend the established assumption of the coast as a liminal space into the political arena. As earlier research into borders, frontiers, and islands has shown, these liminal spaces are both marginal and central from the perspective of the state.[16] By definition, they are geographically off-centre and thus more difficult to control. Geographical limits, in this sense, also represent limits of state authority. At the same time, borders are zones of transition, and their permeability makes them more imperative to control. In that sense, they pose a threat to state authority. The situation of the borders between Scotland and England is a case in point: comparably marginal to the kingdom in its entirety, the assertion of state authority was both problematic and vital to the English state.[17] Arguably, this problem is intensified in the case of liquid borders. Whereas the borderlands were recognised in their political instability for centuries, the coast only became a matter of sustained political debate in the late seventeenth century. Unlike in the borders, however, the threats to state authority posed by the seacoasts were more varied, more vague, and more sustained. To explore the nature of these tensions, and the ways that state authority was to be imposed on a liminal space fraught with ambiguities, is where the present study aims to contribute to the theme of coastal history in a conceptual way. To rephrase these interventions: what is the *political* significance of the coast in the context of British history in the eighteenth century? And what does the combined focus on the seacoast and state authority contribute to the conceptual context of the "new coastal history"?

The contention, which also happens to be one of the key arguments of the present study, that it was only around the turn of the eighteenth century that the coast became a politically distinct space and an area of intense state activity, may well raise some eyebrows and it does indeed require some qualification. The English and British coasts had always, to

---

[16] Thomas H. Wilson, Hastings Donnan (eds), *A Companion to Border Studies* (London, 2012); Paul Readman, Cynthia Radding, Chad Bryant (eds), *Borderlands in World History, 1700–1914* (Basingstoke, 2014); David Newman, 'On Borders and Power: A Theoretical Framework', *Journal of Borderland Studies*, 18 (2003), 13–25.

[17] Catherine Ferguson, 'Law and Order on the Anglo-Scottish Border 1603–1707' (Diss., St Andrews, 1981); Mark P. Bruce, Katherine H. Terrell (eds), *The Anglo-Scottish Border and the Shaping of Identity, 1300–1600* (London, 2012); Jenna M Schultz, *National Identity and the Anglo-Scottish Borderlands, 1552–1652* (Woodbridge, 2019). For a contemporary perspective, see Keith Shaw, 'Bringing the Anglo-Scottish Border "Back in": Reassessing Cross-Border Relations in the Context of Greater Scottish Autonomy', *Journal of Borderlands Studies*, 33 (2018), 1–18.

some extent, been areas of state activity. This is perhaps particularly true for the sixteenth century, when foreign invasion was, at times, a very credible scenario. Smuggling, too, was not a new development of the 1700s, nor were fishing disputes and acts of piracy along the Channel coasts.[18] However, neither Henry VIII's nor Elizabeth's south coast fortification plans far outlived the original scares in which they originated; David Cressy has, in this context and for the period up to the mid-seventeenth century, even spoken of "familiar cycles of urgency and neglect".[19] Smuggling and piracy notwithstanding, Customs procedures were often left in sundry hands in the sixteenth century and farmed out to contractors for the better part of the seventeenth. As research by Elton and Beresford has illustrated, for instance, Customs enforcement in the sixteenth century relied on private individuals to no small extent.[20] This chimes with findings from the administrative history of the pre-eighteenth-century Customs: proper book-keeping regularly fell into complete neglect during the sixteenth century for large parts of the outport administration and was entirely out of reach of central administration during periods of Customs farms, leading Elizabeth Hoon to conclude that "only occasionally (...) did crown officers have complete supervision of the collection."[21] Even when they did, however, officeholding was marked by "amateurism", whereas revenue collection was "rather informal" and "there was no overall central administration to ensure a uniform system of control".[22] Perhaps most distinct is the difference where it concerns the Customs administration outside the precincts of the ports: before the 1690s, it was quite simply non-existent, which is to say that the coast (rather than the ports) was virtually unguarded except during periods

---

[18] See, for instance, B. M. Morley, *Henry VIII and the Development of Coastal Defence* (London, 1976); Ann Coats, Alan Lemmers, 'Dutch and English Dockyards and Coastal Defence, 1652–89', in: David Ormrod, Gijs Rommelse (eds), *War, Trade and the State. Anglo-Dutch Conflict, 1652–89* (Woodbridge, 2020), pp. 137–178; John C. Appleby, 'English Privateering during the Spanish and French Wars, 1625–1630' (PhD thesis, University of Hull, 1983); Evan T. Jones, *Inside the Illicit Economy: Reconstructing the Smugglers' Trade of Sixteenth Century Bristol* (London, 2012).

[19] David Cressy, *England's Islands in a Sea of Troubles* (Oxford, 2020), p. 136.

[20] Geoffrey Elton, 'Informing for Profit: A Sidelight on Tudor Methods of Law-Enforcement', *Cambridge Historical Journal*, XI/2 (1954), 149–167; Maurice W. Beresford, 'The Common Informer, the Penal Statutes and Economic Regulation', *The Economic History Review*, 10/2 (1957), 221–238. See also Jones, *Inside the Illicit Economy*.

[21] Hoon, *Organization*, p. 6.

[22] Edward Carson, *The Ancient and Rightful Customs: A History of the English Customs Service* (London, 1972), p. 24; Graham Smith, *Something to Declare: 1000 Years of Customs and Excise* (London, 1980), p. 7.

of alarm; until the end of the seventeenth century at the earliest, it was not subject to regular and centralized administrative control.

Along with this absence of direct governmental oversight over coastal matters, coastal space as such – and unlike individual coastal matters such as fishing, wrecking and other problems – was not subject to any targeted legislative measures either by the Crown or parliament. As William Masterson once concluded in his study of jurisdictions of the coast, the legal novelties of the eighteenth century were in this regard in fact to be considered rather "drastic", whereas there was, in contrast, "nothing novel or unusual" in the way that parliamentary legislation targeted smuggling as late as 1699; this type of legislation had, by then, "not assumed a very definite form" and did not, for instance, aim to delineate any kind of specific legal coastal space.[23] The coast as a legally and politically distinct space, in other words, did not yet exist. Much like the geographic and military frontier of the Channel, it had to be invented in the eighteenth century.[24] There is, therefore, a new quality to such activity from the 1690s forward and it clearly marks a departure from earlier forms of coastal state activity. Essentially irregular and spasmodic interventions made way, by the 1690s at the latest, for permanent, regularly financed and bureaucratically organised attention to coastal matters with clear political and legislative efforts at defining this space.

The Customs and the Fiscal-Military State

Any discussion of state authority in a spatial dimension is directly connected with conceptual discussions about state-building, whether in the British context or elsewhere. How, and to what extent, authority was enforced, even enforceable, beyond the immediate sphere of Whitehall has been the subject of intense debate in the past decades.[25] Curiously,

---

[23] William E. Masterson, *Jurisdiction in Marginal Seas with Special Reference to Smuggling* (New York 1929), pp. 4–5.
[24] Morieux, *The Channel*.
[25] Simon Devereaux, 'The Historiography of the English State during "the Long Eighteenth Century": Part I – Decentralized Perspectives', *History Compass*, 7 (2009), 742–764; Simon Devereaux, 'The Historiography of the English State During "The Long Eighteenth Century". Part II – Fiscal-Military and Nationalist Perspectives', *History Compass*, 8 (2010), 843–865. See also Aaron Graham, Patrick Walsh, 'Introduction', in Aaron Graham, Patrick Walsh (eds), *The British Fiscal-Military States, 1660–c.1783* (London, 2016), pp. 1–26; Philip Harling, *The Modern British State: An Historical Introduction* (Oxford, 2001). Aiming to cover, as it does, an entire century, the introduction cannot do justice to the individual political contexts of British politics

the administration of the Customs, that is, the very agent charged with enforcing authority on the coastal margins, often sits at the heart of such debates about state-building, without any discussion of how the presence of Customs officers on the coasts reflects on the matter of state authority.[26] The crucial question here is obviously what is meant by state-building.[27] In the British case, there are at least two narratives, without there necessarily being an unequivocal distinction. In one strand of research, the British state tends to be studied in terms of its capacity to raise taxes and enforce economic regulations. The ultimate yardstick of how powerful the state was is, in this reading, its ability to wage war and to build and sustain an economic machinery capable of providing the means for it. In John Brewer's rendering, this is the idea of the fiscal-military state.[28] In a second

falling into this larger timespan. Where such discussion is necessary both in terms of context and argument, it will be introduced in subsequent chapters in the relevant places. The introduction, therefore, focuses on conceptual issues of state-building rather than individual, specific narratives of British politics in the period.

[26] On the Customs' role in state-building Michael Braddick, *The Nerves of State: Taxation and the Financing of the English State, 1558–1714* (Manchester, 1996); Ashworth, *Customs*.

[27] See, for instance, Thomas Ertman, 'The Sinews of Power and European State-Building Theory', in Lawrence Stone (ed.), *An Imperial State at War: Britain from 1689–1815* (London, 1994), pp. 33–51; John Brewer, 'The Eighteenth-Century British State: Contexts and Issues', in Lawrence Stone (ed.), *An Imperial State at War: Britain from 1689–1815* (London, 1994), pp. 52–71; Michael Braddick, 'The Early Modern English State and the Question of Differentiation from 1550 to 1700', *Comparative Studies in Society and History*, 38 (1996), 92–111; Robin Ganev, 'Britain's Fiscal-Military State in the Eighteenth Century: Recent Trends in Historiography', *History Compass*, 22 (2024). Recent debates beyond Britain in Stefan Brakensiek, Heide Wunder (eds), *Ergebene Diener ihrer Herren? Herrschaftsvermittlung im alten Europa* (Cologne, 2005); Ronald G. Asch and Dagmar Freist (eds), *Staatsbildung als kultureller Prozess: Strukturwandel und Legitimation von Herrschaft in der Frühen Neuzeit* (Cologne, 2005); Wim Blockmans, Daniel Schläppi, André Holenstein, Jon Mathieu (eds), *Empowering Interactions: Political Cultures and the Emergence of the State in Europe 1300–1900* (Farnham, 2009); Stefan Brakensiek, 'New Perspectives on State Building and the Implementation of Rulership in Early Modern European Monarchies', in Antje Flüchter, Susan Richter (eds), *Structures on the Move: Technologies of Governance in Transcultural Encounters* (Berlin, 2012), pp. 30–41; Héloïse Hermant (ed.), *Le pouvoir contourné: infléchir et subvertir l'autorité à l'âge moderne* (Paris, 2016); John Morrill, 'Dynasties, Realms, Peoples and State Formation, 1500–1720', in Robert v. Friedeburg, John Morrill (eds), *Monarchy Transformed. Princes and Their Elites in Early Modern Western Europe* (Cambridge, 2017), pp. 17–43; Ronald G. Asch, 'War and State-Building', in Frank Tallett, D. J. B. Trim (eds), *European Warfare 1350–1750* (Cambridge, 2010), pp. 322–337.

[28] See John Brewer, *The Sinews of Power. War, Money, and the English State, 1688–1783* (London, 1989). An important precursor was P. G. M. Dickson, *The Financial*

interpretation, however, the state and its capacities are rather measured in terms of the ability to enforce statutory law and maintain political authority over the peoples of Britain. Whether such research is focused on criminal legislation, the poor laws, or the intricate machinery of local officeholding, the question here is less the fiscal performance of the early modern British state and rather its ability to act as a paternalistic regulator of the constitutional and social equilibrium and the common peace.[29] Unlike the fiscal-military narrative, moreover, this second interpretation is much more interested in the spatial distribution of state authority, that is, to what extent statutory regulations were enforceable at the margins.[30]

Revolution in England: A Study of the Development of Public Credit, 1688–1756 (London, 1967). Around the same time, Patrick O'Brien initiated similar research into the patterns of taxation; see Patrick O'Brien, 'The Political Economy of British Taxation, 1660–1815', *Economic History Review*, 41 (1988), 1–32; Patrick O'Brien, Philip A. Hunt, 'The Rise of the Fiscal State in England, 1485–1815', *Historical Research*, 66 (1993), 129–176. More recent discussions include Lawrence Stone (ed.), *An Imperial State at War: Britain 1689–1815* (London, 1994); John Brewer, Eckhart Hellmuth (eds), *Rethinking Leviathan: the Eighteenth-Century State in Britain and Germany* (Oxford, 1999); Christopher Storrs (ed.), *The Fiscal-Military State in Eighteenth-Century Europe: Essays in Honour of P.G.M. Dickson* (Farnham, 2009); Aaron Graham, Patrick Walsh (eds), *The British Fiscal-Military States, 1660–c.1783* (London, 2016); William D. Godsey, Petr Mat'a (eds), *The Habsburg Monarchy as a Fiscal-Military State. Contours and Perspectives 1648–1815* (Oxford, 2022). A succinct overview is Eckhart Hellmuth, 'The British State', in Harry T. Dickinson (ed.) *A Companion to Eighteenth-Century Britain* (Oxford, 2002), pp. 19–29.

[29] The distinction is less clear-cut as presented here and is often a variation in emphasis, with the second variety said to be more interested in the domestic face of the British state. See Anthony Fletcher, John Stevenson (eds), *Order and Disorder in Early Modern England* (Cambridge, 1985); Lee Davison, Tim Hitchcock, Tim Keirn, Robert B. Shoemaker (eds), *Stilling the Grumbling Hive: The Response to Social and Economic Problems in England, 1689–1750* (Stroud, 1992); Paul Griffiths, Adam Fox, Steve Hindle (eds), *The Experience of Authority in Early Modern England* (Basingstoke, 1996); Steve Hindle, *The State and Social Change in Early Modern England, c.1550–1640* (Basingstoke, 2000); Michael J. Braddick, *State Formation in Early-Modern England, c.1550–1700* (Cambridge, 2000); Joanna Innes, *Inferior Politics: Social Problems and Social Policies in Eighteenth-Century Britain* (Oxford, 2009); Nabil Matar, *Britain and Barbary, 1589–1689* (Gainesville, 2005).

[30] Anthony Fletcher, *A County Community in Peace and War: Sussex 1600–1660* (London, 1975); Andrew Coleby, *Central Government and the Localities: Hampshire, 1649–1689* (Cambridge, 1987); Joan Kent, 'The Centre and the Localities: State Formation and Parish Government in England, circa 1640–1740', *HJ*, 38 (1995), 363–404; David Eastwood, *Government and Community in the English Provinces, 1700–1800* (Basingstoke, 1997); Peter King, *Crime, Justice and Discretion in England, 1740–1820* (Oxford, 2000); Peter King, *Crime and Law in England, 1750–1840: Remaking Justice from the Margins* (Cambridge, 2006); Peter King, Richard Ward, 'Rethinking the

Introduction   11

These different approaches ultimately explain the rather peculiar status of the Customs in such interpretations. In the fiscal-military narrative, the Customs administration is regarded as a central object of study, but its structure and its efficiency are typically measured in terms of its fiscal contribution to the Exchequer.[31] It is seen, in other words, in numerical terms, rather than in terms of its involvement in the wider arena of the enforcement of authority.[32] Wherever aspects of its organisation come into view, as they regularly do, it is typically with a view to its fiscal efficiency that issues like bureaucratic structures, sinecurism, patronage, and corruption are of interest.[33] In the second reading of state-building, in the meantime, the Customs administration has received little attention.[34] Although it is true, as a recent collection of essays has argued, that the view of the Customs in historiography is beginning to change and that it is particularly with a view to studies of the local level that the complexity of the Customs as an administrative entity is being appreciated, the overall dichotomy remains largely in place.[35] This represents a missed chance. The administration employed thousands of officers along the very margins of the kingdoms.

Bloody Code in Eighteenth-Century Britain: Capital Punishment at the Centre and on the Periphery', *Past and Present*, 228 (2015), 159–205.

[31] Patrick Walsh, 'The Fiscal State in Ireland, 1691–1769', *HJ*, 56/3 (2013), 629–656; Julian Hoppit, 'Scotland and the Taxing Union, 1707–1815', *SHR*, 98 (2019), 45–70; O'Brien, 'Political Economy'; P. R. Rössner, *Scottish Trade in the Wake of Union (1700–1760): The Rise of a Warehouse Economy* (Stuttgart, 2008).

[32] Brewer himself has recently raised this: "The danger of a purely economic analysis of such bureaucratic activities as revenue collecting or disbursement is that it defines 'efficiency' in purely monetary terms." See John Brewer, 'Revisiting The Sinews of Power', in Aaron Graham, Patrick Walsh (eds), *The British Fiscal-Military States, 1660–c.1783* (London, 2016), pp. 27–34, at p. 32.

[33] See, for instance, Patrick Walsh, '*The Sin of With-Holding Tribute*, Contemporary Pamphlets and the Professionalisation of the Irish Revenue Service in the Early Eighteenth Century', *Eighteenth Century Ireland*, 21 (2006), 48–65; Brewer, *Sinews*, pp. 69–87.

[34] For a few exceptions see David Fleming, *Politics and Provincial People: Sligo and Limerick, 1691–1761* (Manchester, 2010), pp. 163–231; John Brewer, 'Servants of the Public – Servants of the Crown: Officialdom of Eighteenth-Century English Central Government', in John Brewer, Eckhart Hellmuth (eds), *Rethinking Leviathan: The Eighteenth-Century State in Britain and Germany* (Oxford, 1999), pp. 127–147; Colin Brooks, 'Interest, Patronage, and Professionalism: John 1st Baron Ashburnham, Hastings and the Revenue Service', *Southern History*, 9 (1987), 57–66; Maighréad Ní Mhurchadha, *The Customs and Excise Service in Fingal, 1684–1765: Sober, Active and Bred to the Sea* (Dublin, 1999); William B. Stephens, *The Seventeenth-Century Customs Service Surveyed: William Culliford's Investigation of the Western Ports, 1682–84* (Farnham, 2012).

[35] See Graham, Walsh, *Fiscal-Military States*.

These were not only centrally appointed and centrally accountable; they were also responsible for the enforcement of a wide array of economic and criminal legislation.[36]

This unsatisfactory state of research on the eighteenth-century Customs clearly warrants closer study of one of the oldest executive branches of Britain by the eighteenth century. Whereas the fiscal-military narrative is narrow to the point where it misrepresents the organisation, other questions regarding the "articulation, mediation and reception of authority" in the context of an inherently coastal administration have hardly begun to be asked.[37] Such a study, it is proposed, is particularly promising with a view to the preventive branch of the Customs, as it is here that aspects of authority were more acutely at stake than elsewhere in the administration. Unlike the port establishments of the Customs, it was the coastal police forces that were directly concerned with a number of military, criminal, and economic responsibilities that affected the enforcement of authority in a material way. Revealingly, this coastal preventive service has so far largely escaped academic attention altogether.[38]

A study of the political administration of the seacoasts under the auspices of the Board of Customs, however, offers more than the chance to remedy a partial neglect of the Customs in terms of its administrative history. Rather, the coastal focus affords opportunities for a re-evaluation of established narratives of state-building from a little-explored perspective. This is true in at least three different ways. First, such a study is able to reflect on the spatial distribution of state authority and the enforcement of statutory rules at the margins. It offers, in other words, a unique spatial perspective to the centre-heavy discussion on state-building. Secondly, such an approach enables a take on the Customs administration beyond exclusively fiscal rationales and allows for the recognition of responsibilities of an administration that was concerned with much more than the collection of revenue. The coastal preventive service, after all, consistently eludes

---

[36] See the brief descriptions of the wider tasks of the administration by what is still the best administrative history of the Customs by Hoon, *Organization*, ch. 1. Other histories tend to gloss over the differences; see, for instance, Neville Williams, *Contraband Cargoes: Seven Centuries of Smuggling* (London, 1959); Edward Carson, *The Ancient and Rightful Customs: A History of the English Customs Service* (London, 1972); Graham Smith, *Something to Declare: 1000 Years of Customs and Excise* (London, 1980).

[37] Paul Griffiths, Adam Fox, Steve Hindle, 'Introduction', in Paul Griffiths, Adam Fox, Steve Hindle (eds), *The Experience of Authority in Early Modern England* (Basingstoke, 1996), pp. 1–10, at p. 1.

[38] See only Hoon, *Organization*, ch. 5 and Ashworth, *Customs*, ch. 11.

any straightforward fiscal rationales. This recognition, in turn, permits a re-examination of the fiscal-military beliefs about eighteenth-century Britain as they relate to revenue collection more broadly and the Customs in particular. Thirdly, such a perspective is able to throw a fresh light on how the negotiation of authority, usually studied in relation to parish offices and with a view to the keeping of the common peace, played out in a coastal setting and on a local level.

To start with the last point: what was the role of the Customs administration in enforcing law and authority at the coastal margins of the kingdoms? Was this in any way different from the dynamics we are familiar with in the parishes of rural England, Ireland, and Scotland? There is, at first glance, much that supports the assumption of such differences. In the eyes of central government, the stakes were different on the coast from an administrative perspective. Unlike in the parishes, the enforcement of authority in the coastal counties rested on the shoulders of centrally appointed officers with the monarch's very own revenue directly at stake. If anything, the enforcement of the law was more crucial here. At the same time, it seems to have been more difficult to achieve. Smuggling, in particular, posed a threat not only in terms of fiscal losses, but also in the way it threatened stability and the common peace. Unfortunately, smuggling has, aside from its popular appeal, received academic attention mainly in terms of its fiscal effects, i.e., as a form of tax evasion.[39] Aside from this, there has also been an emphasis, in the context of specific strands of social history, to explain the socio-economic rationales of the smugglers themselves.[40] But research into this area has seldom taken a fuller view that encompasses the side of the enforcers

---

[39] See, for instance, Hoh-Cheung Mui, Lorna H. Mui, 'Smuggling and the British Tea Trade before 1784', *The American Historical Review*, 74 (1968), 44–73; Hoh-Cheung Mui, Lorna H. Mui, 'Trends in Eighteenth Century Smuggling Reconsidered', *The Economic History Review*, 28 (1975), 28–63; Julian Hoppit, *Britain's Political Economies: Parliament and Economic Life, 1660–1800* (Cambridge, 2017), pp. 277–305. There are obviously exceptions; see Paul Muskett, 'Military Operations against Smuggling in Kent and Sussex, 1698–1750', *Journal for the Society of Army Historical Research*, 52 (1974), 89–110; Paul Monod, 'Dangerous Merchandise: Smuggling, Jacobitism, and Commercial Culture in Southeast England, 1690–1760', *JBS*, 30 (1991), 150–182.

[40] Cal Winslow, 'Sussex Smugglers', in Douglas Hay, Peter Linebaugh, John G. Rule, E.P. Thompson, Cal Winslow (eds), *Albion's Fatal Tree: Crime and Society in Eighteenth-Century England* (London, 1975), pp. 119–166; John Rule, 'Social Crime in the Rural South in the Eighteenth and Early Nineteenth Centuries', in John Rule, Roger Wells (eds), *Crime, Protest, and Popular Politics in Southern England, 1740–1850* (London, 1997), pp. 153–168; J. A. Sharpe, *Crime in Early Modern England 1550–1750* (London, 1984), pp. 121–142.

of local authority – the preventive service.[41] Crime and deviance, we have learned from the historiography of crime and police history, can only be fully understood if it is considered not as an act of top-down enforcement, but as a form of a negotiation of authority.[42] But negotiation implies at least two parties. In this sense, a fuller understanding of what central government deployed in terms of an answer to coastal crime promises a better understanding of the negotiation of authority in coastal regions, and in the context of smuggling. This enables a fresh light on these processes – much studied in the parish setting – from the perspective of the rather unusual coastal case. Incidentally, such a study also contributes to a more precise understanding of "how the customs service worked in practice".[43]

One of the keys to doing so is to appreciate that the coastal service of the Customs was not, in the main, a revenue-collecting body. It did not follow exclusively fiscal rationales. The Customs administration as a whole is crudely misrepresented if it is taken to be concerned with the collection of revenue only. Next to the navigation laws, it was tasked with a wide range of economic regulations. Assisting the press gangs, detecting foreign spies, registering passengers, apprehending criminals, and enforcing the rules on quarantines and embargoes were likewise on this list of duties. More than the port administrations, this affected the preventive service.[44] To study the administration in terms of its fiscal efficiency and to measure, in the larger context of the fiscal-military debate, the contribution of the Customs only as to how well it performed according to these logics is evidently unsatisfactory. This, however, makes questions regarding its organization not less important, but more so. The overall development of the Customs as an executive bureaucracy, and the related question of the demise of old regime officeholding and the rise of the civil service clearly matter in this respect.[45] Rather than proving the repeated assumption that the Customs service was operating decidedly on the more corrupt side of things, however, such a study can help re-evaluate fiscal-military narratives. If fiscal concerns were

---

[41] An exception is Paul Muskett, 'English Smuggling in the Eighteenth Century' (Diss. Open University, 1996).
[42] Among others, J. S. Cockburn (ed.), *Crime in England 1550–1800* (London, 1977); Sharpe, *Crime*; Michael J. Braddick, John Walter (eds), *Negotiating Power in Early Modern Society: Order, Hierarchy and Subordination in Britain and Ireland* (Cambridge, 2001).
[43] Graham, Walsh, 'Introduction', 22.
[44] Hoon, *Organization*, ch. 1, ch. 5.
[45] See G. E. Aylmer, 'From Office-Holding to Civil Service: The Genesis of Modern Bureaucracy', *Transactions of the Royal Society*, 30 (1980), 91–108; Mark Knights, *Trust and Distrust: Corruption in Office in Britain and its Empire, 1600–1850* (Oxford, 2021); Jonah Miller, *Gender and Policing in Early Modern England* (Cambridge, 2023).

not the only driver of bureaucratic change in the Customs, what else was? How well was the service adapted to performing these other tasks? And to what extent does the organization of coastal policing speak to the nature of coastal enforcement in a social sense? Ultimately, understanding the wider context in which the revenue department of the Customs – central to the interpretation of the fiscal-military state – operated, allows us to draw a much fuller picture of the fiscal-military state in operation, and thereby expose some of the limits of the fiscal rationale and thus contribute to a social history of the fiscal-military state.

Finally, in its coastal focus, the present study offers a unique spatial perspective on the fiscal-military narrative. This is significant, because it has not to date been explored in any particular depth. Whereas recent research has indeed highlighted the necessity to study the fiscal-military state from a geographical perspective – that is, by taking into consideration the plurality of experiences in the British archipelago, but also the entanglements with European developments – any considerations of space are typically confined to an appreciation of how local studies can contribute to the larger picture.[46] Space, in other words, is characteristically considered in its thematic, but not in its conceptual quality. This represents a missed chance. As conceptual research on space and mobility in Britain, Europe, and beyond has shown, these are categories that have a material impact on the way authority played out in specific settings.[47] Taking its cue from this type of comparable research, the study aims to refine the understanding of the impact of fiscal-military rationales on the domestic setting by looking at how they affected political ideas of space by studying, most importantly, the idea of the coast as political space. When did such awareness first arise and for what reasons? More significantly, what were the long-term consequences of this idea, both for the administration and policing of this particular space itself and for how it shaped political discussions and fiscal notions? How did the ambiguity of coastal space – noted throughout the

---

[46] Graham, Walsh, 'Introduction'; Brendan Bradshaw, John Morrill (eds) The British Problem, c. 1534–1707: State Formation in the Atlantic Archipelago (New York, 1996).
[47] Fiona Williams (ed.), *Locating Agency: Space, Power and Popular Politics* (Newcastle-upon-Tyne, 2010); Luca Scholz, *Borders and Freedom of Movement in the Holy Roman Empire* (Oxford, 2020); Andreas Rutz, *Die Beschreibung des Raums. Territoriale Grenzziehungen im Heiligen Römischen Reich* (Köln/Weimar/Wien, 2018); Susanne Rau, *History, Space, and Place* (London, 2019); Dorothea Heitsch, Jeremie C. Korta (eds), *Early Modern Visions of Space, France and Beyond* (Chapel Hill, 2021); Paul Stock (ed.), *The Uses of Space in Early Modern History* (London, 2015); Renaud Morieux, *The Channel. England, France and the Construction of a Maritime Border in the Eighteenth Century* (Cambridge, 2016).

literature – affect political processes, lawmaking, and policing in eighteenth-century Britain?

With these intentions, the study broadly conforms to an exploration of what Joanna Innes has once termed the "domestic face" of the fiscal-military state. She argued that Britain's "increasing orientation towards interstate rivalry, war and empire" directly affected "the ways in which central institutions of government addressed themselves to the task of ordering and governing British society".[48] By studying one particular central institution and by focusing on a specific spatial setting, the study aims to establish a more refined picture of that state's "face" with respect to the significance of the coast. If state building is the central characteristic of British political history throughout the eighteenth century, the coast – as a social, political, economic and military space – can hardly be ignored.

---

[48] Innes, 'Domestic Face', 96. See also Joanna Innes, 'Parliament and the Shaping of Eighteenth-Century Social Policy', *Transactions of the Royal Society*, 40 (1990), 63–92.

1
Jacobitism, Coastal Policing, and Fiscal-Military Reform (1660–1702)[1]

The British Customs administration during the 1690s was in transformation. Staff numbers were on the rise, new regulations governed port business, and systematic coastal policing became part of Customs responsibilities. Rather than simply internal institutional developments, this transformation is intricately linked to broader trends of that decade. The reign of Mary II and William III witnessed profound changes in the nature of the English state. Such changes are typically identified in relation to constitutional developments, European power politics and fiscal-military policies.[2] The manner of the pair's succession tipped the constitution towards a balanced course with the ascension of parliament and the birth of party politics. The revolution settlement also forced England to commit to continued engagement in continental and colonial theatres of war and European dynastic politics. The costs of such commitment in turn provoked domestic changes that are taken to signal the rise of the fiscal-military state, such as increasing volumes of economic legislation, newly formed or re-formed bodies of financial and fiscal organization and a growing civil and military administration. The revenue departments of Customs and Excise are usually considered to be at the heart of such changes. The Excise is in fact regarded as a model case of administrative reform firmly tending towards fiscal efficiency and modern bureaucracy. The Customs, on the other hand, have generally been seen to fall short of such standards both in terms of revenue returns and administrative efficiency.[3] Yet the overall

---

[1] An abridged version of this chapter appeared in *JBS* 61/2 (2022), 290–314.
[2] J. H. Plumb, *The Growth of Political Stability in England 1675–1725* (London, 1967); Henry Horwitz, *Parliament, Policy and Politics in the Reign of William III* (Manchester, 1977); Craig Rose, *England in the 1690s: Revolution, Religion and War* (Oxford, 1999); Julian Hoppit, *A Land of Liberty? England 1689–1727* (Oxford, 2000).
[3] Patrick K. O'Brien, 'The Political Economy of British Taxation, 1660–1815', *The Economic History Review*, 41 (1988), 1–32; John Brewer, *The Sinews of Power: War, Money and the English State, 1688–1783* (London & New York, 1989); Miles Ogborn,

trend of its institutional development with rising numbers of staff, a newly formed preventive service for coastal policing, and growing dimensions of fiscal duties was still considered to contribute to the fiscal-military overhaul of English government structures, its capability for European commitment and the related trend towards monarchical accountability.[4]

Whereas the transformation of the Customs is undisputed, its significance and consequences are not. In a challenge to the fiscal-military interpretation of the Customs championed by John Brewer and partly reiterated by William Ashworth, a growing body of literature has recently debated the alleged inefficiency of the Customs relative to the Excise. Revenue returns from the Customs, both Julian Hoppit and Spike Sweeting have argued, have been systematically underestimated.[5] Furthermore, various case studies demonstrate that the Customs administration was much less corrupt than formerly assumed and that administrative reforms indeed worked towards a more competent and accountable bureaucratic apparatus.[6] Additionally, Patrick Walsh has shown that even if correct, general assumptions about the alleged inefficiency of the English Customs are not necessarily valid for Ireland, where the Customs continued to be the most profitable fiscal branch.[7] Such work evidently contributes to a rehabilitation of the Customs and its performance in the fiscal apparatus. Perhaps ironically, however, such re-evaluations of older empirical work on the fiscal-military state ultimately strengthen its validity as an interpretation. By putting the Customs on a more equal footing with the Excise in the quest for fiscal efficiency and bureaucratisation, the Customs sit even more comfortably in the fiscal-military narrative.[8] What risks being lost in such

---

Spaces of Modernity: London's Geographies 1680–1780 (New York & London, 1998), pp. 158–200; Ashworth, *Customs*, pp. 117–205; Michael Braddick, *Parliamentary Taxation in Seventeenth-Century England* (Woodbridge, 1994), pp. 168–230.

[4] Brewer, *Sinews*.

[5] Julian Hoppit, *Britain's Political Economies: Parliament and Economic Life, 1660–1800* (Cambridge, 2017), pp. 277–305; Spike Sweeting, 'Policing the Ports: The Regional Dimensions of Eighteenth-Century Customs Activity in England and Wales', *Bulletin of the German Historical Institute London*, 40 (2018), 32–67.

[6] Colin Brooks, 'Interest, Patronage and Professionalism: John, 1st Baron Ashburnham, Hastings and the Revenue Service', *Southern History*, 9 (1987), 51–70; Stephen A. Timmons, 'The Customs Service in the West Country, 1671–1692', *The Mariner's Mirror*, 92 (2006), 148–167; William B. Stephens, *The Seventeenth-Century Customs Service Surveyed: William Culliford's Investigation of the Western Ports, 1682–84* (Farnham, 2012); William Farrell, 'The Silk Interest and the Fiscal-Military State', in Aaron Graham, Patrick Walsh (eds), *The British Fiscal-Military States, 1660–c.1783* (London & New York, 2016), pp. 113–130.

[7] Patrick Walsh, 'The Irish Fiscal State, 1690–1769', *HJ*, 56 (2013), 629–659.

[8] Graham, Walsh, *Fiscal-Military States*.

a view are elements and tendencies that diverge from or even contradict the general thrust towards the fiscal-military state in that crucial decade.

One perspective from which the fiscal-military narrative can indeed be questioned is with a view to the one truly momentous alteration of the Customs during the 1690s, namely the establishment of the preventive service. That is what this chapter seeks to do. Without falling back on claims of the relative fiscal and administrative inefficiency of the Customs, this chapter aims instead to locate the preventive service beyond the fiscal-military rationale. Rather than serving primarily or exclusively fiscal ends, it is argued, considerable parts of the administration were geared towards mercantile interests. At the same time, many policies answered the needs of the fragile Williamite regime or resulted from constitutional struggles between crown and parliament. In other words, the Customs, unlike the Excise, cannot solely be seen as an arena of fiscal activity, but was tied to much broader economic and political agendas. Losing sight of these agendas seriously distorts our understanding of the English Customs in this period. Yet in order to uncover this broader context of Customs activities and preventive policing during the 1690s, a better understanding of the events and the underlying motives is needed than is currently available.[9] Thus a second aim of this chapter is to establish basic clarity regarding the early years of the preventive service. A constant feature of coastal activities for well over a hundred years, the when and how and why of its beginnings remain surprisingly hazy.

The Wool Ban and Coastal Policing under Charles II and James II

Government attention to coastal matters during the reign of Mary and William was intense. Various executive departments, in addition to the court itself, conducted surveys of the coasts of England from as early as 1690. These continued throughout the decade and resulted in numerous plans and schemes for a better guard and policing of the coast. Parliament, on the other hand, was just as eager in passing legislation that targeted coastal

---

[9] Neville Williams, *Contraband Cargoes: Seven Centuries of Smuggling* (London, 1959); Edward Carson, *The Ancient and Rightful Customs: A History of the English Customs Service* (London, 1972); Graham Smith, *Something to Declare: 1000 Years of Customs and Excise* (London, 1980). The most detailed account is still Hoon, *Organization*, but the preventive service is treated only superficially. The same is true for Ashworth, *Customs*, pp. 165–183. Histories of the coastguard remain equally superficial; see Bernhard Scarlett, *Shipminder: The Story of Her Majesty's Coastguard* (London, 1971).

activities such as smuggling. Already in 1689, a first Act was passed with at least four more to come within the span of this single decade.[10] Aside from the intensity of such activity, the truly surprising fact is how starkly this contrasts with the years prior to 1689. Certainly, James II's administration had devoted much time and energy to Customs reforms as far as this related to regular port business. Coastal policing, however, remained excluded from such concerns.[11] The common explanation for this is typically found in relation to tariffs. Comparably low import duties during the previous reigns abruptly ended with English engagement in the Nine Years' War. Spurred by the costs of war, tariffs spiked. This, along with the import ban on French goods and the general disruption of trade, prompted a sudden rise in smuggling activities and therefore necessitated stricter coastal policing.[12] In relation to the intensity of overall Customs activity, this explanation obviously holds a certain degree of validity. And yet it only partly explains the markedly different attitudes to coastal policing. Most of the schemes for coastal policing and the majority of parliamentary legislation during William's reign targeted the prohibited exportation of wool. This, however, had already been banned for decades and does not, therefore, explain the sudden obsession with coastal prevention on its own. Because it was entirely banned from exportation, moreover, the policing of wool smuggling was unlikely to produce larger revenue returns, at least not in any direct fashion.[13] Yet if differences in tariffs alone cannot account for the stark contrast in attitudes towards coastal policing, what can?

During the reigns of Charles II and James II, government did not – quite simply – have much interest in coastal policing. It did not need to. As Michael Braddick has shown, Customs activities after the Restoration

---

[10] William and Mary, ch. 32; 7&8 William III, ch. 28; 9&10 William III, ch. 40; 10 William III, ch.16; 11 William III, ch. 13.

[11] Stephens, *Customs Service*; Brewer, *Sinews*, p. 144.

[12] Most accounts attribute the creation of the preventive police to the increase in smuggling, with the increase in tariffs and the disruption of trade assumed to be the main driving force: Ashworth, *Customs*, pp. 165–170; Paul Muskett, 'Military Operations against Smuggling in Kent and Sussex, 1698–1750', *Journal for the Society of Army Historical Research*, 52 (1974), 89–110; Paul Muskett, 'English Smuggling in the Eighteenth Century' (Diss. Open University, 1996), p. 90, pp. 288–289. Few acknowledge that political concerns played a role: Paul Monod, 'Dangerous Merchandise: Smuggling, Jacobitism, and Commercial Culture in Southeast England, 1690–1760', *JBS*, 30 (1991), 150–182; Williams, *Contraband Cargoes*, pp. 87–89. The standard accounts refer mainly to fiscal motivations: Carson, *Customs*, pp. 45–47; Smith, *Something to declare*, pp. 40–42.

[13] On the wool ban Hoppit, *Political Economies*, pp. 216–248; Peter J. Bowden, *The Wool Trade in Tudor and Stuart England* (London, 1962), pp. 184–217.

provided the Crown with steady returns. A comparably small number of Customs officials, largely confined to the main ports, their dependent member ports and creeks, levied the duties enacted by parliament.[14] That the revenue collected by the Customs were voted for Charles II and again for James II by parliament for life obviously meant that the monarchs had an active interest in the system's efficiency.[15] The exportation of wool and, by extension, coastal policing, however, did not figure large on their agenda. To be sure, the export ban, previously in force by royal proclamation only, was finally enacted in 1660 and further tightened in 1662.[16] Yet while parliamentary debate during the 1670s was certainly hot, no further Act followed during the next 27 years and James II confined himself to two royal proclamations, simply restating older provisions.[17] More importantly, on the level of everyday Customs activities, no administrative measures whatsoever were introduced nor, it seems, considered.[18] This is all the more telling when other areas of Customs business did not escape government attention. The 1680s in particular witnessed intense efforts to reform and improve regular Customs operations in the English and Welsh ports. Apart from matters of political loyalty that repeatedly sparked concerns about Customs establishments, these efforts were aimed at stricter efficiency in the ports, which would in turn directly result in larger shares of revenue returned into the Exchequer.[19] Yet because the same was not the case for the enforcement of the wool ban, government simply lacked incentives to devote any resources.

This is not to say that no one felt these incentives. In the absence of government interest, the ban on wool exportation and its enforcement rested predominantly in private hands. For the period to 1671, this was reflected in the overall structure of the Customs administration. During most of the period until 1671, the Customs were farmed out to contractors in return for fixed rents.[20] Any incentives for the improvement of the

---

[14] Michael Braddick, *The Nerves of State. Taxation and the Financing of the English State, 1588–1714* (Manchester & New York, 1996), pp. 49–67. See also C. D. Chandaman, *The English Public Revenue 1660–1688* (Oxford, 1975), pp. 9–36.
[15] Clayton Roberts, 'The Constitutional Significance of the Financial Settlement of 1690', *HJ*, 20 (1977), 59–76, at p. 62.
[16] 12 Charles II, ch. 32, 1660; 14 Charles II, ch. 18, 1662.
[17] Hoppit, *Political Economies*, pp. 221–227; *Eighth Report of the Royal Commission on Historical Manuscripts. Report and Appendix (Part I)* (London, 1881), pp. 127–128, pp. 137–138; Both proclamations in TNA PC 2/72, p. 473 and p. 648.
[18] Hoppit, *Political Economies*, pp. 221–227.
[19] Stephens, *Customs Service*; Timmons, *Customs Service*.
[20] Braddick, *Nerves*, p. 60; Chandaman, *Public Revenue*, pp. 21–29.

Customs therefore lay firmly with the farmers.[21] Yet even after the Customs reverted to governmental management, the export ban continued to be a matter of private, namely mercantile, interest. Whereas the majority of Customs business remained confined to regular port transactions, a few of the outports and the London establishment boasted a small number of Customs ships, so-called "smacks", for the policing of the shore.[22] Yet these efforts were admittedly inadequate and did not account for the large stretches of coast virtually unpoliced. Here, private individuals stepped in. Similar to certain periods in the sixteenth century, coastal policing in the second half of the seventeenth century remained in the hands of the occasional informer or the self-interested entrepreneur.[23] Men such as William Carter indeed showed considerable energy in preventing the exportation of wool and went to great personal and financial lengths. All the Crown and parliament had to do was to grant such men rewards for their service. As these rewards came in the form of moieties of seized and successfully condemned goods, both the energy and costs of such enforcement remained conveniently outsourced. Clearly, neither the administration of Charles nor James was willing to let the inevitable trade-off between efficient policing and investment in staff tip into the wrong direction.

Just how much of a losing bargain coastal policing could turn out to be is aptly illustrated by Carter's case.[24] Carter was a clothier by trade, born around 1630. Other than that, personal information on him is sparse and often can only be gleaned from what is available in his encounters with authorities. Of these, there are many. As early as 1667, Carter started to petition parliament and Charles II for better enforcement of the laws against the exportation of wool and the prevention of illegal trade.[25] In addition, he published several

---

[21] Braddick, *Nerves*, p. 63.

[22] Graham Smith, *King's Cutters: The Revenue Service and the War against Smuggling* (London, 1983), pp. 7–22. See also TNA CUST18/12.

[23] Geoffrey Elton, 'Informing for Profit: A Sidelight on Tudor Methods of Law-Enforcement', *Cambridge Historical Journal*, XI/2 (1954), 149–167; Maurice W. Beresford, 'The Common Informer, the Penal Statutes and Economic Regulation', *The Economic History Review*, 10/2 (1957), 221–238.

[24] On Carter see Williams, *Contraband Cargoes*, pp. 78–80; Kenneth M. Clark, *Many A Bloody Affray* (Rye, 1968); Smith, *Something to Declare*, pp. 40–41; Muskett, 'Military Operations'; Ashworth, *Customs*, p. 167; Rachel Weil, *A Plague of Informers: Conspiracy and Political Trust in William III's England* (New Haven & London, 2013), pp. 95–103.

[25] William Carter, *An Abstract of the Proceedings of W. Carter; Being a Plea to some Objections Urged against HIM* (London, 1694), pp. 1–4. See also William Carter, *An abstract of the proceedings to prevent exportation of wooll un-manufactured* (London, 1689). For the politics of petitioning in this period, see Mark Knights, *Representation*

tracts defending the wool ban on economic grounds. Addressing the king and the nation as a whole, the position expressed in these tracts was still firmly in the mercantile interest of "merchants, clothiers, and drapers, etc.".[26] Over the years, his zeal attracted much attention from the authorities and his opinion was occasionally also heard in parliament and at court.[27] In other quarters, he was ridiculed as "Wool-Carter".[28] What makes Carter somewhat unusual among the many pamphleteers for the mercantile interest in the wool ban is his commitment to action. Starting in 1669, he made several attempts at preventing the exportation of wool himself, either by discovering such practices and prosecuting them in the courts or, first starting in the 1670s, by employing a network of informers and the help of riders and ships to perform a rudimentary policing operation.[29] Occasionally encouraged by parliament and the Treasury and seemingly backed by mercantile interest groups such as the *Company of Merchant Adventurers*, this endeavour – along with his publishing activity – continued well into the 1690s.

To some degree, such activity was successful and Carter was not the only one to think so.[30] Running of wool was prevented and the nation's wealth maintained. In less abstract terms, however, economic success was far less certain, especially for the undertaker of preventive tasks. On a personal financial level, Carter seemed to encounter only losses and was, if we believe his accounts and petitions, truly left out of pocket. This explains why a considerable part of his writing was less about the enforcement of the wool ban than it skilfully pretended, and more about his financial situation. In 1689 he claimed to have lost his estate and a profitable trade over expenses.[31] Repeatedly, he was spelling this out both to fellow merchants and central authorities, for whose benefit he claimed to exert himself.[32] Leaving aside the alleged loss of his estate and trade, preventive action

---

and Misrepresentation in Later Stuart Britain. Partisanship and Political Culture (Oxford, 2005), pp. 109–162; Brodie Waddell, Jason Peacey (eds), *The Power of Petitioning in Early Modern Britain* (London, 2024).

[26] Carter, *Abstract* (1694), preface. In addition to the above, they include [William Carter], *England's Interest Asserted in the Improvement of its Native Commodities; and more especially the Manufacture of Wool* (London, 1669); [William Carter], *The Proverb Crossed, or A new Paradox Maintained* (London, 1677); William Carter, *The Usurpations of France upon the Trade of the Woollen Manufacture of England* (London, 1695).

[27] *Eight Report*, pp. 127–128, pp. 137–138.

[28] Carter, *Abstract* (1694), preface.

[29] Carter, *Abstract* (1694), pp. 1–12.

[30] TNA T1/8, no. 25.

[31] Carter, *Abstract* (1694), preface.

[32] Carter, *Abstract* (1694); TNA T1/6, no. 3; TNA T1/11, no. 23.

indeed incurred considerable costs. An account covering 1687 to 1689 details expenditures totalling nearly £380.[33] In another account from 1691 he stated that he had spent the considerable sum of £1180 over the past twenty years.[34] In several petitions to the king and the Treasury, he claimed to have received little compensation, "being still unpaid several hundred pounds", "but still spending my money dayly in this affaire."[35] Such spending, as the meticulous accounts show, was incurred on several counts, which fall into three categories. These include personal travel expenses between London and the coasts of Kent and Sussex, monies disbursed to his agents such as seamen and horsemen, and the costs of prosecuting seizures in the Court of Exchequer such as clerks' fees and expenses for witnesses. Moreover, these accounts only stated expenses and did not include any salary for his "Labours and Paynes".[36] These "Paynes", as it happens, included heavy debts. Not only did he claim in 1689 and again in 1690 to be in debt at the Exchequer and therefore unable to pursue any trials on successful seizures,[37] his papers also indicate that he had incurred substantial private debts to both men he had employed and men who had invested in his endeavours.[38] His personal situation, apparent from his petitions (though much less so from his polished published writings), was desperate.

Fortunately for Carter, central authorities showed compassion for his case. Between November 1689 and May 1690, he received almost a thousand pounds for his troubles.[39] Presumably, this was because the Treasury and the Board of Customs generally recognised the value of his work.[40] Yet the Commissioners of Customs in particular stressed that, even if they approved of the work being done by Carter and some recompense for him, they did not think that the Treasury was liable for his expenses. It "was never intended that his charge was to be borne by the King".[41] Instead, Carter was to finance his operations out of shares of prosecuted seizures and by what merchants and clothiers had promised him. It was because such promises were not forthcoming and because he had run into debt for what they considered valuable service that they recommended to alleviate

---

[33] TNA T1/6, no. 3.
[34] TNA T1/11, no. 30.
[35] TNA T1/11, no. 23; TNA T1/11, no. 30.
[36] TNA T1/6, no. 3.
[37] TNA T1/6, no. 3; TNA T1/11, no. 23; T1/6, no. 15; TNA T1/8, no. 25.
[38] TNA T1/6, no. 3; TNA T1/11, no. 23.
[39] TNA T1/11, no. 30.
[40] TNA T1/8 no. 25; TNA T1/6, no. 3; TNA T1/14, no. 17.
[41] TNA T1/6, no. 3.

his troubles.[42] Clearly, however, such conditions were very unfavourable for the undertaker. Expenses were likely to outstrip potential rewards, which in turn were dependent on uncertain court cases. Carter in fact indicated that he at least was "finding none ready to adventure in this affaire, (upon these discouraging terms)".[43]

Certainly central authorities were not willing to adventure in this affair. Parliament had acknowledged early on that to depend on private initiative in such matters was imperfect. The House of Lords had recommended in 1669 that the management of these things should ideally be undertaken by Christ's Hospital in London "because the charge for employing persons effectually to prevent this growing evil is too great for any private person."[44] Yet when Christ's graciously declined to undertake this business, no other centrally organised attempt followed until 1690. Financially, it was simply unattractive to do so. If anything, Carter's petitions and detailed accounts of expenses only helped to strengthen that impression. Unlike regular port staff in the Customs, who were often funded not by salaries but by merchants' fees and who levied duties on imports and exports as a matter of course, the Customs Commissioners could easily learn from Carter's experiences that preventive service on the coast was likely to be a heavy investment in staff and court proceedings with only occasional and uncertain returns.[45] As a result, Customs returns were likely to decrease, not increase, with the undertaking of systematic policing. In the face of such odds, the government's position of sitting back and providing incentives for tasks it was itself unprepared to undertake seems sensible.

It is this situation of the careful weighing of options by central authorities that explains the main thrust of much of the mercantile lobbying activity of this period and that unveils the deeply mercantile nature of the interest in coastal policing. True, only a specific section of merchants was concerned: as Bowden has shown, the wool ban rested on the assumption that continental manufacturing was in desperate need of British wool and that the leakage of such wool to the continent gave continental cloth manufacturers advantages over their English counterparts. This assumption was wrong: English and Irish wool was not superior to continental wool; nonetheless, the wool ban did profit certain sections of the English woollen interest. Whereas wool growers, such as in Kent and Sussex, where few

---

[42] Ibid.
[43] TNA T1/11, no. 23.
[44] *Eighth Report*, p. 138.
[45] On remuneration Hoon, *Organization*, pp. 211–219; Ashworth, *Customs*, pp. 157–164. A contemporary view in Henry Crouch, *A Complete Guide to the Officers of His Majesty's Customs in the Outports* (London, 1732).

clothiers were left around 1700, would have welcomed open trade routes to the continent and were clearly willing to seek those routes even under the ban, the manufacturers, clothiers and traders of woollen manufacture, concentrated especially in the West Country, liked the ban because it kept domestic prices for raw materials low. It was clothiers and merchants such as Carter, therefore, that defended the wool ban at all costs. His pamphlets were part of a "sustained and organized propaganda" that attempted to make the clothiers' partial interests a matter of national interest.[46]

Printed tracts in support of the wool ban usually referred to its economic benefits in a mercantilist fashion. By way of this policy, national trade was protected and the entire nation was to profit.[47] Lobbying of parliament and the court relied on similar arguments in the period.[48] The often only thinly veiled hidden agenda of these appeals to the benefit of the entire nation and the common good was to underscore the direct relevance of the policy for the crown's revenue. Carter was a key promoter of this. In his 1669 *England's Interest Asserted*, he spent much space illustrating the potential damage of wool exportation to the nation and, more particularly, to the merchants, all the while laying a particular stress on the losses to the king's revenue, which he estimated to be no less than 100,000 pounds a year. The king, he claimed, would indeed be suffering most, "because so great a Revenue comes directly into him upon the Trade, occasioned thereby".[49] The same tenor is apparent in Carter's petitions to the Treasury. The proceeds of the woollen manufacture, he claimed, accounted for three quarters of the Customs returns. Moreover, "it doth not only give life to all Trades but a Value to all Lands in England by which means all other Branches of his Majesties Revenue are proportionably increased".[50] How could it not be in the king's interest to keep the wool ban intact? How was it not sensible for him to invest in the prevention of the wool exportation? Carter pushed this argument even further in the midst of the Nine Years' War. In his 1695 *Caution to England*, he expressly linked the proceeds of the

---

[46] Bowden, *Wool Trade*, pp. 184–217, at p. 217.
[47] Thomas Manley, *A Discourse shewing that the Exportation of Wooll is destructive to this Kingdom* (London, 1676). Further examples in John Smith, *Chronicon Rusticum-Commerciale; Or, Memoirs of Wool. Being a Collection of History and Argument, concerning the Woolen Manufacture and Woolen Trade*, 2 Vols (London, 1747), pp. 196–381.
[48] *Eight Report*, pp. 127–128; TNA PC 2/72, p. 617. See also Perry Gauci, *The Politics of Trade: The Overseas Merchant in State and Society, 1660–1720* (Oxford, 2001), pp. 195–233.
[49] [Carter], *England's Interest Asserted*, pp. 14–15.
[50] TNA T1/6, no. 3.

woollen manufacture to the ability of a nation to wage war.[51] Obviously, the aim of such lobbying was to convince the court that coastal policing against the exportation of wool, even if costly at first glance, ultimately was in the government's fiscal and the king's very own financial interest. At the same time, it is no less obvious that this was a blunt attempt to bring the king and his administration in line with what primarily constituted partisan mercantile interests.[52]

For the administrations of Charles II and James II, such strategies did not work. Though parliamentary sessions produced many Bills regarding the wool business, actual legislation was negligible and so were James' lifeless proclamations.[53] Beyond the prescriptive level, the record was even bleaker, for except for a few Customs smacks, there was no systematic effort at coastal policing. On the contrary, a number of coastal offices were indeed suspended, or "sunk", with explicit reference to how much thereby was saved to the king's revenue.[54] The unwillingness of the court to invest was unmistakably expressed as late as August 1688. In February, Privy Council discussed a petition from the clothiers, factors and traders in the woollen manufacture explaining that they had entered into an association funded by voluntary contributions whose aim was to prevent the illegal exportation of wool. Since the men appointed for the task were not legally empowered to actually seize any wool they discovered, they asked for a commission from the king to that effect.[55] After referral to the Treasury and the Board of Customs, Privy Council approved of such measures in June and confirmed the commission by royal proclamation in August.[56] Most of its provisions are a striking reminder of the government's general attitude: as "the method taken for prevention of the great abuses therein [exportation of wool] have not hitherto mett with answerable success", a commission formed of an association of traders was empowered to enforce the laws.[57] They were authorized to collect private funds and use them to this end. The king, for his part, was "not doubting but our Loving Subjects will cheerfully and readily assist and promote so usefull and publick a

---

[51] Carter, *Usurpations of France*.
[52] See Chandaman, *Public Revenue*, pp. 10–21.
[53] Hoppit, *Political Economies*, pp. 221–227.
[54] CTB 8 (1685–1689), pp. 429–430, p. 435 (16 & 19 November 1685).
[55] TNA PC 2/72, p. 617. Efforts for such a commission were already under way the previous year and Carter was involved; see CTB 8 (1685–1689), p. 1191 (11 February 1687).
[56] CTB 8 (1685–1689), p. 1825 (20 March 1688). Approval by the Council and proclamation in TNA PC 2/72, p. 688, pp. 725–727.
[57] TNA PC 2/72, p. 725–726.

work".[58] Quite unmistakably, this policy put the admittedly "publick work" of coastal policing once again squarely into the hands of the merchants. After all, it was obviously in their interest so to do, whereas the king's fiscal interest was only indirectly concerned. Since the revenue was secure without such measures, additional policing only amounted to additional costs.

Customs Reforms under Mary II and William III

Things changed after Mary and William succeeded to the throne. The first session of parliament of their reign passed an Act "for the better preventing the exportation of wool" that created improved legal and practical measures for coastal prevention in 1689.[59] In June of that year, the crews of the Dover Customs smacks were increased.[60] Throughout the following winter and spring, surveys of the English south coast revealed the inadequacy of the administrative setup and witnessed the appointment of several riding officers for guarding the coasts of Kent and Sussex.[61] The trend continued. Whereas preventive officers numbered as few as 41 in 1688, the number jumped to 227 by 1702. In comparison to the 144% overall increase in Customs staff in that period, such a rise of over 500% is particularly stark.[62] This shift in the attitude towards coastal policing requires explanation. It can be found, it is argued, in the combination of three distinct trends that, though only marginally related, all favoured the emergence of a preventive coastal police force. The economic impact of the war and its fiscal demands cannot, obviously, be fully eliminated from this equation. Secondly, however, the constitutional upper hand that parliament was intent to maintain in the wake of the Declaration of Rights was another dynamic, for it significantly strengthened the influence of mercantile interests on government policies. Yet the most important factors were political sensitivities at court and in the executive that were specific to William's regime and its perceived instability, namely its responses to Jacobitism.

In comparison to the relative economic stability of previous reigns, England's plunge into European conflict heralded an era of relatively lean years. As Brodie Waddell has shown, the years after the regime change

---

[58] Ibid.
[59] William & Mary, ch. 32. Even before, James' proclamation had been revived, TNA PC 2/73, p. 57.
[60] TNA T11/12, p. 18.
[61] TNA T11/12, p. 112, pp. 162–163.
[62] TNA CUST18/25 and CUST18/59.

witnessed considerable "economic distress".[63] Merchants and traders were the most heavily afflicted, but ensuing increases in the prices of necessities and a worsening currency crisis made sure "that people in every corner of the country felt the pinch of hardship".[64] The war was the main cause of these developments. Apart from the disruption of trade routes, the war's hunger for cash urged parliament and the treasury to look for new sources of income. After all, the war consumed an extraordinary 79% of expenditures.[65] Government loans, the establishment of the Bank of England and the creation of public debt were one way.[66] Another was to squeeze more money out of traditional sources of revenue. Thus, schemes for extending the Excise, increases in the land tax and fresh Customs duties all contributed to wartime spending.[67] For the Customs, this ended the era of comparably low levels of duties, introducing a growing network of high and complicated tariffs.[68] This created more work for customhouse staff. Furthermore, the combination of high tariffs and relative economic distress was a stimulator for illicit trade.[69] Both trends required additions to the establishments of the ports. According to Brewer, Customs staff increased from 1313 in 1690 to 1839 in 1708.[70] More precisely for the reign of William, establishment lists have Customs staff at 1202 in 1688 and at 1727 in 1702.[71] Revenue officers "sprouted like mushrooms".[72] The war also required adaptions in the way that coastal policing was organised. In June 1690, the Dover Customs smacks were replaced by riding officers as coastal cruising

---

[63] Brodie Waddell, 'The Politics of Economic Distress in the Aftermath of the Glorious Revolution, 1689–1702', *HER*, 130 (2015), 318–351; Brodie Waddell, 'The Economic Crisis of the 1690s in England', *HJ*, 66 (2023), 281–302; D. W. Jones, *War and Economy in the Age of William III and Marlborough* (Oxford, 1988); D. W. Jones, 'Defending the Revolution: The Economics, Logistics, and Finance of England's War Effort, 1688–1712', in Dale Hoak, Mordechai Feingold (eds), *The World of William and Mary: Anglo-Dutch Perspectives on the Revolution of 1688–89* (Stanford, 1996), pp. 59–74.
[64] Waddell, *Politics*, p. 325.
[65] O'Brien, *Political Economy*, p. 2.
[66] Charles Wilson, *England's Apprenticeship 1603–1763* (London, 1965), pp. 206–225; Peter George Muir Dickson, *The Financial Revolution in England: A Study in the Development of Public Credit 1688–1756* (Aldershot, 1993), pp. 46–58.
[67] Brewer, *Sinews*, chapter 4.
[68] Brewer, *Sinews*, pp. 211–213; Hoon, *Organization*, pp. 25–37; Ralph Davis, 'The Rise of Protection in England, 1689–1786', *Economic History Review*, 19 (1966), pp. 306–317.
[69] W. Owen, *A Free Apology in Behalf of the Smugglers, So far as their Case affects the Constitution* (London, 1749), p. 21.
[70] Brewer, *Sinews*, p. 66.
[71] TNA CUST18/25 and CUST18/59.
[72] Plumb, *Growth*, p. 122.

was rendered unfeasible by the war. This also saved money.[73] All things considered, fiscal necessities resulted in administrative growth in the Customs and impacted ideas of coastal policing.

But this explanation leaves explanatory gaps when it comes to the preventive service. Even though the Treasury believed that policing on land served fiscal interests better and despite concerns over increases in smuggling, riding officers were not introduced elsewhere for as long as the war lasted. Numbers stagnated until 1697.[74] Concerted schemes of coastal prevention only emerged near the end of the war. In the meantime, these efforts continued to be piecemeal. Secondly, such efforts remained tied to the wool interest. Officers established for coastal duties in 1699 were officiating "for the wooll business".[75] The connection between the wool ban and the fiscal necessities of the war effort, however, was a loose one at best. The Wool Act of 1689 is a good example. Rather than serving fiscal needs, it highlights the constitutional significance of parliament and the reinforcement of the mercantile lobby.

The Bill "for the better Prevention of the Exportation of Wool" was first read in the Commons on 14 March 1689.[76] This was just weeks after the passing of the Declaration of Rights and yet before the coronation of Mary and William in April. Moreover, though it was foreseeable by that stage, it was also before the declaration of war with France in May. Even if receiving royal assent only in August, after England had entered the war, the content of the Act bore no signs of that circumstance.[77] Rather, it was a direct continuation of mercantile interests expressed at the end of James' reign, inasmuch as the main provisions of the Act are strikingly similar to the 1688 commission granted by James.[78] Both created a commission of merchants to enforce the wool ban.

The Act, moreover, formed part of a larger trend. As Tim Keirn and Perri Gauci have shown, the wool lobby gained a strong influence in parliament after the Glorious Revolution. During the 1690s, parliament was flooded with mercantile projects by traders, clothiers and wool factors, with as

---

[73] TNA T11/12, p. 155, pp. 162–163.
[74] There is a modest growth of 117% from 1688 to 1697, which corresponds to the overall growth of the Customs of roughly 120%; TNA CUST18/25, CUST18/40.
[75] TNA CUST18/51, p. 15.
[76] JHC 10 (1688–1693), p. 47 (14 March 1689).
[77] JHC 10 (1688–1693), p. 270 (20 August 1689).
[78] The Commissioners appointed by James addressed William in February 1689, TNA PC2/73, p. 8.

much as 82 textile bills considered during the decade.[79] Partly, this was due to the economic crisis, but parliament was also in a better position after 1689 to participate in the formulation of government policies. For one, it was more accessible, for it was sitting more frequently and this was, of course, part of its enhanced power. At the same time, the quasi-contractual nature of the revolution settlement combined with William's fiscal needs gave parliament new leverage. It was directly used with a view to the king's revenue when parliament broke with tradition and refused to grant the Customs for life.[80] The struggle over William's finances was certainly the most prominent case of parliamentary confidence, but it was also visible elsewhere. For as similar as the 1689 Wool Act was to the 1688 commission in terms of content, there was one striking difference. Whereas the latter was granted by the monarch, the Wool Act was statutory legislation. Yet the individuals named in the commission for executing the Wool Act were not only merchants, but to a certain extent also MPs. Even if the Wool Commission created by the 1689 Wool Act did not take any practical action until after the war, this still constituted a serious infringement of parliament on the executive side of government.[8] Constitutional issues aside, however, the 1689 Wool Act – as direct an expression of mercantile interests as one can imagine – did lead to new measures of coastal policing with, according to some claims, as many as 300 riding officers around 1699.[82] As in previous reigns, therefore, mercantile support of the wool ban continued to be an important factor for coastal policing.

Whether these two factors would have sufficed to put systematic coastal policing on the agenda of the executive, however, is doubtful. Given that it was only adopted as a policy after monetary pressures had somewhat abated after 1697 and likewise given that mercantile pressures – at least initially – only succeeded to secure a Wool Commission with no connection to the executive, the decisive factor must clearly be sought elsewhere.

---

[79] Tim Keirn, 'Parliament, Legislation and the Regulation of English Textile Industries, 1689–1714', in Lee Davison, Tim Hitchcock, Tim Keirn, Robert B. Shoemaker (eds), *Stilling the Grumbling Hive: The Response to Social and Economic Problems in England, 1689–1750* (New York, 1992), pp. 1–24; Gauci, *Politics of Trade*, pp. 195–233.

[80] E.A. Reitan, 'From Revenue to Civil List, 1689–1702: The Revolution Settlement and the 'Mixed and Balanced' Constitution', *HJ*, 13 (1970), 571–588; Clayton Roberts, 'The Constitutional Significance of the Financial Settlement of 1690', *HJ*, 20 (1977), 59–76.

[81] Robert M. Lees, 'The Constitutional Importance of the "Commissioners of Wool" of 1689. An Administrative Experiment of the Reign of William III', *Economica*, 40 (1933), 147–168 and 41 (1933), 264–274.

[82] Smith, *Memoirs of Wool* II, pp. 166–167.

The critical influence was neither fiscal nor mercantile, but a direct result of the political instability of William's regime. The legitimacy of William's succession was, by everyone's standards, dubitable and the exiled James II continued to maintain his – legally speaking – superior claim to the English throne.[83] This would have been less of a problem, had not the issue of succession possessed a shared line of antagonism with the battle lines of the Nine Years' War. After all, it was France, the war enemy of the League of Augsburg, that supported James' claim. In other words, the Jacobite threat was not a matter of a few exiled noblemen but could potentially rely on the strength of the French Army – even if James' Irish expedition in 1690 illustrated early on where the limits to such support were. Beyond external issues, allegiances to the exiled king were also a matter of concern on domestic grounds, as some parts of the English elite and some segments of the army evidently harboured feelings of loyalty to the exiled king. Oaths of allegiance, quickly introduced by the Williamite regime, only served to abate Jacobite fears to some extent. This was especially so because Jacobite threats of invasion and insurgence often failed to materialise, such as when the English and Dutch navies lost control of the channel after the defeat at Beachy Head in 1690, again in the winter 1691–92 and in the aftermath of the assassination plot.[84] In the absence of clear indicators of the real extent of domestic and foreign opposition to William's rule, the extent of the Jacobite threat remained a matter of conjecture, thereby nurturing "a world of gossip, suspicion, and secrecy".[85] As Hoppit has emphasized, it was "the perceived and not the real scale of the Jacobite threat to William's regime that mattered"; William was "forever worried by the possibility of plots, risings, and invasions."[86]

In this political climate, much attention was fixed on the south-east coasts. To some extent, this was a logical response. It was through the Essex, Kent and Sussex ports that most traffic with the continent – open and clandestine, loyal and treasonous – was channelled. For all the government knew, there was no place on that coast "that is not infested with ill minded people to the Government".[87] It was here, therefore, that any attempt at preventing

---

[83] Paul Hopkins, 'Aspects of Jacobite Conspiracy in England in the Reign of William III' (Diss. Cambridge, 1981); Eveline Cruickshanks (ed.), *Ideology and Conspiracy: Aspects of Jacobitism, 1689–1759* (Edinburgh, 1982); Paul Monod, *Jacobitism and the English People, 1688–1788* (Cambridge, 1989).

[84] Hoppit, *Land*, pp. 37–39, pp. 136–141; John Ehrman, *The Navy in the War of William III 1689–1697: Its State and Direction* (Cambridge, 1953), ch. X.

[85] Hoppit, *Land*, p. 39; Weil, *Informers*.

[86] Hoppit, *Land*, p. 138.

[87] BL Add. MS 33924, fol. 84.

Jacobite designs was most promising. At least to a certain degree, however, attention to the domestic scene was also a makeshift response. Presumably, William and his Secretaries of State would have preferred to surveil Jacobite invasion schemes closer to their breeding ground at the court of St. Germain. William's intelligence service was, however, comparably weak and ineffective.[88] In view of this deficiency, authorities focused their attention more closely on the domestic scene, which also served the additional purposes of ascertaining the loyalty of officials at critical posts along the coast and providing – to use modern parlance – counter-intelligence.

Throughout the first years, when William's grasp on the executive was still tenuous, such sensitivities were quickly picked up on by mercenaries, informers and adventurers of often dubious reputation, who sensed the insecurities of the Williamite regime.[89] Among them was William Carter. At first sight, Carter only continued his preventive activity. Apart from his vigorous petitioning to the Treasury for payment of his debts, he continued to enforce the wool ban. In December 1690, he was granted the assistance of four men with horses for his efforts.[90] In early 1691, Carter was further ordered to be encouraged in his activity by Privy Council.[91] At the end of March, he was even appointed messenger extraordinary for the prevention of wool smuggling.[92] Such endorsement of Carter by the authorities was in line with his services in the 1680s and yet it still looks somewhat odd, seeing that there were misgivings at the Treasury about continuing him in government service.[93] Apparently, Carter had sensed the changing climate at court and had adapted. In a petition to the King in the spring of 1691, he had shifted the weight of his argument from a focus on the problem of wool to an express concern with French and Jacobite designs. Despite efforts to prevent this, he maintained, the French held correspondence with "Ill affected" English subjects while "Dangerous Corresponding" was carried on that provided ample opportunities for disaffected persons to come and go as they pleased.[94] Whether he was interested in such activity or not, Carter was willing to make his case with whatever means available. The explanation for the support he received from Privy Council may indeed lie in the fact that, again, he did not stop at talking about such things.

[88] Hopkins, 'Aspects', pp. 154–170. For an earlier period see Alan Marshall, *Intelligence and Espionage in the Reign of Charles II, 1660–1685* (Cambridge, 1994).
[89] Weil, *Informers*, chapters 2, 3 and 4.
[90] TNA T11/12, p. 270; TNA T1/11, no. 25, no. 26.
[91] TNA PC 2/74, p. 124, p. 138.
[92] TNA PC 2/74, p. 143.
[93] TNA T1/11, no. 30.
[94] TNA T1/14, no. 17.

Beginning in spring 1691, Carter was employed as an agent of the Earl of Nottingham during the latter's first tenure as Secretary of State. In this role, he commissioned agents to go into France and provide Nottingham with intelligence about the French fleets and garrisons.[95] Carter effectively tried to frame wool smuggling as a "security issue" to further his own interests.[96]

To the authorities, such an ambiguous position may have been less troubling than Weil suggests, for to the men in office as well as to their agents on the ground, smuggling and traitorous correspondence were two sides of the same coin that could, ideally, be countered by the same methods. If anything, it is surprising that the close proximity of the spheres of counter-intelligence and coastal prevention has so far mostly been overlooked. To be sure, both Hopkins and Monod have noted that in contemporary imagination – if not always in reality – the hatching of Jacobite plots and the running of contraband were inextricably linked.[97] To stop the latter was to weaken opportunities for the former, many observers believed. Yet the degree to which contemporary responses and practical solutions to such problems seamlessly mixed both issues has so far escaped attention. To many contemporary observers, these were not separate issues at all. Fighting the smuggling trade provided the government with a grasp on something real as a means to prevent something more serious, yet much more elusive. This is not to say that such men did not, as Carter did, have their own agenda in proposing schemes of prevention. Yet beyond those individual interests and on a more abstract level, the genesis of schemes for systematic coastal prevention can unmistakably be found in counter-intelligence schemes. Both were fixated on prevention and coastal surveillance.

Nowhere is this more apparent than in the case of Richard Kingston. Previously studied for his role in Jacobite intelligence, there are many connections to ideas of coastal prevention.[98] According to Hopkins, Kingston was "the best agent the Government ever had", whereas Weil has highlighted his decidedly dodgy profile.[99] He worked for several highly placed

---

[95] Finch III, p. 41, p. 52, p. 87, p. 161, p. 177, p. 375. See also Weil, *Informers*, pp. 95–103. Carter had agents in France before 1689, but this was in the wool interest; see CTB 8 (1685–1689), pp. 1819–1820 (19 March 1688).

[96] Weil, *Informers*, p. 101. See also Finch III, p. 52 and his letter to Trumbull in BL Add. MS 72569, fols 150–151.

[97] Hopkins, 'Aspects', pp. 141–142; Monod, *Jacobitism*, pp. 113–115; Monod, 'Dangerous Merchandise'; Finch V, *Introduction*, pp. xxxviii–xliii.

[98] Weil, *Informers*, pp. 188–216; Paul Hopkins, 'Sham Plots and Real Plots in the 1690s', in Eveline Cruickshanks (ed.), *Ideology and Conspiracy: Aspects of Jacobitism, 1689–1759* (Edinburgh, 1982), pp. 89–110.

[99] Hopkins, 'Plots', p. 92; Weil, *Informers*, chapter 5.

officials around William, such as his trusted advisor, the Earl of Portland, and several of the Secretaries of State such as Nottingham, the Duke of Shrewsbury, John Trenchard and William Trumbull. In this role, he infiltrated Jacobite networks and provided intelligence of their activities to the government.[100] In July 1695 he was, however, also sent on a tour to inspect the English south coast from London to Brighton. Chiefly this was "to settle your Honour [Nottingham] a correspondence there"[101], yet he also reported on the loyalty of the officers and the state of the forts along the coast, both of which appeared "much perverted". Jacobite plots were so advanced, he claimed, that only "the extraordinary care of the Government can prevent it". Such issues he related to the smuggling trade that neither the Customs officers nor the dragoons stationed on that coast were, he asserted, able or willing to prevent. Those smugglers in fact "glory in being called Jacobites" and "drive this common trade of smugling persons as well as goods."[102] In his assessment, therefore, smuggling and treason were closely related. This perception also informed his proposals for preventing this.

Already in 1692, the Earl of Portland had forwarded "suggestions for an intelligence service" to the hand of Nottingham, which were probably Kingston's. Among other things, he proposed a watch on the roads towards the borders of Scotland "as also on the sea-coasts, from Gravesend along, what lyes towards France" which could be effected cheaply, if the revenue officers could be made to undertake such things.[103] In another set of proposals for Secretary of State William Trumbull from 1695, Kingston and one Captain Barron developed a more elaborate way of policing that same stretch of coast.[104] A ship was to be stationed at Gravesend to search all ships, including English and Dutch men-of-war. With this, "great service" would be performed "both in respect of the better security of his Majesties Customs and the more effectually preventing the escape of dangerous persons".[105] Furthermore, as it was obvious that both evils flourished due to

---

[100] Finch IV, p. 113, p. 196, p. 330, p. 352, p. 408, p. 437, p. 457, p. 499 and *passim*.
[101] BL Add. MS 72570, fol. 18.
[102] BL Add. MS 72570, fols 50–51.
[103] Finch IV, pp. 160–161. Weil attributes this convincingly to Kingston, see Weil, *Informers*, p. 197.
[104] Barron's proposal in BL Add. MS 72569, fols 16–17. Kingston commented on this proposal, see BL Add. MS 72570, fol. 12. There is a second proposal in BL Add. MS 72569, fols 18–19, similar to Barron`s. It could be from Barron or one that Kingston claims to have written and that was forwarded by Nottingham to Portland, see Commission on Historical Manuscripts, Report on the Manuscripts of the Marquess of Downshire, vol. 1 (London, 1924), pp. 483–484. It could also be by Mr Wells of Horsham, that Kingston mentions; see BL Add. MS 72750, fol. 6 and fol. 8.
[105] BL Add. MS 72569, fols 16–17.

the "negligence or disaffection" of the Customs officers, it was necessary to encourage these officers with rewards, remind them of their duties and further to "cause frequent surveys upon the coast" and a "strict inspection" of such officers.[106] The civil magistrates needed to be encouraged to support such duties where possible, troops needed to be stationed on the seacoast and ships had to be ordered to cruise coastal waters.[107] Above all, such a setup required a superior officer in charge of these operations. This newly formed office ought to "have the Character of Surveyor General of the Coast of Kent and Sussex".[108] All these measures were emphatically meant "for the better obstructing the owling trade and this other of Intelligence which for the most part are inseparable".[109]

The significance of these proposals does not lie in the practical measures they proposed. Some of that – in the form of orders, personnel, and tactics – was already in place. In September 1690, William had ordered that officers of the Customs should not suffer persons to come and go into and out of England without passes.[110] In addition, the Wool Acts provided that Customs officers were to prevent the running of goods and these commands had been revived by way of royal proclamation.[111] Privy Council had also ordered JPs to enforce these laws and had advised Admiralty to have ships cruise on the south coast in February 1690 and again in August.[112] From as early as 1690, there was talk of involving the militia in the defence of the coast.[113] Indeed, it was ordered that companies of dragoons should be stationed at various posts along the coast.[114] Nottingham engaged personally in this task, using Abraham Stock, the postmaster at Dover and his trusted agent, to devise the best ways of placing these soldiers.[115] Specifically, these dragoons were to assist the Customs in Kent.[116] In many of these measures, the same blurring of the lines between coastal prevention and counter-intelligence is visible. The few riding officers already on coast duty since 1690 were ordered, in 1696, to help discover suspected persons on the coast. They were, however, to keep this a secret and to "give it out" that they were after "seizing of goods not persons".[117]

[106] BL Add. MS 72569, fols 18–19.
[107] BL Add. MS 72569, fols 16–17 and 18–19.
[108] BL Add. MS 72569, fols 16–7.
[109] BL Add. MS 72569, fols 18–9.
[110] BL Add. MS 72569, fol. 19.
[111] TNA PC 2/73, p. 57.
[112] TNA PC 2/73, p. 385, p. 525. See also T1/18, no. 74; T1/22, no. 54.
[113] BL Add. MS 42586, *passim*.
[114] TNA T1/43, no. 27.
[115] BL Add. MS 33924, fols 84f.
[116] TNA PC 2/75, p. 279.
[117] BL Add. MS 72569, fol. 125.

There are, in fact, several individuals whose service for the government sat somewhere between the two tasks. Carter is one example and so is Stock, who, aside from his service as postmaster and informer to Nottingham, also provided the latter with intelligence regarding movements of the French fleets or carried out more specific tasks such as an inquiry into suspicious tampering with the Dungeness lighthouse.[118] Telling is also the case of John Macky, a Scotsman, who informed Nottingham and Portland of the invasion plans in 1692.[119] As a reward, he was made riding surveyor on the coast near Harwich to discover and apprehend "dangerous persons".[120] Some years later, he was put in charge of the Dover packet service.[121] On the whole, it is clear that pieces of what Barron and Kingston had in mind were already in place by 1695. And yet their ideas signalled the necessity for a new approach which government officials could not overlook.

What the schemes from 1695 suggested was the necessity for a systematic and centrally organised approach to coastal surveillance. The current state of things was piecemeal and it was dependent on the activities of a number of officials in different executive departments and with different informal agents. This was neither systematic nor was it accountable. Internal rivalries and party interests flourished.[122] Agents hired as spies often connived at smuggling; others played a double game or ruthlessly pursued private interests.[123] As it stands, even Kingston or Barron agreed that this made for an ineffective approach. The second point that their proposals inadvertently stressed was that there was indeed no department better placed to serve both the interest of the revenue and the interest of internal security than the Customs. Not by accident, Trumbull, receiver of these schemes, forwarded them to the Treasury within days, suggesting that an "effectual course" with a view to the Customs should be considered.[124]

Given that in the quest to prevent Jacobite plots many eyes were fixed on the coast, it is no surprise that much pointed to the Customs. But this sits awkwardly with an understanding of the Customs as a primarily fiscal agency. It is important to reiterate, therefore, that this was not the case. Given that revenue is the only quantifiable Customs activity, it is tempting

---

[118] Finch III, p. 101, p. 110, p. 163, p. 197.
[119] John Macky, *Memoirs of the Secret Services of John Macky, Esq. During the Reigns of King William, Queen Anne, and King George I*, 2nd edition (London, 1733), pp. 1–4.
[120] CSPD, William and Mary (1693), p. 126 (6 May 1693); CSPD, William III (1699–1700), p. 222 (8 June 1699).
[121] Macky, *Memoirs*, p. 7; TNA T1/43, no. 67; T1/84, no. 80.
[122] Hopkins, 'Aspects', pp. 153–241.
[123] Finch V, *Introduction*, pp. xxxviii–xliii; Weil, *Informers*, pp. 140–187; TNA T1/24, no. 62.
[124] TNA T1/34, no. 10. The Treasury also received them: BL Add. MS 72570, fol. 6, fol. 8.

to reduce its activity (and efficiency) to numbers. Contemporaries, however (along with historians like Hoon, Braddick and even Brewer), were (even if grudgingly) aware that the Customs were more than that.[125] Even in terms of economic policies, the implementation of trade laws, Navigation Acts, embargoes and quarantines fell into Customs duties. Beyond the economic sphere, Customs officers assisted the press gangs or apprehended criminals. Most importantly, the Customs was an agency that employed hundreds of royal officers around the coasts of the kingdom and their loyalty to the Crown as well as their influence in local affairs carried much weight. "Considering the Influence that they generally have upon others in the OutPorts (Especially by their Conversaccion and Example)", a memorandum from 1704 read, officers should, in addition to being men "of Integrity and fidelity in their Respective Imployments", also be "men of Stedfast Inclinaccion and affection to the Government".[126] But the prevention of traitorous correspondence was an entirely different matter and it is doubtful that many would have seen this as a natural task of the Customs before William's reign. Yet William's administration was increasingly persuaded that Jacobite plots were a problem partly linked to the coast and the smuggling trade. Because of this, schemes for preventing traitorous correspondence could hardly do without a reference to the officers of the Customs. The question is rather why, against this background, the Customs were not, in the first years of William's reign, at the centre of efforts for coastal surveillance.

The answer is that William and his advisors did not believe the Customs to be reliable. According to Weil, the Customs were a "weak link in England's defence against Jacobite infiltration".[127] This was perhaps especially so in the south-east, as local officers were likely to be sympathetic to local trading interests disrupted by the war with France. Because Customs officers were also subjects with their own views on loyalty, the Customs administration – inherited, as it was, from the previous monarch – caused concern about sheltering Jacobites. In this regard, it was similar to concerns about the Post Office.[128] Godolphin, Lord of the Treasury for much of William's reign, expressed the opinion in 1694 that "the commission of the Customs cannot be made worse than it is at present". Board members were corrupt or could credibly be linked to Jacobite sympathies. Similar concerns were expressed regarding parts of the wider Customs administration and this was little surprise given that some commissioners had a

---

[125] Hoon, *Organization*, pp. 37–44, Braddick, *Nerves*, p. 58; Brewer, *Sinews*, p. 101.
[126] TNA T1/89, no. 135.
[127] Weil, *Informers*, p. 74.
[128] Weil, *Informers*, pp. 76–86, Hopkin, *Aspects*, pp. 162–170.

known "bias towards employing under-officers disaffected to your [William's] government".[129] Shrewsbury also believed that these under-offices were "filled generally with the most declared Jacobites of the country" and that therefore a change was "absolutely necessary in point of state".[130] True as this was in the summer of 1694, the ensuing purge of the Customs posts improved William's opinion of the administration. To be sure, the purge was also a product of the raging conflict of party, as Godolphin observed.[131] And even after 1694, the Customs was not held in the highest of esteems in some quarters. Kingston, for his part, had little faith in the organization, suggesting to Nottingham that matters left to the Customs would inevitably be "slubberd over and come to nothing".[132] Yet the trust that was posed in the administration in the following years suggests that the purge at least partly restored the faith in the reliability of the Customs.

Thus the conditions for systematic coastal policing were only met by 1695. Although the executive was slow in stepping up its efforts, a new approach was gradually emerging. In 1696, parliament passed a second Wool Act.[133] In December 1696, provisions for a "more than Ordinary Watch upon the coasts of Kent & Sussex" were made "by the King's express Command" and ostensibly as a direct reaction to the schemes forwarded by Trumbull. This was "to prevent the Communication and passage of Intelligence and passengers to and from France".[134] In January 1697, five new riding officers were appointed on the Kent coast "for preventing of Trade & correspondence with France".[135] In February, Henry Baker, one of the solicitors of the Treasury, was appointed by the Treasury to supervise preventive measures against the wool trade on the Kent and Sussex coasts.[136] Just days later, early in March, Baker received an additional order from Trumbull, further specifying his task. Here, the running of wool was, once again, understood to be an indicator of something more sinister. Baker was to prevent the "dangerous correspondence with the King's enemies" who

---

[129] CSPD, William and Mary (1694–5), pp. 179–186 (15 June 1694).
[130] William Coxe (ed.), *Private and Original Correspondence of Charles Talbot, Duke of Shrewsbury, with King William, the Leaders of the Whig Party, and other Distinguished Statesmen* (London, 1821), p. 51 (Shrewsbury to King William, 20 July 1694). See additionally TNA T1/8, no. 19.
[131] *Ibid*. See also Horwitz, *Parliament*, pp. 133–134.
[132] BL Add. MS 72570, fol. 85.
[133] 7&8 William III, ch. 28.
[134] TNA T1/41, no. 50.
[135] TNA T11/13, p. 320, p. 325.
[136] TNA T11/13, p. 330. Background on Baker in Stephen Baxter, *The Development of the Treasury 1660–1702* (London & New York, 1957), pp. 249–254.

used the illicit coastal traffic for their designs.[137] Over the next months, Baker surveyed the coast repeatedly.[138] Here and there, new riding officers were appointed, stricter orders given and additional ships set on coastal cruises until finally, in the autumn of 1699, a new systematic setup was introduced.[139] In a scheme that bore striking resemblances to the plans discussed in 1695, Baker was appointed Supervisor of Riding Officers of Kent and Sussex by King William, who took an active interest in these matters.[140] Simultaneously, a systematic guard of the coast by a large number of riding officers and cruisers was incorporated into the Customs administration.[141]

In appearance, this new setup was a compromise. Coastal prevention, as it was instituted in 1699, operated in the wool interest. There were good reasons for this. The woollen lobby in parliament was unrelenting; after 1696, another three Wool Acts were passed.[142] In addition, the Board of Trade, evaluating English trade balances and the importance of the wool trade, readily agreed that something needed to be done.[143] Increases in smuggling and illegal trade with French goods supported such a view.[144] But for the government, the same evidence pointed in a different direction. The unsuccessful yet no less frightening assassination plot of 1696 and the uncovering of a Huguenot smuggling network in 1698 could just as easily be understood as calling for more systematic efforts at preventing traitorous correspondence.[145] The interest that William took in this matter and the rather explicit instructions to Baker indicate that this setup was permeated with political considerations and that, at least at the beginning, coastal policing was to some degree about the prevention of dangerous correspondence.

---

[137] CSPD, William III (1697), pp. 51–52 (8 March 1697).
[138] TNA T1/56, no. 29, no. 41; T1/60, no. 74. See also his report to the Board of Trade, TNA CO388/7 (12 January 1699).
[139] TNA T11/13, pp. 389, 390, 404, 416, 428, 430, 436, 441; T 11/14, 23, 30; TNA PC 2/77, pp. 104, 111, 122, 159, 162; T1/51, no. 77.
[140] CTB 15 (1699–1700), p. 20 (1 November 1699).
[141] TNA PC 2/77, pp. 190–191; T29/11, p. 173 (6 September 1699). T11/14, pp. 41–42 (22 September 1699).
[142] 9&10 William III, ch. 40; 10 William III, ch. 16; 11 William III, ch. 13.
[143] JHC 12 (1697–1699), pp. 425–440 (18 January 1699); TNA PC 1/1/171.
[144] TNA PC 2/76, pp. 503, 509, 564.
[145] Weil, *Informers*, chapter 7; Williams, *Contraband*, pp. 87–88; Ashworth, *Customs*, p. 168. The Treasury had evidence that agents involved in the assassination plot were also involved in smuggling, CTB 19 (1704–1705), p. 133 (14 February 1704).

Bureaucratisation and Fiscal Reform

It cannot be overstated that the establishment of a preventive police in the Customs in 1699 was an entirely new departure. It was to be a continuous feature of Customs activity for the next 120-odd years. However, what risks being overstated with such a claim is the extent to which the way in which this was done was new. The fiscal-military narrative not only makes a claim as to why the state apparatus grew in this period, but also how, and the underlying process is taken to be one of growing bureaucratisation. Brewer, like Aylmer before him, stressed the hesitant arrival of new forms which frequently tended towards an accommodation between the old and the new rather than the wholesale disposal of older forms. Once again, the model case was the Excise, whereas the Customs supposedly continued a higher level of older (and, by implication, less efficient) forms of administration.[146] But given that the motives of bureaucratic change can be understood beyond the dictates of fiscal efficiency, perhaps a closer look at the ways in which the bureaucracy changed is also warranted. To what extent did the government embark on an entirely new course? What elements of bureaucratic modernisation can be discerned? In trying to understand the character of what emerged, it is instructive to keep the motives for change in mind. The government was willing to test new ideas on bureaucratic efficiency where its interests were involved. This was in regard to the problem of traitorous correspondence and constitutional struggles. Here, new features even rivalled those introduced in the Excise. In other areas, however, there is clear evidence of reluctance and inability to reform. The balance sheet was mixed, but it is important to bear in mind for what reasons.

There is much that speaks against a coherent process of bureaucratisation. As in other areas, party politics and patronage were rampant.[147] As Kingston's tour illustrates, beyond the concern over Jacobites there was a second concern, just as pressing, over political allegiances. Kingston's report shows that offices, in the Customs as elsewhere, were frequently awarded not based on qualification but on affiliation.[148] Godolphin, too,

---

[146] G. E. Aylmer, 'From Office-Holding to Civil Service: The Genesis of Modern Bureaucracy', *Transactions of the Royal Society*, 30 (1980), 91–108; Brewer, *Sinews*, pp. 69–85, 101–114; John Brewer, 'Servants of the Public – Servants of the Crown: Officialdom of Eighteenth-Century English Central Government', in John Brewer, Eckhart Hellmuth (eds), *Rethinking Leviathan: The Eighteenth-Century State in Britain and Germany* (Oxford, 1999), pp. 127–147.
[147] Baxter, *Development*, pp. 90–100; Hoon, *Organization*, pp. 195–242.
[148] BL Add. MS 72570, fols 42, 44, 50–51.

during the purge of 1694, was aware that appointments were made "to gratify party and animosity".[149] There were also difficulties in dealing with corruption. In May 1699, two men complained about Joseph Beverton, riding officer at Canterbury, for blackmailing honest traders. They thought "that the officers who are at present concerned to look after the owling trade make it their business not to prevent it, but to make an advantage to themselves".[150] Similar claims were made against Richard Maidstone, commander of the Whitstable boat, in 1698.[151] These were old problems. In 1686, Walter Devereux, commander of Sandgate Castle, informed the Treasury that he was offered a bribe by the owlers to look the other way.[152] Information from February 1688 suggests that he took it.[153] Yet after 1690 he was in the preventive business as a riding officer.[154] Even Henry Baker, most senior of the preventive officers, did not escape the charge of corruption. In May 1700, Devereux voiced severe allegations of illegal practices against Baker.[155] In a hearing before the Treasury, Baker was eventually cleared of such allegations.[156]

There certainly was widespread corruption in the Customs.[157] Yet to some degree, the proliferation of such complaints in a new administrative setup is of little surprise. Not only were there new opportunities for collusive practices, but there was also the availability of new offices to be handed to clients. For these clients, such offices, equipped with handsome salaries, were tempting. Indeed, at the root of many allegations seems to have been the vying for office. The two men complaining against Beverton in 1699 promised to produce their own "scheme for preventing the owling trade" and begged the Treasury to wait for that scheme "before they appoint new officers for that purpose."[158] Devereux, too, while he voiced his allegations against Baker, was drafting competing schemes for the preventive service.[159] It was little wonder that he believed that everything that Baker "affirms

---

[149] CSPD, William and Mary (1694–5), pp. 179–186 (15 June 1694).
[150] TNA T29/11, p. 115.
[151] TNA T1/57, no. 56, no. 66, no. 67.
[152] CTB 8 (1685–1689), p. 64 (19 March 1685); CTB 8 (1685–1689), p. 818 (7 July 1686).
[153] TNA PC2/73, pp. 22, 30, 43. Devereux answered by complaining against his accusers, *ibid.*, p. 60.
[154] TNA T1/8, no. 59; T1/18, no. 41, no. 43.
[155] TNA T1/69, no. 13, no. 38; T1/70, no. 8.
[156] CTB 15 (1699–1700), pp. 113–115 (23 July 1700).
[157] Hoon, *Organization*, pp. 195–242; Baxter, *Development*, pp. 90–100; Stephens, *Customs Service*; TNA T1/8, no. 19.
[158] TNA T29/11, p. 115.
[159] TNA T1/60, no. 12; T1/69, no. 35, no. 61.

to be true is generally false". [160] For several years, Devereux clung to the belief that he would have been the better person in Baker's station.[161] To some degree, therefore, corruption and patronage were a side effect of a growing bureaucracy. Yet it remains that little was done to root this out systematically.

Looking at general patterns of employment for the preventive service in these years also reveals that old practices died hard. The Treasury continued, for example, to encourage policing by private parties after the preventive service was established, even if to a lesser degree than in Carter's days.[162] More importantly, the Treasury did not always introduce coastal policing by employing new staff. Instead they resorted to schemes already practised under James II, when coastal duties were heaped onto the existing port staff. Establishment lists of the Customs before 1689 show that when a supplementary watch on the coast was required, regular port staff were provided with horses and boats.[163] This aggregation of duties in one person was inefficient. After 1698 the Treasury continued, in some cases, to follow the same practice. When the new setup arrived, it was reserved for certain regions. An establishment "for a stricter guard of the western Coast", for instance, listed few new officers in the Devon and Cornish ports; in most cases, regular waiters and searchers were provided with allowances for horses.[164] The same can be observed in a scheme for the coast between Beaumaris and Carlisle, for the port of Milford and the stretch between Newcastle and Bridlington.[165] On the Scottish Borders, too, a similar rationale was applied. Instead of appointing new officers, the Treasury handed out commissions to Excise men, "whereby the charge of establishing new officers [...] has been avoided".[166]

Such reluctance to root out older bureaucratic forms is balanced by what was practised in other regions. In Kent and Sussex, the service was put on much stricter terms than what the Customs administration in general is usually credited for. In appointments of new officers, there was a clear eye to sufficient ability and "good character".[167] At the same time, dismissal as punishment was strictly enforced.[168] Frequently, officers were engaged on a

---

[160] TNA T1/70, no. 8.
[161] CSPD Anne (1702–1703), pp. 190–191 (19 July 1702), p. 293 (13 November 1702).
[162] TNA T11/14, p. 338; T1/13, no. 47; T1/33, no. 29; T1/86, no. 63.
[163] TNA CUST18/12; CTB 8 (1685–1689), p. 64 (19 March 1685).
[164] TNA T11/13, pp. 461–464.
[165] TNA T11/14, pp. 53, 149; T1/38, no. 86.
[166] TNA T11/13, p. 404. See also T11/14, pp. 24–25.
[167] TNA T11/14, pp. 33, 34, 44, 69, 70, 98, 284; T1/63, no. 30.
[168] TNA T11/13, p. 257 and *passim* in T11/14; T1/66, no. 41.

trial basis before – "having given good testimony" – being properly established.[169] Such establishment entailed, perhaps for the first time, adequate salaries. Whereas in most counties, riding officers received yearly between £30 and £60, in Kent and Sussex the handsome sum of £90 was common.[170] Unlike before, when coast business was largely unspecified, both riding officers and commanders of Customs cruisers and Admiralty ships were also provided with instructions.[171] In a further step to achieve bureaucratic coherence, the Treasury was much less willing to engage outsiders. A request by Carter was turned down specifically because the Treasury had already "appointed persons at certain salaries for this service."[172] Among further administrative measures that clearly equalled those of the Excise, riding officers were to keep journals of their transactions, which in turn were to be controlled by an "itinerant collector".[173] Additionally, ordinary riding officers in Kent and Sussex were put under the direction of a Supervisor of Riding Officers, who received an additional salary for such responsibility.[174] To prevent as much as possible collusion on the part of the officers, these were preferably to be bachelors and they were – similar to Excise men – to be "rolled" from station to station at regular intervals.[175] If it is hard to say whether all of this was enforced coherently and consistently, it nonetheless speaks for the willingness of the Board of Customs and the Treasury to introduce notions of bureaucratic efficiency.

The question of how far the government was willing, in this new setup, to enforce stricter notions of bureaucratic efficiency was to a certain extent, therefore, rather a question of where it was willing to do so. Explaining these priorities is necessarily an exercise in conjecture, since we lack univocal explanations from the authorities. Once again, three motives have some probability. Kent and Sussex were hot spots of wool manufacture and illegal exportation played a larger role here than elsewhere.[176] At the same time, the government remained deaf to concerns expressed by Baker and the Board of Trade that the successful suppression of wool smuggling in

---

[169] TNA T11/13, p. 182.
[170] TNA T11/14, pp. 41–42, 53, 155.
[171] TNA T1/63, no. 21; T11/13, p. 451; CO388/7, 26 January and 15 March 1699; CSPD William III (1697), p. 471 (12 November 1697).
[172] TNA T1/11, no. 30.
[173] TNA T1/64, no. 33
[174] TNA T1/63, no. 21
[175] TNA T1/63, no. 21; T11/13, p. 451. Objections to Baker's proposal by Devereux in T1/60, no. 12. Devereux had been dismissed as a riding officer for refusing to be 'rolled', see T11/13, 257.
[176] Ashworth, *Customs*, pp. 166–168; Bowden, *Wool Trade*, pp. 41–106.

Kent and Sussex was prone to push the smugglers elsewhere.[177] The seriousness of this particular concern is therefore somewhat doubtful. Secondly, there are good reasons to assume that the government continued to be worried about Jacobitism. True, the war was over. Yet James II was alive and, in the absence of security in the question of succession, his claim to the throne continued to be a threat. Tensions with France, moreover, never entirely abated between Ryswick and the death of Charles II of Spain.[178] As in Scotland, the southern counties of England were, as Monod has shown, also a haven of Jacobite sentiments among the landed gentry.[179] It is likely, therefore, that William and his government continued to be worried about Jacobite plots and invasion plans with a view to Kent and Sussex. It was only here, after all, that the preventive service of the Customs was consistently complemented by Admiralty cruisers and troops of dragoons.[180] If smuggling was the foremost concern in government circles, then notorious regions such as East Anglia would not have been excluded from the strict coastal crackdown visible in Kent and Sussex. On the surface, such measures still answered the need to fight the owling trade. After all, the geographical focus on Kent and Sussex also served the interest of the "wool interest", as it subjected a region with many wool growers to the interest of clothiers, mainly in the south-west and East Anglia, who needed cheap wool for domestic manufacturing.[181] And yet the instructions to Baker, his detailed accounts and comments in the Treasury and the Board of Customs illustrate that "intelligence and correspondence with France" continued to be an important concern.[182]

Finally, there is a third factor that relates to the wool interest. The Wool Commission empowered by the Act of 1 William and Mary, chapter 32 did not take any action until after the war. However, in July 1698 – coinciding with efforts at the Treasury – a number of the commissioners met at the Guild Hall in London and decided to take action. They commissioned a sloop to cruise against wool smugglers and sent officers to the Scottish Borders,

---

[177] TNA CO388/7, 12 January 1699 (Baker to the Board of Trade); PC 1/1/171 (Report by the Board of Trade, 28 October 1702).
[178] Rose, *England*, pp. 144–151.
[179] Monod, 'Dangerous Merchandise'.
[180] CTB 14 (1698–1699), p. 96 (16 June 1699); CTB 15 (1698–1699), p. 102 (30 June 1699). TNA PC1/3/50; John Childs, *The British Army of William III, 1689–1702* (Manchester, 1987), p. 177; Muskett, 'Military Operations'; TNA T1/54, no. 8.
[181] Bowden, *Wool Trade*, pp. 41–76.
[182] TNA T1/58, no. 8; T1/60, no. 74; T1/83, no. 107. Baker's accounts in TNA AO3/1101/1.

into the West Country and into other maritime counties.[183] According to John Haynes, a subscriber to the Wool Commission and a pamphleteer in support of its cause, these men "did wonderful good service".[184] According to one account, the Wool Commission employed around 300 riding officers.[185] This, however, is probably hugely exaggerated. Another statement from the commissioners has the number closer to 100 officers.[186] Moreover, these were not officers in the strict sense but had received deputations from the commissioners without any salary whatsoever.[187] In all probability, these were men desperate for employment who were ready to profess their willingness to enforce the wool ban. Indeed, there were complaints that the Commission had deputed "necessitous and broken Persons, who committed many violent Actions". The zeal of such "abusive officers" – especially in the absence of any pay – must seriously be doubted.[188] Sure enough, "there being no possibility of obtaining Money out of the Exchequer to pay the Officers for their good services", soon enough "the Officers were forced to decline acting".[189]

Haynes, in his later writings, blamed the Treasury for such developments, for the "true reason" for which the Commission stopped acting, and "the only thing that baffled all their Designs and Projects" was that the Treasury was not willing to grant them any money.[190] Indeed, the Commission lobbied parliament and Privy Council repeatedly. In July 1698, they petitioned Privy Council, which forwarded the matter to the Treasury, but no money was forthcoming.[191] In the next year, a petition was laid before parliament, which set up a committee to investigate the matter. Despite some reports in parliament during that session, no decision was taken and,

---

[183] John Haynes, *A View of the Present State of the Clothing Trade in England* (London, 1706), pp. 41–52.

[184] Haynes, *View*, p. 48. Haynes also authored *Great Britain's glory: Or, An Account of the Great Numbers of Poor Employ'd in the Woollen and Silk Manufactures, to the Increase of Trade, the Enlargement of the Revenues of the Crown, and Augmenting our Navigation* (London, 1715).

[185] Smith, *Memoirs of Wool* II, pp. 166–167. Lees suggests that these figures are drawn from the accounts of the Commission rendered to parliament, but this is speculation. Lees, *Importance*, p. 160.

[186] CTB 14 (1698–1699), p. 85 (23 May 1699).

[187] Haynes, *View*, p. 50.

[188] JHC 13 (1699–1702), pp. 13, 703. The complaints were later confirmed by parliament, ibid., p. 783.

[189] Haynes, *View*, p. 48.

[190] Haynes, *View*, p. 60.

[191] TNA PC 2/77, p. 204; CTB 14 (1698–1699), pp. 180–181 (9 November 1698). The Treasury argued that things were being managed by the Customs and thought additional expenses unadvisable, see T1/74, no. 74.

again, no money disbursed.[192] Haynes claimed that this was because the session of parliament simply ended before a decision could be taken, but it is more likely that parliament thought the many instances of "corrupt and indirect practices" committed by the officers deputed by the Wool Commission were destructive to the wool trade.[193] Haynes, at least, was able to receive some reimbursement for his personal troubles.[194]

In its petitions, the Wool Commission made the claim, familiar from Carter's writings, that coastal prevention was in the king's interest and that the illegal exportation of wool cost him huge amounts of money in customs.[195] The argument was still valid, but times had changed. Government had already stepped up its own efforts at coastal prevention and if it is true, as has been suggested above, that this was both for more important and more covert motives than wool smuggling, then the government cannot have been happy at entrusting this to the hands of a few merchants. More importantly, the Treasury was jealously guarding its executive rights against any outside meddling.[196] Godolphin, during his tenure, was certainly keen on keeping the prerogatives of the Treasury intact.[197] With a view to the petition of the Wool Commission, the Treasury was aware that the Commission had – from a legal point of view – a "concurrent power" with the Customs concerning the exportation of wool and its prevention.[198] Yet despite the fact that the Board of Customs was willing to admit that, especially in regard to the Scottish Borders, it would be sensible to allow the Wool Commission some money, the Treasury was unwilling to make such an order.[199] More explicit still, when John Haynes petitioned for a position as a Supervisor of Riding Officers, the Treasury had his past activities on behalf of the Wool Commission thoroughly checked and arrived at a damning verdict.[200] Yet if the Treasury was serious about not needing the Wool Commission, then it was to some extent forced to find redress for the problems that the Commission had repeatedly pointed out, not least

---

[192] JHC 13 (1699–1702), pp. 41, 465, 705, 783.
[193] Haynes, *View*, p. 61; JHC 13 (1699–1702), p. 783.
[194] CSPD William III (1699–1700), p. 214 (1 June 1699); CTB 14 (1698–1699), p. 96 (16 June 1699); CTB 16 (1700–1701), p. 354 (9 August 1701).
[195] Anon., *The Deplorable Case of the Chief and other Agents or Officers that have been deputed...* (s.l., s.d.); also in TNA SP34/2/23.
[196] On the rise of the Treasury see Baxter, *Development*.
[197] CSPD, William and Mary (1694–5), pp. 179–186 (15 June 1694).
[198] CTB 14 (1698–1699), p. 85 (23 May 1699).
[199] TNA T11/14, p. 24; CTB 14 (1698–1699), p. 5 (23 May 1699); T1/74, no. 74.
[200] TNA T1/82, no. 26. This was in 1702. He tried again in 1719, only to be rejected on the same grounds, see TNA T1/224, no. 1, I–IV.

48 Coastal Policing in Eighteenth-Century Britain

with a view to the Scottish Borders.[201] Incidentally, the trafficking of English wool into Scotland was also a concern to Trumbull because of its apparent connections to Jacobites.[202] This made the Scottish Borders appear just as vulnerable as the southern coast. Some of the additional measures relating to Scotland,[203] but also the ones relating to Kent and Sussex can thus be understood as a means to discredit the view that the Wool Commission was "the only sure and effectual means" to enforce the wool ban.[204] Finally, given that the Wool Commission was also an infringement of parliament on the executive side of government, any endorsement of its activities by that government would have been highly controversial. William himself cannot have had any sympathies for the further strengthening of parliament's hand when he had been – during the years following the Peace of Ryswick – seriously at odds with the House over the question of a standing army.[205]

Conclusions

In the quarter ending midsummer 1688 – in the last months of James' reign – the number of preventive officers on the Customs establishment was 3.4% in relation to the total numbers of staff. In the quarter ending midsummer 1697 – in the months before the Peace of Ryswick, when fighting had stopped – those same numbers are not very different: preventive numbers were at 3.7%. Moreover, the overall growth of the Customs department was similar to the modest growth in preventive staff. The real divergence follows after 1697. In the quarter ending midsummer 1702 – just after William's death in March – preventive staff made for 13.1% of the numbers and 16.4% of the costs of the Customs establishment. This is even more striking if one excludes the London establishment – with its costly central office – from the equation: compared to the overall outport numbers, the preventive service accounted for 17% of the numbers and 24.6% of the costs. To put it differently: while the department had grown from 1202 officials in 1688 to 1727 officials in 1702, the preventive staff accounted for more than 35%

---

[201] Haynes, View, pp. 42, 55; TNA PC 2/77, p. 292.
[202] CSPD William III (1697), p. 477 (12 November 1697). Trumbull thought that "a commerce of such dangerous consequence to us ought by all means to be timely prevented, if possible".
[203] TNA T11/13, p. 404; T11/14, pp. 333, 390; T1/55, no. 54.
[204] Haynes, View, p. 28.
[205] Lois G. Schwoerer, 'The Role of King William III of England in the Standing Army Controversy', JBS, 5 (1966), 74–94; Lois G. Schwoerer, 'No Standing Armies!' The Antiarmy Ideology in Seventeenth-Century England (Baltimore, 1974).

Jacobitism, Coastal Policing, and Fiscal-Military Reform   49

of that growth. From a few riding surveyors and Customs smacks in 1688, numbering 41 in total, the service had swollen to 227 officers in 1702. Striking as they are, these numbers are a conservative estimate. For reasons of clarity, they only include officers solely devoted to coastal duties and do not account for the growing number of port officers equipped with horses and boats to perform additional coastal duties. Also, they only include Customs staff registered on the official establishment list and do not account for the large number of officers paid by incident.[206] The real proportions were, if anything, higher. After William's reign, the numbers still show a modest rise, but the figures at the end of Anne's reign – in 1714 – indicate a stagnation of growth both in total as well as of preventive staff.

Table 1: Customs Staff Numbers and Costs (England and Wales), 1685–1714.

Customs staff numbers	1685	1688	1697	1702	1714
Staff (London)	370	366	501	513	558
Staff (Outports)	749	836	940	1214	1312
Staff (total)	1119	1202	1441	1727	1870
Staff (Prev. Officers*)	68	41	54	227	280
Customs costs°	**1685**	**1688**	**1697**	**1702**	**1714**
Costs (London)	6124	5076	5605	5958	7278
Costs (Outports)	5163	5651	6987	9951	10848
Costs (total)	11287	10727	12592	15909	18126
Costs (Prev. Officers)	675	420	728	2612	3056

* To avoid ambiguity, only officials solely devoted to coastal duties are considered as preventive officers, such as riding surveyors, riding officers and the Customs smacks and their crews. The continuously rising number of port officials provided with horses and boats for coastal policing is not included.

° Total costs for the respective midsummer quarter, rounded sums in £. Whenever proportions of preventive costs exclusively to outport costs are given in the text, the costs of the smacks on the London establishment (typically at Gravesend) are excluded.

The above figures are derived from TNA CUST18/19, 18/25, 18/40, 18/59, 18/105.

While bare figures tell us little about the causes of such developments, these numbers still underscore the arguments of this chapter. The reign of William saw profound changes to the revenue service of the Customs,

---

[206] Hoon, *Organization*, pp. 198, 218.

most notably the establishment of a preventive coastal police within the span of just a few years. The correlation of this development to the war and to fiscal demands, however, is far from straightforward. For one thing, the decisive changes occurred after the war. Secondly, preventive staff was costly and therefore prone to diminish Customs returns. Of the overall rise in establishment costs from 1688 to 1702, preventive staff accounted for 42%. Consistently, the establishment lists show that preventive staff – with highly salaried riding officers and costly Customs smacks – was much more expensive in relation to their mere numbers than port staff. Their share of costs is always higher than their proportion in numbers.[207] Furthermore, they were much less productive in fiscal terms than regular port staff. They did not collect duties. Returns, if any, came in the form of penalties on the import or export of prohibited or highly taxed goods, but these were contingent on successful condemnation in the Exchequer – itself a costly and uncertain procedure. Given that smuggling in the 1690s concerned mainly the import of French goods and the export of wool, both of which were prohibited, Customs returns by way of legal import or export were still not going to rise even if the preventive service was successful in its task. Fiscally, the preventive service did not make much sense. The general attitude of the Treasury after 1698 – when changes were inevitably underway – supports this view. They were extremely reluctant to expend more than strictly necessary for the service. They repeatedly declined to establish a systematic Customs cruisers' scheme due to its cost.[208] They stubbornly haggled with Baker over the costs of his scheme of riding officers and attempted to cut the costs at all corners.[209] From their point of view, this was only sensible. When Baker's reduced scheme was finally adopted, it still cost £4880 per annum, roughly 8% of the entire establishment in 1699.[210] Clearly, Baker made substantial seizures and was fairly successful in court.[211] But the money necessarily expended on prosecution and the uncertainty of returns still made for an unreliable base of income.

Contrary to the general view of the Customs in this period, therefore, changes in the department cannot solely be attributed to fiscal pressures.

---

[207] Total staff numbers and total costs compared to the proportion of preventive staff and costs shows the relation at 3.4% to 3.9% (1688), 2.7% to 5.8% (1697), 13.1% to 16.4% (1702) and 15% to 16.9% (1714). The difference is more pronounced if only outport figures are considered, for example 5.1% to 9.5% (1697) and 17% to 24.6% (1702). See CUST18/25, 18/40, 18/59, 18/105.
[208] TNA T1/55, no. 75; T1/69, no. 61.
[209] TNA T1/58, no. 8; T1/60, no. 79; T1/45, no. 4a; T1/64, no. 33, no. 42.
[210] TNA T1/60, no. 79; CUST18/49.
[211] TNA CO388/7, 12 January 1699; T1/57, no. 57.

Jacobitism, Coastal Policing, and Fiscal-Military Reform 51

More tariffs certainly accentuated the need for stricter enforcement, which in turn required more staff. The heavy investment in a coastal police that accounted for over a third of the overall growth in the Customs and whose fiscal balance was prone to be negative must be attributed to a combination of other factors. The woollen interest and concerns in the highest political offices about the dangers of Jacobite infiltration each contributed to reforms in the revenue departments. To isolate one of these factors as decisive remains difficult. Perhaps intentionally, statements from each interested party tended to be equivocal: just as the clothiers and wool manufacturers claimed that such efforts would also improve the internal security of the Williamite regime, politicians at court recognised that creating a coastal police against elements subverting the regime had the additional benefit of pleasing an important fraction of the merchant community and an interest group in parliament. With the realisation, around 1695, that stricter coastal policing was politically called for – driven home by the events of 1696 and 1698 – the subsequent dedication of resources to Kent, Sussex and the Scottish Borders reflected both concerns equally. The exact shape of this new branch of the Customs was clearly modelled on schemes first conceived in counter-intelligence plans and for a time, this may have been the overriding concern in the executive. But the government was prudent enough to see the opportunity for killing two birds with one stone.

This is not to say that coastal policing did not benefit fiscal objectives in the long run. When smuggling shifted – by the eighteenth century – to goods such as tea, tobacco or brandy, the government's revenue was much more directly at stake.[212] At the moment of its inception, however, other motives prevailed and these frequently resurfaced during subsequent decades, particularly in relation to war and in the context of the Spanish War of Succession.[213] Bearing this in mind ultimately helps to see the preventive

---

[212] Ashworth, *Customs*, pp. 170–183.
[213] BL Add. MS 61607, fols 115–116; BL Add. MS 61608, fols 11–26; CTB 22 (1708), pp. 365–366 (16 August 1708). See for subsequent decades John B. Hattendorf, 'England in the War of the Spanish Succession' (Diss., University of Oxford, 1979); A. Thomson, 'Louis XIV and the Origins of the War of the Spanish Succession', *Transactions of the Royal Historical Society*, 5th ser., 4 (1954), 111–134; Matthias Pohlig, *Marlboroughs Geheimnis. Strukturen und Funktionen der Informationsgewinnung im Spanischen Erbfolgekrieg* (Köln/Weimar/Wien, 2016); Matthias Pohlig, 'Speed and safety. Infrastructuring the English postal service to the Low Countries during the War of the Spanish Succession', in Matthias Pohlig, Michael Schaich (eds), *The War of the Spanish Succession. New Perspectives* (Oxford, 2018), pp. 343–368. On the general transformation of political culture in these decades Andreas Gestrich, Michael Schaich (eds), *The Hanoverian Succession: Dynastic Politics and Monarchical Culture* (Farnham, 2015).

service and the Customs in a different light. Rather than portraying the Customs as an economically inadequate and fiscally deficient agency when measured against fiscal-military parameters, its failure to meet those standards perhaps calls for a questioning of these parameters. Any reduction to solely fiscal concerns understates the range of activities of a supposedly fiscal agency such as the Customs and, by extension, oversimplifies the complexities of the origins of the fiscal-military state. After all, even during the 1690s, the growth of state institutions was possible where no additional revenue was to be achieved and where such growth went directly against the dominant urge for a positive fiscal balance sheet.

2
Littoral Space and Coastal Mobility

This chapter advances a simple argument. From the moment designated coastal legislation and administration started to impact on the physical geography from the 1690s, the coast became a politically distinct space. Whereas geography had influenced social and economic realities in coastal regions for centuries, it was only with the designated attempts at ordering littoral space and controlling coastal mobility that this also became true in a political sense. The coast, in legal and practical terms, became an area of state activity and, thereby, a space apart. By looking at how legislators and administrators attempted to order coastal space with designated sets of laws and new bodies of coastal officers from the late seventeenth century onwards, the chapter aims to illustrate this larger argument by a number of smaller points.

Once the coast appeared on the political map of the United Kingdom in the context of political concerns specific to the reign of Mary and William (chapter 1), there was no returning to a state of ignorance. And yet for a long time, ignorance as to what the coast was and where it began or ended was not eliminated from legislation. With increasing amounts of legislation targeting coastal areas, there was not necessarily an awareness of how best to control coastal space. Such regulation was, secondly, often profoundly at odds with priorities in the executive. This was only natural, given that enforcement was a different matter from legislation. It is argued here, however, that these differences not only derived from different positions in the governing apparatus but originated in diverging understandings of space. Legislators tended to conceive the coast as something linear that required a sealing-off of certain movements and a restraint of certain activities attempting to cross the coastal line. Administrators, on the other hand, more acutely appreciated that the coast was to be understood as a deeper space, extending beyond the geographical tideline. They realised that enforcement hinged on familiarity with coastal spaces that eluded political or legislative delineations. Additionally, there was disagreement between central administrators and outport officials as well as individual riding officers: central bodies remained wilfully ignorant of physical realities on the ground. While statutory law and grand schemes of prevention rapidly encroached on coastal areas, these arrangements often failed to appreciate the complexity of coastal mobility. Finally, as a look at Scotland, Ireland and the Isle of Man shows, a uniform and expansive view of coastal space was profoundly at odds with the continuing fragmentation of fiscal spaces in the British archipelago well into the eighteenth century. Taken together, these results show that while the coast became an area of state activity to a hitherto unprecedented degree, attempts at state-building nevertheless remained incomplete even by the end of the eighteenth century.

Legislating Coastal Space

Three sets of statutory legislation started to impact on coastal mobility from around 1690.[1] The Wool Acts targeted certain forms of coastal movements, i.e. those connected to the logistics of wool export. Around 1700, Smuggling Acts started to extend these concerns to other types of smuggling, such as the illicit import of tea, tobacco and brandy. Secondly, existing legislation on vagrancy was brought to bear on coastal space. Finally, beginning with George I's reign, the control of coastal mobility was extended beyond movements on shore to include the coastal waters. In a sequence of Hovering Acts, specific types of movement of specific types of vessels were gradually restricted. Each in its own way, these sets of legislation sought to disable undesired types of mobility on the coast. They did so by subjecting actions that were deemed potentially indicative of criminal intent to a generalised form of suspicion whenever they occurred in proximity to the shore. At the same time, such legislation gradually enabled the tailored use of state authority in coastal regions.

The early legislation on wool displayed a marked focus on the mobility of goods. The Wool Acts passed in the reign of Charles II forbade the exportation of sheep or wool out of any port of England and Ireland. With the exception of a limited freedom of transport from the port of Southampton

---

[1] See on migration, vagrancy and other forms of everyday mobility, Peter Clark, 'Migration in England during the Late Seventeenth and Early Eighteenth Centuries', *Past and Present*, 83 (1979), 57–90; Peter Clark, David Souden (eds), *Migration and Society in Early Modern England* (London, 1987); David Hitchcock, 'Editorial: Poverty and Mobility in England, 1600–1850', *Rural History*, 24 (2013), 1–8; Steve Hindle, *On the Parish? The Micro-Politics of Poor Relief in Rural England, 1550–1750* (Oxford, 2004); Patricia Fumerton, *Unsettled: The Culture of Mobility and the Working Poor in Early Modern England* (Chicago, 2006); David Hitchcock, *Vagrancy in English Culture and Society, 1650–1750* (London, 2016).

to the islands of Jersey and Guernsey, no specific geographic provisions were made.[2] With the 1689 Wool Act, more specific spatial considerations entered the law. The Act required any wool carried into a five-mile zone from the shoreline to be entered into a register. In case of violation, horses, waggons and carriages were forfeit. On a larger scale, the Act limited the ports of export from Ireland and the English ports in which Irish wool could be imported.[3] The next Act extended these provisions to the Scottish Borders and appropriated the penalties to geographical circumstances. Legislation now ordered a summary penalty for the inhabitants of hundreds where offences were committed.[4] Gradually, the legislation acquired sensitivity for spatial issues. Because of frauds in Romney Marsh, the 1698 Act ordered for Kent and Sussex that all wool lodged within ten miles of the coast was to be registered with port officers. The same now applied to the Scottish Borders.[5]

This focus on wool was soon extended. At the same time as the Wool Acts were passed, the vagrancy laws were brought to bear on coastal mobility, as the opportunities for illegal export of wool were improved by the presence of "loose, idle & Disorderly persons that lye sculking along the Coasts".[6] In February 1690 and June 1698, Privy Council ordered JPs and other local magistrates "to put in execution with the utmost severity, the severall Statutes now in force against all Idle Persons, Rogues, Vagabonds & Sturdy Beggars".[7] Dating back to Tudor and Stuart reigns, the vagrancy statutes of 1572, 1597, 1601 and 1604 introduced severe punishment for people who, instead of remaining in their respective parishes, took to wandering the roads.[8] In 1662, just after the Restoration, a system of certificates for the monitoring of seasonal work was set up, and JPs were vested with powers to remove persons found idling to their home parishes, to workhouses, or to the plantations, thus ridding afflicted parishes of "rogues and vagabonds".[9] Such legislation was further refined in 1700 and 1714 and provided local magistrates with ready ways to rid the coasts of idle subjects.[10]

---

[2] Charles II, ch. 18.
[3] William and Mary, ch. 32.
[4] 7&8 William III, ch. 28.
[5] 9&10 William III, ch. 40.
[6] TNA PC 2/77, p. 192.
[7] *Ibid.* and TNA PC 2/73, p. 385.
[8] A. L. Beier, *Masterless Men: The Vagrancy Problem in England, 1560–1640* (London, 1985).
[9] Charles II, ch. 12.
[10] Hitchcock, *Vagrancy*, chapter 3.

With the reign of George I, attention shifted to the coastal waters. In a sequence of three acts, from 1718, 1719 and 1721 respectively, the hitherto unrestricted movement of ships was gradually constrained. Vessels under the size of 15 tons were forbidden to import spirits into any port of Great Britain. Similarly, fishing boats were barred from taking in merchandise from vessels at sea. The 1718 Act also defined and banned the practice of hovering, namely the lying of a ship off the coast "and not proceeding on her voyage (...), wind and weather permitting".[11] The next Act passed in the following session increased the tonnage limit to 30 and extended the hovering ban from the individual port limits to a general coastal zone of two leagues from the shores of Britain and Ireland.[12] With few exceptions, the use of rowing boats with more than four oars was forbidden in the southern coastal counties.[13]

Subsequent acts extended such limitations. In 1736, 1763 and 1779, the size and type of ships liable to rummage and seizure within the two league distance was specified; the 1736 Smuggling Act also introduced a four-league distance in which ships could not break bulk. Any coasting vessels could also now be searched by Customs officers.[14] In 1784, the hovering limit was extended to four leagues and certain types of boats – mainly the smaller and faster types such as cutters and wherries – were forfeit when entering these limits.[15] Finally, in 1794, coastal movement of certain boats was constrained by the introduction of restricted areas, such as within a supposed straight line from Lizard Point in Cornwall to Prawle Point in Devon or from Cromer in Norfolk to Flamborough Head in Yorkshire.[16] Such restricted areas were accompanied by prescriptions on the build and rigging of vessels as well as the visibility of ships' names and the hoisting of flags in order for the officers to more easily identify offenders.

From 1721, the mobility of people was severely restricted. The 1721 Smuggling Act held that more than five persons carrying weapons or going in disguise and moving contraband within 20 miles of the coast were guilty of felony.[17] The Waltham Black Act of 1723 reserved even severer punishment for going in disguise.[18] The 1746 Smuggling Act similarly deemed

---

[11] George I, ch. 11.
[12] George I, ch. 21.
[13] George I, ch. 18.
[14] George II, ch. 35; 3 George II, ch. 22; 5 George III, ch. 43; 19 George III, ch. 69.
[15] George III, ch. 47; See also 27 George III, ch. 32.
[16] George III, ch. 50.
[17] George I, ch. 18.
[18] E.P. Thompson, *Whigs and Hunters: The Origin of the Black Act* (London 1975); Frank McLynn, *Crime and Punishment in Eighteenth-Century England* (London, New York 1989), pp. 172–201.

the blackening of faces in proximity to the shore a serious offence.[19] It was the 1736 Smuggling Act, however, that held the most serious restrictions on mobility. Because "divers dissolute and disorderly persons frequently appear in great gangs near the sea coasts", the Act enabled JPs to commit persons with firearms and in company of three to gaol. Similarly, two or more armed or disguised persons found passing within five miles from the coast with horses or carriages and carrying more than six pounds of tea or brandy were to be "deemed and taken to be runners of foreign goods". Arrest was possible even in the absence of proof that the goods had paid no customs. A third provision was even vaguer: any person found "lurking, waiting, or loitering, within five miles from the sea coast" with an intent to assist in the running of goods could be asked to "give a satisfactory account of themselves, and their callings". Failing this, they could be sentenced to hard labour.[20] Evidently, in their language and in the penalties assigned to those "loitering" on the coast, these laws were similar to those against vagrancy. Yet they were meant to enforce executive control and limit undesired mobility specifically in coastal spaces.

The spaces thus demarcated by parliamentary legislation were unquestionably linear. The Acts interspersed the map of the United Kingdom with straight lines, corridors and radii of varying size and depth. The linchpin of these was invariably the coast. Irrespective of the irregularities of the shoreline, legislation conceived of it as a clearly defined benchmark for the definition of spaces on either of its sides. From a legal perspective, different rules applied within these spaces. The question is what happened when such idealized notions of space met with reality.

The limits prescribed by parliament were insufficient in that they recurrently revealed legal loopholes. In a statement before the Commons in 1746, one Barnaby Bland, officer in the Customs, described a "Defect in the Laws relating to the Seizure of Vessels". Whereas vessels illicitly importing tea were liable to seizures regardless of size within the legal limits, vessels allegedly running brandy were not liable to rummaging if above 40 tons.[21] Such problems were framed by witnesses as problems of enforcement, but parliament correctly understood them to be legal deficiencies. The 1783 revenue committee, for example, was rather outspoken about such defects. Whereas it was a felony to wound an officer attempting to board a ship within port limits, they observed, there was no such penalty for doing the same without the port limits. To protect the officers, an extension of the limits was necessary. Horses and carriages were only subject to forfeiture

---

[19] George II, ch. 34.
[20] George II, ch. 35.
[21] JHC 25, p. 107.

when they were actually being used to convey contraband. Thus the stationing of waggons was as indicative of criminal intent as it was unprosecutable by law.[22] Time and again, it was found that "the Laws against this pernicious Trade are not sufficient to prevent it".[23] As late as 1785, the collector at Cowes found the Wool Acts insufficient in that they only mentioned Kent and Sussex. They should, ideally, cover all "Counties bordering on the Sea Coasts of the Kingdom".[24]

There were also practical problems to applying the laws. The 1783 committee found that the loitering clause in the 1736 Act enabling the arrest of persons lurking within five miles of the coast was "impracticable". As "Persons of this Description chiefly assemble" in the night, when it was impossible to obtain warrants from JPs, they often went unobstructed about their business.[25] Other problems resulted from the legal proof that many activities within the legal limits required. Frequently it was not feasible to find proof that ships had broken bulk within hovering distances. Goods seized in such cases had to be released.[26] Moving of wool was also difficult to prove to be intended for illegal export, "however suspicious the Circumstances of the Case may be".[27] Not without irony did one George Bridges remark in 1744 that this was the stone on which all legislation against smuggling was "split upon". "For, what Man living can swear to the *Intention* of another Man, unless he sees his *Intention* brought into Action? and then Action shapes our Matter and Form, by which the *Intention* is discovered: But, by the way, I must tell you it is then too late, the Ship is gone".[28]

On some stretches of coast, moreover, the two-league hovering distance was no obstruction to smuggling. From Great Yarmouth it was reported in 1783 that this limit "is evidently too small" as vessels could "lay in the offing without the limits" and, observing the coast to be clear, "can put for

[22] 'Third Report'.
[23] *The Report of the Committee appointed to inquire into the Frauds and Abuses in the Customs, to the Prejudice of Trade, and Diminution of the Revenue*. Reported on the Seventh of June 1733 by Sir John Cope, printed in *Reports from the Committees of the House of Commons*. Reprinted by Order of the House. Vol. I, Miscellaneous Subjects: 1715–1735 (1803), pp. 601–654, at p. 633.
[24] TNA CUST 61/6, 29 January 1785.
[25] 'First Report', pp. 215–278.
[26] *The Report of the Committee appointed to inquire into the Frauds and Abuses in the Customs*, p. 635.
[27] TNA CUST 61/6, 29 January 1785.
[28] George Bridges, *Plain Dealing: Or the Whole Method of Wool-Smuggling Clearly Discover'd, And the Weakness of the Laws in Force, put in a clear Light* (London, 1744), p. 5.

the Land and gain it within an Hour".[29] From Cowes, it was said that if the hovering distance was extended to three leagues, it might be "some check" on the smugglers.[30] William Stiles argued in 1800 that the best approach was "to do away the present limited distances".[31] Indeed, the answer to such faults was for parliament to extend the limits and strive, wherever loopholes were discovered, for a more universal ambit of the laws. With Acts passed after 1800, the limits were settled at 8 and then, in 1805, at one hundred leagues.[32] This corresponded with opinions on the ground. In 1804, the collector at Cowes reasoned that it was best "to abolish the limits altogether", for in his opinion "Limits on the Coast operate more as an encouragement and safeguard to the Smuglers than as a Terror or Risk".[33]

Such gradual encroachment of the laws did not, however, go uncontested. Particularly the Act of 1736 sparked a long debate in parliament.[34] Its opponents protested the imprecision of its spatial delineations. They took umbrage at the clause that allowed rummaging of ships within port limits: "What may be meant by the limits of the port, I do not know, but I am certain it is a term so vague and indeterminate, that it must occasion an infinite number of contests". This would, in turn, be "a great hardship upon our merchants"; precise limits were needed.[35] Such precision was also urged relative to the clause that made the assembly of three armed persons a felony. Whereas the 1721 Act had required officers to prove that persons were found passing within a certain distance to the sea, the Bill's opponents protested that such proof was abolished by the present clause. If anyone was "only passing from one inland town to another, but unluckily happened to be within five miles of any navigable river, which includes many inland parts of England, [...] he thereby forfeits his estate and liberty".[36] To make actions a felony that formed an essential part of the rights and liberties of English gentlemen – namely, to carry arms and to go freely about their ways – was putting the constitution in grave danger. A clause that allowed arrest "without limitation of time or place" was simply unacceptable.

[29] TNA CUST97/25, 20 October 1783.
[30] TNA CUST61/6, 23 October 1783.
[31] TNA T64/153, p. 60.
[32] William E. Masterson, *Jurisdiction in Marginal Seas with Special Reference to Smuggling* (New York 1929), pp. 72–90.
[33] TNA CUST61/17, 31 December 1804.
[34] *The Parliamentary History of England, from the Earliest Period to the Year 1803*. Vol. IX, A.D: 1733–1737 (London, 1811), pp. 1225–1268; *The London Magazine and Monthly Chronologer* 1736, pp. 714–734.
[35] *The Parliamentary History*, p. 1239.
[36] *The Parliamentary History*, p. 1263.

In the event, the advocates of the Bill won the day: it passed without amendments. They defended the above clauses as adequate to the heinous nature of the crime, harmless to innocent people and, what was more, necessary to fight the growing evil of smuggling. As to port limits, their speaker took "it to be a term as well understood among merchants and seafaring men, as any term whatever: I suppose every firth and navigable river, must be within the limits of some port; and with respect to our ports upon the ocean, I suppose the limits of each port extend to the place where ships bound for that port usually come to anchor."[37] As far as the advocates of the Bill were concerned, such objections to the spatial provisions of the Bill were unfounded.

But they were not. The Customs officers' powers for stop and search frequently caused legal disputes.[38] Also, the port limits in every port were not as well defined as members of parliament thought. Late in December 1727, the collector of Great Yarmouth informed the Customs Board that there was "a tract of the sea shore in the County of Norfolk of about 20 miles extent, that is not as yet set forth to be in any Port." This area was notorious for smuggling, and its undefined nature was likely to produce seizure disputes.[39] Despite several surveys, this state of affairs continued for another ten years.[40] The matter was eventually settled in 1738, when, after a redrawing of the limits, "no chasm is left between Port & Port". At the same time, port limits in Norfolk and Suffolk were extended: whereas previously the distance was set individually for each port at a water depth of 14 fathoms, this was universally extended to the seaward to a limit of four leagues, so that "anchoring places on the whole coast will be included".[41] This was more reliable, as the depths varied and the legal bounds were in some places fairly near the shore, whereas in others "the bounds might be said to be indefinite". Though this way it was more difficult for Customs men clearly to determine the exact distance to the shore, it was much easier for informers, who, witnessing frauds from land, had no means of establishing the distance by depth, "but they can always nearly tell what distance from the Shore the fact was committed".[42]

---

[37] *The Parliamentary History*, p. 1251.
[38] TNA CUST97/3, 14 and 23 April 1718; CUST97/4, 31 March 1720, 18 April 1721, 8 May 1721.
[39] TNA CUST97/5, 1 November 1728.
[40] TNA CUST97/6, 16 April 1729; CUST97/7, 14 July 1732; CUST97/10, 16 October 1736, 25 October 1736.
[41] TNA CUST97/11, 4 December 1738.
[42] TNA CUST97/11, 18 December 1738; 4 May 1741.

As these examples show, coastal spaces demarcated by parliament were as homogenous and clear in the statute book as they were blurry in practice. They were not as unambiguously defined as their application required. They were hard to determine on the ground and too crude to account for local particularities. And the application of legal provisions often posed practical difficulties, because prosecutions required proof that movements had taken place within those spaces. Finally, the legal distances fell forever short of the necessities. The obvious remedy of extending those limits, however, met with opposition. With a view to this situation, the 1783 committee concluded that it appeared "impossible to provide better Laws than are already in Force". In a resigned appraisal of legislative measures, the report stated that, "there are other obvious Measures of Coercion, which depend rather upon the executive Power than on any new Provisions to be recommended to the Legislature".[43] Much, as this conclusion suggests, depended on the executive and actual enforcement.

Coastal Space in the British Archipelago

Priorities in the executive were different from legislative notions. Drawing legal limits onto the maps of the Great Britain was neither difficult nor expensive. Enforcement was a different matter. There were never sufficient resources to pay equal attention to every stretch of coastline. Some places were heavily protected. Others were virtually unguarded. But what places were these? Appointments from the early 1700s onwards already reveal specific patterns. They are even more evident when looking at later establishments. But the underlying rationales of these choices made by central authorities are best understood with a view to Ireland, the Scottish Borders, the Isle of Man and the south-east of England.

At the end of the seventeenth century, the majority of the English and Welsh coastlines were unguarded. The Commissioners of Customs and the Treasury were aware of this, yet often responded with hesitation. In May 1686, the collector of Great Yarmouth reported that he had "been upon the Coast of Norfolke as farre as Wells and doe finde […], that it is in a manner wholly unguarded, there being noe officer from Yarmouth to Cley which is forty miles, and in that forty miles, 22 landing places".[44] Indeed, the Board had pursued a course of reluctant investment during the 1670s and 80s. In 1676, the two surveyors were instructed "often to visit the Coast both to

[43] 'Third Report', pp. 10–11.
[44] TNA CUST97/1, 31 May 1686.

the Northward, and Southward".[45] Two years later, one Mr. Anguish was to "endeavour to settle a correspondence in all such suspitious places whereby you may have notice of all such practices."[46] Nicholas Webb, officer at Norwich, was equally told to settle a "Correspondence [...] to gain Intelligence". He was also to visit public houses at Norwich where carriers coming from "any Maritime Place" were lodging.[47] Only in 1681 was the watch on the coast supplemented with additional officers.[48] Though these measures indicate a growing awareness of the lengths of unguarded coastlines, they also speak to the restraint of such efforts. Coastal vigilance was left to part-timers and informers.

Matters stood similarly in Sussex and Kent before 1699. In a tour from Gravesend along to Chichester, Henry Baker revealed a decidedly patchy situation.[49] In the Isle of Sheppey, there was "noe officer at all in any part of this island". Affairs at Whitstable, Herne Bay and Reculver were similar. The Isle of Thanet, furthermore, saw a great deal of smuggling that "cant be prevented withoute a better Guard on that Coast". From Ramsgate to Sandwich there was, again, "noe manner of Rideing officer, or soe much as a horse kept". Things were better at Deal, Dover and further west. But here, too, establishments were inadequate. The situation worsened in Romney Marsh and between Winchelsea and Hastings, where the one officer stationed was "no more a Guard for his Ride on the Coast, than an honest man on the Road is against five Highwaymen". Seaford was worse, for there was "a bold open Coast and noe officer near itt", just as there was none between Newhaven and Shoreham. At Littlehampton, there was one boatman who was "of nor more use for this service, than a Gull on the beach". By the end of 1699, Baker had managed to arrange for a seamless watch on these same coastlines.[50]

The example of Kent and Sussex spread. Soon the Scottish Borders were reviewed by the collectors at Berwick and Carlisle.[51] Formerly, the borders were inspected by officers of the Customs as well as Excise men. In February 1698, a surveyor had been appointed to supervise these efforts; this was complemented with another set of riding officers.[52] Around this time, the western ports – Portsmouth, Southampton, the Isle of Wight,

---

[45] TNA CUST97/74A, 4 August 1676.
[46] TNA CUST97/74A, December 1678.
[47] TNA CUST97/74A, 26 August 1680.
[48] TNA CUST97/74A, 4 August 1676.
[49] TNA T1/63, no. 21.
[50] TNA T11/14, pp. 41f.; TNA T1/76, no. 46.
[51] TNA T1/55, no. 54; T1/60, no. 80.
[52] TNA T11/13, p. 404; T11/14, p. 333, pp. 390f.

Weymouth, Exeter, and the ports down the Devon coast and around the Cornish peninsula, including Dartmouth, Plymouth, Falmouth, Penzance and St Ives – were put under stricter guard. In September 1699, additions were made on the Lincolnshire coast;[53] in December, preventive officers were appointed from Beaumaris to Carlisle;[54] in November 1701, the coast from Newcastle to Bridlington also received extra officers for the "better Guard of the several Rivers, Bays & Creeks";[55] finally, appointments were also made in Hampshire, Dorset, Devon and Norfolk.[56]

By the end of William's reign, this arrangement seemingly covered all of England and Wales. This impression is supported by the new 1698 establishment of sloops for the coastal waters. Whereas Kent and Sussex were guarded by three sloops in addition to the Gravesend smack, altogether fourteen sloops were proposed for the rest of the English and Welsh coast to guard "the whole Coast of England".[57] This establishment at sea, however, was not put into practice at this stage. With regards to the shore, it is important to note that the exact nature of investment reveals significant regional differences. Whereas in Kent and Sussex it was new appointments of officers with explicitly preventive titles – such as riding officers or riding surveyors –, other regions either had existing funds reallocated to preventive officers or were granted officers who combined preventive tasks with port business. In the western ports, for example, new preventive officers were only settled on the Isle of Wight and some Cornish ports, whereas elsewhere it was established officers who received allowances for horses or increased salaries for additional preventive tasks.[58] Aside from Kent and Sussex, the entire south received few new preventive officers. On the stretch between Beaumaris and Carlisle on the north-western coast, in contrast, a larger share of new preventive officers was established at ports such as Chester, Liverpool, Lancaster or Whitehaven.[59] In the north-east, too, a higher number of preventive officers was appointed in 1701. Whereas it is uncontroversial, in other words, that the heaviest emphasis was and remained on the south-east, it seems that it was on the Scottish Borders, in the north-east and in the north-west, where the strongest departure from former arrangements during these early years of the preventive service occurred.

[53] TNA T11/14, p. 44.
[54] TNA T11/14, p. 53.
[55] TNA T11/14, pp. 149, 155.
[56] TNA T11/13, pp. 397, 403, 406, 408, 428; T11/14, pp. 42, 97, 287.
[57] TNA T1/51, no. 77; T1/55, no. 75; T1/56, no. 12.
[58] TNA T11/13, pp. 461–463.
[59] TNA T11/14, p. 53.

The patterns of these early years are confirmed by establishment records for the rest of the century (see Table 2). Most preventive staff are recorded for the south-east, from Kent through Sussex and Hampshire to Dorset. Next were regions particularly open to smuggling from the continent, such as Devon and Cornwall (from France), Essex and Norfolk (from the Netherlands) and Yorkshire (from Scandinavia). Given the political dominance of England over the British archipelago, one should assume that the further one moved to the north and west, the less preventive staff should have been required. This is not confirmed by the establishment lists. Whereas the Welsh coastline remained virtually unguarded, Cumberland and Northumberland as well as Lancashire and Cheshire did have a considerable number of preventive staff in the period. This is despite the relatively low levels of Customs receipts of ports such as Whitehaven or Lancaster. Throughout the period, moreover, it was coastal stretches such as these that were patrolled by navy vessels and occasionally reinforced by the military. What were the guiding rationales for these deployment patterns? The south-east has already been looked at in chapter 1, but what were the guiding principles for the north-west and north-east? These cannot be explained from an English perspective, but can only be understood with a view from Scotland, Ireland and the Isle of Man.

"So many Seas": Scottish Prevention and English Trade

The Act of Union of England and Scotland spawned a host of administrative problems. Little was regulated in terms of the everyday conduct of political business. Among other issues, the assimilation of the revenue schemes of both kingdoms was to be regulated. This was difficult ground. In fact, "the setting up in this Place [Scotland] that great and ingenuous Fabrick of the Customs of England which has been erecting there by degrees almost an age" was enough to frustrate even the most willing of administrators.[60] The Treasury knew little about Scotland and Godolphin depended on the English revenue boards for suggestions.[61] After some debate, separate Scottish

---

[60] TNA T1/123, no. 4.
[61] On the Union and the Customs P. W. J. Riley, *The English Ministers and Scotland 1707–1727* (London, 1964); Philipp Robinson Rössner, *Scottish Trade in the Wake of Union (1700–1760): The Rise of a Warehouse Economy* (Stuttgart, 2008). On smuggling Jack Sybill, 'Customs, Tobacco and Smuggling in South-Western Scotland', *Journal of the Sydney Society for Scottish History*, 2 (1994), 52–75; T. C. Barker, 'Smuggling in the Eighteenth Century. The Evidence of the Scottish Tobacco Trade', *The Virginia Magazine of History and Biography*, 62 (1954), 387–399; Robert C. Nash, 'The English and Scottish Tobacco Trades in the Seventeenth and Eighteenth Centuries. Legal and Illegal Trade', *The Economic History Review*, New Series 35 (1982),

Table 2: Preventive Officers on the English Establishment by County, 1702–1802 (Sources: TNA CUST18/59, CUST18/105, CUST18/213, CUST18/400, CUST18/530).

County	1702 men	1702 ships	1714 men	1714 ships	1742 men	1742 ships	1782 men	1782 ships	1802 men	1802 ships
Kent	46	2	56	3	66	3	184	7	72	3
Sussex	51	2	52	2	75	2	182	5	130	3
Hampshire	11	1	16	1	33	2	81	3	63	2
Dorset	10	1	34	2	9		97	3	48	1
Devon	26	2	36	2	38	2	125	5	41	1
Cornwall	32	3	55	3	22		188	7	76	2
Somerset	/		/		1		4		1	
Gloucestershire	8	1	9	1	9	1	8		3	
South Wales (Swansea)	2		1		17	2	1		2	
West Wales (Milford Haven)	2		2		4		1		35	1
North Wales (Beaumaris)	1		1		1		3		6	
Cheshire	1		4		2		2		2	
Lancashire	19	1	7		8		6		15	
Cumberland	5		5		6		36	1	20	
Northumberland	11	1	12		11		62	2	41	1
Durham	2		/		2				6	
Yorkshire	11		11		23	1	30	1	16	
Lincolnshire	3		4		6		15	1	10	
Norfolk	8	1	7	1	43	3	49	2	39	1
Suffolk	/		/		19	1	7		7	
Essex	9	1	1		32	2	96	3	58	2
	258		313		427		1177		691	

Customs and Excise boards were established and the Scottish Customs were managed by three Englishmen and two Scots.[62] On the ground, port establishments were adjusted to the management of the English outports. And while many Customs men on the Scottish side feared that positions were being taken away from them so that English ministers could satisfy the demands of patronage, English officials worried that Scottish officers were both too unfamiliar with the English way of collecting revenue and too familiar with local circumstances not to be heavily entangled in corruption.[63] Both fears, as subsequent developments showed, were absolutely warranted.

The first establishment of the Scottish Customs in 1707 included four riding surveyors and twelve riding officers.[64] These officers were to be divided into four districts.[65] Because of the "Large Firths and inlets", boats and smacks were to be employed.[66] Because of frequently "tempestuous weather", three "strong" sloops were built and ordered to cruise the Scottish coast. One was to guard the far north – from Skye on the west coast to Inverness in the east. A second sloop was to patrol the Firth of Forth, ranging as far as Berwick and Inverness. A third sloop, finally, was to focus on the Firth of Clyde, once again ranging as far as Skye in the north and the Solway in the south.[67] Alongside these Customs sloops, some private shipowners seem to have been contracted for coastal prevention.[68] Early in 1708, it became clear that additional firepower was needed on the west

354–372; Valerie Wallace, 'Presbyterian Moral Economy. The Covenanting Tradition and Popular Protest in Lowland Scotland, 1707–c.1746', *SHR*, 89 (2010), 54–72; Jacob Price, 'Glasgow, the Tobacco Trade, and the Scottish Customs, 1707–1730: Some Commercial, Administrative and Political Implications of the Union', *SHR*, 63 (1984), 1–36. On the uncertainties of the Scottish board about rules see T1/101, no. 103 (instructions), T1/102, no. 61 and no. 101 (salaries), T1/102, no. 96 (prosecutions); T17/1, pp. 96–98. The best summary account of the economic impact of the Union is C. A. Whatley, *Scottish Society 1707–1830: Beyond Jacobitism, towards Industrialisation* (Manchester, 2000). See also his 'Economic Causes and Consequences of the Union of 1707', *SHR*, 68 (1989), pp. 150–181. Most recently Hannes Ziegler, 'Smuggling and the Customs Administration in Post-Union Scotland, c.1707–1724', *SHR*, 103 (2024), 436–458.

[62] Alexander Rigby, James Isaacson, Lionel Norman (England); Robert Dickson, William Boyle (Scotland).
[63] Riley, *English Ministers*, pp. 37–59.
[64] TNA T17/1, pp. 165ff. (Establishment Michaelmas 1707).
[65] *Instructions for the Collectors and other Officers Employ'd in HER MAJESTIES Customs, in the North-Part of Great-Britain* (Edinburgh, 1707), Appendix 43.
[66] TNA T1/102, no. 101.
[67] TNA T1/105, no. 29; T1/106, no. 13; T17/1, pp. 219–221.
[68] TNA T1/102, no. 76; T1/103, no. 96.

coast and three men-of-war under Admiralty commands were appointed.[69] In the same vein, soldiers were occasionally stationed in coastal areas.[70] Steps were also taken for a proper communication between Customs and Admiralty and a strict supervision of coastal officers.[71]

All of this amounted to considerable costs: whereas the initial 1707 establishment cost £9,735 per year, costs had risen to £12,446 in 1710. Together with incidents, expenses stood at £17,758.[72] Given that the average customs receipts from Scotland were around £20,000 – a mere 2% of the British totals – this was expensive.[73] But it was in line with the idea of the Scottish Board to make the system work, "cost what it will". They acknowledged that the Scottish returns did not justify such expenditures, but thought these efforts justified by the "prevention of a much greater damage to the whole Island".[74] Thus the initial pattern of events conformed to Defoe's observation that the physical geography of Scotland would require "a little army of officers" for preventive tasks.[75] Over the course of the following years, diminishing net returns revealed the true dilemma of the Scottish Customs. For one thing, widespread fraud was thought to diminish returns significantly. There were vivid reports of corruption among the officers.[76] Merchants, "country people", JPs and lairds were believed to connive at these practices.[77] Sir Alexander Rigby, most active of the Commissioners, did not escape charges of corruption either.[78] Smuggling, too, was a growing concern.[79] Such reports fuelled a steady growth of the establishment after 1707. The Board, realising the enormity of their task, grew desperate: "Wee do what in us lies [...], for the naturall situation of this Countrey doth very much perplex us, having so many and such large inletts, which are

[69] TNA T1/106, no. 71; T1/107, no. 15, no. 53; T1/113, no. 18; T17/1, pp. 351–352, 384–385.
[70] TNA T1/102, no. 97; T1/106, no. 70; T1/107, no. 9.
[71] TNA T1/107, no. 60.
[72] Riley, *English Ministers*, pp. 126–129.
[73] Rössner, *Scottish Trade*, p. 40; Price, *Glasgow*, pp. 7–8.
[74] TNA T17/1, p. 97; TNA T1/102, no. 101.
[75] Daniel Defoe, *The History of the Union between England and Scotland with a Collection of Original Papers Relating Thereto* (London, 1709, repr. 1786), p. 577.
[76] TNA T1/105, no. 8; T1/113, no. 44; BL Add. MS 70047, fols 16–37; TNA T1/121, no. 15.
[77] TNA T1/105, no. 29; T1/106, no. 60; T1/110, no. 7, no. 38; T1/240, no. 45. For descriptions of an insider, see William Mackay (ed.), *The Letter-Book of Bailie John Steuart of Inverness 1715–1752* (Edinburgh, 1915). See also BL Add. MS 70048, fol. 165.
[78] TNA T1/114, no. 19; Riley, *English Ministers*, pp. 132–134; "A Short History of The Custome House Affairs of North Brittaine Since the Union to the Fifth of May 1709" in BL Add. MS 30229.
[79] TNA T1/107, no. 9, T1/108, no. 24; T1/113, no. 40, no. 43.

as it were, so many Seas."[80] Consequently, more preventive officers were appointed.[81] While doing little to raise the revenue, their salaries further diminished returns.

At this point, Godolphin stepped in and asked the Scottish Board to reduce the costs of their establishment.[82] They put up an elaborate defence, citing preventive duties and the decay of Scottish trade as reasons for the meagre returns. They also argued that they had only the seventh part of officers compared to the English Customs for securing the revenue in a country that was "more difficult to Guard against Frauds", the "circumference of our Coast" being larger as well as "much more accessible, and difficult to watch" than in England. Ultimately, however, they complied.[83] The establishment of August 1710 saved more than £3,000.[84] It did away with riding officers altogether, they having not "answered the End of their appointment". Port officers with horses and Excise men with deputations were to replace them. The sloops were struck off because they were "very expensive, and of little or no use" and "not at all fit" for the Scottish coasts.[85] The English Commissioners' strong objection to the abolition of designated coastal officers went unheard.[86]

When Godolphin was replaced by Robert Harley, this changed little in the management of the Scottish Customs. Rather, the pattern of events until 1710 was to repeat itself after 1711. Corruption among the Customs men and smuggling remained recurring issues, despite a large-scale purge of the lower ranks in 1710/11.[87] An investigation in 1712 revealed widespread frauds at Prestonpans; another in 1718 detailed a sorry state of affairs at Inverness.[88] As a direct result of these findings, the reduced establishment began almost immediately to grow again. In February 1714, a riding surveyor, five riding officers and a sloop were appointed for the guard of the south-western coast. An entirely new establishment the following month – requested by Harley in response to frauds – included additional preventive boats. In the next year, a sloop

---

[80] TNA T1/116, no. 4.
[81] TNA T17/2, pp. 95, 129; T1/114, no. 30.
[82] TNA T17/2, p. 174; T1/117, no. 4.
[83] TNA T1/123, no. 4; BL Add. MS 70047, fols 40–43.
[84] TNA T17/2, pp. 200–209; see also CTB 24 (1710), pp. 408–413.
[85] TNA T17/2, pp. 207–209. On the performance of these officers see T1/126, no. 37.
[86] TNA T1/123, no. 4; TNA T1/157, no. 2; BL Add. MS 70047, fols 64–65, 67–68, 83–84.
[87] TNA T1/127, no. 2, no. 37; T1/131, no. 48, no. 55; see also the report from 1715 in T1/185, no. 63.
[88] TNA T1/145, no. 43; T64/238. Reactions to the Inverness report in T17/4, p. 294. Frauds were also discovered at Leith, Bo'ness, Aberdeen, Montrose, Orkney, Shetland see T1/146, no. 33; T1/151, no. 15; T1/240, no. 45; T17/7, pp. 70–71.

was built for the Firth of Forth and additional landcarriage men with a riding surveyor were hired.[89] Land and navy forces were also frequently required.[90]

Matters were finally put on a new level under the management of Robert Walpole from 1721. Throughout the second half of the decade, frauds continued to be reported and the Treasury under Walpole, Stanhope and Sunderland made efforts at checking corruption among the Customs men. Things came to a head in the election year 1722, when English merchants intensified their pressure on the English administration about frauds in Scotland.[91] Humphrey Brent, former Scottish Commissioner, was sent to inspect Glasgow and other ports.[92] At the same time, parliament abolished the separate Scottish Customs Board and in 1723 an extensive inquiry was launched into the Scottish administration. It recommended large-scale changes to coastal policing. The inspectors professed "great surprise" about how poorly the coasts were guarded. Boats were recommended at Bo'ness, St Andrews, Montrose, Aberdeen, Fraserburgh, Inverness, Thurso, Fort William, Port Glasgow, Ayr, Wigtown and Dumfries. Also, more riding officers were needed at St Andrews, Montrose, Aberdeen, Fraserburgh, Inverness and Glasgow in addition to six riding officers south of Dumfries and Edinburgh to guard the borders. A number of new sloops were built in addition to the two existing ones.[93] Changes were quickly implemented. Four riding surveyors were appointed to supervise the Firth of Clyde and the area west and south-west of Glasgow.[94] In June 1724, the Treasury ordered seven sloops for the western and eastern coastlines.[95] In June 1725, William Hamiltoun was appointed riding surveyor commanding ten riding officers for prevention on the west and south coast.[96]

The geography of these appointments owes something to English mercantile pressures. From the Union to the reforms under Walpole, English comments on preventive measures in Scotland were regularly made with a view to potential consequences to English trade. In 1709, the English Customs Board ventured the opinion that the losses in the Whitehaven tobacco

[89] TNA T17/3, pp. 22–23, 476, 537, 539; T17/3, pp. 29–87.
[90] TNA T1/137, no. 24; T1/146, no. 13.
[91] Price, *Glasgow*; Anon., *The Case of the Merchants Trading in Tobacco, at Whitehaven, in the County of Cumberland* (c.1715); Anon., *Reasons humbly offered for Regulating the Importation of Tobacco into this Kingdom, for the Preservation of the Revenue, and the better Carrying on of the said Trade* (1722).
[92] TNA T17/6, pp. 194, 332. Brent's final report in T64/240.
[93] George I, ch. 21; Instructions for the 1723 inquiry in T17/6, pp. 336–341, 367. The reports in T1/250, no. 9.
[94] TNA T17/6, pp. 194–196.
[95] TNA T1/252, no. 70; T17/7, pp. 184–186, 416–421.
[96] TNA T17/7, pp. 370–371, 382, 406, 415.

trade were a result of the Union.[97] Subsequent surveys unfailingly stressed this particular point. When four riding surveyors were appointed early in 1722, this was because by frauds in Scotland "the merchants in England have also been greatly discouraged in their Trade."[98] Shortly thereafter, frauds in Scotland were perceived as a "great loss and Damage to the fair Importers of Tobacco from Virgina and Maryland into England."[99] The building of the seven sloops in 1724, was justified by the perception that frauds otherwise carried on were "to the detriment of the Trade in South Britain."[100] Such views were not exclusive to the early 1720s. Around 1711, too, it was alleged that "in the management of the Customs in *North Britain*, the Revenue and Trade of *England* may suffer considerably."[101]

Anti-smuggling appointments reflect these views. In the establishments, the heaviest investment had – by the farmers of the Customs before the Union – been in the south-east and on the borders. Some islands had been further sublet by the farmers and most were treated as outside the Scottish fiscal ambit. The islands, the north, and the north-west were thinly policed, if at all.[102] In 1707, this was continued: most officers acted south of a line between Glasgow and Peterhead.[103] This was especially the case for the initial establishment of preventive officers in 1707, whose four districts had a clear imbalance towards the south and east with no officer stationed north-west of a line between Inverness and Glasgow.[104] It is true that this balance tipped in favour of the north and west after 1710.[105] But the north-west comprised a larger area and was more difficult to police. Additionally, the investment in preventive officers was still heavier in the south-east during the period. Recommendations of the 1723 survey amounted to a redeployment from the north-west to the south-east.[106] Simple arithmetic informed this view: "The situation of the North West part of this Country is more commodious for embezlements [frauds], then for a regular Trade. The Islands are so contiguous to Ireland, and afford such shelter, that the whole Revenue now collected would not pay the Salaries to such a number of Officers as might be sufficient for guarding the Islands, Coast, Creeks,

---

[97] TNA T1/121, no. 10.
[98] TNA T17/6, p. 195.
[99] TNA TT17/6, p. 332.
[100] TNA T17/7, p. 185.
[101] BL Add. MS 70047, fol. 83. My emphasis.
[102] BL Add. MS 70047, fols 86–87.
[103] TNA T17/1, pp. 165–172.
[104] *Instructions for the Collectors and other Officers Employ'd in HER MAJESTIES Customs, in the North-Part of Great-Britain* (Edinburgh, 1707), Appendix 43.
[105] Riley, *English Ministers*, p. 202.
[106] TNA T1/250, report no. 6.

Firths and Inlets." Rather than preventive officers, a system of securities was more likely to check illegal importation into Scotland.[107] Whenever preventive officers were appointed, the focus was on the south-east.[108]

This also affected policy at the borders. Watches on the borders, an important feature of both the Scottish farmers and the English Customs administration before 1707, were eliminated from the Scottish establishment with the Union.[109] In England, however, they remained. Just before the Union, the English establishment listed three riding surveyors and four riding officers at Newcastle, Berwick and Carlisle.[110] On the express command of the Treasury, these were continued after the Union. More than ten years later, at least five of them were still in place.[111] In 1718 and 1721, new riding officers and surveyors were appointed.[112] Ultimately, it was the 1723 survey that settled matters in a more definite way. Arrangements before the Union, the reports stated, "should have been continued" considering the "laying open the Borders at the Union" and the ensuing supply of England "with Goods at an underrate". At both Edinburgh and Dumfries, riding officers were settled for border duties. On the English side, more riding officers were appointed and the arrangement of officers consolidated near the borders.[113] In the eyes of the English ministry, it was the borders and the south-east that were of primary concern with a view to smuggling and prevention.

"The most suspected parts of our coast": Irish Coastal Policing

The constitutional situation of Ireland vis-à-vis the English government, combined with the Navigation and Wool Acts of the Restoration Period and William's reign confined Ireland to a "second-class status" and "a sort of mercantilist colony" in the wider context of the British Atlantic Empire.[114] This situation did have a tangible impact not only on legal trade

---

[107] BL Add. MS 70047, fols 86–87.
[108] BL Add. MS 70047, fols 64–65; TNA T17/6, pp. 194–196; T1/248, no. 38; T1/250, no. 9.
[109] Riley, *English Ministers*, pp. 55, 126.
[110] TNA CUST18/77, Lady Day 1707.
[111] TNA CUST18/115, Midsummer 1717.
[112] CUL, Ch(H), Political Papers 40, reports no. 7 and no. 14 ; T11/15, pp. 318, 411; T11/17, pp. 61, 86.
[113] CUL, Ch(H), Political Papers 40, reports no. 6 and no. 7.
[114] James Guilfoyle, 'Ireland, Mercantilism, and the Navigation Acts, 1660–1686', in Douglas Kanter, Patrick Walsh (eds), *Taxation, Politics, and Protest in Ireland, 1662–2016* (Basingstoke, 2019), pp. 19–42, at pp. 21 and 23. On the status of Ireland in the wider British (imperial) context see also Charles Ivar McGrath, *The Making of the Eighteenth-Century Irish Constitution: Government, Parliament and the Revenue, 1692–1714* (Dublin, 2000); Martyn J. Powell, *Britain and Ireland in the Eighteenth-Century Crisis of Empire* (Basingstoke, 2003).

but also on illicit trade, which was less profitable and therefore less prevalent.[115] Because of this, the Irish Customs was a more successful operation in relative terms than in England: whereas the English Customs returns stood perennially in the shadow of Excise returns in the 18th century, in Ireland the Excise was "the poor relation".[116] Irish Customs also contributed more to the British totals than Scotland ever came near to and was able to provide for the upkeep of a strong contingent of the British Army.[117] In this well-established story of the relative merit of the Irish Customs in the British fiscal-military apparatus, little attention has been paid to coastal arrangements. They are, however, rather telling regarding the geographic priorities they reveal.

The existing documentation of the Irish Customs is worse than for Scotland or England, because the outport letters are lost. Much can be gleaned from the Commissioners' minutes and their communications with the Treasury, however.[118] The serially available establishments lists are also helpful.[119] Matters are, however, complicated by the fact that the nomenclature of offices in the Irish preventive branch is both ambiguous and not correspondent to either England or Scotland. Land officers largely figure under the term of "coast officer", which, according to Maighréad Ní Mhurchadha, may indicate an overlap with a land- or tidewaiter's port duties.[120] Fortunately, a manuscript from 1690 shows that preventive officers were

---

[115] L. M. Cullen, *Anglo-Irish Trade 1660–1800* (Manchester, 1968), pp. 139–154; L. M. Cullen, 'Smugglers in the Irish Sea in the Eighteenth Century', in L. M. Cullen, *Economy, Trade and Irish Merchants at Home and Abroad, 1600–1988* (Dublin, 2012), pp. 118–136. Older studies include F. G. James, 'Irish Smuggling in the Eighteenth Century', *Irish Historical Studies*, 7 (1961), 299–317.

[116] Patrick Walsh, 'The Fiscal State in Ireland, 1691–1769', *HJ*, 56/3 (2013), 629–656, at p. 639.

[117] *Ibid.*; Patrick Walsh, 'Enforcing the Fiscal State: The Army, the Revenue and the Irish Experience of the Fiscal-Military State, 1690–1769', in Aaron Graham, Patrick Walsh (eds), *The British Fiscal-Military States, 1660–c.1783* (London/New York, 2016), pp. 131–158. On the army also Charles Ivar McGrath, 'Waging War: The Irish Military Establishment and the British Empire', in William Mulligan, Brendan Simms (eds), *The Primacy of Foreign Policy in British History, 1660–2000: How Strategic Concerns Shaped Modern Britain* (Basingstoke, 2010), pp. 102–118.

[118] Walsh, 'The Fiscal State'; Walsh, 'Enforcing the Fiscal State'; Patrick Walsh, 'The Sin of With-Holding Tribute, Contemporary Pamphlets and the Professionalisation of the Irish Revenue Service in the Early Eighteenth Century', *Eighteenth Century Ireland*, 21 (2006), 48–65. See also D. A. Fleming, *Politics and Provincial People: Sligo and Limerick, 1691–1761* (Manchester/New York, 2010), ch. 5.

[119] TNA CUST20/56ff.

[120] Maighréad Ní Mhurchadha, *The Customs and Excise Service in Fingal, 1684–1764: Sober, Active and Bred to the Sea* (Dublin, 1999), pp. 15, 31.

not usually employed on other duties.[121] A large-scale survey of 1733, on the other hand, confirms that coast officers were considered preventive officers.[122] Though they need to be treated with caution, numbers used below are a reliable approximation.

The Irish Customs were similar to the English Customs, but not the same. Farmed out, as in England, for part of the Restoration, the Irish Customs reverted to government management in 1682, more than ten years after their English counterpart. Originally controlled by the Irish executive, the farming out period had weakened those ties and left the Irish Commissioners with a more independent position. Administrative interference, however, was exerted via the English Treasury from 1682 onwards, at least in important policy matters; in staffing matters, on the other hand, the Irish Commissioners were often able to hold their own.[123] This arrangement ensured that the Navigation Acts of the Restoration period – forced onto the Irish legislature since 1662 and designed to restrict Irish access to the plantation trade – were actually complied with from the 1680s, after a period of "large-scale violations".[124]

Irish matters, however, were handled differently than in England: instead of separate revenue Boards, the Irish Commissioners – seven in number – controlled both branches of the revenue. Excise districts, inland and coastal, overlapped with port districts and a certain amount of intersection of administrative duties was inevitable – especially in smaller establishments. After heavy disruption of the government machinery during the Williamite Wars and stimulated by the fiscal demands of the Nine Years' War, the Irish Customs continued to evolve into "a more modern, professional and productive revenue system".[125] Among other indicators of the rise of bureaucratisation, the overall establishment grew continuously – if

---

[121] BL Add. MS 4761, fols 93–125, at fol. 99.
[122] David Dickson, 'Edward Thompson's Report on the Management of Customs and Excise in County Kerry in 1733', *Journal of the Kerry Archaeological and Historical Society*, 7 (1974), 12–20. See also Fleming, *Politics*, p. 166.
[123] Charles Ivar McGrath, 'The Irish Revenue System: Government and Administration, 1689–1702' (Diss. University of London, 1997), p. 89; Guilfoyle, 'Ireland, Mercantilism, and the Navigation Acts', p. 26; Seán Egan, 'Finance and the Government of Ireland, 1660–1685' (Diss. University of Dublin, 1983), chap. IX. On the politics of patronage more generally, see Patrick Walsh, *The Making of the Irish Protestant Ascendancy: The Life of William Conolly, 1662–1729* (Woodbridge, 2010), pp. 125–152; Thomas Bartlett, 'Viscount Townshend and the Irish Revenue Board, 1767–1773', *Proceedings of the Royal Irish Academy*, Section C, 79 (1979), 153–175.
[124] Guilfoyle, 'Ireland, Mercantilism, and the Navigation Acts', p. 35.
[125] McGrath, 'Irish Revenue System', p. 6.

less dramatically than in England – during William's reign.[126] In many ways, changes to the Irish Customs throughout the 1690s were the same as in England during the same period.[127]

There is one parallel to English developments, however, whose significance has escaped attention. In comparing the 1693 and the 1709 establishments of the Irish Customs, McGrath demonstrated the general growth of the department. He attributes the overall rise of 33% to "increasing revenue yields arising from a developing economy, increased trade, and new parliamentary duties".[128] It is significant, however, where in the service this growth occurred. Most of the growth, in fact, is due to preventive staff. Whereas no riding surveyors existed in 1693, by 1709 there were 6. From 10 riding officers, numbers had grown to 42. In relative terms, this was the largest increase in any type of officer. Boatmen – support staff routinely employed for preventive duties – had also increased significantly. Thus the largest increase between 1693 and 1709 occurred in preventive staff, accounting for up to two-thirds of the overall growth of the Customs establishment outside the central office.[129] As most of this growth had already occurred by 1702, this development is in perfect parallel to what happened in England during the same period.[130]

As on the English scene, part of the answer was wool. The 1699 Wool Act, prohibiting the export of wool manufacture from Ireland and channelling raw wool to England, forced the English Treasury to engage in its enforcement.[131] Regardless of whether the initiative for the Wool Act resulted from party political readjustments after the conclusion of the Nine Years' War or more directly from mercantile pressures exacted on the English parliament, wool certainly was, as L. M. Cullen has put it, "a political commodity".[132] If there was enough of a lobby to enact a wool export ban on Ireland against the wishes of William's government, then it was only to be expected that

---

[126] McGrath, 'Irish Revenue System', p. 180.
[127] Next to administrative differences, the legal situation was different. See Thomas Bacon, *A Compleat System of the Revenue of Ireland, in its several Branches of Import, Export, and Inland Duties* (Dublin, 1737); R. V. Clarendon, *A Sketch of the Revenue and Finances of Ireland and of the Appropriated Funds, Loans and Debt of the Nation from their Commencement* (London/Dublin, 1791).
[128] McGrath, 'Irish Revenue System', p 180.
[129] McGrath, 'Irish Revenue System', pp. 361–362.
[130] TNA CUST 20/69 (Lady Day Establishment 1702).
[131] See Cullen, *Anglo-Irish Trade*, pp. 140–143.
[132] Louis M. Cullen, 'H.M.S. "Spy" off the Galway Coast in the 1730s: The Politics and Economics of Wool Smuggling', *Journal of the Galway Archaeological and Historical Society*, 65 (2013), 27–47, at p. 27.

there were strong pressures to enforce it.[133] Thus, in 1699, the Irish Revenue Commission found itself in much the same situation as the English Board: lobby groups had pressed for a mercantilist policy that required substantial investment in enforcement measures with only indirect returns into the Exchequer. John Locke, a member of the Board of Trade involved in the discussions about the 1699 Act, had expressly cautioned against the measure by pointing out that it would be impossible to prevent smuggling.[134] He was right. As in England, the expenditures for enforcing the ban quickly mounted. The statute required the Admiralty to have several men-of-war and sloops cruise the coasts of England and Ireland for enforcing the ban, particularly in the Irish Sea. At the same time, Irish port districts – predominantly in the north-east – were strengthened with additional preventive officers and it was these additions that accounted for most of the growth in preventive staff until 1702.[135]

Over the following decades, this increase steadily continued. Yet there are several things worth noting. First of all, at no point did coastal policing reach the levels seen in England, and the Irish Revenue Board together with the Treasury displayed a certain ease towards smuggling. As late as 1759, stretches of up to 50 miles of coastline were entirely unguarded.[136] The smuggling trade was, as Cullen has shown, "of relatively little importance".[137] As in England, the problem of wool smuggling was in all probability an exaggeration fuelled by the wool manufacturers.[138] To this was added a reluctance by the Irish Commissioners to comply with projects initiated in London, either because they wished to maintain administrative control or because Irish officials displayed a "lack of enthusiasm" towards legislation formulated by the English parliament and thus "failed to approach enforcement problems with either the zeal or the thoroughness found at Westminster".[139]

Whatever the reasons for it, the effects of this attitude are clearly visible. In 1703, just after preventive staff levels had been raised, Thomas Knox approached the Duke of Ormond, Irish lord lieutenant, with a proposal to

[133] H. F. Kearney, 'The Political Background to English Mercantilism, 1695–1700', *The Economic History Review*, 11/3 (1959), 484–496; Patrick Kelly, 'The Irish Woollen Export Prohibition Act of 1699: Kearney re-visited', *Irish Economic and Social History*, 7 (1980), 22–43.
[134] Kearney, 'Political Background', p. 488.
[135] By 1702, appointments were centred on the Belfast district. See TNA CUST20/69.
[136] Fleming, *Politics*, p. 168.
[137] Cullen, *Anglo-Irish Trade*, p. 139.
[138] Cullen, *Anglo-Irish Trade*, pp. 140–143; Cullen, 'Politics and Economics of Wool Smuggling'; McGrath, 'Irish Revenue System', pp. 159–160.
[139] James, 'Irish Smuggling', pp. 311, 312.

prevent the running of wool from Ireland. He envisioned an informal preventive force on the Irish south coast at a cost of £1500 per year, independent of regular Customs staff "whose Employ being only to Inspect Shipps Loaded in Ports Cannot Prevent those Clandestine Proceedings". The Irish Commission, however, expressed confidence in their current staff and dismissed Knox's remarks about the levels of wool smuggling as unfounded allegations.[140] Yet Knox persevered and, after travelling to London, gained the support of the British Treasury, who intervened on his behalf. In 1704, the Irish Commissioners were obliged to furnish him with a commission for surveying the Irish coasts regarding the need and suitable forms of additional coastal policing. Over the course of two years, Knox repeatedly surveyed the southern and northern coastlines, travelling several hundred miles in the process, and drew several maps as well as "formed a Scheme of Officers for to guard those Coasts".[141]

Overall, Knox's efforts between 1704 and 1706 are similar to the services performed by Henry Baker on the English south coasts. The difference was that Knox's scheme never came to fruition. The Irish Commissioners rebutted his proposals: "As we were at first of opinion that the Petitioners office would be of little or no use […] so we are now by Experience convinced thereof and we do humbly conceive that the Coasts of this Kingdom are so well Guarded by the Established Officers in the respective Ports, by Four General Surveyors and other officers who continually ride the Coasts, that there is no need of an Extraordinary officer for that purpose". Neither was there any need for Knox's scheme.[142] That same confidence of the Irish Revenue Commissioners is still visible 20 years later. Confronted with allegations of underestimating the owling trade by an ex-officer in 1723, the Board defended its efforts as absolutely sufficient. Discrediting the officer as "a Person of vile Character", guilty of frauds, the Commissioners protested that they had always prevented the running of wool "with the utmost diligence and zeal". They had doubled officers on "the most suspected parts of our coast" and had built an armed sloop; they had prosecuted all seizures and had offered large rewards for the discovery of frauds. All this was done, they contended, to such effect, "that we believe the smugling Wooll trade does not continue in this Kingdom in near as great a degree as formerly."[143]

If investments in preventive policing remained modest in Ireland throughout the period, it is worth considering where they were considered

[140] TNA T1/87, no. 79.
[141] TNA T1/100, no. 27.
[142] TNA T1/101, no. 8. See also TNA T14/8, pp. 398, 426. Other proposals in T1/102, no. 48.
[143] TNA T1/243, no. 3.

necessary. For there is a second development noteworthy in the patterns of preventive coastal policing after 1702, and this relates to its geography. The early establishments of preventive officers had favoured the northeast. Dublin and its member ports did, of course, have a special place due to its volume of trade and had already listed preventive officers on its establishment in 1690, when no other port had had any.[144] It is the pattern of growth after 1702 that is remarkable. Next to Dublin's exceptional position, accounting for around half of the Irish gross revenue throughout the century, it was the south-west and the Munster ports specifically that accounted for large shares of Ireland's trade. Though there was a decline between 1698 and 1798, receipts from Munster contributed at least 25% of the Irish totals and Cork alone accounted for between 15 and 20%. Notably, in the first half of the century, Ulster ports remained a distant third and Connaught an even more distant fourth. Belfast contributed only around 5% in the first and around 9% in the second half of the century; only in the second half of the century, moreover, did Ulster start contributing more than 10% of the totals, namely 16% in 1774 and 21% in 1798.[145] At first glance, this situation is reflected in staff levels. The number of revenue officers employed in the provinces and port districts corresponds to the levels of receipts when considered in absolute numbers.[146] The most obvious explanation for this is that less trade required less staff.

Table 3: Total Customs Staff on the Irish Management, 1702–1782 (Source: TNA CUST20/69, 20/81, 20/110, 20/149).

	1702	1714	1742	1782
Leinster	162	206	292	549
Ulster	89	109	155	407
Munster	157	179	274	639
Connaught	26	26	46	70

A more complicated picture emerges, however, if numbers of preventive staff are distinguished from port staff. This reveals striking divergences in the correlation of staff levels and revenue receipts. The general trend over the course of the century shows preventive staff commanding a rising percentage of the overall staff levels (see Table 4). Incidentally, these numbers

[144] TNA CUST20/58.
[145] Patrick Walsh, 'Patterns of Taxation in Eighteenth-Century Ireland', in Douglas Kanter, Patrick Walsh (eds), *Taxation, Politics, and Protest in Ireland, 1662–2016* (Cham, 2019), pp. 89–119, at pp. 100–101.
[146] See Walsh, 'Enforcing the Fiscal State'.

are often similar to the Dublin establishment, whose situation mirrored the overall trend. Munster, on the other hand, always remained below the national average, especially in the beginning of the period, despite it occupying a comfortable second place regarding customs receipts and, by implication, trade volumes. The numbers for Connaught – because they remain rather small in the general picture – are a bit off the mark, but they indicate that regions with smaller amounts of legal trade still required substantial investments in preventive coastal policing.[147] As in England and Scotland, this often resulted in a negative balance sheet for such ports and it shows where administrators considered the negative impact of preventive staff on illegal trade a more critical investment than a positive balance from legal trade.[148] In Ireland, this is particularly striking with a view to Ulster and the north-eastern ports. Ulster, distant third in gross customs receipts, always had an unusually high percentage of preventive officers, exceeding the national average by a fair amount. Even in the latter part of the century, the percentage of preventive officers on the Ulster establishments remained exceptionally high. Larne, previously part of the Belfast establishment, listed 45 preventive officers compared to 19 port officers in 1782.

The reasons for the concentration of coastal policing in the north and east are obvious. The area was particularly open for shipping to and from the north-west of England and the Scottish south-west. Despite the perpetual clamour regarding the smuggling of wool, authorities in both Ireland and Scotland were aware that the real problem was the relatively unhindered trade carried on in this particular triangle stretching across the Irish Sea. It was here that navy ships were continuously wanted and requested.[149] Thus the smuggling of Irish victuals into Scotland and the illicit trade in tobacco, brandy and tea was a heavier consideration for the Irish and Scottish Commissioners as well as the English Board and the Treasury than wool ever was. It was "these mischiefs", as the Irish Commissioners thought, that "with great concerne we have for sometime past found too true"; and it was precisely for preventing "these mischiefs", that extra coastal officers were appointed "to guard our Northern Coasts".[150] As in northern England and southern Scotland, furthermore, the problem of preventing smuggling into northern Ireland can be traced to one place in particular: the Isle of Man.

---

[147] Though Fleming has observed this disparity for the district of Limerick, he offers no explanation; see Fleming, *Politics*, p. 167.
[148] Sweeting, 'Policing the Ports'.
[149] TNA T1/107, no. 15, no. 53, no. 60.
[150] TNA T1/121, no. 4; T1/248, no. 38.

Table 4: Ireland: Preventive Staff (ps) relative to Customs Staff Totals (ts) by Port and Region, 1690–1782 (Sources: TNA CUST20/58, 20/69, 20/81, 20/110, 20/149).

		1690	1702			1714			1742			1782		
		ps	ps	ts	%	ps	ts	%	ps	ts	%	ps	ts	%
Ulster	Ballyraine	/	/	/		/	/		/	/		2	24	
	Belfast	0	9	36		10	40		11	48		21	96	
	Coleraine	0	2	10		4	11		7	23		7	26	
	Donoghadee	0	1	9		2	6		5	11		5	12	
	Killibegs	0	0	5		2	9		4	14		6	17	
	Larne	/	/	/		/	/		/	/		45	64	
	Londonderry	0	2	20		6	28		8	40		10	62	
	Newry	/	/	/		/	/		/	/		7	79	
	Strangford	1	3	9		5	15		7	19		8	27	
		1	17	89	19,1	29	109	26,6	42	155	27	111	407	27,2
Munster	Baltimore	0	0	10		1	12		4	26		2	82	
	Cork	0	1	57		2	58		4	76		42	208	
	Kinsale	0	1	13		1	19		4	24		13	60	
	Limerick	0	1	19		3	21		8	41		7	61	
	Ross	0	1	8		1	11		0	17		1	19	
	Tralee	0	0	8		5	13		11	18		40	56	
	Waterford	1	1	27		2	31		4	40		24	109	
	Youghall	0	1	15		3	14		5	32		4	44	
		1	5	157	3,1	18	179	10	40	274	14,5	133	639	20,8

Table 4 (continued)

		1690 ps	1702 ps	1702 ts	1702 %	1714 ps	1714 ts	1714 %	1742 ps	1742 ts	1742 %	1782 ps	1782 ts	1782 %
Leinster	Drogheda	0	1	15		2	16		3	24		7	26	
	Dublin	9	16	122		20	144		32	191		95	457	
	Dundalk	1	2	9		6	20		7	32		3	13	
	Wexford	1	2	12		4	18		9	30		10	35	
	Wicklow	0	2	4		1	8		7	15		7	18	
		11	**23**	**162**	**14,1**	**33**	**206**	**16**	**58**	**292**	**19,8**	**122**	**549**	**22,2**
Connaught	Galway	0	0	18		2	17		5	26		10	25	
	Newport	/	/	/		/	/		1	10		1	14	
	Sligo	0	1	8		2	9		2	10		16	31	
		0	**2**	**26**	**7,6**	**4**	**26**	**15,3**	**8**	**46**	**17,3**	**27**	**70**	**38,5**
	Irish totals	**47**		**434**	**10,8**	**84**	**520**	**16,1**	**148**	**767**	**19,2**	**393**	**1665**	**23,6**

"That Warehouse of Frauds": The Isle of Man

Experiences from Ireland, Scotland and northern England all pointed to the Isle of Man. In fact, Mann – that infamous "warehouse of frauds" – was the central nexus of the contraband trade in the Irish Sea and ultimately the reason why much of the preventive efforts in England, Scotland and Ireland went that way. The constitutionally and fiscally exceptional situation of the island until 1765 required the Scottish, English and Irish Customs Board to surround the Irish Sea with an expensive perimeter of fiscally unproductive preventive officers, soldiers, and navy vessels. "This Island," a 1751 article in the *Gentleman's Magazine* grumbled, "may be looked upon as a FORTRESS in the hands of our enemies, draining us of our specie [...], and also continually annoying us in the most sensible part, our trade and commerce". Why, it went on, should the Isle of Man "have remained so long in a manner independent of Great Britain"? The only question was "whether we ought to dispossess them or not".[151] As this suggests, there was an urge to integrate the Isle of Man into the fiscal ambit of Great Britain. Superficially, this was achieved by 1765. This process and its consequences, however, reveal two things. Parliament and the executive were firmly attached to an expansive and linear notion of space: annexing the Isle of Man was understood to simply obliterate a gap in the circumference of British fiscal and political authority. Developments after 1765 show, however, that this notion failed to grasp geographical realities and the easy permeability of legal notions of space and fiscal borders.

In the context of the British archipelagic empire, the Isle of Man had an exceptional status.[152] Mann was, since Henry V had given it to Sir John Stanley in 1405, in the possession of the Earls of Derby. The Island was therefore "part of the Crown, but not of the Realm of England".[153] This meant that the king's writ did not run in the island, which was also outside the fiscal ambit of England. Mann – under the rule of the Derbys and, when the line failed in 1736, under the Dukes of Atholl – passed its own laws and regulated its own Customs tariffs. This created a peculiar situation from the

---

[151] *Gentleman's Magazine*, May 1751, pp. 201–202.
[152] C. W. Gawne, *The Isle of Man and Britain Controversy 1651–1895: From Smuggling to the Common Purse* (Douglas, 2009); Frances Wilkins, *The Isle of Man in Smuggling History* (Kidderminster, 1992); John R. Dickinson, 'The Overseas Trade of the Isle of Man, 1576–1755', *Transactions of the Historic Society of Lancashire and Cheshire*, 154 (2005), 1–30; R. C. Jarvis, 'Illicit Trade with the Isle of Man, 1671–1765', *Transactions of the Lancashire and Cheshire Antiquarian Society*, 58 (1947), 245–267; L. M. Cullen, 'Smuggling in the North Channel in the Eighteenth Century', *Scottish Economic and Social History*, 7 (1987), 9–26.
[153] Jarvis, 'Illicit Trade', p. 246.

late 17th century onwards, when, in the context of the French Wars, England witnessed a steep rise in Customs tariffs and prohibitions on French goods. Mann continued to impose relatively low tariffs and remained open to French imports. From this point, the Island naturally saw an influx of goods and merchants intent on capitalising on the fiscal and geographical situation of the island. This need not necessarily always have been illicit forms of trade. As both labour and provisions were cheap, the island was a perfect magazine for the stapling of goods. At the same time, the island also became an "Asylum of Broken Merchants and others of Desperate or Low Fortunes".[154]

This situation posed a number of problems for the English, as well as the Irish and Scottish Customs administrations. The first problem was Mann's geographical situation at the very heart of the archipelago. No contemporary commentator failed to notice "how prejudicial it must be to the Revenues of these Kingdoms, to suffer a small Island, so conveniently situated between the Three, inhabited chiefly by Vagrants, Rebels to his Majesty, and outlaw'd Smugglers, to carry on that illicit Trade of Smuggling."[155] Its position "nearly in the Centre of the Channel"[156] meant that it offered easy access to all the surrounding coasts. As Charles Lutwidge, riding surveyor for Cumberland, remarked:

> The Isle of Man from its natural Situation lies so convenient for smuggling, t'will be almost impossible to make any Laws so effectual as entirely to put a stop to it. There are four principal Ports, viz. Douglas, Derbyhaven, Ramsey, and Pieltown, from the two first the Coasts of Cornwall Wales Cheshire and Lancashire are supplied; from Ramsey the Coast of Cumberland and the Coasts of Scotland along the Solway Firth, which has been for some years past very great; and from Pieltown the Highlands and West of Scotland, and the North of Ireland.[157]

Smugglers from the Isle of Man thus operated with a fair share of advantages. As collectors around Mann complained, smugglers could land "in any place and at any time".[158] The coast and hinterland of Cumberland, the Whitehaven collector grumbled in 1736, was well supplied with "Brandy

---

[154] CUL, Ch(H), Political Papers 41, no. 64.
[155] Stephen Janssen, *Smuggling Laid Open, in all its Extensive and Destructive Branches. With Proposals for the effectual Remedy of that most iniquitous Practice* (London, 1767), p. 240.
[156] BL Add. MS 38462, fol. 23.
[157] BL Add. MS 38462, 1 April 1764, fol. 76.
[158] TNA CUST 82/1, 29 July 1720.

Rum Tea and Tobacco Soap and other High Duty Goods illegally imported". It all came from Man which "lies opposite and in open view of this Coast" so that boats could make a quick journey to "any place almost on the open shore". They could choose the tide they wanted and the place they preferred "just as suites best" and then be gone in a matter of hours "without the knowledge of any preventive officer".[159] As other reports – from Whitehaven and Dumfries, Beaumaris and Liverpool – suggest, the smugglers' geographical advantage enabled them to smuggle, quite literally, at liberty.[160]

This was exacerbated by a second problem, namely that the British Customs could not enforce their regulations in the ports of the island. Aside from the fact that parliament could not impose tariffs on the Isle of Man, oversight over Customs processes in the ports would still have allowed the English executive to check certain types of fraud. The English Customs Board did have officers on Man since the late 17th century, but even then, the exercise of their office had been hindered by local forces, including Manx officers.[161] British officers were not even allowed to seize contraband.[162] Manx officers even took the liberty of imprisoning a number of mariners of the Revenue sloop *Sincerity* in 1750.[163] This situation made it impossible to gain any understanding of what wares entered or left the island and what part of it could be assumed to be legal. In 1726, therefore, parliament passed an Act that forbade the import of goods from Man to Britain that were not the produce of the island.[164] But this only discouraged the honest merchant and did little to quell smuggling. Goods from France and Spain, Sweden and the Netherlands, Hamburg and the West Indies continued to pour in. Additionally, the paperwork of the Customs was left to local officers, so that the English Customs men were unable to ascertain whether the paperwork of ships sailing from Man was in order. Smuggling vessels could thus be provided with cockets for coastal trade between different Manx ports simply to prevent their being seized by the Customs at

---

[159] TNA CUST82/3, 23 October 1736.
[160] Rupert Jarvis (ed.), *Customs Letter-Books of the Port of Liverpool 1711–1813* (Manchester, 1954), 11 October 1715, 8 November 1715, 19 August 1726, 22 February 1740, 4 November 1750; TNA CUST82/1, 10 July 1718, 29 July 1720, September 1720; CUST82/2, 27 February 1731; CUST78/1, 11 June 1757, 16 June 1757; CUST78/2, 14 May 1763; NRS CE51/1/3, 25 September 1759, 2 October 1759, 10 December 1759; TNA T1/388/104.
[161] Wilkins, *Isle of Man*, pp. 12–13.
[162] Jarvis, 'Illict Trade', p. 233.
[163] TNA CUST82/6, 12 January 1751; T1/342/96; BL Add. MS, fols 202–203; Jarvis, *Customs Letter-Books*, 24 July 1750, 23 October 1750; Janssen, *Smuggling Laid Open*.
[164] Geo I, ch. 28.

sea. Except for the occasional spy and informer, Man was, to the British executive, a smuggling warehouse with a closed account book.[165]

This had implications for coastal prevention on all coastlines open to Man. The Irish Commission and the Boards in London and Edinburgh poured substantial means into guarding these coasts. It would have been necessary, some felt, to station preventive officers "almost in sight of one another".[166] In addition, private parties, the army and the navy supplied additional watches, but this, too, proved futile.[167] "It is an Army could scarce do it."[168] Local inhabitants, keen to profit from the illicit trade, supported smuggling runs; and the smugglers were willing to use force.[169] As elsewhere, the officers also operated under legal restrictions. If they seized contraband at sea, it carried "a Great Expence to the Crown" and was difficult to condemn, because it moved outside legal seizure limits.[170] If "the Cruisers and Kings Ships had absolute and positive Orders to seize all small Vessels that were laden with contraband Goods if found out of the Limits of the Ports of the Island, it would be a great Terror and the surest means of putting a Stop to running". As the law stood, however, seizure outside port limits was illegal and the smugglers knew exactly where these limits were.[171] When goods were seized within port limits, on the other hand, captains were often able to provide (falsified) papers that showed their being bound for legal destinations.[172] "As the Law now stands", one experienced officer concluded, "there is no way to prevent Smugling".[173] The same frustration can still be found in the minds of modern observers of the situation: "The Commissioners of Customs were such sticklers for the law. They required everything to be proved – even against a smuggler. They were never prepared to steal a fast one over even the meanest citizen."[174]

Smugglers also profited from their ingenuity. Knowing that the *Sincerity* cruiser on the Whitehaven establishment did not have legal powers to seize

---

[165] TNA T1/132, no. 15; CUST 29/3, 23 February 1765; Wilkins, *Isle of Man*, pp. 36–40.
[166] Cit. Jarvis, 'Illicit Trade', p. 252.
[167] TNA CUST 29/3, 15 October 1761; T1/248, no. 38; CUST 82/1, 24 September 1718; CUST 82/2, 10 August 1731; CUST 82/5, 1 September 1744, 3 September 1746; CUST 82/9, 31 May 1763, 7 July 1763. For the Customs sloops, see Rupert Jarvis, 'The Customs Cruisers of the North-West in the Eighteenth Century', *Transactions of the Historic Society of Lancashire and* Cheshire, 99 (1949), 41–61.
[168] TNA T1/132, no. 15.
[169] TNA T1/110, no. 7; CUST 82/1, 24 September 1718; CUST 82/6, 8 May 1752.
[170] CUL, Ch(H), Political Papers 41, no. 64; TNA CUST 78/1, 16 June 1757.
[171] TNA CUST 82/6, 8 May 1752.
[172] BL Add. MS 38462, "An Impartial Enquiry", fol. 26.
[173] CUL, Ch(H), Political Papers 41, no. 64.
[174] Jarvis, 'Illicit Trade', p. 261.

smugglers on the Scottish side of the Solway, smugglers made sure to be close to the Scottish side when running up the Solway.[175] And the smugglers were typically also a step ahead when it came to technical advantages. Not only were the small open boats used by the smugglers able to outsail the cumbersome revenue cruisers, they also knew how to navigate the shoals and sands of the Solway.[176] Whitehaven illustrates this situation perfectly. When the establishment had consisted of boats and a cruiser early in the century, the smugglers had operated with wherries "that were all excellent sailors such as the boat durst not face and the other cruisers cud not come up with". When the Customs changed to cruising with similarly built sailers, the smugglers switched to "open Boats with good oars, which draw little water, thrust into any place, over any bank and can easily if it do not blow outrow the cruiser which is built for sailing and rather too heavy to be managed by oars, with any success".[177] This process of adapting to the opponent's sailing outfit went back and forth over the next decades, with the smugglers typically one step ahead. Faced with such ingenuity, revenue men knew "of no method to put a stop to them".[178]

The situation was impossible. The Irish and British Customs combined, it was computed in the 1760s, lost around £300,000 by way of these frauds.[179] Hence, around 1764, a serious campaign got under way to rent, buy or annex the island from the Duke of Atholl. Plans for a lease of the Manx Customs had been discussed in the 1690s, but were abandoned.[180] In 1710 and 1711, plans were discussed for firmer legislative action. This, too, was abandoned after the Earl of Derby had complied with passing legislation to quell the smuggling trade.[181] Yet even at the time, the insufficiency of such measures was recognised. In scrutinising Manx legislation of 1712, the Customs Board found it necessary that Admiralty ships should cruise the channel. Moreover, they thought, "it will be necessary that more Officers be established on that Part of the Coasts of South Brittain that lies over against the Isle of Man in regard the said Coast is very open and favourable for such Clandestine Practices".[182] For many, the idea of a lease

---

[175] TNA CUST82/6, 7 April 1749; 8 May 1752.
[176] TNA CUST82/6, 27 July 1750, 8 May 1752.
[177] TNA CUST82/2, 26 May 1731.
[178] TNA CUST78/2, 14 May 1763. See also CUST82/8, 20 February 1756.
[179] BL Add. MS 38462, 1 July 1764. For earlier computations see T1/123, no. 41; CUL, Ch(H), Political Papers 41, no. 64.
[180] Jarvis, 'Illicit Trade'; various documents in BL Add. MS 38462.
[181] TNA T11/15, p. 161 (18 February 1710), T1/121, no. 10; T1/127, no. 2; T1/133, no. 5, no. 65; T1/147, no. 46; CUL, CH(H), Political Papers 44, no. 9; BL Add. MS 38462.
[182] BL Add. MS 38462, fols 154f. See also TNA T1/147, no. 48.

of the island had advantages. Part of the cost, some argued, "may be saved by Lessening preventing Officers upon the Coasts".[183] With the smuggling trade thus prevented, "the expence of officers would rather be less, and the Revenue would be considerably increased".[184]

Getting Man under British fiscal control emerged as the principal idea of stopping the damage to the revenue and lessening the costs of establishments around Man. In 1759, the Treasury commissioned reports requesting information on the smuggling logistics, the costs of preventive establishments and the income of the Duke of Atholl from Manx Customs. These inspections were made "in as private a manner but with as much care and accuracy and with as much dispatch as possible".[185] At the same time, the Treasury began negotiations with the Duke of Atholl, who earned around £7,500 in Manx Customs annually, about a potential sale of the island. When negotiations stalled, parliament took to the legislative road and passed two Acts annexing the island to Great Britain; Atholl was compensated with £70,000.[186] At once, Britain took possession, replacing civil officers and sending a military detachment to "Convince the Natives it is really annexd to the Crown of Great Britain".[187] Charles Lutwidge, formerly riding surveyor of Cumberland, was sent to Man as surveyor general. In addition to setting up the Customs to the British model, he was to survey the "Coasts of the said Isle both by Sea and Land, and all the Ports, Creeks, and Harbours" and take "precautions for the Security of the Revenue".[188]

If the expectation of the British executive had been that this would stop the illicit trade from the Isle of Man, they were disappointed. After the annexation, the Board inquired if the situation had changed for the better. Initial reports were encouraging. From Dumfries, Greenock and Rothesay, collectors reported that smuggling was "almost entirely checked and put to a stop".[189] The Cardiff collector knew that the smugglers "were much disgusted at finding the alteration" in the Isle of Man.[190] Other reports were less positive. Whitehaven reported that smuggling was still very much

[183] TNA T1/132, no. 15.
[184] CUL, Ch(H), Political Papers 41, no. 64. See also BL Lansdowne MS 707/3, 1753.
[185] TNA CUST29/3, 13 February 1759, 14 February 1759, 23 February 1765; CUST82/9, 18 May 1764, 29 May 1764; T1/437, fols 41, 381–386, 414; T1/392/16–20; T1/434/61; T1/434/67; BL Add. MS 38462, fols 212–216.
[186] Wilkins, *Isle of Man*; Jarvis, 'Illicit Trade'.
[187] BL Add. MS 38462, fols 257–258.
[188] TNA T1/437, fols 169–173; CUST29/3, 14 May 1765, 30 August 1765; BL Add. MS 38462, fols 257–258.
[189] NRS CE51/1/3, 1 September 1766; GCA CE73/1/1, 1 June 1766, CE60/1/4, 1 September 1766.
[190] TNA CUST72/1, 20 August 1766.

practised, but expressed the pious hope "that the consequences of the said act will appear daily more and more to the advantage of the revenue." Tellingly, Whitehaven was also to report whether any illicit trade was now carried on with "Scilly, Jersey, Guernsey, Alderney and Sark".[191] The Board was apprehensive that the annexation of Man would boost smuggling further south.[192] They were not wrong: Exeter reported that smuggling from Guernsey, Alderney and Jersey had increased. Scilly was now "greatly frequented and in a manner substituted to serve the Purposes for which the Isle of Man was famous".[193] On the Scottish west coast, Arran and Bute began to take on the role previously held by Man.[194] Similar evasions were visible in Ireland. The Irish Commissioners feared that the change would relocate smuggling operations from the north of Ireland to the south and west. The change "so wisely calculated for many salutary Purposes, will give greater Latitude" to smuggling elsewhere. "The good Effects intended (so far as relates to Ireland) by that Regulation, have not, nor cannot take place", unless preventive forces were strengthened in the south-west.[195]

But Man, too, remained notorious. From Beaumaris it was reported that a "new Mode" or new "method of Smugling" was practised "ever since the Isle of Man was annexed to the Crown". Smuggling ships were now much larger and better armed. Clearly, the ease of previous days was gone, but smugglers could still make the running of contraband worth their while.[196] Contrary to the Board's expectations, therefore, the cost of preventive staff could not sensibly be reduced. Establishments around the Isle of Man in England, Scotland and Ireland continued to grow. It also became necessary to police the Irish south-west coast more strongly and cruisers now became necessary around Scilly, Guernsey, Jersey, and Alderney.[197] Man, too, required an increasing number of preventive staff. The first establishment in 1765 had only consisted of port staff proper, but several boats and riding officers were subsequently established.[198] Until the end of the century, inquiries confirmed that smuggling was widespread and the preventive

[191] TNA CUST82/10, 22 August 1766.
[192] TNA CUST82/10, 6 July 1765.
[193] TNA CUST64/6, 25 August 1766.
[194] GCA CE60/1/4, 21 December 1764; CE82/1/11, 7 May 1791, 13 June 1791; CE73/1/1, 20 March 1766, 8 June 1770. Frauds often involved salt for the herring fishery; see GCA CE74/2/6, 28 August 1797.
[195] TNA T1/437, fols 142–143, 144.
[196] TNA CUST78/3, 21 May 1767, 20 February 1769.
[197] TNA CUST29/3, 5 March 1767, 20 October 1768, 22 April, 12 May, 7 June 1769. See also BL Add. MS 38463.
[198] *The Report of the Commissioners of Inquiry for the Isle of Man* (1792), Appendix B, nos 42–43, Appendix D, nos 28–29.

setup inadequate. A 1791 inquiry into the Manx Customs exposed a sorry state of affairs. Supervision of preventive staff was almost non-existent; fraud, corruption, and smuggling were widespread.[199] The report concluded

> that smuggling in general cannot be put a stop to, unless this island be guarded by cruizers, and the coasts and interior parts of the island watched by sufficient number of tide officers, and active resolute riding officers. Even after these are established land officers will be of little use, unless they are supported by military.[200]

The annexation of Man – widely believed to solve the problem of smuggling in the north-west – did not meet the expectations of the British executive. They were misled by a political notion of space that suggested the possibility to exercise authority by increasing the spatial ambit of the law and the executive. By swallowing Man into the realm, the opportunity for smuggling and the connected expenses for preventing it would, it was believed, significantly decrease. That this was not the case shows, yet again, that legal and political notions of space remained ignorant of how fluid and permeable such borders were.

Coastal Mobility

Little remains said at this point about how legislative measures were enforced and how the grand schemes played out in a local setting. In a number of areas, there was in fact disagreement between executive commands and local priorities and this was linked to spatial considerations. The physical and geographical realities on the coasts of Britain often ran counter to what central authorities demanded and yet these realities were not always allowed to supersede abstract rationales. What follows is intended to highlight these spatial tensions by looking at the patterns of movement and the rationales behind the stationing of preventive officers.

Mobility
Central authorities were obsessed with the mobility of preventive officers. Appreciative of the fact that illicit mobility could occur anywhere at any given time, central authorities attempted to cover as much ground as

---

[199] *The Report of the Commissioners* (1792), Appendix B, nos 59, 62, 67, 71. See also Wilkins, *Isle of Man*, pp. 111–116.
[200] *The Report of the Commissioners* (1792), Appendix D, no. 22.

continuously as possible. Hence the instructions for riding officers and surveyors demanded the near impossible:

> In Order to perform the Duty hereby required of you, you are not only in the Day-time to patroul in your Station, to observe what suspicious Vessels are on the Sea, or hovering on the Coast within your District, but you are also every night, as often as is practicable, [...] to patrole to and fro, from one End of your District to the other, till Day-light.[201]

Instructions to cruiser captains stressed the same point.[202] The importance of this is underscored by the untiring frequency of reminders sent from the Board to outport collectors and individual officers.[203] "The state of the Moon or Weather" was no excuse to be "less alert on duty".[204] Noncompliance, moreover, meant trouble for the officers.[205]

In addition to individual instructions, the Board was aware that such solitary efforts were doomed unless coupled with a close coordination of such movements and a constant flow of information between the officers. Hence the instructions to all officers aimed at a close-knit network of mutual exchanges:

> You are always to hold a good Correspondence with your Brother-Officers, both to the East and West of you, and freely communicate such Intelligence as you shall receive, or Observations you make, to each other, that you may the better concert Measures together, to detect the Smuglers; and always endeavour to cultivate Friendship with one another, that the King's Service may be the better perform'd by your Unanimity.[206]

As this shows, solitary actions were deemed ineffective. In the summer of 1762, for instance, it was reported that Thomas Bell, commander of the king's boat at Seafield (Ayr) "never has been in use to act in Concert with the rest of the officers for the good of the Revenue [...], notwithstanding he

---

[201] TNA CUST141/4, p. 17.
[202] TNA CUST97/74a, 1 April 1714. See also Henry Crouch, *A Complete Guide to the Officers of His Majesty's Customs in the Out-Ports* (London, 1732), p. 7.
[203] TNA CUST59/71, 3 February 1737. See also CUST59/3, 26 September 1730; CUST59/71, 12 February 1734, 22 October 1734; CUST59/72, 24 July 1740. Similar reports from Maldon in CUST101/1, 18 April 1732, 9 November 1732.
[204] 469 TNA CUST29/7, 5 May 1821.
[205] TNA CUST73/62, 20 November 1717.
[206] TNA CUST141/4, 18. Similarly for cruiser captains in TNA CUST97/74a, 1 April 1714.

has your Honours Directions so to do." Because he refused to give signals to his fellow officers on shore, the Board professed itself to be "very much dissatisfied with your Indolent [Sic!] Conduct with regard to the Revenue".[207] Both constant movement and constant exchange of intelligence were designed to arrive at a comprehensive coverage of all parts of the British coast as continuously as humanly possible.

Such designs met with considerable obstacles. Both officers on shore and at sea often claimed to be unable to perform the services required of them. Next to illnesses, bad weather and family business, which often rang of unwillingness rather than inability, many officers were physically obstructed by natural circumstances or manmade opposition. Officers at Shoreham, for example, were unable to patrol westwards, because the ferry over the Adur was frequently impassable.[208] Officers at Portsmouth, on the other hand, could never leave the city whenever the gates were shut for the night and if they did, were unable to go eastwards because of the flats.[209] At Dunwich, the king's boat had to be beached as a matter of course and was unable to put to sea in south-easterly winds for want of proper shelter.[210] Similarly, when a boat was proposed to be established at Cheriton, in southern Wales, for the officers "to keep to their duty upon the Water", it was observed by the collector at Swansea that "the place appointed for the said Boat is so much exposed to the Weather that it's Impossible to keep a boat there".[211] In nearly every port, certain demands for continual patrols were physically impossible.[212]

To this was added the obstructions thrown in the way of officers by the smugglers. Their mere presence regularly meant, as the collector at Dumfries put it in 1759, "that the officers dare hardly look out of their own Doors".[213] Behind this was, in fact, a deliberate strategy on the part of smugglers. Often stopping short of physically harming the officers, they tampered with the free movement of the officers. In 1747, the riding officer at Caister-on-Sea was repeatedly barred from going south to meet with an agent coming from London. Armed smugglers simply forced him to dismount and remain with them before sending him back whence he came,

---

[207] NRS CE51/1/3, 25 August 1762, 18 September 1762.
[208] TNA T1/63, nos 21, 93.
[209] TNA T1/63, nos 21, 95.
[210] TNA CUST97/7, 24 May 1732.
[211] TNA CUST73/1, 23 April 1733.
[212] See also reports by the Kent and Sussex supervisors in TNA T1/63, no. 21; T1/224, no. 1, LXXXV.
[213] NRS CE51/1/3, 10 December 1759.

"without doing any other Injury than that of putting him in fear."[214] In January 1751, the mariners of the king's boat were imprisoned by the authorities on the Isle of Man for making a seizure.[215] Such attempts to stay the movement of state agents was occasionally carried to further extremes. An often employed strategy was to lure officers from the places of illicit landing of goods by "false Intelligence".[216] In other cases, authority was deliberately dislocated when the smugglers, often of French origin, kidnapped riding officers and either kept them on board their ships for a time, later to be released as far away as Ireland, or shipped them to France, where these men faced a long, expensive, and troublesome homeward journey.[217] Such was the fate of Peter Harrold, for example, a boatman at Great Yarmouth who, on boarding a smuggling vessel, was carried away to Holland and was only able to return a full two months later.[218] On the whole, it is clear that the comprehensive and continuous patrolling of every single stretch of British coastline was an administrative fantasy.

"the most likelysh places"

If central demands were regularly impossible to put into action, they were also frequently seen as disadvantageous to the service by local administrators. Equipped with better knowledge of the local geographies, their opinions often contradicted the instructions by central authorities in terms of the most advantageous stationing of individual officers and the extent of their districts. As the final say remained with central authorities, their adaptation often involved negotiation between central and local administrators. In some cases, this proved successful. In others, central administrators remained inflexible and, their geographical blindness notwithstanding, insisted on their own interpretations of how good service was to be achieved.

The Board of Customs was routinely in touch with the outport collectors regarding the stations of individual officers. In certain intervals, the Board received lists of preventive officers of each port from the collectors, typically including their stations and a brief evaluation of whether such stations were to the benefit of the revenue.[219] Sometimes, this information was requested with a view to making changes. For instance, the Board

---

[214] TNA CUST97/14, 10 December 1747.
[215] TNA CUST82/6, 12 January 1750.
[216] NRS CE87/1/5, 25 November 1777.
[217] TNA T1/47, no. 15; TNA T1/55, no. 24.
[218] TNA CUST97/4, 3 July 1724, 5 August 1724.
[219] TNA T11/18, p. 206.

occasionally wanted to know whether a post was actually necessary.[220] At other times, the Board's intention was redeployment. When it requested a list of officers at Weymouth in August 1751, including "the place of Residence of each officer and their District", the collector was to reflect which officers could be spared.[221] In response, the Weymouth collector assured the Board that the six riding officers were "placed at the most likelysh places for Run Goods along the Sea Coast and we Immaging if either of those officers should be take from the place where they are now fix'd it would be giving the smugglers a greater liberty of carrying on their illegal practices".[222] The collector even requested an additional officer. Though it does not seem that the Board obliged, it did refrain from making changes to the stationing of officers.[223] When changes were inevitable, they were occasionally made in unison: when the preventive boat at Plymouth was sent from Oreston to the mouth of the Yealm on a trial basis in July 1804, the collector agreed with the Board that "the Revenue has been materially benefited by the removal".[224]

Routine consultation of the local collectors, however, did not necessarily mean that the Board followed their opinions. When the Weymouth collector reported in 1717 that the smacks at Poole and Dartmouth had been of "very little service", he argued that they needed to be laid aside and replaced with riding officers. Specifically, the collector asked that a riding officer be placed at Sherbourne (Dorset), to prevent the running of goods towards Bristol in the north and Winchester in the east. Such an inland station was certainly unusual and the Board was quick to disperse any hopes for such a station, thinking it not advisable "to appoint an officer at Sherbourne being so far distant within land". Despite clear evidence that smuggling operations frequently extended their networks far inland, often as far as London, the Weymouth collector ultimately had to make do with an officer at Dorchester.[225]

In perhaps the most common of local complaints, the districts of individual officers were deemed too large. Just as common were cases in which officers were thought to be stationed in the wrong places. Sometimes, these complaints were interlinked. At Annan, on the Scottish side of the Solway, it was deemed impossible for one officer to patrol the entire stretch between the mouth of the Annan and the mouth of the Sark. If an officer

---

[220] See, for instance, TNA CUST59/69, 10 August 1700.
[221] TNA CUST59/74, 29 August 1751.
[222] TNA CUST59/8, 4 September 1751.
[223] *Ibid.*
[224] TNA CUST66/4, 6 July 1804, 3 July 1805.
[225] TNA CUST59/1, 18 March 1717, 27 May 1717; CUST59/2, 3 September 1720.

was stationed "in a more centrical part on the shore", such as Torduff point, "where a good deal of smuggling is carried on", it would serve the revenue much better, not least because it respected local geography.[226] When such requests met with disapproval from the Board, local supervisors became frustrated. "There is so many inlets upon the Coast", the Cardiff collector frequently protested during the 1740s, that it was "morally impossible" to suppress smuggling if he was not given more resources.[227]

Most disagreement between the Board and local collectors resulted from the fact that the latter claimed better knowledge of both local geography and the logistics of local smuggling operations. This is true almost anywhere on the coast but can easily be shown in relation to the Solway Firth and the Moray Firth. Particularly before 1765, the collectors of Whitehaven were full of concerns regarding the smuggling from Man, which usually targeted the Solway. In the frequent applications for officers, different types of boats and different stations, the Whitehaven collectors made their case on the back of profound geographic and logistical knowledge. In May 1752, for instance, the Whitehaven collector requested a boat at Bowness-on-Solway and represented that the few riding officers at Carlisle were unable to prevent the running of goods into England via the Solway. The sloop stationed at Whitehaven was unable to pursue the Manx sailing boats into the shallow waters of the Solway. A boat at Bowness would admittedly be limited by the strong tides, but if combined with two boats at Silloth-on-Solway and Cardurnock Point "to act in concert", it would increase the security of that coast.[228] From the Scottish side, too, there were concerns regarding the security of the Solway. As late as 1788, the Dumfries collector argued that the sloop stationed at Carsethorn was unable to prevent smuggling along the Solway. For not only were the smuggling vessels preferring the English side of the firth, the water being deeper, but there were also no boats stationed on that side of the Solway. Since the captain of the Carsethorn sloop only held a Scottish commission for his service, he was unable to pursue these smugglers who passed "under his Eye on the opposite side of the Firth". As a remedy, the Board was to grant the captain an English commission or station additional boats on the English side of the Solway.[229] In the event, nothing systematic was done to combat Solway smuggling. By

---

[226] NRS, CE51/1/3, 25 February 1769.
[227] See TNA CUST72/1, 17 June 1749, 21 July 1749, 20 November 1750, 10 November 1752. Similar requests at Beaumaris; see CUST78/2, 14 May 1763.
[228] TNA CUST82/6, 8 May 1752.
[229] NRS CE51/1/5, 17 April 1788.

1802, matters had only got worse, because the sloop formerly at Carsethorn had been discontinued.[230]

Whereas in this case the Board neglected to act despite the well-informed requests of local officers, the guarding of the Moray Firth followed the reverse logic of an active involvement by the Edinburgh Board against the better judgement of local collectors. Throughout the 1770s, the Aberdeen collector was questioned by the Edinburgh Board about the very few seizures of the boats at Peterhead and Portsoy. The collector was able to reassure the Board that the Portsoy boat would "have success" once the commander got "a little acquainted in the country", but this did not work for the Peterhead boat.[231] Twice, during spring 1770, the collector had to answer for the failures of this vessel. In both instances, the collector referred to the difficult station of the boat which – for want of proper allowances for the crew – was only able to cruise "within a few miles on each hand" of Peterhead. The smugglers, knowing this, avoided Peterhead and made their landings near Collieston in the south or Fraserburgh in the north. The commander of the boat therefore needed the means to roam the coast in a wider district, extending into the Moray Firth "as discretion and Intelligence may direct him".[232] A few weeks later, the collector argued again that the boat's cruise "be not in a narrow Circle, but that he be at different places", for a small district was "such a Barr to success that the ablest Commander and Crew in the Kingdom would have little Chance".[233] Despite such pleas, the boat remained at Peterhead. Less than two years later, however, the captain of the Peterhead boat was ordered to repair to Cromarty, on the northern edge of the Moray Firth. To this, the collector at Aberdeen, as well as the commander, objected, claiming that "Boats may be necessary in many parts of the Murray Firth but at none more so than at Peterhead". No land officer could protect the firth in the same way and if a boat must be stationed inside the firth, it should be at Portknockie.[234] The station at Peterhead, local administrators argued, was a "judicious one as ships coming on that part of the Coast commonly make these head lands in the course of things".[235] Yet the boat was sent to Cromarty regardless.[236]

Such disagreement between port collectors and the Boards in Edinburgh or in London was sometimes superimposed by a shared distrust of

[230] NRS CE51/1/7, 19 July 1802.
[231] NRS CE87/1/5, 10 December 1777.
[232] NRS CE87/1/5, 17 February 1770.
[233] NRS CE87/1/5, 27 April 1770.
[234] NRS CE87/1/5, 17 March 1772.
[235] NRS CE87/1/5, 17 February 1770.
[236] NRS CE87/1/5, 17 March 1772.

the concerns of more inferior officers. When Hugh Harsnett, riding officer at Lymington, proposed different stations for the nearby riding officers, the collectors of both Poole and Southampton rejected this as "very prejudiciall" to the revenue. The present stations, where the officers were able to "consult together", were better. It seemed to them that the entire proposal "tends more to some private advantage than the Publick service of the Crown".[237] Though it is unclear what this advantage might have entailed, a case from the summer of 1762 at Weymouth throws more light onto the concerns of inferior officers. In spring, the petition of riding officer Henry Weston, stationed at Abbotsbury, had reached the Board, which asked for removal to the Isle of Portland. Upon review by the Weymouth collector, this was granted because he "was bred to and always used the Sea". In his stead, the riding officer at Portland, John Moies, who "was not brought up to or hath used the Sea" was removed to Weston's former station at Abbotsbury.[238] Shortly thereafter, Moies complained to the Board about the removal, arguing that he had been removed to the station of Portland "by way of rewarding his activity and Diligence' and that he had had the "greatest success" in making seizures there. Removing him to Abbotsbury where "very little smuggling is carried on and few seizures are made" would rob him of the "greatest advantage of his employment". Having gained the station of Portland because of his diligence, the removal to Abbotsbury "would turn out a punishment instead of a reward".[239] Evidently, the concerns of inferior officers regarding their stations overlapped only partly with those in higher office – the primarily preventive instrument of seizures was regarded by the lower ranks as perks.

The proper stationing of preventive officers was therefore guided by different rationales depending on the administrative location of such opinions. The lower ranks tended to see to their own advantage and primarily seek a profitable station. Though these tended to be stations where a lot of illegal traffic was carried on and thus were also high on the agenda of superior outport administrators, the private advantages sought by the preventive officer were also seen as potentially problematic by the latter because they could – and often did – entail collusion. Though collusive agreements were also not beyond the occasional collector, these officials aimed at making the preventive service compatible with the local geography. Because this frequently entailed a modification of general rules formulated by the central administration, it led to disagreements between the centre and local

[237] TNA CUST62/59, 28 April 1718.
[238] TNA CUST59/10, 24 May 1762.
[239] TNA CUST59/76, 27 July 1762. The answer in CUST59/10, 2 August 1762.

administrators. After all, the London and Edinburgh Boards were seldom willing to adapt, let alone relax general directives for the sake of local peculiarities. The tension was as fundamental as it was unresolvable. By 1815 it was common opinion that "the Commissioners of the Customs can never be proper Judges of the fittest Stations and therefore must depend on the Informations of inferior Officers, whose Judgement is too often guided by their own Convenience and Comfort."[240]

Conclusions

The coast, from the 1690s, was becoming a political space in its own right. At the same time, it was also increasingly a politically distinct space, with specific rules and regulations impacting everyday mobility in a routine manner. Parliamentary legislation and political debate began to understand the coast as an area of state activity, to be subjected to its own political rules. As contemporaries were aware, such rules were a serious threat to the liberties of the people, as they could essentially result in the forfeiture of "estate and liberty" for what were otherwise and elsewhere entirely unsuspicious actions.[241] The ordering of littoral space and the controlling of coastal mobility were, in other words, matters of state-building.

As the chapter has shown, however, state-building in coastal space remained profoundly incomplete in the period in question. This was for three reasons: first, whereas coastal space could be defined as political by legislative measures and thereby subjected to the grasp of administrators, the resources of the executive departments dealing with such matters were severely limited. Not all spaces could be policed with the same intensity, and this was because despite being part of the revenue administrations, coastal policing was both costly and not fiscally productive in a direct way. Secondly, there was, between the legislature and the various administrative levels involved with coastal policing, a profound confusion as to what exactly constituted coastal space and how it was accordingly to be administered. The simple and linear understanding of coastal space in evidence in parliament was noticeably in conflict with the physical and geographic realities on the ground. The complexities of the latter were such that even between different levels of the revenue administration, there were consistently strong disagreements as to how best to police these spaces. This ambivalence and complexity of coastal space thus constituted a real limit to

---

[240] BL Add. Ms 38262, fol. 196.
[241] *The Parliamentary History*, p. 1263.

any straightforward imposition of authority as envisaged by parliament and by central administrators. Finally, as the situation of Scotland, Ireland and the Isle of Man underscores, the political dominance of England over the British archipelago did not automatically eradicate the economic and political contestation of coastal space as long as fiscal state-building remained incomplete. In a sense, therefore, the discovery of the coast as an area of state activity, rather than constituting an uncontested imposition of central authority, underscored the geographical limits of British state-building in the eighteenth century.

3
Coastal Administration and the Art of Enforcement

In the historiography of the fiscal-military state, much emphasis is placed on whether the bureaucratic apparatus of the Customs was equal to its tasks of raising revenue, enforcing trade regulations, and policing revenue crimes. Analysed in a framework that evokes comparisons with the Excise and introduces numerical 'efficiency' as a yardstick, the Customs are largely seen to fall short of these tasks. As it is corruption and smuggling in particular that tend to be seen as responsible, much blame is heaped on either the outdated bureaucratic structure of the Customs as giving ample opportunity for sinecurism, collusion and negligence or the branches concerned with coastal policing as responsible for large-scale Customs evasion. Chapters 3 and 4 are an attempt to approach the administrative setting of the Customs from a different angle, with the aim of challenging the straightforward, but misleading assumption of fiscal efficiency typically adopted in modern scholarship.

The present chapter is aimed at a better understanding of the bureaucracy. It is argued here that an undue focus on fiscal efficiency misrepresents the purpose of this branch of service. To make this point, it is necessary to reintroduce a number of administrative complexities that characterised the mechanics of coastal policing in the eighteenth century but have subsequently been obscured by modern notions of bureaucracy. Even at the centre of the executive, different ideas about the purposes of coastal officials prevailed. Nominally part of the Customs, other departments regularly imposed their own agendas on these officials. To ignore these influences is to discount activities for which fiscal 'efficiency' was not a factor. The chapter also illustrates that there was no lack of administrative mechanisms to supervise and control local officials. The problem was that the nature of central directives often made compliance disadvantageous, dangerous, and sometimes outright impossible. For officers on the ground – even if willing to comply – many policies paid little heed to their everyday experiences and at times ran counter to effective enforcement. As the seizure procedures illustrate, enforcement required cooperation between different agents of the state in the localities and thus necessitated complex negotiations between different areas of law-enforcement that exceeded Customs competences and official Customs concerns. The prevailing assumption of exclusive competences is at the roots of later misapprehensions of the purposes, the mechanics, and the 'efficiency' of coastal policing.

The Preventive Service and the Executive

It tends to be assumed that the eighteenth-century Customs was a uniform body regarding its purposes and its organisation. It is equally often taken for granted that the administration of the Customs was predominantly concerned with Customs business and uniformly acted as a fiscal agency concerned with the raising of revenue. Both views are misguided. A closer look at the administration shows that alongside regular port establishments typically assumed to represent the Customs as a whole, there existed distinct branches such as the preventive service that had little to do with the raising of revenue. It is with a view to this branch, moreover, that one must realise that fiscal duties were but a part of the Customs administration. Executive control was influenced from outside the Treasury and the Customs Board. Within the Customs, the preventive service occupied an exceptional position, and different rationales applied here than elsewhere. A better understanding of the different purpose of the service forms the basis for a more even-handed evaluation of its administrative efficiency.

Executive Control
The routine administration of the English and Welsh Customs was conducted by the Board of Customs.[1] In 1671, it had six Commissioners, later ranging between five and nine. Headquarters were in the Long Room on the upper floor of the Customs House, situated just upstream of the Tower on the northern bank of the Thames. Except between the 1720s and 1740s,

---

[1] The best account is Hoon, *Organization*. Ashworth's account is more focused on everyday interactions; see Ashworth, *Customs*, chapter 8. For the Board also W. R. Ward, 'Some Eighteenth Century Civil Servants: The English Revenue Commissioners, 1754–98', *HER*, 70/274 (1955), 25–54; J. E. D. Binney, *British Public Finance and Administration 1774–1792* (Oxford, 1958). For Ireland Patrick Walsh, 'The Fiscal State in Ireland, 1691–1769', *HJ*, 56/3 (2013), 629–656. On the Treasury Henry Roseveare, *The Treasury 1660–1870: The Foundations of Control* (London, 1973).

there existed a separate Scottish Board in Edinburgh.[2] Irish business was conducted by the Irish Revenue Board, overseeing both Customs and Excise business.[3] In each case, Commissioner posts were highly salaried positions and typically no sinecures. A certain amount of rotation and division of duties was practised, and individual Commissioners stood out for their zeal and attention to detail, but the Commissioners typically acted in concert and as an executive body. Routine administrative business was guided by the work of a secretary and carried out by scores of clerks, registrars, and solicitors at the Customs House.[4] Theoretically, the Board was the sole executive authority over routine business, from appointment procedures and implementation of parliamentary statutes to the handling of Customs business proper, that is, the processes of import and export in the port of London as well as the outports. In addition, they decided upon legal matters and handled communications with merchants and petitioners.

The source of the Board's authority, however, lay elsewhere. It was the Treasury that held ultimate authority over the revenue boards and it routinely interfered in Customs business in matters great and small. The original Customs patent granted ample powers, but they remained dependent on the Treasury. Powers not covered by patent needed to be confirmed by warrant from the Treasury. This included routine procedures such as payment of salaries, the conclusion of seizure cases, or the appointment of officers.[5] The Treasury, recipient of constant petitions from merchants, officers and other departments, also referred such cases routinely to the Customs. Routine exchange was conducted via letters and by the Commissioners waiting on the Treasury Lords. The relationship seems to have

---

[2] On the Scottish setup, see P. W. J. Riley, *The English Ministers and Scotland 1707–1727* (London, 1964); Philipp Rössner, *Scottish Trade in the Wake of Union (1700–1760): The Rise of a Warehouse Economy* (Stuttgart, 2008). See also *Instructions for the Collectors and other Officers Employ'd in HER MAJESTIES Customs, in the North-Part of Great-Britain* (Edinburgh, 1707).

[3] See Charles Ivar McGrath, 'The Irish Revenue System: Government and Administration, 1689–1702' (Diss. University of London, 1997); Patrick Walsh, 'The Irish Fiscal State, 1690–1769', *HJ*, 56 (2013), 629–659; D. A. Fleming, *Politics and Provincial People: Sligo and Limerick, 1691–1761* (Manchester/New York, 2010), ch. 5; Maighréad Ní Mhurchadha, *The Customs and Excise Service in Fingal, 1684–1764: sober, active and bred to the sea* (Dublin, 1999). See also Thomas Bacon, *A Compleat System of the Revenue of Ireland, in its several Branches of Import, Export, and Inland Duties* (Dublin, 1737).

[4] Hoon, *Organization*, pp. 92–121.

[5] For Treasury control of Customs matters Hoon, *Organization*, pp. 45–91. Communication to the Customs Board in TNA T11/1ff. (Out-Letters to Customs).

been harmonious, with only occasional frictions.[6] Whereas the Customs Board could not take decisions even on several routine matters, the Treasury typically followed the Board's opinions. Furthermore, the Treasury was dependent on the Board for information. As Hoon has suggested, however, Treasury influence in Customs matters appears to have increased over the century, with the Treasury progressively interfering in matters such as appointments.[7] This was because Customs positions, dotted with sinecures, were an important pool for patronage. The Customs Board, on the other hand, was carefully guarding their prerogatives. The best example is incident officers. Unlike established officers, they were not appointed by Treasury warrant but by the Board's authority alone, effectively granting an executive tool free from Treasury interference.[8]

Such recluses of authority notwithstanding, the Customs Board was "a body of ministers through whom a higher controlling power operated to secure the enforcement of trade laws, yet who were themselves responsible for the due execution of such laws."[9] Because of their minor position, the Customs Board depended on the Treasury to work as an intermediary to other departments, such as parliament, Privy Council, Admiralty or the Secretary at War. Hoon has given this matter some attention, but it has been one-sided. Whereas she has detailed on what occasions the Treasury secured support for the Customs in matters within the remit of their duty, comparably little attention has been paid to how other government departments, including the Treasury, interfered with the Customs in matters outside the nominally fiscal remit of the Customs Board.[10]

Aside from revenue collection, the Customs was a tool to oversee the implementation of Navigation Acts and trade laws. All paperwork ensuring that trade complied with statutory law passed through the hands of the Customs officers quite simply because they constituted the only body of central officers at the borders of the kingdoms. A considerable part of Customs work was thus not the raising of duties but the handling of paperwork. Even where it concerned duties, it was also often outside the remit of the Customs, such as lighthouse duties or the sixpenny fee in support of

---

[6] Hoon, *Organization*, pp. 45–91.
[7] Ibid.
[8] *The Fifteenth Report of the Commissioners Appointed to Examine, Take, and State, the Public Accounts of the Kingdom* (London, 1787), p. 22: "Judgement upon the Propriety or Necessity of the Payments incident to the Management of the Customs, and the Sanction thereof, must be confided to and rest with that Board, to whom the important Charge of conducting this Department is intrusted."
[9] Hoon, *Organization*, p. 60.
[10] Hoon, *Organization*, p. 46.

Greenwich Hospital under the Admiralty.[11] These were considered routine tasks that formed a natural extension of Customs work in port. More challenging to the view of the Customs as a fiscal agency was the assignment of coastal tasks. These were both wide-ranging and foreign to fiscal concerns. Quarantine matters were routinely placed under the care of the Board, as was the enforcement of embargoes. Less regular tasks included aid for ships in distress as well as the securing of wrecks. Privy Council also required the Customs to secure criminals, as well as suspected spies or prohibited books. Admiralty orders, moreover, often had Customs officers guard the coasts against enemy vessels, inspect the packet boats, report sightings of enemy movements on the coasts, carry military intelligence, stop and search individuals moving near the shores, and assist with the Admiralty business of impressing seamen for the fleet. Secretaries of State formed another source of orders, often relating to the gathering of intelligence or the arrest of individuals. To various central bodies, the Customs was the ideal enforcer and conveyor of information along the coast.[12]

As most of these tasks were coastal in nature, they were principally entrusted to the preventive service. In fact, these matters were placed on the Customs *because* the preventive service existed; despite its high cost and dubitable fiscal efficiency, that was in part also why the service was continued throughout the century. After all, unlike port staff, this was a mobile coastal service that guaranteed the coastal presence these tasks required. The preventive service was, above all, a coastal enforcement unit rather than a fiscal tool. Executive control formally rested with the Board of Customs; it was by means of the Treasury, however, that the service was put to a series of tasks relevant to government as a whole.

The Place of the Preventive Service

The preventive service was formally part of the regular Customs administration. Yet preventive business was different from the duties of regular port staff. Outsiders found the existence of the preventive service perplexing. The Commissioners on the first proper audit of the Customs in 1784 concluded that these officers evidently "constitute a peculiar and extensive Branch of Service". But from the paperwork, they were unable to ascertain quite how extensive it was, since "many Persons are concerned in the Conduct thereof, who are Officers of the Customs, and were none of them included in the Lists of Officers returned to us". This was because many acted "upon extra and casual Service", so that no "definite Number" could

---

[11] Hoon, *Organization*, pp. 37–44.
[12] See Hoon, *Organization*, p. 37; Fleming, *Politics*, ch. 5.

be stated.[13] Both nominally and on a practical level, the preventive service was a branch apart.

As the Commissioners noted in 1784, many officers on preventive duties were not included in the establishment lists. This was because they were on incident payment and rarely entered the staff lists. Typically overlooked, this has grave consequences for the evaluation of the extent of the service. To give but one example: the establishment of 1742 listed four riding surveyors and four riding officers at Great Yarmouth. The incident list submitted to London that same year, however, reveals the real number to be fourteen.[14] As these lists were reported to the Board with changing form and regularity and because for many ports the outport records are today lost, it is now impossible to ascertain the exact figures for the preventive service at any given time. Yet the Board's choices in such appointments are telling. Rather than having preventive staff on the establishment, which required a Treasury warrant, many preventive officers were paid on incidents, that is, by actual service out of the income of a port. If this is to suggest that many preventive officers were only a temporary feature of the outports, this is not so. In most regions, they were quarterly continued.[15] But payment by incidents gave the Board flexibility: service could be altered at pleasure, as could be the place of service otherwise fixed by Treasury warrant. More importantly, it handed the Board a tool outside Treasury control.

This flexibility was necessary because these officers were not, in a strict sense, fiscally productive. Preventive officers did not collect any duties as a matter of course and they did not handle any paperwork relating to import or export. Unlike many of the port staff, therefore, they did not receive fees, but had to be fully salaried.[16] The nature of their service, moreover, did not allow for the existence of sinecures either among the established or among the incidental officers.[17] Officers in the preventive service also required no training and a very limited set of skills; advancement based on training or seniority was also not an option for preventive staff as it was in port offices. Except for a few individuals, the preventive service must be considered low-ranking in the context of the Customs on the margins of the usual

[13] *Fifteenth Report*, pp. 17, 29.
[14] TNA CUST18/213; CUST97/12, 8 August 1743.
[15] See incident payment lists in TNA CUST58/12, 28 January 1784; CUST73/1, 14 December 1730.
[16] On the discussion about fees Spike Sweeting, 'Capitalism, the State and Things: The Port of London, circa 1730–1800' (Diss. Univ. of Warwick, 2014), pp. 109–114; *Fourteenth Report of the Commission for Stating the Public Accounts* (1785).
[17] On sinecures see also Sweeting, 'Capitalism', p. 151; *Fourteenth Report of the Commission for Stating the Public Accounts* (1785).

hierarchy. Additionally, while the remit of their duties was nominally very narrow, typically only consisting of coastal patrols, their service involved a wide range of legal, social, economic, and military matters.[18]

Features typical for the eighteenth-century Customs administration were less prevalent or took a different shape in the preventive service. The reason for as well as the result of these differences was a much stricter insistence on service actually performed than elsewhere in the administration. This is most clearly visible in matters of dual officeholding and patronage. Both features were prevalent throughout the administration and to some extent, they were tolerated.[19] Not in the preventive service, however.

Dual officeholding was pervasive in the Customs. Officers appointed by royal patent could deputise their work to the willing and it was quite common for one man to take on several deputations.[20] This was frowned upon but tolerated. In the preventive service, however, this was actively discouraged. In June 1710 it was reported that Jeffrey Haford, Sandwich collector, was also acting supervisor of riding officers in east Kent, "which duties are inconsistent", the first requiring residence, the latter requiring constant travel. Haford was accordingly relieved of the latter duty.[21] The same rule was applied to the Irish establishment. Smaller ports would frequently see one port officer perform the various duties of tidewaiter, jerquer, warehouse keeper and others. It was only the riding officers who were employed "distinctly", because their duty did not allow for sundry port duties.[22] If the service deviated from that norm, it prompted questions.[23] As much as the Board was inclined to overlook dual officeholding in other parts of the administration, such practices were actively prevented in coastal officers.

That same stress on performance is in evidence regarding patronage. An accepted and, to some extent, functional instrument of eighteenth-century administration, patronage was quite pervasive in the Customs, where the existence of sinecures and the possibility of deputising lucrative positions drew much attention from patrons, brokers, and clients alike.[24] Seeing that

---

[18] TNA CUST141/4.
[19] See John Brewer, *The Sinews of Power. War, Money, and the English State, 1688–1783* (London, 1989), pp. 101–102.
[20] Hoon, *Organization*, pp. 200–201.
[21] TNA T1/128, no. 3.
[22] BL Add. MS 4761, fols 94–125.
[23] TNA CUST97/15, 20 August 1748; CUST82/3, 6 January 1739, 20 January 1739.
[24] Hoon, *Organization*, pp. 195–204. On the abuse of deputations and patronage William B. Stephens, *The Seventeenth-Century Customs Service Surveyed: William Culliford's Investigation of the Western Ports, 1682–84* (Farnham, 2012), pp. 1–34;

the preventive offices required little in the way of training, were fully salaried, and possessed of a fuzzy description of duties, they may seem ideal assets in the patronage market. But the evidence points another way. It is true that there were voices claiming that "their [the officers'] Appointments are Favors from their Members [of parliament], and much more Attention being paid to their Interest as Votes, than to their Abilities and Education for the Duty of their Offices."[25] On further inspection, however, these oft-quoted remarks are *made* by a high-ranking preventive officer, but he makes explicit reference to *port* staff. Thus, while it is undeniable that in some areas and during election periods in particular, officers tended to be picked according to party allegiance, this practice was clearly less prevalent in the preventive service than elsewhere.[26] Only in rare cases are political connections obvious.[27]

It was normal, moreover, that candidates should be presented either by way of a petition or by recommendation. Where else would one find suitable candidates? The first establishment of riding officers in Kent and Sussex in 1699 consisted of Treasury recommendations, personal recommendations, former soldiers deserving of a government post and some recommendations by individuals such as Marlborough. Most were simply recommended as being "fitt" for such employment.[28] This pattern was typical for preventive appointments. Many preventive officers were put on such stations following a petition and as a reward for past services, typically in the military or navy.[29] In other cases, officers entered service if they could reasonably claim to have experience in fighting the smuggling trade, for instance, by way of private prosecutions or informal service.[30] In case of petitions, the Board typically proceeded with caution, frequently inquiring into the background of individuals.[31] Usually, applicants had something to

---

Hannes Ziegler, 'Customs Officers and Local Communities: Informing in Late Seventeenth-Century England', in María Ángeles Martín Romera, Hannes Ziegler (eds), *The Officer and the People: Accountability and Authority in Premodern Europe* (Oxford, 2021), pp. 325–348.

[25] *Eighteenth Century Documents*, p. 246.
[26] Richard Saville (ed.), *The Letters of John Collier of Hastings 1731–1746* (Lewes, 2016), pp. xiii–li.
[27] TNA CUST82/4, Collector to Board 17 February 1742, 26 May 1742, Board to Collector 16 July 1742, 21 October 1742, 14 January 1743.
[28] TNA T1/63, no. 30.
[29] TNA T1/18, no. 3; T1/43, no. 67; T1/87, no. 79; T1/84, no. 80; T1/173, no. 45.
[30] TNA T1/81, no. 25; T1/87, no. 61, no. 79, no. 146; T1/131 no. 52; See BL Add. MS 61603, Add. MS 61614 for various patronage requests in 1716 to 1720 for Customs posts, often rejected.
[31] TNA T1/82, no. 26; CUST148/12, p. 429.

speak for themselves in terms of experience or merits rather than simply suggesting a case of favours exchanged. If the Customs was, in the context of eighteenth-century, a convenient reservoir of patronage, the target were not the low-ranking, time-intensive preventive positions.

The Many Purposes of the Preventive Service
As the forebear of the modern coastguard, it is unsurprising that coastal officers should have been responsible for aiding ships in distress. Coastal shipwreck was a lasting feature of coastal life. On the Norfolk coast, the winter season regularly witnessed several shipwrecks each year.[32] One should be careful, however, to read too much benevolence into such tasks of the preventive service, as the practice seems to have focused less on life-saving for its own sake as on the rescue of precious cargoes washed ashore. Popular myth indeed has it that the rescue of shipwrecks by the general population was often not about the saving of lives, but rather the extinguishing of what little life remained so as to be able to claim the wreck, in accordance with popular practice, as flotsam and jetsam. The reality, as Cathryn Pearce has shown, was less barbarous, even in Cornwall.[33] But it is true that the scramble for wrecked goods was a violent business. It was not an uncommon sight for preventive officers finding "vast crowds of people of both sexes" in pursuit of wrecked goods.[34] At the same time, any seizure of the goods by local manor lords resulted in legal process.[35] It was the purpose of the preventive service, therefore, to set watches over the wrecks and secure the goods in the next Customs warehouses. This was an invidious and often dangerous task with only the weakest links to any fiscal agenda.[36]

In another respect, too, preventive officers provided for a coastal watch-force. For fear of the spread of infectious diseases, either in humans or cattle, Privy Council frequently required arrivals from certain ports to quarantine at designated places. Similarly, embargo orders issued by Privy

---

[32] TNA CUST 97/2, 11 February 1709.
[33] Cathryn Pearce, *Cornish Wrecking, 1700–1860: Reality and Popular Myth* (Woodbridge, 2010).
[34] TNA CUST 82/8, 21 January 1757.
[35] TNA CUST 59/1, 5 January 1716; CUST 89/4, 22 April 1763; CUST 82/6, 18 May 1750; CUST 97/7, 31 May 1732, 15 August 1732; CUST 97/16, 15 August 1750; T1/114, no. 34; T1/122, no. 10; T1/159, no. 6.
[36] For instance, TNA CUST 59/10, 16 January 1762; CUST 72/77A, January 1713; CUST 82/8, 21 January 1757; CUST 97/2, 11 February 1709; CUST 97/10, 15 September 1738; CUST 97/19, 23 December 1766; CUST 97/21, 3 March 1774; NRS CE 87/1/3, 30 January, 4 February 1752.

Council required surveillance of naval movements near the shore.[37] Any paperwork relating to such orders was typically handled by port officers, but compliance was supervised by the preventive service.[38] Theoretically, many counties operated a system whereby JPs were responsible for setting those watches from the local population, but eagerness to perform such service was limited.[39] In a typical sequence, the collector would be informed of the danger of "the Plague". He would "forward this account along the coast as expeditious as may be" and require preventive officers to stop designated ships from landing. At the same time, collectors informed JPs, who in turn were required to appoint "sea watches" for the same purpose.[40] The results were patchy. In 1785, it was complained that the Customs at Dover suffered quarantine ships to come into port for illicit business "regardless of the dangerous consequences attending the having communication with Ships liable to Quarantine".[41] Similarly, a quarantined captain at Great Yarmouth had allegedly been allowed "to come on shore, visit his Family and lay with his wife (…) regardless of the orders relative to the plague".[42] Notwithstanding the breaches, preventive officers were regularly watching the coasts for potential breaches of quarantine.

Orders from the Board, the Treasury, Privy Council and individual Secretaries of State also required the preventive officers to perform policing operations. Often these were orders to apprehend individual smugglers. In the 1730s, it became common to require preventive officers making a seizure to transmit affidavits with names and detailed descriptions of the smugglers.[43] This was because preventive officers were alleged to "often secret the persons concerned in the running the Goods and pretending they are unknown". Following the 1736 Smuggling Act, officers were ordered to apprehend or, failing to do so, to "discover" such persons. Any

---

[37] See the respective minutes in TNA CUST29/1–7, containing several general orders as well as orders relative to particular cases and the orders transmitted from the Treasury to the Customs in T11/19, p. 239. See also CUL, Ch(H), Political Papers 41, no. 55.

[38] TNA CUST59/2, 9 September 1720; CUST59/72, 11 June 1741; CUST59/73, 8 July 1743, 8 September 1743; CUST59/77, 19 December 1771; CUST97/4, 26 October 1720; CUST97/25, 30 October 1784; CUST97/26, October 1786; CUST97/76, 20 July 1753; NRS CE87/1/5, 19 March 1770.

[39] TNA CUST97/4, 7 November 1720, 21 June 1721; CUST59/2, 24 October, 29 October, 7 November 1720; T1/131, nos 25, 49.

[40] TNA CUST97/14, 31 May 1747; CUST82/1, 19 November, 20 November 1720.

[41] TNA CUST54/1, 4 May 1785; a similar case in CUST59/77, 12 March 1772.

[42] TNA CUST97/20, 1 December 1770.

[43] TNA CUST59/71, 16 June 1737. An earlier example in CUST97/74a, 25 September 1679.

"false account" or failure to produce a full account was made punishable.[44] It was impossible that the officers "should not be able to discover the names and places of abode of some of them at least".[45] And the Board was not squeamish when it scented foul play.[46]

What is striking in this development is that riding officers and captains were required to name and apprehend criminals in an increasingly proactive manner. If the Board heard of a particular offender being in the whereabouts of a particular port, preventive officers were to go after that person.[47] As the smuggling laws coming into force under Walpole and in subsequent years had made smuggling a felony, this can hardly be understood in terms of fiscal activity of the preventive service, but rather as a partial repurposing of the Customs to a crime-fighting agency. It went after smugglers not as fiscal offenders, but as felons. The preventive service constituted a force responsible for upholding authority in a wider sense:

> In addition to the arguments in favour of the continuance of this force, arising from the proofs of its efficiency in promoting the direct objects of its institution, there are incidental benefits attending it, to which, in our opinion, considerable importance must be attached. Those who are acquainted with the remote districts on the coast [...], will immediately understand the nature and value of the advantages which are to be derived from the establishment of stations on the parts of the country least frequented, where the residence of a number of men of regular conduct, and subject to constant superintendence, is found to produce a manifest improvement in the general habits of the people in the neighbourhood, and at the same time to afford a highly useful support to the local authorities, in the maintenance of good order and the general enforcement of the laws.[48]

It was consistent with such developments that other state departments should have relied on the preventive service in a similar manner. When Customs officers were to look out for suspected criminals, it was typically for crimes that relied on coastal mobility. Such crimes were typically of a treasonous nature. It was not uncommon for Secretaries of State to send

---

[44] TNA CUST59/71, 26 March 1737. See also CUST97/14, 30 March 1747.
[45] TNA CUST59/73, 24 March 1747.
[46] TNA CUST97/13, 14 September 1745, 18 September 1745, 24 September 1745, 14 October 1745.
[47] TNA CUST59/73, 1 September 1746.
[48] *Tenth Report of the Commissioners of Inquiry into the Collection and Management of the Revenue arising in Ireland, Scotland, etc. Ports of Ireland, Preventive Coast Guard, Quarantine, etc.* (London, 1824), p. 21.

orders "to look out diligently after one [xy] who is expected from France hither, there being ground to believe that he may bring with him books and papers of a dangerous nature";[49] or to seek and detain "a Woman supposed to pass by the name of [xy] and to be concerned in carrying on a Treasonable correspondence".[50] In the context of war, moreover, central authorities were eager to hear from the coasts about *any* suspicious movement of persons. Coastal officers acted for the purpose of "detecting or putting a Stop to Correspondence with her Maj. Enemies".[51] Similar orders were given in Scotland after 1707.[52] A circular letter to the outports from 1715 read:

> There being just cause to suspect that some disaffected persons in severall parts of this Kingdom doe secretly carry on seditious traitorous designs against His Majestys Government the Commissioners have therefore thought fit in a more particular manner to recommend it to you to use your utmost Care and diligence to detect all secret practices whatsoever which may at any time be carrying on in your Parts to the disturbance of the Government to give them an daily and full account thereof.[53]

Local officers frequently sent reports about suspicious encounters to the Board in London.[54] It was, however, often difficult to distinguish fact from rumour. Did the strange proceedings on a Norfolk beach in October 1745 indicate that an invasion was imminent?[55] Was the person making enquiries on the Suffolk coast in December 1745 a spy?[56] Did the frequent sighting of ships off the southern coasts, reported from places such as Romney, Rye, Folkestone or Deal during 1744 and 1745, signify that the French were about to land troops?[57] Was there any truth to reports of squadrons of French ships amassing near Scarborough, Newcastle, or Dover in the spring of 1709?[58] Were the French ships meeting with unknown persons on the

---

[49] TNA CUST59/70, 17 July 1716. See also TNA CUST97/14, 22 May 1746.
[50] TNA CUST97/16, 16 and 19 October 1751. A similar case in T1/128, no. 3. See also NRS CE87/1/3, 26 September 1751; GCA CE82/1/1, 5 October 1751.
[51] BL Add. MS 61596, fols 97–98, 159–160; BL Add. MS 61507, fols 115–116; BL Add. MS 61608, fols 11–26; CTB 22 (1708), pp. 365–366 (16 August 1708); T1/83, no. 107; T1/100, no. 29.
[52] TNA T1/107, no. 60; T1/113, no. 18.
[53] TNA CUST97/74a, 17 September 1715; CUST59/70, 17 September 1715.
[54] For similar orders, see TNA CUST59/73, 26 September 1745, 4 December 1745; CUST97/75, 4 December 1745, 14 December 1745.
[55] TNA CUST97/13, 21 October 1745, 23 October 1745.
[56] TNA CUST97/13, 28 December 1745.
[57] BL Add. MS 28157, fols 154, 187, et *passim*.
[58] BL Add. MS 61546, fols 126, 133, 138.

Sussex coast near East Dean or on the Dorset coast indicative of treasonous proceedings? Was the suspicion warranted that the Dover packet boats were bringing in "popish Books"?[59] Exactly because of their routine occupation of riding and watching the coasts, it was preventive officers who were expected to separate the unusual from the ordinary.

The line between the lookout for criminals and the gathering of military intelligence was fluid. In the context of hostilities with France, Customs men were frequently enjoined, "in case an enemy should appear on the Coast", to inform the commanders of nearby regiments.[60] Most often such orders remained general, as when officers were drilled to look out for "any of the Enemys ships" or to give "regular constant and immediate accounts of any Intelligence" relating to "Hostile Preparations of the French to land on the Coast".[61] In other cases, officers were instructed to look out for sightings of a particular squadron of French vessels.[62] Here the preventive service became an important instrument of military affairs.

But the preventive service also more directly served in military matters. The Customs frequently assisted the press gangs in local villages and port towns. Occasionally, of course, the Customs had trouble with their own officers – theoretically exempt – being picked up by the press gangs.[63] More often, however, it was the Customs service that served to identify, list, and name suitable candidates in the outports.[64] At times, in addition, the Customs men were to pick up arms in defence of the kingdom, as in Whitehaven in 1745: "we and several other officers now bear arms and do duty by turns".[65] Perhaps most directly, the Customs contributed to war efforts by their preventive establishment at sea – sloops and cruisers – being commandeered by the navy to perform auxiliary roles.[66]

---

[59] BL Add. MS 61608, fols 11–21; Add. MS 61609, fols 7–10. Another concern was to apprehend deserters; see TNA CUST97/75, 25 November 1745.

[60] TNA CUST97/30, 7 May 1798.

[61] TNA CUST97/73, 10 August 1745; CUST54/147, 5 September 1755, 20 September 1755, 6 November 1755, 16 July 1756; CUST97/76, 5 September 1755; CUST58/75, 16 July 1756.

[62] TNA CUST59/73, 4 September 1743.

[63] TNA CUST59/72, 11 July 1739; CUST97/22, 20 December 1776; T1/8, no. 9; GCA CE60/1/2, 29 November 1757.

[64] TNA CUST54/147, 11 January 1757; CUST59/71, 12 December 1734.

[65] TNA CUST82/5, 2 October 1745, see also 1 September 1744, 6 February 1745, 14 November 1745.

[66] TNA, CUST59/73, 7 December 1745; CUST97/24, 5 September 1781; T11/23, p. 46; CUST29/4, 'Cruizers', 20 August 1779, 3 December 1779, 4 September 1781, 10 May 1782, 19 October 1782.

The Vigilant and the Negligent

When Sir William Musgrave, Commissioner between 1763 and 1785, evaluated the quality of each part of the Customs service, his evaluation of the preventive service was scathing:

> These Riding officers are therefore of very little Service tho' a great Burthen to the Revenue and of late Years parliamentary Interest has recommended Apothecaries, Brewers & other Tradesmen to these employments who never ride but when their own occupations require it and fabricate Journals for the rest of the time. And it is generally reported that many of them are the relation of & even that some of them are the Agents & Collectors for the Smuglers.[67]

In their vividness, these comments have done much to taint the image of the preventive service in the eyes of contemporaries and historians. Riding officers, the story goes, were unusually corrupt and ineffective even in the context of a Customs service flawed by sinecures, corruption, and patronage. These comments also point to the failure of a number of bureaucratic techniques of control. Both this failure and the general remissness of preventive officers are usually taken to be important explanatory factors in the volumes of smuggling in the period: with a service so negligent, was the alleged ease of running contraband any wonder?[68]

This chapter argues that such an equation should be read with caution. For one thing, these bureaucratic measures of control have never been studied in detail.[69] Secondly, whereas it is beyond doubt that smuggling continued despite the existence of the preventive service, the exact impact of this form of prevention on the actual levels of smuggling is difficult to measure – not least because the amount of smuggling itself is beyond exact computation. In the absence of this possibility, a better understanding of the performance of the preventive service is the only viable means of evaluating its efficiency.

To do so, a few key areas need to be analysed. What qualifications were needed in riding officers and sloop commanders, and what principles guided the appointments by the Customs and the Treasury? What were

---

[67] *Eighteenth Century Documents*, pp. 254f.
[68] Brewer, *Sinews*, p. 101.
[69] Even in Hoon's detailed account of the Customs in the eighteenth century, the preventive service is only touched upon, see Hoon, *Organization*, 176–185. Ashworth has similarly devoted only few pages to preventive officers, see Ashworth, *Customs*, chapter 10.

Customs authorities doing to prevent corruption and collusion of their officers on the ground? As has already become apparent in the description by Musgrave, there were several mechanisms to ensure sufficient ability and honesty of the officers. Some principles operated at the appointment stage and concerned the age, character, family status and qualifications of the officers. Other mechanisms took effect when officers were appointed, such as oaths of office, personal securities and restrictions on where officers could serve. A further set of bureaucratic techniques were meant to control conduct in office. These included rolling procedures, the keeping of journals, and supervision structures. All this was not only up to date when compared with the allegedly more efficient Excise, it also went a long way in achieving bureaucratic efficiency – further, at least, than Musgrave was willing to concede.

"fitly Qualified for that Imployment"

Appointments in the preventive service of the Customs were made on the basis of certain social indicators rather than professional skills, physical abilities or political suitability. Because the duty of a riding officer or a sloop commander required little in the way of technical skills usually expected from port staff, the Board looked for more personal qualities in the preventive service. Honesty, youth, activity, and zeal were thus more important than professional skills. Yet such personal qualities were not easy to establish in any objective manner. The Board needed to rely on social mechanisms such as personal reputation, sureties and oaths. Beyond this, officers were ideally both young and unmarried. At the same time, the Board lacked the resolve to rigorously enforce this. Thus it proved flexible regarding most objective criteria, provided the appointee possessed a proper character and was able to provide the required securities.

Of strictly professional requirements for the preventive service, there were few: riding officers needed to be able to ride, and sloop personnel needed seafaring experience, being ideally "bred to the sea".[70] Both also needed to be able to read and write to handle instructions, reports and journals. Not everyone, however, passed this test.[71] No knowledge of accounting techniques was required and legal expertise was only necessary to the extent that officers were expected to understand the Acts of Parliament in relation to the Customs and able to act lawfully and according to

---

[70] TNA CUST 82/3, 6 January 1739; CUST 59/10, 24 May 1762.
[71] For instance, TNA CUST 82/4, 26 May 1742. An order to Campbeltown in 1791 specifically asked the collector to stop employing people who could not write; see GCA CE82/2/5, 28 September 1791.

the rules prescribed by the Board of Customs. The latter, however, does not seem to have been a strict requirement. Only of supervisors of riding officers was it expected that they were "versed in the Customs and Penal Laws so as to be able on occasion to instruct, as well as inspect their [the ordinary riding officers'] behaviour".[72] For all others, rudimentary knowledge was seemingly enough.

In terms of personal qualifications, the ideal candidate was "young", "brisk", "sober" and "active".[73] Often, however, appointments remain silent as to the qualifications of individual candidates. Instead, the personal "character" operated as a marker for individual qualifications. Both in appointments and regular surveys, the character of an officer thus frequently decided his administrative fate. If outport collectors deemed someone an "esteemed man fitly Qualified for that Imployment", "very knowing and diligent" or indeed "a very hardy, robust diligent and honest Man", the Board had little choice but to accept such information.[74] If the Board claimed that a "due knowledge and Choyce of the officers" was one of its chief duties, there was still no circumventing the expertise of local administrators.[75]

Of personal attributes, only youth was an objective criterion. But this was a preference rather than a strict directive. Of the riding officers employed in Kent between 1736 and 1743, the average age was 45.8 years. The average time already served by these same officers was 10.3 years, making the average hiring age around 35 years. In 1743, altogether 15 of the 34 officers were above 50, whereas none was younger than 30. The case of George Herbert, who served in Kent until the age of 75, is not exceptional.[76] Elsewhere, too, riding officers tended to be old.[77] And it was not necessarily perceived as a problem. George Herbert repeatedly received favourable evaluations. If others were dismissed because of old age, it was usually because this coincided with other personal deficiencies.[78] Only in 1782 did the Board order that no persons over the age of 45 should be admitted to be a riding officer because it required "Spirit, Activity, and labour to perform the Duties

---

[72] TNA CUST82/4, 15 February 1744.
[73] TNA CUST72/3, 23 October 1783; CUST97/2, 27 December 1704; CUST97/20, 1 March 1770; CUST148/13, p. 5.
[74] TNA CUST97/4, 5 October 1722; CUST82/1, 29 April 1715; CUST97/2, 29 November 1704; CUST59/69, 11 June 1700; CUST97/74a, 27 April 1710; CUST59/1, 18 March 1716.
[75] TNA T1/4, no. 52.
[76] Statistic derived from the officer lists in TNA CUST148/11.
[77] NRS CE51/1/3, 5 July 1761; TNA CUST97/74a, 27 April 1710; CUST97/11, 15 December 1738.
[78] TNA T1/250, nos 9, 158; CUST148/13, p. 35; CUST97/74a, 27 April 1710.

thereof with any reasonable Hope of Success."[79] Around the same time, however, entry was restricted to the age of 21 and above.[80] Youth, therefore, was an administrative preference, but not a strict criterion of entry or continuance.[81]

The same flexibility is apparent regarding the marital status of the officers. Originally, Henry Baker had proposed that riding officers be bachelors so as to make them less prone to be part of social networks and to make it easier for officers to move from their native place.[82] This maxim was often reiterated. In September 1717, the Weymouth collector asked that officers "be men that are [...] unmarried" that do not "have the Clogg of a family".[83] But this rule, too, was only laxly applied. All over the service, officers were married and had large families "to maintain" – sometimes with as many as nine children.[84]

Rules on double-employment were stricter. By the Board's orders, officers were plainly instructed "not to keep Publick Houses or be otherwise concerned in Trade contrary to their Instructions".[85] Officers were "not to follow any other Business or Profession whatsoever, but to apply yourself entirely to the Service of the Revenue".[86] This rule was enforced: when it was reported in May 1727, that the riding officer at Sherringham "keeps a farm, deals in foreign goods and otherways misbehaves", this prompted an immediate inquiry.[87] Similarly, when it was alleged that the sloop commander at Great Yarmouth was often ashore to tend to his farm, an inquiry was launched.[88] In such instances, officers were given occasion to defend themselves against accusations and occasionally also allowed time to remedy failures and thus avoid the Board's "displeasure".[89] But the Board

---

[79] TNA CUST29/5, 16 October 1782; see also CUST97/80, 17 July 1783. The same cap was introduced for commanders and mates of cruisers, see CUST29/6, 13 December 1793. The cap was subsequently reduced to 35 years, but only in 1819; see CUST29/7, 21 July 1819.

[80] TNA CUST29/5, 9 September 1788. This rule was enforced: CUST59/76, 23 October 1784.

[81] See TNA CUST29/7, "Ages and Capacities". Examples in GCA CE60/1/2, 16 August, 20 September 1755.

[82] TNA T1/60, no. 12. See the subsequent orders in TNA PC2/77, p. 190; T11/13, p. 451.

[83] TNA CUST59/1, 28 September 1717. See also BL Add. MS 18903, fol. 89.

[84] TNA CUST148/13, pp. 5, 6, 27, 30; T1/149, no. 48; CUST89/6, 12 October 1779; CUST97/10, 16 October 1738; NRS CE51/1/3, 5 July 1761; GCA CE60/1/4, 3 July 1765.

[85] TNA CUST31/1, 16 April 1743.

[86] TNA CUST141/4, p. 20.

[87] TNA CUST97/5, 12 May 1727.

[88] TNA CUST97/2, 7 April 1708.

[89] TNA CUST148/13, pp. 2, 35, 36.

considered such conduct a serious breach of duty and did not hesitate to dismiss officers not complying.[90]

Having met the entry criteria, officers were expected to give warranties to the Board for their conduct. Specifically, all officers were to be "under oath and security".[91] Aside from a general clause about the faithful discharge of the office, the oath also forbade the taking of any "Reward or Gratuity, directly or indirectly".[92] Noncompliance was a serious breach of duty. The 1723 investigation into the Scottish establishment contained a long report on who had and who had not taken the oath of office among the Scottish officials.[93] On top of the individual social bond of the oath, the Board also required each officer to name at least two sureties. These were to be given by persons "of substance Credit and reputation".[94] As early as 1700, the Board ordered that "upon no Pretence whatsoever [should] any Person be employed without first giving Security".[95] A certificate of the sufficiency of such sureties was sent to an examiner each year.[96] He was to inquire into all proposed securities as to their suitability.[97]

Only after such checks were officers handed a deputation by the Board. For the duration of their service, this acted both as acknowledgement of duties and proof of employment. Serious trouble awaited those who presumed to act in a particular capacity without deputation,[98] or who lost them.[99] Upon any employment ending, the Board made sure to order collectors "to call in the deputation and cancel it and transmit it to us".[100] On the whole, qualification for an office in the preventive service, both upon admission and during tenure, was regulated predominantly by social factors, chief among which was the individual "character" of a person, his word and the sureties he was able to give, rather than any objective criteria such

---

[90] TNA CUST97/11, 5 October 1739; CUST82/1, 3 December 1718. See also T64/139, fol. 1 and T64/140, fol. 1.
[91] TNA CUST82/3, 1 April 1735; CUST82/6, 27 July 1750.
[92] TNA CUST141/4, p. 20. See also Ashworth, *Customs*, pp. 358–364.
[93] TNA T1/250, no. 9, report no. 3. Scottish officers were also required to take an "Oath on Government".
[94] TNA CUST97/4, 15 May 1723.
[95] TNA CUST29/2, 31 August 1700.
[96] TNA CUST31/1, 3 November 1735; CUST29/3, 2 November 1758. Examples in CUST97/74b, fols 141–142; CUST69/59, 21 February 1734.
[97] TNA CUST29/3, 23 September 1768; CUST29/4, 5 February 1782.
[98] TNA CUST82/12, 20 September 1774; CUST97/2, 27 December 1704, 8 January 1705; CUST97/3, 13 April 1715.
[99] TNA CUST29/4, 11 January 1780.
[100] TNA CUST82/3, 24 January 1735; CUST97/75, 29 January 1744.

as age and family status or indeed physical or professional skills. The latter criteria could disqualify a man, but they were not sufficient to qualify him.

"more integrity than which is usual in this Age"
Personal qualities were more important to the Board than professional skill because the toughest test on officers was likely to be a test of character. "Can anyone believe", a Customs memorial asked, "that a Collector or other officer, unless he has more integrity than which is usual in this Age, will detect his Brother, uncle, or other Relation of any fraud committed to the prejudice of the Revenue?"[101] Collusion, fraud and embezzlement were perennial worries for the Board, for the monetary advantages were tempting. If these were linked to social bonds, the revenue, it was believed, was doomed. The Board's most central maxim in this regard, therefore, was that officers "were to be present in the community, but not of it".[102] Or, as the Treasury expressed this sentiment in 1766: "Natives of the Place & too long residence even for Foreigners in the same Place exposes the Officers of the Customs to Connections and influence that may hurt the Revenue".[103] To the authorities, it was only common sense "to preserve the Men, as much as possible, from too frequent or too long an Intercourse with the Inhabitants of the Coast" and to prevent them forming "local Connections".[104] As early as 1696, the Treasury had formed the rule that officers should not be employed in places where they were "related or habituated".[105] Even before, the Board had aimed to appoint "persons of integrity & not of this place".[106]

Theoretically, this applied to all officers. In practice, it proved unworkable. The order was "totally neglected".[107] Occasionally there are indeed mentions of officers being deliberately placed in stations to which they were "strangers", but there is no evidence to suggest systematic implementation of the non-native rule.[108] The 1723 investigation in Scotland reported a general neglect of the rule and concluded that "Officers have been too

---

[101] BL Add. MS 18903, fols 88–89.
[102] John Brewer, 'Servants of the Public—Servants of the Crown: Officialdom of Eighteenth-Century English Central Government', in id., Eckhart Hellmuth (eds), *Rethinking Leviathan: The Eighteenth-Century State in Britain and Germany* (Oxford, 1999), pp. 127–147, at p. 139.
[103] Treasury to Board of Customs, 17 December 1766, cit. Hoon, *Organization*, p. 207.
[104] 'Third Report', p. 10; TNA CUST 29/4, 13 June 1788.
[105] *Eighteenth Century Documents*, pp. 260–261. See also TNA CUST 29/2, 15 May 1714, 27 May 1714, 8 July 1714.
[106] TNA T 64/139, fol. 3.
[107] BL Add. MS 18903, fols 88–89. See also TNA T1/250, no. 9; Hoon, *Organization*, p. 207.
[108] TNA CUST 97/4, 5 October 1722; CUST 59/2, 25 May 1720; T1/250, nos 9, 159.

frequently employed in Ports where they have had Friends and Relations in the Neighbourhood and it is not naturally to be expected these should exert themselves with that necessary Vigour as Strangers probably would in detecting and preventing Evil Practices."[109] The exception to this was the preventive service. Because it was "a work of time to beget such a confidence between the smuggler and the officer as will be necessary for a mutual trust of each other", it was considered good practice that at least the "waterguard and the preventive land officers were rolled annually from Port to Port".[110]

Indeed, rolling, the removing of officers from station to station at regular intervals, was considered the principal method for making sure that officers were neither related nor habituated in the places where they served. Prior to the establishment of the preventive service, this was already regarded as a fine bureaucratic tool in the Excise. On the recommendation of Charles Davenant, rolling procedures in the Excise branch were used to achieve both a universality of administrative techniques and to ensure the honesty of officers.[111] But contrary to the relatively bad press the Customs received in regard to such forward-looking bureaucratic features, rolling procedures were used in the preventive service from the start.[112] The first to advocate them was Henry Baker.[113] Even before 1698, traces of this procedure are evident in relation to riding officers.[114] In August 1698, the principle was formally included in the authorisation of Baker's scheme, ordering that officers "be changed in six or twelve Months at least".[115] That September, word reached Baker that the Commissioners of Customs had complied with that order in a letter that not only informed him that the "Rolling of the Riding Officers" was "put in immediate execution", but also stated the times at which the various officers were to be rolled.[116]

But even at this stage, the rolling of officers was not uncontroversial. The Board itself advised that the rolling be done "in such manner as may be without prejudice to the service" and that officers "may remove with least inconvenience to the Service".[117] Serious objections had been raised in 1699

---

[109] TNA T1/250, nos 9, 196.
[110] BL Add. MS 18903, fol. 89.
[111] Ashworth, *Customs*, pp. 117–130; Miles Ogborn, 'The Capacities of the State: Charles Davenant and the Management of the Excise, 1683–1698', *Journal of Historical Geography*, 24 (1998), 289–312; Hoon, *Organization*, p. 239.
[112] See Brewer, *Sinews*, pp. 101–102.
[113] TNA T1/63, no. 21.
[114] TNA T11/13, p. 257.
[115] TNA T11/13, p. 451; PC2/77, pp. 190–191.
[116] TNA T1/56, no. 41.
[117] *Ibid.*

by Walter Devereux. He held that "the removall of officers frequently was of known Prejudice". Officers thus removed, he argued, necessarily lodged in public houses and were constantly amongst the offenders they were to police.[118] He was also concerned that frequent removal would inhibit officers in acquainting themselves with local situations and making contacts with informers. Later observers, too, thought it was necessary for officers "to cultivate a friendship with the Country People to have their Assistance on Occasion".[119] Stations in a familiar place were also considered advantageous in a geographic sense; officers were simply more likely to possess a decent knowledge of local geographies and the "different ways of carrying on their [the smugglers'] illicit Traffick".[120] Officers with families were burdened with great costs upon every removal.[121] And many officers refused to be rolled or appointed in strange places for exactly such reasons.[122] At least for the latter case, the Board had a clear answer: "I answer that the force of this objection lyes against the appointing Persons who have families to such Imployment not against their being rolled as proposed".[123]

Such objections notwithstanding, the Treasury followed Baker's advice in 1698. Still, evidence of systematic rolling in practice is sparse. Rather than ordering removes on a regular basis, they appear to have been made on specific occasions. Collectors were asked in 1703, for instance, whether they thought any "alteracions or removes ought to be made amongst" their officers.[124] Individual removes are also in evidence in Kent and Sussex in the 1710s, 30s and 40s.[125] Such occasional removals of officers are scattered throughout the outport records for the rest of the century for both England and Scotland.[126] In most of these instances, any sense of a systematic

---

[118] TNA T1/60, no. 12.
[119] TNA CUST59/1, 28 September 1717.
[120] TNA CUST58/13, 23 October 1784. This consideration is also in evidence for the crews of revenue cruisers; see CUST29/4, 22 December 1787.
[121] BL Add. MS 18903, fol. 89.
[122] TNA CUST82/2, 10 June 1730; CUST97/7, 24 May 1732; NRS CE87/1/5, 17 February 1770.
[123] BL Add. MS 18903, fol. 89.
[124] TNA CUST98/1, 28 August 1703.
[125] TNA T1/138, no. 49; CUST148/13, pp. 18, 30, 34, 39, 41, 45, 58, 67; CUST148/12, pp. 445, 449.
[126] TNA CUST59/71, 18 June 1734; CUST59/76, 27 July 1762; CUST82/9, 21 September 1759; CUST98/1, 19 September 1732; CUST97/10, 25 October 1738; CUST97/77, 16 March 1767; 5 May 1770; NRS CE87/1/8, 15 June 1787. See also the Treasury warrant from June 1761, permitting the Board to remove the crews of revenue cruisers; see TNA CUST29/3, 5 June 1761. For Ireland, see Fleming, *Politics*, p. 182. For Scotland, see, for instance, GCA CE60/1/15, 27 January 1783.

purpose is missing: removes were made if and when something appeared amiss or when a survey revealed a different stationing to be more likely to benefit the revenue. To claim that the practice of rolling was not in use in the Customs, however, would be misleading.

In support of this, there is also occasional evidence of more systematic uses of the rolling procedure. A few years after establishments had been arranged for Scotland after the Union, for instance, the Treasury authorized the Scottish Board in 1714 to remove officers from one port to another "where you shall judge it to be for the service of the Revenue".[127] Similarly, in the course of the 1723 survey of the Scottish Customs establishment, the investigation filed a report with a "list of officers proposed to be removed to other ports and of officers proper to be removed from other ports to supply their places".[128] Finally, in 1710, there was a large-scale rolling procedure in Kent and Sussex after the model proposed in 1699. That very same year, the preventive service on the Scottish Borders was similarly subject to alterations of the officers' stations.[129] Whether these were individual cases or whether they point to a systematic use of rolling procedures now obscured by the incompleteness of the records remains difficult to tell. But they do suggest that rolling remained an important bureaucratic tool in the arsenal of the Customs.

"to Certify the respective Duties performed"

The most important tool of executive control for the preventive service was the journal. Coastal officers were to record their every movement and observations daily in a printed blank journal inspected by their superiors. The journal translated the everyday actions of coastal officers into a standardized form of bureaucratic accountability. This was expected to keep officers active, vigilant and honest. To some extent, this worked. But the journal as a bureaucratic tool was full of ambiguities. If prevention was the aim of the administrative effort on the coast, the journals' contents would, in the best of scenarios, be utterly insignificant. The aims of coastal prevention were best served if nothing happened. Furthermore, the insignificance of the journal entries could easily be forged to conceal inactivity and fraud. A well-kept journal could therefore potentially signify both an active officer and successful prevention – or the exact opposite.

---

[127] TNA T17/3, p. 122.
[128] TNA T1/250, no. 9, report no. 2.
[129] TNA T1/128, no. 3; T11/15, pp. 309–314, 318.

With the introduction of regular coastal policing during the 1690s, the journal became a standard feature of the lives of coastal officeholders.[130] On his inspection of the Sussex and Kent coasts in 1699, Henry Baker recommended that each officer keep a journal, inspected by "Trusty persons" once a fortnight.[131] Commanders of Customs vessels, too, were instructed to keep journals.[132] This type of journal was exclusive to the preventive officers.[133] There is some evidence in this early period that orders were not always complied with, either because officers refused or because the practice fell into disuse at individual ports. But the Board was quick to admonish the respective officials whenever such remissness came to light.[134]

Regulations were further standardized in 1718 when the secretary of the Board, Charles Clarkesse, informed the outport collectors that a new "Forme for more regularly keeping" the journals had been devised. Journals were printed in London and outports were supplied with blank journals upon request. All preventive officers were from now on to follow this form. It included a column for the date; another in which to insert between what places the officers had patrolled or what place they had attended; a further section was to record wind and weather. A last column, finally, was reserved for "observations":

> Particularly what Officers met & where; What Informations he received of Goods run, or to be run; and what method he took to prevent the Same; What Seizures made, What Ships he observes on the Coast & which way they sail, & what notice of such ships he gave to the next Officers; what Signals he Observes from the Commander of the smack, and also whatever happens in the Day, Evening or night, that may be fitt for the Commissioners' knowledge.[135]

As with other bureaucratic instruments – and particularly in view of the later loss of almost all journals from the Customs records of the period – there is no telling to what extent these rules were followed. The outport records make frequent reference to the journals, but the practice may well have been followed in some ports and rapidly forgotten in others. It is noteworthy

---

[130] In some cases this was in use earlier, see TNA CUST97/1, 27 January 1686, 31 May 1686; CUST97/74a, 27 November 1679.
[131] TNA T1/63, no. 21.
[132] TNA CUST59/69, 10 August 1700; CUST29/2, 18. November 1713; CUST97/74a, 1 April 1714.
[133] TNA CUST31/1, 10 November 1716.
[134] TNA CUST97/2, 20 October 1708; CUST97/74a, 21.10.1713; T11/16, pp. 109–112.
[135] TNA CUST59/70, 31 May 1718. See also CUST62/59, 31 May 1718; CUST73/62, 31 May 1718; CUST72/77A, 31 May 1718; CUST29/1, 9 April 1718; CUST31/1, 31 May 1718.

that another set of similar instructions was issued in 1735. As in 1718, the Board supplied all outports with blank journals printed in London along with printed instructions for the riding officers and supervisors, insisting that they ought to record their "whole Duty and Observations, both by Day and by Night", in which they ought always to be "very particular".[136]

Despite this stress on journals, there was an awareness that they did not automatically prevent fraud. A Board minute from 1744 stated that "it is the highest Breach of Duty in an Officer to make fictitious Entries in his Journal".[137] The danger was real. At Weymouth, a riding officer was dismissed for falsifying his journal in June 1735; at Great Yarmouth, the supervisor of riding officers was found "guilty of making false Entries in his Journals" in August 1747 and dismissed accordingly.[138] It is from such evidence that William Musgrave suspected officers to fabricate their journals as a matter of course.[139]

Yet his comment should be read with caution. Musgrave had access to the entire Customs archive.[140] In the above comments, however, Musgrave relied exclusively on the reports of John Collier, Surveyor General of the riding officers in Kent during the 1730s and 1740s.[141] In these reports, Collier did indeed make reference to falsified journals, occasional slackness in journal entries and other forms of administrative negligence.[142] To conclude, however, that all riding officers were of the negligent sort was to distort the scale of the problem. Officers neglecting their duties were perfectly common in all departments.[143] They were also, in Collier's reports, infrequent when viewed in their entirety. Most notably, however, it was the journals that were at the basis of this form of control because they were the single most important source of information for Collier in inspecting the riding officers. Collier used the regular keeping of the journals itself as

---

[136] TNA CUST97/75, 20 August 1734, 31 May 1735; CUST97/8, 23 September 1734; CUST82/3, 9 April 1735. Instructions in CUST141/4, p. 26.
[137] TNA CUST29/1, 2 May 1744.
[138] TNA CUST59/71, 10 June 1735; CUST97/75, 22 August 1747. Another case in CUST97/19, 19 March 1766.
[139] *Eighteenth-Century Documents*, pp. 254–255.
[140] See, for instance, BL Add. MS 8133A–C, 8134, 8135.
[141] TNA CUST148/11–13.
[142] See TNA CUST148/13, p. 35.
[143] Michael Braddick, 'Administrative Performance: the Representation of Political Authority in Early Modern England', in Michael Braddick, John Walter (eds), *Negotiating Power in Early Modern Society: Order, Hierarchy and Subordination in Britain and Ireland* (Cambridge, 2001), pp. 166–187; María Ángeles Martín Romera, Hannes Ziegler (eds), *The Officer and the People: Accountability and Authority in Pre-Modern Europe* (Oxford, 2021).

evidence of activity and service; he was also able to judge by the contents of the journal whether individual officers had done their duty; and Collier regularly compared and cross-checked the journals. Musgrave's criticism of the efficiency of the journals was not, therefore, a fair one. If anything, the Collier reports show that administrative control worked and that it did so *because* of the journals.

The reason was that the journals were read. Proper supervision did exist and it operated on various levels. As early as 1699, Baker had recommended appointing an "itinerant collector of journals" to the Board. The task fell to the supervisors of riding officers in their districts.[144] In addition to keeping journals of their own, supervisors were to inspect their inferiors and "write down on the Back of each of their Journals all material Observations" such as absence or neglect of duty.[145] Copies of these journals together with the supervisor's journal were to be submitted monthly to the collector of the respective ports, who were to "peruse and examine" them and – after making their own observations on whether supervisors had acted "Carefully, Dilligently, and faithfully" –, send them to London.[146] Assessment was to be "without favour or Affection".[147] All journals were sent quarterly to London.[148] There the journals were again assessed by designated examiners from 1719 onwards.[149] Any refusal to produce the journals was considered a "high offence and contempt of this Board and punished accordingly."[150]

In the waterguard, the system was similar. From around 1700 onwards, commanders as well as mates of boats, smacks and sloops were to keep a journal and present the same to the head officials when coming into port. These officers were then to report to the Board "whatever you find remarkable at any time".[151] In 1713, this was put on a more regular basis by requiring the commanders to deliver their journals monthly, while port officials were to send them quarterly to London with their observations.[152] A different system was introduced around 1740, when the Board appointed a Surveyor of Sloops and Boats who was to inspect the journals of all commanders and

[144] TNA T1/64, no. 33.
[145] TNA CUST141/4, p. 27.
[146] TNA CUST97/75, 20 August 1734.
[147] TNA CUST59/70, 10 November 1716, 20 November 1717; CUST73/62, 20 November 1717.
[148] TNA CUST31/1, 13 December 1733.
[149] TNA CUST31/1, 30 September 1719. These posts were discontinued in 1781 and 1790, after which time the Board's clerk prepared the journal for the perusal of the Board; see CUST29/4, 28 November 1781, 19 January 1790; CUST29/5, 28 November 1781.
[150] TNA CUST29/3, 19 March, 8 April 1774.
[151] TNA CUST59/69, 10 August 1700.
[152] TNA CUST97/74a, 21 October 1713. See also CUST29/1, 24 January 1727.

mates.¹⁵³ By 1742, the Board employed an examiner in London for that very purpose. But collectors were still required to make their own observations before passing the journals on to London.¹⁵⁴ By 1767, the London official was called an Inspector of Sloops and Boats.¹⁵⁵ The same course was taken in Scotland.¹⁵⁶

The keeping of journals – regardless of their content – was deemed very important; noncompliance first prompted a stop of pay and ultimately dismissal. So did cases of misconduct and negligence. As in other systems of accountability, however, the crucial factor was to detect such misconduct. How well did the system work?

The first level of control was the supervisor. Better paid than ordinary officers, he was supposed to visit the preventive officers in his district. "Once every week (or oftener if occasion require)" and as often as possible "by night". Twice per month, supervisors were also to survey their entire district.¹⁵⁷ In addition, they were reviewing the journals in connection to specific incidents.¹⁵⁸ Every month, the supervisor was to send the journals of his officers as well as his own to either the collector of his port or to the Surveyor General. Whether all of this was done consistently is difficult to establish. A recurrent problem was that districts were too large.¹⁵⁹ In general, therefore, inspections tended to be too rare, especially at night.¹⁶⁰ In other cases, observations made on the journals of riding officers were deemed too superficial.¹⁶¹ On the basis of such negligence, some supervisors were even dismissed.¹⁶² As early as 1714, it was found that neither officers nor supervisors returned their journals punctually in Kent and Sussex.¹⁶³ Later orders specified that salaries were to be stopped if journals were not forthcoming.¹⁶⁴ An order of 1741 stated, further, that salaries were to be paid only once all the journals had been received by the collector.¹⁶⁵ This was strictly enforced: when the supervisor at Great Yarmouth, one Mr.

[153] TNA CUST97/75, 23 June 1740.
[154] TNA CUST59/73, 7 April 1743; CUST29/2, 19 August 1742; CUST31/1, 7 April 1743.
[155] TNA CUST59/77, 2 July 1767; CUST82/10, 2 July 1767; CUST29/3, 30 June 1767.
[156] NRS CE14/2, p. 25.
[157] TNA CUST59/71, 30 May 1735. See also CUST97/8, 13 September 1734; CUST148/13, p. 42.
[158] TNA CUST148/12, pp. 51, 97–98, 101–102, 357; CUST97/10, 13 August 1737.
[159] TNA CUST82/4, 23 November 1743.
[160] TNA CUST97/74b, 23 March 1727; CUST59/4, 19 June 1736.
[161] TNA CUST82/3, 18 March 1736; CUST59/4, 19 June 1736.
[162] TNA CUST82/3, 18 November 1738.
[163] TNA T11/16, 7 January 1714.
[164] TNA CUST59/71, 11 October 1735.
[165] TNA CUST59/72, 26 November 1741.

Knott, did not produce all journals of his officers, his pay was immediately stopped.[166] As we cannot suppose that any officer would remain in office for long if he was not complying with this order, it is reasonable to assume that this system generally worked. Mr. Knott, after being repeatedly unable or unwilling to produce the journals, was dismissed without further ado.[167]

Another level of supervision were the port officials, usually collector and comptroller. They were to acknowledge the receipt of the journals, review them and send them to London with their observations. The Board considered this level of control very important. It argued in 1741 that the principal officers of the port "have not only a power, but it is their Duty from time to time [...] to enquire into and observe the behaviour of every Officer within their Port."[168] This specifically applied to the preventive officers acting at a distance from the port. When the Great Yarmouth collector admitted in 1748, for instance, that he had "never seen" the journals, the Board sternly reminded him that it was "not intending that their Respective Supervisors and Surveyors General should be the only Checques upon them in the Execution of their Duty".[169] Most collectors seem to have taken this to heart.[170] But there is also evidence of slackness and obstinacy. In March 1723, the Great Yarmouth collector sent the journals, supposing "them to be true". Being an officer "above Stairs" with "a multitude of business on our hands and no time to ride abroade" he could not possibly be asked, he wrote, to ascertain the truth of the matter.[171] Similarly, in 1799, the Plymouth collector argued that the stations of the officers were "so remote and so distant" that he had it not in his power to certify whether "they have attended at the various times and places as mentioned in the Journals."[172] He was "obliged to be at our Desk in the office to execute our Personal Duty", therefore it was "impossible for us to Certify the respective Duties performed by them", at least "from personal knowledge". At the same time, he acknowledged that the "duties actually performed" by the riding officers very much depended on proper supervision.[173]

---

[166] TNA CUST 97/13, 29 December 1744.
[167] TNA CUST 97/13, 31 January 1745.
[168] TNA CUST 59/72, 26 November 1741.
[169] TNA CUST 97/75, 12 July 1748.
[170] TNA CUST 97/8, 20 July 1734. A similar case at Peterhead in NRS CE87/1/5, 27 April 1770.
[171] TNA CUST 97/4, 20 March 1723. See also CUST 97/4, 15 December 1721.
[172] TNA CUST 66/1, 18 January 1799.
[173] TNA CUST 66/2, 22 April 1801. Further disputes in CUST 97/2, 20 October 1708; CUST 97/3, 13 October 1718, 23 November 1719; CUST 97/4, 22 February 1720.

Journal controls on the ground were often done in a "hasty quick manner".[174] It was different for the examiners in the London Customs House. These inspections were thorough. For both the riding officers and their supervisors, as well as the commanders and mates of the Customs sloops, the examiners noted times of unusual absence from duty, time spent at home instead of on patrols or on cruises as well as any lack of details in noting the times and places of such patrols or cruises.[175] They noticed things such as officers not acting when they had information about a smuggling operation or even missing a meeting with fellow officers.[176] Supervisors were reprimanded for failing to make proper observations, not visiting officers as often as they should, staying at home for too long, or suffering inferior officers to be off duty without leave.[177] As for the journals themselves, any deviation in format or frequency from the required method by the outport officers was noticed and admonished.[178]

These various layers of supervision in effect resulted in the implementation of four eyes principles and different layers of control. The Board further encouraged this by administrative cross-checks. Not only did it rely on supervisors controlling their inferiors, but also encouraged the officers to do the same, enabling the Board to measure the activity of both.[179] Riding officers were also to record when and where they had met other officers in adjacent districts to allow for cross-checks of the journals so that "one officer will be a Cheque on another".[180] In order for the supervisors to establish whether officers had truthfully reported the sighting of ships, moreover, they were "to have recourse to the Journall of the Commander of the Sloop as he shall Desire". The collectors, too, were to compare journals of officers with those of the sloop captains to detect discrepancies.[181] Perhaps most common was the rule, however, that journals of riding officers stationed in the vicinity of each other were to be compared with one another, both as a matter of course and in relation to particular incidents. This instruction

---

[174] TNA CUST82/4, 23 November 1743.
[175] TNA CUST97/74b, 14 June 1726; 23 March 1727; CUST82/4, 26 May 1742; CUST59/4, 19 June 1736.
[176] TNA CUST97/75, 06 October 1744.
[177] TNA CUST97/74b, 14 June 1726, 23 March 1727; CUST82/3, 18 March 1736; CUST82/4, 23 November 1743; CUST59/4, 19 June 1736; CUST59/77, 18 April 1769.
[178] TNA CUST97/2, 20 October 1708; CUST97/3, 13 October 1718, 23 November 1719; CUST97/4, 22 February 1720.
[179] TNA CUST97/4, 22 February 1719. See also TNA CUST148/13, p. 42.
[180] TNA CUST59/1, 28 September 1717.
[181] TNA CUST97/75, 20 August 1734.

operated on every level: supervisors, collectors, and the London examiners, respectively.[182]

What was, however, impossible to remove from the entire process was the ambiguity of ostensibly correct, but entirely nondescript journal entries. When it was observed, for instance, that the journals on a particular stretch of coast recorded nothing but trifles when there were, at the same time, clear indications that smuggling was rife in that area, authorities tended to send exhorting messages to the respective ports, expressing their "surprise" at the quietness of the journals in an ostensibly turbulent station.[183] Dull journals generally made for suspicious reading. Entries such as the ones in the journal of Abraham Pike, supervisor of riding officers at Southampton, for January 1803 may have been entirely innocent. But they perfectly underscore the ambiguity of the journals as bureaucratic tools of accountability:

> Went to Vernhill on discoveries. No success.
> Surveyed the East coast to Beacon, saw nothing for the Service.
> Went to Thorley on discoveries, no success.
> Surveyed the West coast to Bourn, nothing occured.
> Went to Hurn on discoveries, no success.[184]

"to Instruct and Direct, as well as to Punish and Correct"

Ambiguity was a problem for the Customs Board. Particularly with a view to the performance of its officers, the Board needed to establish clarity. It did so by supplementing the lack of clarity in practice with a dualistic language of officeholding. According to the Board, there were only two types of officers: the vigilant and the negligent. This distinction was coupled with the view that they alone were "the Imediate Judge of the officers behaviour". Challenges to this exclusive responsibility from above – such as the Treasury – or below – such as collectors – were fended off with the assertion that the Board's "business it has alwaies been to Instruct and Direct them [officers], as well as to Punish and Correct them by Suspension Dismission or otherwise".[185]

This dualism is particularly pervasive in the Board's instructions: to the riding officers it let it be known that "a diligent and faithful Discharge of your Duty shall always meet with all due Encouragement and Assistance

---

[182] TNA CUST97/8, 13 September 1734; CUST82/11, 12 January 1771.
[183] TNA CUST73/3, 30 October 1773; CUST59/77, 22 May 1770.
[184] Hampshire Archives and Local Studies, 25A03. Similar impressions in TNA CUST148/12, p. 357.
[185] TNA T1/4, no. 52.

[...], so also will your Neglects meet with suitable Returns."[186] More explicit still are the instructions issued to commanders of revenue sloops:

> As on the one hand, we are determined to probe the conduct of the Preventive Officers, and punish them according to their demerit, deeming laxity and negligence where found [...] to be a sufficient ground for not retaining them in our service; so on the other hand, that vigilance and faithful Duty [...] may not be deprived of fair and due Reward.[187]

More than any other word or phrase, vigilance encapsulated the expectations of the Board towards their officers; similarly negligence stood for all that was reproachful in an officer. Accordingly, it was these words that kept reappearing.[188]

Obviously, this did not eradicate the problem of ambiguity per se. Regularly, the Board was in fact receiving mixed signals: whereas official reports insisted on the good service of its officers, these same reports often indicated a large amount of smuggling on individual stretches of coast. Faced with such contradictions, the Board often chose to assume negligence. On receiving reports of smuggling, it reminded officials that this "could not possibly be to such degree if the preventive officers did their duty as they ought."[189] In such instances, the Commissioners also claimed to have reason to believe "that this Trade is too much encouraged by the Neglect if not Connivance of the officers". Therefore, officers were encouraged to use their "utmost Care and Vigilance" and reminded that the Board would have particular regard for the vigilant, whereas it would punish those "they shall find either unfaithfull or negligent".[190] Negligence, in fact, was seen as just as sinful as fraud. Whereas the collector at Great Yarmouth thought that his officers were honest and "not in Combination either with the Masters or Merchants to deprave the Revenue", it was nonetheless clear to the Board that there was a "general Remisseness and want of skill or zeal in them", which amounted "in effect to the same and the Revenue is liable thereby to be as greatly prejudiced as if there was a want of honesty".[191] Because

---

[186] TNA CUST141/4, p. 29.
[187] TNA CUST143/16, p. 150.
[188] TNA CUST59/70, 24 July 1716; CUST59/4, 11 October 1737; CUST59/72, 24 July 1740; CUST59/9, 25 November 1741; CUST73/7, 30 October 1773; CUST82/3, 18 November 1738; CUST54/1, 30 December 1784.
[189] TNA CUST59/70, 10 November 1716.
[190] TNA CUST59/70, 24 July 1716. See also GCA CE60/1/37, 13 January 1810.
[191] TNA CUST97/75, 12 July 1748.

it could not possibly determine the cause of inefficiency in many cases, the Board tended to assume the worst. Although the number of preventive officers was "so very great", the Board wrote, "there is little or no effect from their being employed either by preventing the said frauds or seizing the goods". Unless the Board found "much greater services rendered", the Board would "look upon them as useless persons consequently no longer deserving any salary from the crown."[192]

All communications of admonishment carried a threat. To keep preventive officers "to a strict performance of their duty", collectors were instructed to "acquaint the several officers if they are found remiss for the future, we shall dismiss them on the next complaint."[193] The threat was real: evidence of fraud, collusion or negligence was punished. Often, however, the Board exercised discretion. It frequently opted for a temporary stop of pay and connected a full reinstatement to the remedying of specific failures.[194] As in the matter of admissions, the Board was dependent on information from the outports. Rather than a direct examination by the Board, the fate of allegedly negligent officers thus depended on the testimony of fellow officers. To retain control of such local procedures, the Board imposed rules for collectors on how to proceed in cases of misconduct. Upon receiving notice of it, the collector was to draft "a full Charge" of these matters. The officer in question was then allowed "reasonable time" for giving his answer to the charge. Upon receipt, a day was to be appointed where the officer and the complainant were to meet "face to face". By this procedure, "the truth" of the matter was to be "the better discovered". The collector then was to make his own observations and transmit them to the Board, who would, in all instances, retain the right to decide the case.[195]

Straightforward as this procedure was, it did leave room for local administrators to interject either against or on behalf of the accused. As in admissions, "character" played a key role here. Confronted with an "unaccountable proceeding" in a seizure case, one Mr. Ward, riding officer at Whitehaven, was charged but ultimately retained "he having hitherto had a very fair Character". It may have helped that upon being charged he "owns his mistake and appears very sorrowful for it".[196] In many cases, if

---

[192] TNA CUST82/6, 10 June 1749; CUST59/74, 10 June 1749, 23 October 1750; CUST97/76, 31 August 1756; CUST59/75, 31 August 1756.
[193] TNA CUST97/74b, 14 June 1726.
[194] TNA CUST97/13, 29 December 1744, 14 September 1745, 18 September 1745, 24 September 1745, 14 October 1745, 23 October 1745, 14 November 1745, 25 November 1745, 4 January 1746.
[195] TNA CUST59/70, 18 July 1717.
[196] TNA CUST82/1, 23 June and 15 August 1718.

an officer had failed to live up to the bureaucratic standards, but could be shown to be an "Industrious striving man", chances were that he could hope for forgiveness, provided "he will not be guilty of the like anymore".[197] Any offender not wholly lost to the Commissioners' idea of vigilance thus could sometimes expect pardon. Serious or repeated offences, on the other hand, were understood as a sign of bad character and resulted in being deemed negligent and prompt dismissal.[198]

The Art of Enforcement

If bureaucratic frameworks for supervision and control show that the preventive service was a much better run operation than previously assumed, it remains that administrative efficiency is not an end in itself. Administrative efficiency does not equal administrative success. And yet the question of success or failure itself poses a problem. As the first part of this chapter has illustrated, it was perennially unclear even in Whitehall what purpose this administrative branch of the Customs served. Reducing the question of success to criteria solely connected to the service's anti-smuggling capacity therefore fails to accommodate the full range of ways in which preventive coastal policing could potentially be seen as a success – or indeed as a failure. Even with a view to its most overt purpose as an anti-smuggling agency, measuring success is far from straightforward. In this capacity, the aim of the service – manifested in its very name – was the prevention of illicit activities. Yet arriving at any clear sense of how much smuggling the service prevented was and is impossible. As the case of the journals has shown, administrators could do everything to ensure diligent service and still be none the wiser about how well this worked. For this reason, administrators increasingly fixated on the number, the frequency, and the returns of seizures as a measure of success. This was easier, but it was paradoxical: if prevention was the aim of the service, then a fixation on seizures was to measure success with something that should not, if prevention was successful, exist in the first place.

Seizing contraband, moreover, was much less straightforward than it sounds. Legally, preventive officers commanded extraordinary authority to seize suspected goods, but they were still dependent on the local magistrates to do so lawfully. This required precise legal knowledge and negotiation skills; it also risked countersuits and malicious prosecutions.

---

[197] TNA CUST97/11, 15 December 1738; CUST97/13, 29 December 1744.
[198] TNA CUST82/3, 18 November 1738; CUST148/12, p. 51.

The power to seize goods, was also hampered by the preventive officers regularly being outnumbered. Only with private help or the assistance of the army and the navy were officers frequently able to seize (and retain) contraband. Finally, the prosecution of seized goods before JPs or in the Court of Exchequer was a precarious undertaking: private money needed to be spent and it was extremely time-consuming; furthermore, the outcome of the process was far from secure. All this was exacerbated by the fact that, rather than unanimously working together, all those involved in a particular seizure – Customs officers, local informers, the military and the navy – tended to work in competition with each other when it came to seizure rewards. Seizures, rather than a straightforward administrative act, required the mastering of a complex art of enforcement that went far beyond the administrative brief of a preventive officer.

The Right to Seize

Seizures were, by the standards of 18th-century law enforcement, a complicated legal business, subject not only to fine-grained differentiations but also to frequent changes over the course of the century.[199] Officers could either seize goods on suspicion or upon receiving information. The first scenario involved officers meeting with goods on the seaside under circumstances that suggested illicit activity. Those goods were seized, weighed and gauged, entered into the next Customs warehouse and only released on proof that the Customs had been paid. The second scenario involved officers being informed about illicit goods being stored in private houses, taverns, ships, etc. Officers could only search private property and seize goods after informing their superiors and with a peace officer present. To call in such help, a writ of assistance was required. As in the first scenario, the goods then entered the warehouse. Depending on their rank, seizing officers were then to inform the collector of the port or the London Board directly of all circumstances of the seizure, such as the manner, time, place, and witnesses present. The Solicitor of the Board would then review the legality of the case and either order a discharge of the goods (if the case was weak or the seizure wrong), a composition, or a prosecution.

Prosecution was traditionally conducted in the Court of Exchequer, but since the late 17th century, a growing number of statutes allowed for prosecution of cases before the Justices of the Peace. The Board expected the seizing officer to prosecute the case for a share of up to one half of the

---

[199] The following is based on Hoon, *Organization*, pp. 270–289; Henry Crouch, *A Complete Guide to the Officers of His Majesty's Customs in the Out-Ports* (London, 1732), pp. 279–320.

penalties.[200] Prosecution was expensive and uncertain, however, so officers unable or unwilling to bring the action were allowed to relinquish their share; the prosecution was then conducted at the charge and to the sole benefit of the Crown.[201] Although there were minor differences between an Exchequer prosecution and those before JPs, the procedure was similar. Goods were appraised and publicly proclaimed. If goods were not claimed, they were condemned and sold, and the proceeds divided between the seizing officer and the King, according to the statute under which the seizure had been made. If they were claimed, the case went to trial. If successful, the goods were condemned and sold in the Exchequer sales held four times a year. The proceeds were again divided between the officer and the Crown. If the officer had made the seizure upon an information, he was obliged to reward the informer with a share, usually a third of his own share.[202] If soldiers had assisted the seizure, they received a portion of both the officer's and the King's share.[203] Admiralty crews instrumental for a seizure received either one half or two-thirds of the proceeds of a successfully condemned seizure.[204]

This, in the simplest terms, was the seizure procedure that officers were expected to navigate as a matter of course. What did ordinary officers know about this? There were those among the ranks that acquired great skill and were able to profit greatly, but for most inferior officers an understanding of the intricacies of seizures remained shaky. For them, the entire procedure was bedevilled with discouragements at almost every turn. Certainly not the least of these was to know what exactly constituted an illicit transportation of goods and when a seizure might be in order. Henry Crouch thought that no part of the procedure was "less understood" and preventive officers in particular so "extremely ignorant (...), that they scarce know any Cause of Seizure". This was because "few of the inferior Officers ever saw, or if they did,

---

[200] A contemporary summary in John Crookshanks, *Instructions for the Collectors and other Officers Employ'd in HER MAJESTIES Customs, etc. in the North-Part of Great-Britain* (Edinburgh, 1707), Appendix no. 60. Shares were subject to changes and differed depending on the statute under which the seizure was made. Compare with the 1784 *Rules and Regulations for the Distribution of the Officers Shares of Seizures* issued by the Edinburgh Board, summarising the regulations then in force, NRS CE14/1, 20 May 1784.

[201] TNA CUST59/71, 1 September 1736; CUST82/3, 1 September 1736; CUST97/9, 16 January 1735; CUST97/75, 1 September 1736; CUST31/1, 23 February 1741. Before 1736, all seizures were to be made in the name of the seizing officer. This led to many seizures not being prosecuted; see CUST29/2, 19 July 1716.

[202] TNA CUST59/70, 20 November 1717.

[203] TNA PC1/3/50; T11/16, pp. 427–430.

[204] TNA T11/18, p. 231; CUST97/74b, 25 June 1723; CUST54/147, 16 June 1757; CUST59/76, 18 June 1763, 6 November 1764.

are capable of studying or digesting the Laws of the Customs, so as to make themselves Masters of this Part of the Business".[205] Even then, as a memorial to Walpole stated, "it can't be supposed that an officer in the Customs can bee learn't in the Rules and practice of the Exchequer". In fact, it was doubtful, according to this memorial, whether any officer "has for these fifteen years past knowne anything of a Recognizance or read a word thereof".[206]

This certainly rings true. The laws on smuggling were contained in a dizzying number of statutes, all of which provided different legal circumstances under which a seizure was legal. Depending on the type of goods, their location or the location of the vessel, the way they were packed, their direction of travel and the time of the day or year, a seizure could be either legal or illegal.[207] From these abstract rules, officers needed to infer what behaviour gave reasonable grounds for suspicion. The unlading of tea on a moonlit beach required little skill to discern its unlawful nature, but most cases were not that simple. The carrying of wool at the seaside, for instance, was forbidden if done with an *intention* of illegally exporting it. But how, the collector of Cowes objected, were officers supposed to tell whether the carriers harboured such an intention? Unless it could somehow be proved, "we apprehend doubtful if a seizure could be supported" by the mere carrying of wool.[208] The Board itself decreed that no person should be stopped "on the Road on Suspicion only" and that ships only be detained if "Proofs are very clear, or upon very Strong Circumstances".[209] Officers were warned to be "extremely careful how they stop goods", for if these turned out to be legal, it would result in "an action on the case [...] attended with

---

[205] Crouch, *Complete Guide*, p. 279. Crouch's volume is part of a genre of advice literature for Customs officials. See Crookshanks, *Instructions*; Anon., *The Rules of the Water-Side: Or, the General Practice of the Customs* (London, 1714); Richard Hayes, *Rules for the Port of London: Or, the Water-side Practice* (London, 1722); Henry Crouch, *A Complete View of the British Customs* (London, 1725). Crouch's volume was officially used by the Board for the instruction of officers and sometimes updated; see TNA CUST 29/3, 6 March 1770.

[206] CUL, Ch(H), Political Papers 44, no. 55.

[207] In a well-intended attempt to provide clarity on the hundreds of regulations then in force, William Hunter's *Pocket-Book*, first published 1765, inadvertently underscored the complexity of the matter by providing endless lists of statutes and regulations, see William Hunter, *The Tidesman's and Preventive Officer's Pocket-Book, Explaining the General Nature of Importation and Exportation, so far as concerns them in the Execution of the Water Guard Duty* (London, 1771), pp. 112–150.

[208] TNA CUST 61/6, 29 January 1785. See on this particular point also George Bridges, *Plain Dealing: Or the whole Method of Wool-Smuggling clearly discovered, and the Weakness of the Laws in Force, put in a clear Light* (London, 1744), p. 5.

[209] TNA CUST 29/2, 17 January 1743; CUST 31/1, 30 August 1740; CUST 29/5, 15 December 1780.

the expense of 50 or 100l. to the officer, besides the disgrace."[210] Crouch, writing in 1732, thus thought it best if preventive officers could refer to a "Pocket-Volume" containing all the causes of seizure.[211] In reference to this, William Hunter published such a volume to prevent officers incurring "trouble and disgrace". This was only in 1765, however. His book consisted of more than 200 pages of lists and tables often irrelevant to the business of seizures. It hardly qualifies as a pocket volume.[212] Meanwhile, inferior officers had to rely on their instructions for guidance on seizures.

The focus of the instructions, however, was less on the causes of seizures and more on due administrative process. The 1734 printed instructions are a rare example of details on what goods could be seized under what circumstances, but they, too, placed a heavy stress on due procedure.[213] So did written instructions issued by the Board.[214] The closest superior officials came to explaining the causes of forfeiture was by passing down new statutes.[215] It was left to inferior officers to penetrate the legal prose. In all other respects, orders focused on making seizures correctly. The Board was adamant that seizures needed to be accompanied by sufficient legal proof, backed by witnesses of reputation.[216] Exact accounting and warehousing were considered just as important.[217] Seizure accounts, the Board insisted, had to be "very particular" as well as "full and distinct".[218] Such emphasis resulted from the Board's preoccupation with successful prosecution: there was lingering anxiety that administrative blunders committed by inferior officers could "frustrate or invalidate the cause of a good and legal seizure".[219] To an extent, inferior officers shared such concerns. They, too, had an interest in successful prosecutions. For them, however, the danger of getting things wrong was more existential.

---

[210] Hunter, *Pocket-Book*, p. 209.
[211] Crouch, *Complete Guide*, p. 279.
[212] Hunter, *Pocket-Book*, p. 2.
[213] TNA CUST141/4.
[214] TNA CUST69/59, 12 February 1736; CUST82/3, 26 March 1737, 16 June 1737; CUST97/74a, 4 August 1711; CUST97/75, 26 March 1737; CUST98/1, 4 August 1711.
[215] TNA CUST59/71, 27 May 1736, 19 June 1736; CUST61/6, 5 June 1784; CUST82/9, 3 June 1763; CUST97/11, 21 November 1741; CUST97/75, 3 July 1736.
[216] TNA 31/1, 24 April 1721, 8 July 1732; CUST29/2, 20 February 1741; NRS CE14/2, 25 October 1732. See also Hunter, *Pocket-Book*, p. 177.
[217] TNA CUST29/2, 15 July 1713; NRS CE14/2, 18 November 1718.
[218] TNA CUST31/1, 8 November 1733; 26 March 1737; CUST29/2, 8 March 1758.
[219] Hunter, *Pocket-Book*, p. 177.

Most threatening to officers were "vexatious and litigious law-suits".[220] Regarding the causes of seizures and proper administrative process, inferior officers were continuously at risk of being sued. Things could go wrong at every turn. Often, the officers faced suits for the seizure of goods without a peace officer or a writ of assistance. The latter was not necessarily the fault of the officers. There were few writs in any given port and often not ready at hand.[221] This made them valuable assets: in 1770, the Norfolk riding officer Paul Nightingale was dismissed for selling his writ in London.[222] A few years earlier, the collector had complained that they were in need of more writs, his own being in "latin and so much worn as not to be ligible and we apprehend the validity of it is disputable". For want of a writ, the captain of the cruiser had "oftentime been obliged to run the Risque of searching houses without one or borrow from the Riding Officers".[223] The risk was real: officers were regularly charged with searching houses without writ; others earned the displeasure of the Board for searching people on the road "by day and night" without either a writ or a constable present or "on conjecture only".[224] The legality of a seizure often stood on a knife's edge. In a case from Dorset, for instance, the validity of writs not made out in the seizing officer's name was questioned. As the Weymouth collector reported in December 1719:

> The Petty foggers and nut crackers of the Law in this Country give out that a Writt of Assistance directed to the Commissioners of the Customs and such Persons as are by them deputed is not a sufficient Power to authorize any Particular Officer deputed by said Commissioners to break up and Enter any House with a Constable and other Peace Officer and I believe the smuglers will try that Point with us the next assizes having already sued one of our officers and his assistants.[225]

---

[220] TNA CUST 59/2, 16 October 1719. See also John Walter, '"Law-Mindedness": Crowds, Courts and Popular Knowledge of the Law in Early Modern England', in Michael Lobban, Joanne Begatio, Adrian Green (eds), *Law, Lawyers and Litigants in Early Modern England. Essay in Memory of Christopher W. Brooks* (Cambridge, 2019), pp. 164–184; Douglas Hay, Francis Snyder, 'Using the Criminal Law, 1750–1850: Policing, Private Prosecution, and the State', in Douglas Hay, Francis Snyder (eds), *Policing and Prosecution in Britain 1750–1850* (Oxford, 1989), pp. 3–53; David Lemmings, *Law and Government in England during the Long Eighteenth Century: From Consent to Command* (New York, 2015), pp. 56–80.
[221] TNA CUST 97/2, 4 March 1705.
[222] TNA CUST 97/77, 8 December 1769, 22 March 1770.
[223] TNA CUST 97/14, 27 November 1746.
[224] TNA CUST 29/2, 1 June 1714; CUST 97/5, 16 August 1727; CUST 29/5, 7 May 1776.
[225] TNA CUST 59/2, 30 December 1719.

Because of such supposed loopholes, lawyers acting on behalf of merchants and smugglers often found Customs officers to be easy prey. Uneducated in legal matters and without the assistance of the Board's solicitor, inferior officers often had to capitulate in local courts over matters they did not sufficiently understand. In other cases, actions were defeated by biased juries. When one Samuel Bayly, Surveyor at Norwich, found contraband on one Mr. Arnold – a "great Smuggler" – and brought the case at the next Quarter Sessions, Bayly was in for a surprise. The JPs – well-informed by Arnold and his friends – decided to discharge Arnold because "officers could not stop and search any man on the road, without the assistance of a Constable that it was contrary to the Liberty of the Subject".[226] Unlike the Customs men, Arnold had also been aided by a "noted Attorney to manage the Cause". In another attempt to convict Arnold, the collector hired legal counsel who agreed that Bayly had only done his duty. The judge thought the same and told the jury "that they must find it for the King". The jury, however, "brought in their Verdict for the Defendant which in the Judgement of thinking people there was contrary to their Oaths and Duty and shew'd how little respect they had either for His Majesty His Revenue and His Officers".[227] This was not an isolated case. Local juries tended to sympathise with local men: "Little Justice can be Expected from Session Jurys which are Generally the Worst of men".[228]

Many prosecutions against officers were indeed "unjust and vexatious Claimes", that is, motivated by "Revenge", meant to "distress" and "plague" the officers.[229] In other cases, accusers had a point, for example, when officers falsified the circumstances of a seizure so as to make it appear legal or when a bloody encounter between officers and alleged smugglers turned out to have been started by the Customs men.[230] More often than not, however, the fault lay with things beyond the control or the knowledge of the officers. When Customs men wrongly seized calicoes in Cambridge early in 1722, the matter should legally have ended in the return of the goods to the owners in return for a fee. Due to administrative misunderstandings

---

[226] TNA CUST97/3, 14 April 1718, 23 April 1718. On the wider context see Jonah Miller, 'The Touch of the State: Stop and Search in England, c.1660–1750', *History Workshop Journal*, 87 (2019), 52–71.

[227] TNA CUST97/4, 31 March 1720. Similar difficulties were reported from Norwich; see CUST97/4, 18 April 1721, 8 May 1721.

[228] TNA CUST59/2, 6 April 1720, 30 April 1720.

[229] TNA CUST97/11, 11 August, 8 October 1741; CUST97/12, 11 August 1744; CUST97/2, 13 August 1708; GCA CE60/1/2, 16 June 1756.

[230] TNA CUST82/3, 24 January 1735; CUST97/28, 16 August 1791; CUST97/7, 18 July 1733.

between the seizers and the collector at Great Yarmouth, however, the matter spiralled into what the latter called a "Disasture". Mistakenly, the goods were condemned and put up for sale, upon which the collector was sued by the owner of the calicoes. In an embarrassing turn of events, he had to hide from arrest and was charged with paying heavy compensation. And he bitterly lamented the lack of support from the Board:

> If we be not supported [...] it will have a mischevious effect in Our Officers seizing of Goods there being a great many of that Smuggling Tribe who will be as willing to Hamper them as Harwood has unjustly us, and that it will frustrate the End of the Law if the Officers be not supported in the Execution of their Duty therein. [...]
>
> And we do humbly hope the Honourable Court of Exchequer will be so favourable in the Incouragement of Officers as not upon Little Occasions or Mistakes, to Suffer them to be worried by such Litigious fellows and Notorious Enemies to his Majesties Revenue as the Smugglers are known to be.[231]

Perhaps the most common problem was a want of proof that goods were indeed illegal. As the Whitehaven collector reported in 1756, officers often "dare not for fear of actions at law seize [...], lest [the goods] might happen to have paid the duties".[232] Even if everything indicated that a particular cargo was contraband, officers needed to secure sufficient proof, otherwise they risked being sued for trespass or the unlawful stopping of a vessel. Such proof could be hard to come by: "A proof of running is the most difficult thing that can be attempted".[233] When a vessel was detained near Great Yarmouth in the summer of 1731, everything indicated the ship to be on a smuggling mission. The officers "have a great Opinion that they shall get such proofe as will condemn the Goods" and were able to procure two witnesses. Soon, however, "contrary to our Expectations they [i.e. the witnesses] gave us the Drope and have not since been heard of". The prosecution against the captain was dropped and the officers anxiously pleaded with the Board to prevent the captain suing them for wrongful seizure.[234]

---

[231] TNA CUST97/4, 2 March 1722, 12 March 1722, 30 April 1722.
[232] TNA CUST82/8, 24 December 1756.
[233] NRS CE87/1/6, 14 February 1778; TNA CUST89/6, 22 January 1782; CUST97/6, 13 January 1728; CUST97/5, 13 November 1728.
[234] TNA CUST97/7, 13 August 1731, 19 August 1731, 23 August 1731, 05 November 1731; CUST97/6, 13 January 1728; CUST97/9, 18 July 1735; CUST97/11, 11 August 1741, 08 October 1741. Problems with witnesses were a regular feature of seizure prosecutions and the Board therefore ordered in 1780 that officers were to inform the Board "whenever they discover their Witnesses prevaricate from their first Information,

All this tended to "greatly discourage" officers.[235] If they were not supported despite a "complayence in them with every thing that may be reasonably expected", they "must be ruined with vexatious and Litigious law suits".[236] But the Board was reluctant to engage in the legal defence of its officers. Its solicitor provided legal expertise to outport officials when needed, but regulations for a legal defence were strict. If the Board found that a lawsuit resulted from unaccountable proceedings – such as not informing the Board of a search or without sufficient proof and information – officers stood alone.[237] In case officers promised "satisfactory proof" of a seizure "and fail upon trial and if it shall appear they have therein wilfully misled the Board", they also had to bear the costs of the suit.[238] The same was true if officers prosecuted against the advice of the Board.[239] Finally, officers could only be defended at the Crown's charge if the administrative process before trial was without flaws and if they relinquished any right to a share of the seizure.[240]

Given such unfavourable odds, it is hardly surprising that many officers treaded with caution. Even if the Board often paid for the officers' legal defence, such support was dependent on the Board's goodwill.[241] Many officers tended to be "intimidated" from doing their "duty in the seizure of forfeited goods and thereby few seizures be made".[242] It was thus common sense that inferior officers "cannot be too wary" in view of "vexatious Claimes".[243] It seems probable – understandable even – that most officers would have confined themselves to acting only against the most obvious forms of illicit activity. After all, they were trapped in an enforcement dilemma: if they were found to be lukewarm in their duty, they risked censure from the Board. Too much vigour, however, carried the risk of getting entangled in costly litigation that – given the large sums involved – could easily become ruinous. A certain half-heartedness was, in many cases, the more prudent course.

---

or refuse to appear in Court or abscond, or die, on pain of being charged with all such costs as shall accrue after any of those Events have happened and have been concealed from the Board in breach of this order", CUST29/5, 15 December 1780.

[235] TNA CUST59/2, 06 April 1720.
[236] TNA CUST59/2, 16 October 1719.
[237] TNA CUST29/2, 09 June 1710, 23 November 1733, 17 January 1743; CUST29/5, 26 November 1779.
[238] NRS CE14/2, 13 December 1750.
[239] TNA CUST29/2, 26 June 1725.
[240] TNA CUST29/2, 20 August 1718, 10 June 1719; CUST29/3, 21 January 1774.
[241] TNA CUST97/3, 18 July 1733; CUST97/6, 13 January 1728; CUST97/9, 18 July 1735.
[242] TNA CUST97/2, 11 June 1708.
[243] TNA CUST97/2, 13 August 1708.

The Power to Seize

Caution on the part of the officers was also a result of the risks that enforcement carried for their wellbeing – and even their lives. It was not hyperbole when a riding officer near Dumfries reported, in 1759, that the officers "dare hardly look out of their own Doors".[244] Regions suited for the landing of goods were regularly plagued with large gangs of smugglers – sometimes as many as 300 individuals, armed "with swords, pistols Blunderbusses Carbines and Quarter Staffs".[245] Countless pleas and petitions vividly illustrate "the audacious treatment the officers receive from the smugglers when they make the least attempt to seize any part of their Goods, by their being very much beat".[246] The Board drew up impressive lists of officers being beaten, wounded and killed in the exercise of their duty.[247] Some officers "cannot doe their duty as they ought for fear of being murdered".[248] To central authorities, it was clear that these men needed help. It was less forthcoming, however, than some accounts suggest.[249]

Magistrates were obliged to assist the Customs men but were notoriously reluctant to do so. Numerous are the incidents in which constables refused to help. Customs men suspected that parish officers frequently were "in amity with the smugglers if not immediately concerned with them".[250] The Weymouth collector felt that the parish officers colluded with the smugglers, being "comely lined together in the smuggling trade".[251] And the Aberdeen collector grumbled that magistrates were very "backward in giving us assistance in searching for and finding out unentered and prohibited Goods" which "must prove a sad Clog upon us in the Execution of

---

[244] NRS CE51/1/3, 10 December 1759.

[245] NRS CE87/1/8, 28 December 1786; TNA CUST58/12, 8 May 1784; CUST59/1, 4 March 1718; CUST89/6, 29 March 1779; CUST97/14, 10 December 1747.

[246] TNA CUST97/24, 25 November 1780. A similar report from Beaumaris CUST78/1, 7 October 1758.

[247] See, for instance, TNA CUST148/12, pp. 577–622; *The Report of the Committee appointed to inquire into the Frauds and Abuses in the Customs, to the Prejudice of Trade, and Diminution of the Revenue*. Reported on the Seventh of June 1733 by Sir John Cope, printed in *Reports from the Committees of the House of Commons*. Reprinted by Order of the House. Vol. I, Miscellaneous Subjects: 1715–1735 (1803), pp. 601–654, at p. 610; CUL, CH(H), Political Papers 41, nos 23, 25, 59; ESRO, SAY252–259, SAY260–267, SAY279–283.

[248] TNA CUST148/12, pp. 365–366.

[249] For suggestions that the army was a decisive factor in enforcement, see J. A. Houlding, *Fit for Service: The Training of the British Army, 1715–1795* (Oxford, 1981), pp. 77–89; Paul Muskett, 'Military Operations Against Smuggling in Kent and Sussex, 1698–1750', *Journal of the Society for Army Historical Research*, 52 (1974), 89–110.

[250] TNA CUST97/12, 16 October 1742.

[251] TNA CUST59/2, 9 June 1719.

our Duty."[252] In court, too, magistrates often proved a disappointment.[253] One reason was that parish officers were likely to be sued for involvement in wrongful seizures.[254] When executing a warrant against a smuggler, one constable at Ellenfoot was "so terrified" by the conjuring tricks of an alleged attorney that he never dared exercise the warrant.[255] Especially in the wake of the 1736 Act, the Board was therefore keen to advertise that any JP "vexatiously prosecuted on account of putting the said act in execution they will be defended at the charge of the revenue".[256]

A second reason was that parish officers owed their office and loyalty more to the community and less to the far-away institutions of the Crown that the Customs represented.[257] From Dorset it was even reported that communities "in many places elect for Constables and Tythingmen such Persons as are notorious Smugglers".[258] The reality, of course, may have been less malign: the revenue was far from popular among large parts of the population and parish officers – villagers themselves – may simply have shared a common sentiment. Rather than siding with the revenue against a communal prevalence of anti-Customs feelings, parish officers tried to use discretion in such matters, aiming to find a middle course.[259] In other cases, such as an assault on Customs men employed by the Mayor of Hythe, the implications were more sinister.[260] Yet whatever the reason for their reluctance, parish officers evidently preferred to steer clear of revenue matters, despite fines being introduced for not assisting the revenue.[261]

---

[252] NRS CE87/1/2, 10 December 1742.
[253] TNA CUST59/71, 16 March 1738; CUST97/5, 17 August 1726; CUST78/1, 16 June 1757.
[254] TNA CUST97/75, 10 June 1737. Parish officers risked, for instance, being sued for trespass; see CUST59/77, 7 November 1772; CUST29/3, 9 August 1763.
[255] TNA CUST82/5, 18 June 1746. The attorney claimed that the warrant was unlawful for it named the constable's residence by the commonly used "Canonby" instead of the proper name of the town, "Crosscanonby".
[256] TNA CUST97/75, 3 July 1736.
[257] See Keith Wrightson, 'Two Concepts of Order: Justices, Constables and Jurymen in Seventeenth-Century England', in John Brewer and John Styles (eds), *An Ungovernable People: The English and their Law in the Seventeenth and Eighteenth Centuries* (New Brunswick, NJ, 1980), pp. 21–46; Hannes Ziegler, 'Customs Officers and Local Communities: Informing in Late Seventeenth-Century England', in María Ángeles Martín Romera, Hannes Ziegler (eds), *The Officer and the People: Accountability and Authority in Premodern Europe* (Oxford, 2021), pp. 325–348.
[258] TNA CUST59/2, 16 October 1719.
[259] TNA CUST59/5, 4 September 1738.
[260] TNA T1/18, nos 14, 50; PC2/74, pp. 383, 396, 408, 425, 428.
[261] Regarding fines, see Hunter, *Pocket-Book*, p. 208.

Feebler still was the hope by central administration that the "country people" would help the officers solely by virtue of being subjects of the Crown. Such unworldly views contrast starkly with perceptions by outport staff. "The whole inhabitants of the Country", one read from Dumfries in 1791, "are friendly to the Smugglers rather than to the Revenue officers".[262] "Our greatest efforts are often ineffecutall", the Weymouth collector wrote, because of the "Countenace given the Smugglers by the Country People".[263] Local people were indeed involved with smuggling at all stages. They "miserably betrayed" the Customs men by giving "immediate notice" of the officers' approach, often by signals or lights.[264] Others were concerned in the landing of goods, being "constantly in waiting" "with Carts and Horses". Thus the country people – "many of whom follow no employment, but this illicit practice" – were ill chosen as enforcers of the Customs.[265] There are, occasionally, cases where local men could be persuaded to assist the revenue. But they, too, needed to be protected against "discouragements" of the smugglers.[266] In the spring of 1734, a Norfolk collector gained the help of "some Country Gentlemen" and "twenty stout country fellows". But they demanded to know what rewards they would receive and what care would be taken to protect them from lawsuits, as there was "a good Deal of uneasiness among the People" for not receiving rewards on former occasions. Several of the men frankly declared "that they can make a much better account by aiding the Smugglers than they received by aiding the Officers". Central administrators may have balked at this, but these were the terms with which local administrators were faced:

> I am sure that by what I can Judge of the ill Humour of the Country on that account, the officers are not like to be aided by the Country again till they are satisfied or it is Publickly known what part the Country shall have of Seizures made by their assistance.[267]

It is also doubtful if keener assistance by "the country people" would have amounted to much. Powerless in the face of large gangs, many petitions of riding officers stressed the necessity for armed assistance.[268] "To the great

---

[262] NRS CE51/1/5, 16 August 1791.
[263] TNA CUST59/1, 4 March 1718; similar reports in CUST59/2, 9 June 1719, 16 October 1719.
[264] TNA CUST98/5, 9 June 1716; CUST82/1, 24 September 1718.
[265] TNA CUST89/1, 23 October 1783; CUST78/5, 20 October 1783.
[266] TNA CUST59/1, 29 October 1718, 18 April 1719.
[267] TNA CUST97/8, 27 February 1734, 21 June 1734, 24 June 1734.
[268] Requests from Great Yarmouth in TNA CUST97/20, 21 August 1769; CUST97/21, 22 June 1772, 7 August 1772, June 1774; CUST97/22, 1 June 1775, 17 March 1777;

terror of his Majestys officers", some gangs were known to be "Publickly declareing they are under no fears from the Civill Power, nothing but a military Power they Dread".[269] The Board, the Treasury, and Privy Council were aware of this, and their answer frequently was to procure the assistance of the army and the navy.[270] The use of military personnel for civil duties stretched back to the 1690s, when the Wool Acts required the Admiralty to have men-of-war cruise the southern coasts and Privy Council ordered the War Office to quarter dragoons in Kent and Sussex to assist the newly established preventive service. What started as a measure confined to the south-eastern shorelines soon spread to other regions after the turn of the century.[271] Admiralty vessels were stationed in coastal waters to prevent the smuggling trade, with at times as many as 43 individual ships assigned.[272] Similarly, detachments as large as several hundred soldiers were quartered in the vicinity of the coast, predominantly in Cornwall and Devon, Dorset and Hampshire, Sussex, Kent, Essex as well as the Norfolk and Suffolk coastlines.[273] All military and naval commanders received instructions to assist preventive officers against well-armed smuggling vessels and gangs.[274]

CUST97/23, 16 May 1778; CUST97/24, 25 November 1780; TNA CUST97/25, 11 June 1784. Similarly WO1/877, 1 August 1782, 20 May 1783, 23 May 1783. Weymouth reported in 1718 that "nothing but a military force can support the officers in the due discharge of their dutys." CUST59/1, 4 March 1718.

[269] TNA CUST82/5, 29 January 1746; CUST97/8, 24 June 1734.

[270] Hannes Ziegler, 'Competition in Coastal Water: Customs Sloops and Admiralty Cruisers in Eighteenth-Century Britain', *Journal for Maritime Research*, 23/1 (2021), 1–17; Hannes Ziegler, '"Very Prejudicial to the Service of the Revenue": The British Army on Coastal Duty in Eighteenth-Century East Anglia', *British Journal for Military History*, 7/1 (2021), 46–63; Louis M. Cullen, 'H.M.S. "Spy" off the Galway Coast in the 1730s: the Politics and Economics of Wool Smuggling', *Journal of the Galway Archaeological and Historical Society*, 65 (2013), 27–47; Houlding, *Fit for Service*, pp. 77–89; Muskett, 'Military Operations'.

[271] For navy involvement, see 10&11 Will. III, ch. 10, 1699 and the respective orders of Privy Council in 1690, PC2/73, pp. 385, 525. For the use of the military, see TNA PC2/75, p. 279; TNA PC2/77, pp. 190–192; PC1/3/50; T1/43, no. 27; T1/54, no. 8; TNA T1/56, no. 29; T1/63, no. 21; WO5/32, p. 207.

[272] This was the case in the early 1760s; see TNA ADM1/3866, 10 September 1765. Other such moments are the early 1730s or the late 1740s; see ADM1/3865, 15 August 1734, 26 November 1748.

[273] Houlding, *Fit for Service*, pp. 79–81. Houlding is relying on the War Office's marching orders. See, for instance, the marching orders for Norfolk and Suffolk from the 1730s to 1750s, TNA WO5/32, pp. 132, 207, 212, 236, 404; WO5/33, pp. 62–63, 70, 241–242, 284; WO5/40, p. 413; WO5/41, pp. 55–59, 515–516; WO5/42, pp. 169–170. See also requests for troops from December 1772 in WO1/875, pp. 33–36.

[274] Instructions for the navy cruisers in TNA CO388/7, 26 January and 15 March 1699; CSPD William III (1697), p. 471 (12 November 1697); TNA CUST97/75, 15 August

To some extent, this worked. Where military forces were deployed, smugglers reined in their activities or moved elsewhere.[275] Armed assistance also increased chances of seizures.[276] But in stressing the concurrent effort at fighting the smuggling trade, it is often overlooked to what extent the rationale of both navy and army conflicted with the logics of the revenue. When the Admiralty and the War Office stated that military officers on revenue duties were subject to directives of the Customs men, these commanders often disagreed. Given the subordinate place of the Customs in the executive, this is hardly surprising. Communications between both War Office and Admiralty were coordinated via the Treasury.[277] Customs men, were also untrained civilians and of low social status in its inferior ranks and thus never enjoyed a high reputation vis-à-vis the ethos and status of officers of either navy or army. Beneath a thick layer of cooperative rhetoric from central authorities, therefore, cooperation on a practical level was anything but straightforward.

Tensions with the Navy were particularly stark. Instructions to naval commanders encouraged communication and cooperation. In November 1716, Admiralty cruisers on coastal duties were reminded "for the More effectual performance of this Service to hold a constant Correspondence with the Officers who command the Ships which are appointed to Cruise next to you."[278] In Scotland, too, commanders were to keep constant communication with the officers of the Customs.[279] In that spirit, the Admiralty cruiser *Fly*, commanded by Captain Oates to cruise between Great Yarmouth and Flamborough Head was instructed to hold a "constant correspondence" with the Customs officers in 1734. More particularly, Captain Oates was "to the utmost of your Power to assist the Custom House Officers in the Execution of their Duty" and "any Vessels which may be Imployed to Cruise on the Coast by the Commissioners of His Majesty's Customs".[280] A corresponding charge was given to Customs men: when Admiralty ships were settled on a stretch of coast, they were to "settle such a Correspondence with the Commanders of these Sloops as may most conduce for his

---

1734. From the 1760s onwards, instructions became more standardized, see T1/402, fols 94–95. A printed version in ADM1/3866, undated. For the army briefs, see the marching orders in WO5.

[275] See, for instance, WSRO, Goodwood 156, G59.
[276] See, for instance, TNA CUST97/22, 2 August 1775.
[277] See, for instance, TNA ADM1/4283 and ADM1/3865–3867; WO1/827; WO1/875–877.
[278] TNA CUST59/70, 10 November 1716.
[279] TNA T1/107, no. 60.
[280] TNA CUST97/75, 15 August 1734. Oates' initial instructions in ADM1/3865, 15 August 1734.

Majesties Service".[281] In case of the *Fly*, the Norfolk officers were "Carefully to Correspond with the said Commander for the Service on all Occasions and to be aiding and assisting to him and take care he be treated by them and you with all possible Civillity and Respect".[282] The Board of Customs and the Lords of Admiralty thus feted the ideal of a harmonious and synergetic effort of their agents.

Yet the relationship of Customs and navy was profoundly conflictive. Customs officers were frequently engaged in seizing contraband on navy vessels, prompting the opposition of navy officers.[283] The Customs, on the other hand, faced problems when their officers were picked up by the press gangs.[284] The navy was also jealously guarding its rights to fly the jack and pennant on their ships.[285] In terms of coastal prevention, too, the concurrent service of both forces was imbued with animosities. Admiral Edward Vernon – then in command of the North Sea Squadron – complained in 1745 that the Customs cruisers suffered the smugglers to carry on a traitorous correspondence with the French.[286] Customs officials, meanwhile, protested that Admiralty ships did not "exert themselves" as much as needed.[287] It was to their "Indolence and Inactivity" that "the increase of this iniquitous trade is in a great measure owing".[288] Navy men also did not like taking orders from Customs officials. "It hath long been a matter of great lament," the Scottish Commissioners protested in 1708, "that the Commanders [of men-of-war] have been Superior to all Observation but that of the Admiralty only."[289] The incident at Ely in 1764 is a case in point: the commander of the navy cutter *Alarm*, cruising on preventive duties, simply refused to disclose his reasons for coming into port to the Scottish Board, finding himself "excused from giving any answer."[290]

---

[281] TNA CUST97/74b, 8 February 1728; CUST97/76, 31 May 1763.
[282] TNA CUST97/75, 15 August 1734.
[283] TNA ADM1/3865, 5 February 1735, 13 September 1743, 26 February 1746; CUST54/147.
[284] TNA CUST59/71, 21 August 1735; ADM1/3865, 17 October 1741. Sometimes Customs men were impressed while on warships; see ADM1/3865, 15 October 1741.
[285] TNA ADM1/3866, 25 November 1772. A more comprehensive report in ADM1/3865, 6 November 1730.
[286] TNA CUST59/73, 14 December 1745; CUST97/75, 14 December 1745.
[287] TNA CUST97/7, 16 August 1732; CUST97/5, 26 April 1728; ADM1/3866, 21 October 1767.
[288] TNA CUST89/4, 4 April 1768; see also the letter from 30 May 1774.
[289] TNA T1/107, no. 60. See Margarette Lincoln, *Representing the Royal Navy: British Sea Power, 1750–1815* (Aldershot, 2002); N. A. M. Rodger, 'Honour and Duty at Sea, 1660–1815'. *Historical Research*, 75 (2002), 425–447.
[290] TNA T1/514, fols 255–259.

Frictions between the Customs and the army were similar. Here, too, military officers were strictly held to cooperate with the revenue and – as far as revenue matters were concerned – subordinated to the authority of Customs men.[291] But this, too, was beset with difficulties and "misunderstandings between those soldiers and the officers of the Customs".[292] Customs men suspected that the soldiers had no interest in performing the cumbersome "coast duty" and were more interested in making a little profit from the smugglers by looking the other way.[293] Other conflicts were due to the different rationales of Customs and army. As General Henry Hawley suggested, the problem was that military officers resented being put under Customs authority and disagreed with the disposition of their troops along the coast in a way that was regarded as entirely unmilitary.[294] The coastal duty would subject the soldiers "to the calls of the Revenue Officers, on every trivial or false information" and prevented them "to render effectuall assistance in any real occasion of importance."[295] The military clearly preferred preventive officers to act as "advanced Spyes" in service of the dragoons, thus reversing the hierarchy in revenue matters.[296] Needless to say, the Customs disagreed.

On the whole, the preventive service certainly profited from the assistance of the navy and the army. After all, the preventive service could hardly do without either a "Superior Naval Force" or a "Superior Military Force".[297] The service did not, however, profit as much as many historians have suggested. In 1716, John Saxby, supervisor of riding officers in Kent and Sussex argued that many seizures "would have been made without the Dragoons", leading the Customs Board to conclude "that the Dragoons have not answered the service at first intended."[298] In 1784, the War Office admitted that "the Revenue has not hitherto derived all the benefit that might have been expected from the assistance of the Troops employed on the Coast Duty".[299] Too great were the differences between the rationales of these various agents and too great was, on the other hand, the mutual

---

[291] See the respective marching orders TNA WO/5 and the Board's minutes in CUST29/3, 20 July 1763; CUST29/5, 11 April 1780, 24 November 1780, 17 April 1784, 27 January 1787.
[292] TNA PC1/3/50.
[293] TNA T1/224, no. lxxxv.
[294] TNA PC1/5/111.
[295] TNA WO4/125, 22 May 1784.
[296] Ibid.
[297] TNA CUST98/1, 29 December 1719.
[298] TNA T1/224, no. lxxxv.
[299] TNA WO4/125, 22 May 1784.

mistrust resulting from cases of corruption and collusion with the smugglers. The physical ability to seize contraband, even if theoretically enhanced by armed assistance, always remained problematic and further suggested a cautious approach to seizures.

The Pains of Prosecution and "Trivial Shares"

Problems did not cease with a successful seizure. Bringing a case to prosecution required time and money. It was possible, furthermore, that the proceeds of a successful condemnation did not sufficiently compensate for such spending, because the officers always competed with other agents – informers, navy men, soldiers, Excise officers – for these returns. The Board, keenly aware of the discouraging terms for inferior officers, did its best to prevent any legal or illegal shortcuts through the seizure procedure.[300]

How much time and money prosecutions consumed is best illustrated on a micro-level. In January 1779, the Stockton collector listed expenses for prosecuting four smugglers, ranging from £6 to £22 each. Although three cases were prosecuted at the Crown's charge, preventive officers were involved in preparing the prosecution and required to actively expend time and money. Such expenses could later be reclaimed. In the above cases, for instance, Walter Parker, riding officer at Redcar, was involved in preparing the prosecutions. In the case of the smuggler James Reighley, Parker had expended £3; in the case of Adam Armstrong, this amounted to more than £9 and again nearly £4 for the prosecution of John Williamson. These expenses alone amounted to more than a third of his annual salary of £40. They included riding charges, horse hire, the conducting of defendants or witnesses to court, and fees for assistants. Of these charges, however, the majority were only partly allowed by the Board and several disallowed altogether. The accounts also show Parker spending several days per month from August 1778 to January 1779 on these prosecutions. For Reighley's case alone, he had ridden 64 miles and had travelled another 172 miles for Williamson's case. Finally, for Armstrong's case, he had spent altogether

---

[300] Summary accounts of seizure prosecutions in TNA T64/143 and T64/144 from 1723 to 1732. On Exchequer prosecutions and its mechanisms Margaret R. Hunt, 'Wives and Marital "Rights" in the Court of Exchequer in the Early Eighteenth Century', in Paul Griffiths, Mark S. R. Jenner (eds), *Londinopolis. Essays in the Cultural and Social History of Early Modern London* (Manchester, 2000), pp. 107–129; J. M. Beattie, *Crime and the Courts in England, 1660–1800* (Princeton, 1986); Robert B. Shoemaker, *Prosecution and Punishment: Petty Crime and the Law in London and Rural Middlesex, c.1660–1725* (Cambridge, 1991); James Cockburn, *A History of English Assizes, 1558–1714* (Cambridge, 1972).

326 miles on the road.[301] To this was added the "fatigue" of attending the Assizes, sometimes for days.[302] As cases prosecuted at the Crown's charge did not reward the seizing officer with a share of the penalty, Parker was truly left out of pocket.

The Board, when considering money spent by its officers, indeed tended to be parsimonious, especially when it deemed charges unnecessary. Yet what the Board considered excessive was often a necessity on the ground. Walter Parker, for his part, got increasingly frustrated. In October 1779, he described how he had been unable to find anyone willing to execute the Board's arrest warrants against several smugglers and had finally done so himself "at the hazard of his Life". This action had earned him the hatred of the community, who had "vowed Revenge" and had, to his "Great terror", broken into his house. He also complained that the Board had "thought proper to disallow a great Part" of his charges, making him "a considerable losser on account of performing" the Board's orders.[303] The story was similar elsewhere. In 1786 the collector at Great Yarmouth pleaded with the Board to allow officers their expenses. The hire of waggons to secure seizures could only be got at a high price, if at all. If the Board was to disallow such expenses, the consequences were, the collector insisted, catastrophic:

> The expense of bringing a small seizure to the warehouse, particularly by those officers most remote from the Port, added to those of Condemnation etc. will make their share for seizing so trivial, that it will not indemnify them for the Expences attending Information, nor encourage them to expose themselves to the Resentment of the most daring set of men that live.[304]

Expense accounts are detailed when the officers could reasonably claim compensation. This was the case, for instance, if suits were conducted at the Crown's expense.[305] As compensation was not ordinarily allowed in an officer's prosecution, expenses are less detailed. But they were likely to be similar. In 1787, riding officer Chris Cutting sent a desperate petition, claiming that his salary was not enough to cover expenses, which he incurred

---

[301] TNA CUST89/6, 29 January 1779, 16 March 1779, 1 September 1779.
[302] TNA CUST59/2, 19 March 1719.
[303] TNA CUST89/6, 12 October 1779.
[304] TNA CUST97/26, 9 June 1786. Other cases in CUST97/5, 6 August 1726; CUST97/9, 10 December 1735; CUST97/10, 30 September 1736; CUST97/11, 30 November 1739. The complaint in 1786 was a result of new orders issued by the Board in 1780 that disallowed expenses incurred in conveying goods to the warehouses; see CUST29/5, 25 November 1780, 16 November 1781.
[305] TNA CUST29/2, 19 March 1716; CUST97/7, 15 September 1731.

Coastal Administration and the Art of Enforcement 147

"whether I make Seizures or not". In the way of seizures, moreover, he had, he declared, almost 800 casks of spirits in the warehouse, seized since January 1785. "And having disbursed for Informations etc. £130 for the same and have received nothing, being obliged to borrow Money to perform the Service untill I can get no more Credit".[306] The amount of expenses and the duration during which they remained unsettled, therefore, could – and did – land officers in debt.[307] Long delays were also problematic if goods were perishable. While the "great Charge of Condemnation" increased with long warehousing, their "Decay" lessened the goods' value, so "that the officers getts Little or nothing which cannot but be a mighty discouragement to them".[308] The consequence was, ultimately, "destruction to his own [the preventive officer's] private Property".[309]

Nor did the payout mean that officers were fully compensated. Sale of the goods in the Exchequer sales did not secure ideal prices.[310] More importantly, officers were required to share their rewards. Apart from the Crown's share, officers were held to reward those that had a key role in making the seizure. Typically, this either involved informers or soldiers assisting in the apprehension of a seizure. Each were entitled to a share of the reward, and in the case of informers, this came exclusively from the officer's part of a seizure. The Board insisted that these shares be paid fully and punctually.[311] After all, informers lured by monetary incentives were the only way of interesting "the country people" in the enforcement of otherwise unpopular policies. Officers not paying their informers thus faced disciplinary action.[312] The Board, moreover, had to remind officers to give "all reasonable encouragement to any Person who shall Discover" illicit activities.[313] Fair and speedy rewards to informers were considered "of more Consequence than at first Sight it may appear".[314] Similarly, because the army was often reluctant to do coast duty, fair and swift payment of shares was considered crucial.[315] In the case of the army, the reluctance to share the rewards also led to officers choosing to take as few men as

---

[306] TNA CUST97/26, 15 March 1787.
[307] TNA CUST97/5, 23 May 1726; CUST97/11, 25 November 1740; CUST97/13, 29 December 1744; GCA CE60/1/4, 10 September 1766.
[308] TNA CUST97/2, 13 August 1708.
[309] TNA CUST97/25, 28 May 1783.
[310] See Hoon, *Organization*, pp. 278–289.
[311] TNA CUST29/3, 20 July 1763.
[312] TNA CUST29/2, 15 May 1723, 11 January 1725.
[313] TNA CUST59/70, 20 December 1717.
[314] *Eighteenth Century Documents*, p. 293.
[315] Ziegler, 'British Army'; TNA CUST29/5, 15 February 1783. At times, this also involved the local militia; see TNA CUST97/23, 19 June 1779.

possible with them – with the obvious result that the men were in fact too few to overcome the smugglers.[316] Whereas the Board aimed to optimize enforcement, officers sought to augment personal returns. Quick to discourage such behaviour, the Board ordered that "seizures lost through the avarice of the Officer not employing sufficient assistance such loss to be imputed to the Officer."[317]

Officers' returns were also imperilled by competition, namely by the Admiralty and the Excise. Violent clashes and legal disputes between Customs and navy were common, as agents of both competed for the rewards of seizures made in conjunction or by one side outwitting the other. "Misunderstandings and disputes", the Board summarised, "have sometimes happened and probably may again about the right of seizures".[318] For preventive officers, the outcome of a dispute could mean the difference between a reward and empty hands. The same was true in conflicts with the Excise. These arose because some goods were customable as well as excisable and the officers of both branches of the revenue had equal rights to seize. Conflicts thus evolved around who had seized a particular set of goods first and what assistance or information had been given.[319] The Board aimed at ensuring "that all officers may have their just share of every seizure".[320] Inferior officers, on the other hand, tended to assert – with a view to agents of the Excise – that "there is very little dependance uppon their Integrity" and even the Board was aware that there was a "want of confidence and agreement betwixt the officers".[321] Given that officers stood to lose substantial rewards, such hostility is perfectly understandable.

Finally, even within the Customs administration, there was dispute and competition over shares of seizures. Walter Parker, in 1779, had to fight a long battle for a seizure of goods that – owing to his inattention – had been snatched up by the crew of the Customs cruiser.[322] These were common squabbles. Especially at sea, it was difficult to establish whether – in the run-up to a seizure – the activities of nearby vessels counted as having

---

[316] TNA CUST31/1, 17 January 1740; CUST59/71, 26 March 1737; CUST97/75, 26 March 1737; ESRO SAY288–294.
[317] NRS CE14/2, 13 February 1715.
[318] TNA ADM1/3866, October 1766.
[319] TNA CUST62/59, 30 August 1718; CUST89/6, 31 October 1780; CST97/24, August 1781; CUST98/5, 22 September 1724, 28 November 1734; NRS CE87/1/2, 2 December 1743; GCA CE60/1/1, 11 October 1749.
[320] TNA CUST98/1, 4 October 1726; GCA CE73/1/2, 4 September 1775.
[321] TNA CUST62/59, 30 August 1718; NRS CE14/1, 29 March 1773.
[322] TNA CUST89/6, 8 April 1779, 6 May 1779, 5 June 1779, 17 June 1779.

Coastal Administration and the Art of Enforcement 149

given assistance.[323] Officers were often unwilling to acknowledge such support. Others skilfully professed to have given support or information and conspired to procure witnesses to such alleged facts.[324] Onboard the Customs vessels, moreover, strife usually erupted over divisions between crews. Captains were entitled to more than mates and mariners. But seizures also happened to be made without either captain or mate present and the Board usually ruled in favour of those that made the seizure in person.[325] Similarly, for inferior port officers or preventive officers, the greed of superior port officials raised serious problems. Because they could afford to wait out any lengthy prosecution, superiors often coerced inferiors into selling their right to shares for smaller sums than the share was worth.[326] The Edinburgh Board, in 1742, ruled that certificates by inferior officers stating that they had received full shares were to be sent up every six months, but it is doubtful whether inferior officers were in a position not to sign such certificates when asked.[327] But port officials seriously risked the Board's "Censure and Displeasure" if shares were not remitted "to the sole Benefit" of the seizing officers only.[328] Riding officers, meanwhile, disputed this principle, if seizures were made by port officers: "The Riding Officers alledge that such seizures of Goods are sometimes made from their great Labour and attendance in watchings as well by day as lying out exposed in the Night on the Coast".[329]

Given all this, it was logical that preventive officers sought shortcuts and advantages in the seizure procedure. Yet the Board was aware of these and moved to prevent them, especially if they amounted to fraud, as with collusive seizures. These were agreements between officers and smugglers that aimed at an exchange of money from the latter to the former in return for purposefully seizing wrongly or only a small fraction of the real amount of goods.[330] The Board dismissed whoever was found guilty thereof, but their frequency shows the temptation on the part of the officers to forgo a regular

---

[323] TNA CUST82/8, 21 July 1756.
[324] TNA CUST92/11, 10 September 1770, 14 January 1771, 26 January 1771.
[325] NRS CE14/2, 31 July 1777; CE14/3, 17 February 1757; TNA CUST59/71, 14 July 1733.
[326] TNA CUST31/1, 20 April 1734, 18 March 1737; CUST98/1, 8 July 1732; GCA CE82/1/2, 6 October 1769.
[327] NRS CE14/2, 9 December 1742.
[328] TNA CUST29/2, 1 February 1739; 4 October 1752.
[329] TNA CUST59/10, 19 August 1761. Similar cases in CUST97/9, 7 July 1735; CUST97/23, 26 September 1778.
[330] Hunter, *Pocket-Book*, p. 209: "By collusion is meant a deceitful contract or agreement between two or more, for the one to bring an action, etc. against another." See also Anon., *Rules of the Water-Side*, p. 67.

seizure procedure with unsure returns.[331] And the Board also loathed those local agreements that were not necessarily meant to defraud the revenue, but were beyond direct control and authorisation of the Board. It forbade, for instance, the entering into a composition without licence of the Exchequer or cognizance of the Board.[332] Similarly, any "Partnerships or private Arguments between the Officers" relating to seizures were strictly prohibited.[333] For the officers, these were simple means to sidestep seizure procedures or look for ways to alleviate their potential losses. For the Board, it was tantamount to fraud.

Whether preventive officers could make a profit under these circumstances is an open question. For many – in debt and trapped in expensive lawsuits – the opposite seems to have been the case. Others fared better: for Henry Baker, supervisor of riding officers, or Warren Lisle, captain of a cruiser at Weymouth, proceeds of seizures were clearly a considerable source of income. Lisle in particular profited much from his office. In addition to a sloop commanded by himself, he entered into a contract with the Board for another two cruisers at Exeter and seizures often greatly exceeded his costs.[334] But these are not typical cases. Baker was a solicitor at the Treasury and Lisle, too, possessed substantial expertise in Customs matters. Both could easily wait out the results of a prosecution, being well-off in the first place. It is particularly noteworthy, in this respect, that even Lisle deemed the officers' shares, "out of which they bear a proportionable part of the Charges of the Seizure, Prosecution, Condemnation and Disposal thereof", outrightly "discouraging".[335] Matters were worse for ordinary officers or mariners on the Customs sloops. Even George Medcalfe, solicitor of the Customs, admitted that the officers had not "sufficient Encouragement and Protection in putting those Laws in Execution" and that, when it came to prosecutions, "the Encouragement is not adequate to the risk they run".[336]

---

[331] TNA CUST 31/1, 25 May 1714; CUST 29/2, 21 May 1714, 17 May 1723; CUST 82/12, 24 May 1775; CUST 97/4, 8 April 1723; NRS CE51/1/5, 3 October 1791.
[332] TNA CUST 29/2, 13 July 1720; CUST 31/1, 4 September 1744; CUST 59/73, 4 September 1744.
[333] TNA CUST 29/2, 21 May 1740.
[334] TNA CUST 64/6, 14 April 1766; BL Add. MS 8133B, fol. 124.
[335] TNA CUST 64/6, 20 April 1768.
[336] Stephen Janssen, *Smuggling Laid Open, in all its Extensive and Destructive Branches* (London, 1767), p. 64.

"A Good Deal of Chance in Making Seizures"

Given these terms, the surprising fact is that seizures by the Customs, in some years, amounted to considerable sums. In the early 1780s, the average annual total for England and Wales was c. £120,000. Net payments into the Exchequer – i.e. the king's share after the deduction of charges – could, in good years such as 1775 or 1778, easily reach six-digit figures, with the gross total up to twice as large. On average, the 1760s saw net payments between £40,000 and £50,000, with a significant rise in the 1770s, when net payments reached between £70,000 and £90,000.[337] Between 1777 and 1779, moreover, the average king's share of seizures made by cruisers alone stood at £51,000, whereas the annual expenses of these forty-one cruisers came, in the same period, to roughly £30,000.[338] Most cruisers in the western and northern ports had positive seizure balances compared to expenses.[339] But such figures should not be overstated. Net payments into the Exchequer were – unlike receipts from duties – a volatile affair. A net receipt of £76,000 in 1781 was followed by net receipts of around £30,000 in successive years. At such times, seizure receipts accounted for barely 1% of total Customs proceeds.[340] This was merely a tenth of what England's second and third ports, Bristol and Liverpool, produced and these again were dwarfed by the London receipts.[341] It is important to bear in mind, furthermore, that the gross total of seizures in 1782 – around £120,000 – was still less than half of the management costs of the English and Welsh Customs establishment, which, in 1782, stood at £257,600.[342]

---

[337] BL MS 8133B, fols 238, 240. All these and the following figures are for England and Wales only.
[338] Ibid., fols 115, 118.
[339] Ibid., fols 124, 126. This balance could easily become negative as it depended on the success of a cruiser in any given season; see also CUST97/10, 20 October 1738. For remittances into the Exchequer from seizure proceeds, compare also the figures from CUST37/2, with a detailed breakdown of costs for the later 1760s.
[340] BL Add. MS 8133C, fol. 124.
[341] BL Add. MS 8133A; Add. MS 8133C, fol. 110.
[342] BL Add. MS 8133C, fol. 135. This shortfall was lessened, to some extent, by the fact that a number of cruisers were contract vessels, paid out of successful seizures; see Add. MS 8133N, fols 122, 126.

Table 5: Customs Returns and Management Charges (England and Wales), 1778–1782 (Source BL Add. MS 8133A, 8133B).

	Net totals (£)	Net seizures (£)	Net receipts London (£)	Net receipts Bristol (£)	Net receipts Great Yarmouth (£)	Management Charges (£)
1778	2,270,659	128,463	1,515,765	152,199	23,173	281,635
1779	2,577,190	74,916	1,713,355	186,426	19,873	295,064
1780	2,788,167	64,246	1,865,088	196,418	29,169	300,700
1781	2,867,924	76,495	2,019,431	186,485	19,741	282,900
1782	2,897,585	36,022	1,864,385	239,375	23,075	257,672

Table 6: Customs Receipts and Seizures Receipts (England and Wales), 1760–1784 (Source BL Add. MS 8133C).

	Net totals (A)	Net seizures (B)	%		Net totals (A)	Net seizures (B)	%
1760	2,007,166	37,232	1.85	1772	2,589,510	63,914	2.47
1761	1,906,621	40,469	2.12	1773	2,505,926	66,909	2.67
1762	1,900,828	42,411	2.23	1774	2,640,398	72,628	2.75
1763	2,293,323	43,719	1.91	1775	2,574,853	93,822	3.64
1764	2,212,080	42,607	1.93	1776	2,576,253	95,851	3.72
1765	2,321,111	49,879	2.15	1777	2,309,565	80,459	3.48
1766	2,497,940	49,659	1.99	1778	2,270,659	128,463	5.65
1767	2,415,271	59,421	2.46	1779	2,577,190	74,916	2.91
1768	2,483,618	38,602	1.55	1780	2,788,167	64,246	2.30
1769	2,693,759	54,673	2.03	1781	2,867,924	76,495	2.67
1770	2,607,289	61,145	2.34	1782	2,897,585	36,022	1.24
1771	2,704,106	61,977	2.29	1783	2,883,764	35,444	1.23
				1784	3,355,170	28,531	0.85

In the larger picture of Customs receipts, seizures were a minor variable. Why, then, the apparent obsession with seizures by central administrators? There are two reasons for this. Seizures were of symbolic value. Given the impression – in the executive, parliament, and the wider public – that smuggling was pervasive, seizures signalled the recovery of money otherwise irretrievably lost. As both punishment and deterrent, it was a triumph over "the most daring set of men that live".[343] Secondly, for central administrators, seizures were the only countable measure for the success against smuggling. This attitude was most keenly felt by the preventive service. It was seizures – or the lack thereof – that served as the ultimate yardstick of activity.[344] When, in 1770, it appeared that no seizures had been made by the boat stationed at West Lulworth, the Board expressed its surprise and exhorted the officers to "exert themselves more effectually".[345] Similarly, in the 1770s, officers at and around Aberdeen were asked to explain "the Causes of their want of success on serving the revenue either by making seizures or securing Dutys".[346] No amount of reasonable justification could, in the final analysis, satisfy the Board. Trouble always loomed "in cases where the Officers appear not to have been successful in making Seizures".[347]

But in light of how the seizure system worked, it remains questionable whether taking seizures as the yardstick for administrative efficiency is an apt perspective. The inferior ranks certainly disagreed. Outport officials – some timidly, some fiercely – argued that seizures were vital, but only part of the picture and that reducing the assessment of the preventive service to seizures was missing its purpose. Prevention – even if impossible to measure precisely – should itself, they argued, be valued as success. Even in light of "very inconsiderable seizures", these men argued, it stood to reason "whether these Officers may not have been a means to prevent" smuggling to begin with.[348] For all the zeal and activity of the preventive service, there was "a Good Deal of Chance in making seizures".[349] The "principal end" of the service was "Publick Protection by Preventing Frauds", whereas making seizures was "a mere contingency". In case the Board fixated exclusively on seizures, the service's numerous other tasks would suffer, as "they cannot be supposed will come within the circle of his [the officer's] attention".[350]

---

[343] TNA CUST97/26, 9 June 1786.
[344] See, for instance, TNA CUST148/13, p. 54 *et passim*.
[345] TNA CUST59/77, 22 May 1770.
[346] NRS CE87/1/5, 17 February 1770, 27 April 1770; CE87/1/6, 14 February 1778.
[347] TNA CUST29/6, 1 December 1796.
[348] TNA CUST59/2, 31 January 1729.
[349] NRS CE87/1/5, 27 April 1770; CE87/1/6, 14 February 1778.
[350] TNA CUST97/25, 28 May 1783, 30 October 1784.

Conclusions

The eighteenth-century Customs was primarily a fiscal agency, and it occupies a prime place in the study of the fiscal-military state as one of the central agencies tasked with raising revenue to conduct British military campaigns in Europe and beyond. In this perspective, the Customs is typically seen to fall short of the administrative efficiency attributed to the Excise, which also resulted, for most of the century, in a higher revenue output. The present chapter corrects this perspective in two important ways. It shows, firstly, that whereas fiscal concerns formed a large part of Customs activity, they were by no means exclusive. Rather, and in particular with a view to the coastal preventive service, the Customs was tasked with a range of enforcement activities hardly matched by any other bureaucracy in the period. These activities consumed money and time without the expectation of their being fiscally productive. To measure Customs activity in exclusively numerical and fiscal terms, therefore, is to misunderstand both the efficiency and the output of the Customs to a wide spectrum of state activities. By adopting this wider view, the present chapter, secondly, also makes a case for a part-rehabilitation of the bureaucratic performance of the Customs in the period. Rather than attributing poor fiscal performance to corruption, negligence and inefficiency, the chapter shows that the bureaucratic state of the art in the Customs indeed paralleled that of the Excise in many important respects. The reason why this did not result in larger revenue returns was that these bureaucratic tools often related to activities well outside the raising of revenue. The results of this chapter thus complicate a straightforward fiscal-military perspective even on those parts of the executive that were tasked with fiscal matters. Assessing the executive as to its administrative efficiency and performance requires an appreciation of the greater complexity of bureaucratic enforcement. An exclusively fiscal focus, on the other hand, risks misrepresenting and distorting such performance.

4
The Social History of Coastal Policing[1]

From 1747 to 1750, Charles Lennox, the 2nd Duke of Richmond, pursued one of the severest anti-smuggling campaigns in English history. It led to the execution of over forty individuals. And it was triggered by a particularly heinous crime. In 1747, a gang of smugglers had broken into the Customhouse at Poole to rescue a seizure previously taken by the Customs. When an informer attested to the identity of the offenders, he, along with a Customs officer, was abducted, tortured, and killed by the gang. The episode is one of the best-known smuggling stories of the eighteenth century. In large part, this is due to Richmond seeking to publicise the events to garner support for his campaign. Historiography, too, has paid close attention to the campaign and it has since been a central theme in the discussion of eighteenth-century smuggling and the debate on the "crime wave" of the 1740s.[2]

---

[1] Records from the Goodwood Estate Archives, now held in the West Sussex Record Office (WSRO), were consulted and are quoted in this chapter by courtesy of His Grace the Duke of Richmond and Gordon, and with acknowledgments to the West Sussex County Record Office and the county archivist.

[2] Cal Winslow, 'Sussex Smugglers', in Douglas Hay, Peter Linebaugh, John G. Rule, E.P. Thompson, Cal Winslow (eds), *Albion's Fatal Tree: Crime and Society in Eighteenth-Century England* (London, 1975), pp. 119–166; Paul Muskett, 'English Smuggling in the Eighteenth Century' (PhD diss. Open University, 1996); Frank McLynn, *Crime and Punishment in Eighteenth-Century England* (London, 1989), pp. 172–201; John Rule, 'Social Crime in the Rural South in the Eighteenth and Early Nineteenth Centuries', in John Rule, Roger Wells (eds) *Crime, Protest, and Popular Politics in Southern England, 1740–1850* (London, 1997), pp. 153–168; Geoffrey Morley, *Smuggling in Hampshire and Dorset 1700–1850* (Newbury, 1983); Mary Waugh, *Smuggling in Kent and Sussex 1700–1840* (Newbury, 1985); Richard Platt, *Smuggling in the British Isles: A History* (Stroud, 2011); Christopher McCooey, *Smuggling on the South Coast* (Stroud, 2012); Nicholas Rogers, 'Confronting the Crime Wave: The Debate over Social Reform and Regulation, 1749–1753', in Lee Davison, Tim Hitchcock, Tim Keirn, Robert B. Shoemaker (eds), *Stilling the Grumbling Hive: The Response to Social and Economic Problems in England, 1689–1750* (Stroud, 1992), pp. 77–98; Bob Harris, *Politics and the Nation: Britain in the Mid-Eighteenth Century* (Oxford, 2022), pp. 278–323.

Much as we know about the campaign, there remain gaps in how it has been studied. Traditional accounts have depicted the events as a confrontation between agents acting for the common good – the duke, the magistrates, the Customs men – and the villains – the smugglers and murderers. In a recent discussion, the events are seen as a "classic confrontation between public terror on the one hand and a Christian conscience with its wish for law and order, and justice, on the other".[3] Even in the social histories of the 1970s, usually critical of the elite perspective, this juxtaposition has not been questioned. In this interpretation, too, it was a clash "between the plebeian gangs and the forces of the Government."[4] Historiography thus has continued to adhere to contemporary accounts which suggest the existence of a line neatly separating the enforcers from the offenders.[5] Only Muskett has questioned the "over-simplification of the adversarial model" of law enforcement inherent in such accounts.[6]

Two things have remained underrated in how the Richmond episode – and smuggling in general – has been studied. By assigning the Customs men firmly to the side of authority, their rootedness in social communities is neglected. This view, as research on officeholders has shown, is misleading.[7] No more were the Customs officers villains or heroes than the smugglers. They, too, lived in the social realities of coastal communities. If we are to understand the microcosm of coastal authority, we must give equal importance to the social tensions in all these roles. To appreciate this, we must, secondly, go beyond the dualistic view of contemporary political, judicial, and administrative writings. What existing accounts of smuggling continue to underplay is that the crucial areas for the enforcement of authority were

---

[3] McCooey, *Smuggling on the South Coast*, p. 136.
[4] Winslow, 'Sussex Smugglers', p. 158.
[5] See Anon. ('Gentleman of Chichester'), *A Full and Genuine History of the Inhuman and Unparrallell'd Murders of Mr. William Galley, A Custom-House Officer at the Port of Southampton and Mr. Daniel Chater, a Shoemaker, at Fordingbridge in Hampshire, by Fourteen Notorious Smugglers* [...] (London, 1749). Winslow convincingly suggests that the author was the Duke of Richmond himself; Winslow, 'Sussex Smugglers', p. 128.
[6] Muskett, 'English Smuggling', p. 3.
[7] Most recently María Ángeles Martín Romera, Hannes Ziegler (eds), *The Officer and the People: Accountability and Authority in Pre-Modern Europe* (Oxford, 2021). For the English case Michael Braddick, 'Administrative performance: the representation of political authority in early modern England', in Michael Braddick, John Walter (eds), *Negotiating Power in Early Modern Society: Order, Hierarchy and Subordination in Britain and Ireland* (Cambridge, 2001), pp. 166–187. See also the more recent and excellent studies by Mark Knights, *Trust and Distrust: Corruption in Office in Britain and its Empire, 1600–1850* (Oxford, 2021) and Jonah Miller, *Gender and Policing in Early Modern England* (Cambridge, 2023).

not necessarily the contact points of an idealised juxtaposition of officers and offenders. Rather, it was the grey areas in between that mattered. Social figures such as the common informer are key to understanding what incentives operated in that wide spectrum between the official and the criminal, and what forces regulated the grey areas of authority.[8].

This chapter draws on the rich social historiography of early modern Britain along with research on officeholding in order to illustrate the complexity of coastal enforcement. The aims are to question the dichotomic picture of law enforcement presented by authorities, to populate the grey zones of law enforcement and to deconstruct the supposedly straightforward social roles of the officer and the criminal. Examining the corrupted officer, the converted smuggler, and the common informer provides a better view of the social realities of coastal policing. Having thus challenged the prevailing perspective on law enforcement in coastal spaces, the chapter will bring the results to bear on rewriting the history of the Richmond campaign.

Two Concepts of Order

Communities in early modern Britain were tight-knit and compact social units with clearly established internal hierarchies and rules of conduct. Some of these were imposed by church and state; others developed out of local social hierarchies and power relations.[9] Whatever the nature of these relations, however, the local community was "a unit of identity and belonging", in which social rules of conduct were being negotiated without necessarily conforming to the moral and political codes of the lawmakers and policymakers of the nation.[10] Officeholders, too, were no strangers to

[8] For more recent research on smuggling as a grey area, see, for instance, Anna Knutsson, Charlotte Bellamy, 'From Valet to Smuggler: A Microhistorical Study of a French Intermediary in Stockholm, 1775–1832', *Revue d'histoire nordique*, 27 (2018), 115–140; Ryan Mewett, '"To the Very Great Prejudice of the Fair Trader": Merchants and Illicit Naval Trading in the 1730s', *Historical Research*, 93 (2020), 692–714; David Chan Smith, 'Fair Trade and the Political Economy of Brandy Smuggling in Early Eighteenth-Century Britain', *Past and Present*, 251 (2021), 75–111.

[9] Alexandra Shepard and Phil Withington (eds), *Communities in Early Modern England: Networks, Place, Rhetoric* (Manchester, 2000); Phil Withington, *The Politics of Commonwealth: Citizens and Freemen in Early Modern England* (Cambridge, 2005); Michael J. Halvorson and Karen E. Spierling (eds), *Defining Community in Early Modern Europe* (Abingdon, 2008); Beat Kümin, *The Communal Age in Western Europe, c.1100–1800: Towns, Villages and Parishes in Pre-Modern Society* (Basingstoke, 2013).

[10] Keith Wrightson, 'The Politics of the Parish in Early Modern England', in Paul Griffiths, Adam Fox, and Steve Hindle (eds), *The Experience of Authority in Early Modern*

the villages and towns where they held office, but active members of these communities.¹¹ After all, "local officers", it has been maintained, "were the agents of their communities as much as of the crown".¹² Joan Kent has even spoken of "dual pressures" on these officeholders, who were required to render account formally to superior authorities at the end of their term, but also informally throughout their term to their peers and relations within the communities.¹³ Keith Wrightson has framed this in terms of "two concepts of order" that operated at village level and directed the performance of local officeholders. Between the order of the "moralists and legislators" on the one hand, and the order of the "intimate local level" in which "personal considerations" loomed large on the other, local officers were left with the task of mediating between "the national legislative ideal and ambivalent local realities".¹⁴ This required compromises in the enforcement of legislation and necessitated negotiations of two (or more) different, if not distinct, and sometimes incompatible social roles.¹⁵

    England (Basingstoke, 1996), pp. 10–46, at 11. See also Keith Wrightson, *English Society 1580–1680* (London, 1982), pp. 39–65, 149–182; Steve Hindle, *The State and Social Change in Early Modern England, 1550–1640* (Basingstoke, 2002), pp. 204–230.

11 Mark Goldie, 'The Unacknowledged Republic: Officeholding in Early Modern England', in Tim Harris (ed.), *The Politics of the Excluded, c.1500–1850* (Basingstoke, 2001), pp. 153–194; Braddick, *State Formation*, pp. 20–46.

12 Goldie, 'Unacknowledged Republic', p. 166.

13 Joan Kent, 'The English Village Constable, 1580–1642: The Nature and Dilemmas of the Office', *JBS*, 20/2 (1981), 26–49. Reprinted in Clive Emsley (ed.), *Theories and Origins of the Modern Police* (Farnham, 2011), pp. 239–262, at p. 243. See also Joan Kent, *The English Village Constable 1580–1642: A Social and Administrative Study* (Oxford, 1986).

14 Keith Wrightson, 'Two Concepts of Order: Justices, Constables and Jurymen in Seventeenth-Century England', in John Brewer and John Styles (eds), *An Ungovernable People: The English and their Law in the Seventeenth and Eighteenth Centuries* (New Brunswick, NJ, 1980), pp. 21–46, at pp. 23–26. Wrightson's concept is not dissimilar to the idea of acceptance-oriented rule, as proposed by Stefan Brakensiek, 'Akzeptanzorientierte Herrschaft: Überlegungen zur politischen Kultur der Frühen Neuzeit', in Helmut Neuhaus (ed.), *Die Frühe Neuzeit als Epoche* (Munich, 2009), pp. 395–406. See also Stefan Brakensiek, Heide Wunder (eds), *Ergebene Diener ihrer Herren? Herrschaftsvermittlung im alten Europa* (Cologne, 2005); Johannes Kraus, 'War Administration: Subjects, Local Officers, and the Contribution System in the Thirty Years War', in María Ángeles Martín Romera, Hannes Ziegler (eds), *The Officer and the People. Accountability and Authority in Premodern Europe* (Oxford, 2021), pp. 251–272. For the implications on the history of administration, see Stefan Brakensiek, Corinna von Bredow, Birgit Näther (eds), *Herrschaft und Verwaltung in der Frühen Neuzeit* (Berlin, 2014).

15 Braddick, 'Administrative Performance'. On the implications for policing, see J. M. Beattie, *Policing and Punishment in London, 1660–1750: Urban Crime and the Limits*

Such a setting of dual pressures and accountabilities can also be shown to operate for Customs officials, but this has, to date, been much less explored.[16] This is particularly odd given that fiscal ideas were even less prone to be accepted locally than regulations about the public peace.[17] And in the Customs, too, officers were typically recruited from within the communities where they held office. In the context of fiscal policy, where the king's revenue was at stake, central institutions deeply resented the social repercussions of recruiting officeholders locally. It afforded too many opportunities for conflicting social interests, collusion, and corruption. From their perspective, it was common sense "to preserve the Men, as much as possible, from too frequent or too long an Intercourse with the Inhabitants of the Coast".[18] Officers, as John Brewer put it "were to be present in the community but not of it".[19] Customs men, therefore, generally ought not to be employed in places where they were "related or habituated".[20] This was frequently reiterated, but only unevenly enforced.[21] This means that Customs officers were subjected to as many social pressures as parish officers and that, therefore, their performance must be judged not exclusively in terms of compliance to official instructions, but also to how much of their actions resulted from such rootedness in social settings. This is not to say that Customs men were wholly abject to some forms of outright corruption. Corruption, that is, wilful deviations from official instructions, did

---

[16] *of Terror* (Oxford, 2001); Robert B. Shoemaker, *Prosecution and Punishment: Petty Crime and the Law in London and Rural Middlesex, c.1650–1725* (Cambridge, 1991). See Ashworth, *Customs* and Hoon, *Organization*; John Brewer, 'Servants of the Public—Servants of the Crown: Officialdom of Eighteenth-Century English Central Government', in id., Eckhart Hellmuth (eds), *Rethinking Leviathan: The Eighteenth-Century State in Britain and Germany* (Oxford, 1999), pp. 127–147; Hannes Ziegler, 'Customs Officers and Local Communities: Informing in Late Seventeenth-Century England', in María Ángeles Martín Romera, Hannes Ziegler (eds), *The Officer and the People: Accountability and Authority in Premodern Europe* (Oxford, 2021), pp. 325–348.

[17] Cynthia B. Herrup, *The Common Peace: Participation and the Criminal Law in Seventeenth-Century England* (Cambridge, 1987); Malcolm Gaskill, *Crime and Mentalities in Early Modern England* (Cambridge, 2000); James Sharpe, 'Enforcing the Law in the Seventeenth-Century English Village', in V. A. C. Gatrell, Bruce Lenman, Geoffrey Parker (eds), *Crime and the Law: The Social History of Crime in Western Europe since 1500* (London, 1980), pp. 97–119.

[18] 'Third Report', p. 10.

[19] Brewer, 'Officialdom', p. 139.

[20] *Eighteenth Century Documents*, pp. 260–261.

[21] Ashworth, *Customs*, pp. 117–130; Miles Ogborn, 'The Capacities of the State: Charles Davenant and the Management of the Excise, 1683–1698', *Journal of Historical Geography*, 24 (1998), 289–312; Hoon, *Organization*, p. 239.

exist. But it was not just greed that motivated these local officers. Customs officers belonged not to the Crown, but to their own social cosmos.

"The Officers in general are men of but low circumstances"

Customs officers were predominantly recruited locally. This was even cited as a particular advantage for the service.[22] At the same time, it is difficult to clearly establish the social profile of the ordinary Customs man on a preventive post. Most sources tell us precious little about their social background. But such evidence is sufficient to ascertain that they typically belonged to the socially and economically marginal sort. Whereas parish offices required their holders to possess a minimum of social standing in the community, such a criterion did not, could not and need not normally be a concern of the Treasury and the Board of Customs when appointing inferior port or preventive officers.[23] As the appointment typically involved a measure of local recommendation, we must assume that a certain standard applied, but there is nothing to suggest that this routinely included social credit; more often it was specific knowledge or experience, along with circumstances characterising the applicant as deserving. The latter were often facts that marked the applicant as socially weak and economically vulnerable.[24]

The lower ranks were recruited from a spectrum comprising the lower middling sort and the better-off of the meaner sort. Ex-soldiers, artisans, fishermen, seamen, bankrupt merchants, day labourers, cottagers and shopkeepers were the core recruitment groups. If many individuals were able to name some kind of trade or upbringing that would typically be used to mark their belonging to the middling sort, it was predominantly those who had failed in those occupations that ended up in a Customs post. In fact, the appointment in the Customs required these men to forgo their ordinary trade or occupation. "My long continuance in the constant service of the Government", one riding officer remarked "has put me out of any other way of provideing for my selfe, my Dear wife & three children".[25] Some, it is true, were reluctant to devote themselves fully to the revenue. But in such cases the Board was quick to intervene. If other occupations, therefore, would have afforded subsistence, such men would not have vied for a Customs post. There is, in fact, recurrent evidence of preceding failure. This chimes with the observation that candidates were on average in

---

[22] TNA CUST58/13, 23 October 1784; CUST59/1, 28 September 1717.
[23] Goldie, 'Unacknowledged Republic', pp. 164–172.
[24] Muskett, 'English Smuggling', pp. 134–135; Brewer, 'Officialdom', pp. 129, 133.
[25] TNA T1/128, no. 3.

their early to mid-30s – and thus well beyond the enterprising ages of early adulthood – when they entered the service.[26] Existing officers' sureties confirm this. As sureties needed to be "persons of Substance Credit and Reputation", officers were likely to reach up the social ladder for credible securities.[27] If the result, for ordinary riding officers, was a mix of mastmakers, ropemakers, sailmakers, grocers, apothecaries, carters, and yeomen, this puts them on a par with or somewhere below such occupations.[28]

Alongside these, a considerable fraction came from a more hand-to-mouth background. The assessment of the Scottish establishment was that "they are a number of very poor men".[29] Others expressed this with more contempt: "The Inferior Officers [...] are generally speaking so poor, so ignorant, and most of them of such ill characters".[30] Similarly, on the English and Welsh establishment many were in "mean" or "low circumstances".[31] Riding officers "in general" were considered "men of but low circumstances".[32] Most had no resources beyond their salaries and could not normally subsist on personal credit relations for long. If salaries dried up, they were "reduced to great poverty and want" or a "starving condition".[33] "I have nothing else", a Norwich officer lamented, "to support my self and family, but my place."[34] Similarly, once they left the service, most seem to have aimed for the superannuation fund, itself regarded as a less than "tolerable subsistence".[35] "Tis a Melancholly consideration", Lewis Gillart, a superannuated officer in Kent, complained, "to think that ould Age & gray haires which are a Crown of glorey to others must be the occasion of my shame & poverty".[36]

The existence and requirements of the pension fund are themselves to some degree a testimony to the social status of the officers. An officer needed to have paid into it for ten years and needed to be 60 years of age to qualify, unless by an accident he was disabled prior to that age. It was also strictly required that officers had no other means of subsistence. Many did

---

[26] See the officer lists in TNA CUST148/11.
[27] TNA CUST97/4, 15 May 1723.
[28] TNA CUST97/74b, fols 141–142; CUST69/59, 21 February 1734.
[29] TNA T1/107, no. 33.
[30] TNA T1/185, no. 63.
[31] TNA CUST72/1, 26 May 1747; CUST82/6, 4 January 1751; CUST97/14, 30 April 1748.
[32] TNA CUST97/26, 9 June 1786.
[33] TNA T1/149, no. 48; CUST89/6, 12 October 1779; CUST82/1, 23 June 1718, 15 August 1718; CUST97/13, 29 December 1744, 25 November 1745.
[34] TNA CUST97/11, 29 November 1740.
[35] TNA T1/128, no. 3; CUST58/12, 29 December 1783; CUST97/25, 1 October 1784.
[36] TNA T1/128, no. 3.

not, and were indeed "incapable of getting [their] living any other way".[37] In some cases, there is a record of debt.[38] Many petitions, moreover, contrast the existence of a large family with the dependence on a single salary.[39] The ex-soldier and odd day labourer on the farms and in the warehouses, the part-time fishermen and seagoing men must have been the most pertinent social groups.

Salaries are among the better social indicators. Who could and wanted to subsist on the £30 to £90 per year that the posts of riding officer, boatman, and cruiser man typically paid? 50s per month easily surpassed what a craftsman or labourer could hope to earn during the same time.[40] £30 yearly marked a labouring family as relatively well-off, and considering that many occupations were seasonal and occasional, such salaries must have been attractive to that particular social group. As both commercial farming and trade would have resulted in more yearly income than even the £90 at the upper end of the scale, it can only have been those of the middling sort who were – due to misfortune, late birth, or the effects of meagre years – unable to hold on to comfortable subsistence above and independent of wage labour.[41] If such salaries appear somewhat high for a post that required little else but riding and watching, this was because officers should have a "competent salary to live on" to compensate the foregoing of other occupations and to give "noe occasion of taking bribes".[42] For the successful middling sort, such salaries were below what they would have considered "competent". "I was indeed before I had this Place a Hotpresser and had a good Business", one officer explained. This had gained him about £150 per year. "But after [I] dropt by Degrees until wholly dropt, and for near two years before I had this Place, I did not earn enough to maintain my Family

---

[37] TNA CUST58/12, 29 December 1783; CUST97/13, 29 December 1744. On the original setup of the fund, see T11/15, p. 314.
[38] TNA CUST72/1, 29 December 1750; CUST97/11, 25 November 1740, 29 November 1740.
[39] TNA T1/149, no. 48; CUST97/11, 15 December 1738, 6 February 1741.
[40] Jeremy Boulton, 'The "Meaner Sort": Labouring People and the Poor', in Keith Wrightson (ed.), *A Social History of England 1500–1750* (Cambridge, 2017), pp. 310–329, at pp. 311–312.
[41] On the social standing of the middling sort Jonathan Barry, Joseph Melling (eds), *The Middling Sort of People: Culture, Society and Politics in England 1550–1800* (Basingstoke, 1994); Margaret R. Hunt, *The Middling Sort: Commerce, Gender, and the Family in England, 1680–1780* (London, 1996); Henry French, *The Middle Sort of People in Provincial England 1660–1750* (Oxford, 2007).
[42] TNA T1/157, no. 2.

but went backwards continually".[43] The ones enticed by preventive salaries either came from precarious social backgrounds or had faced adversity.

The same is not true for the higher posts. Supervisors typically received £120 per annum and surveyor positions for Sussex and Kent paid as much as £500. Cruiser captains also earned much more than the average riding officer.[44] Captains on contract ships, too, needed the means to supply a ship and a crew. These men clearly belonged to the middling sort and some, such as John Collier, or Henry Baker, even hailed from the lower gentry.[45] The question here is why such men would settle for salaried service. Part of the answer may be that such posts offered something in the way of reputation, influence, and the opportunity to capitalise. Surveyors had considerable influence on appointment processes, and this translated into local influence, both for personal and political reasons.[46] Some posts also lent themselves to considerable profit, as Warren Lisle's career in the Customs shows.[47] Finally, if the lower positions must be deemed a dead end in terms of future careers, superior posts could be used as stepping stones. Baker, starting as solicitor and surveyor for Kent and Sussex, gained the attractive collector post at Chichester.[48] William Culliford, once a surveyor, ended up on the Board.[49]

"A Mixture of Passions, Contradiction and Private Quarrel"

Officers of the preventive service often met with violence in the execution of their duties. This was meant to intimidate or incapacitate them. At the same time, smuggling held a promise of monetary rewards: a preventive officer willing to connive was likely to incur large rewards. The intention of lining one's pocket cannot, therefore, be ignored as a stimulus of deviance. From the perspective of the archive, however, genuine intimidation is hard to distinguish from greed or social obligations when it comes to the outcomes of such stimuli: administrators invariably branded these as

---

[43] TNA CUST97/11, 29 November 1740.
[44] TNA T17/6, p. 214; T11/20, p. 208; T11/22, pp.7 3, 130, 206; Hoon, *Organization*, chapter VI.
[45] TNA T1/141, no. 16; T1/96, no. 93.
[46] See Richard Saville (ed.), *The Letters of John Collier of Hastings 1731–1746* (Lewes, 2016), pp. xiii–li. See also Collier's correspondence with Newcastle in BL Add. MS 32688, Add. MS 32692, Add. MS 32702, Add. MS 32703, Add. MS 32706, Add. MS 32709, Add. MS 32711, Add. MS 32712, Add. MS 32718.
[47] TNA CUST64/6, 14 April 1766; BL Add. MS 8133B, fol. 124.
[48] TNA CUST18/77; T11/14, p. 397.
[49] TNA T1/30, no. 13; T1/38, no. 85; T1/202, no. 1; William B. Stephens, *The Seventeenth-Century Customs Service Surveyed: William Culliford's Investigation of the Western Ports, 1682–84* (Farnham, 2012), pp. 5–7.

negligence, collusion, and corruption. But it is important to separate these. In the first case, officers could not act otherwise. Greed, on the other hand, meant that they were monetarily incentivised to not act honestly. In such cases, deviance was a matter of self-interest. The existence of social ties and pressures, finally, suggests rather that officers were disinclined to act against moral codes more immediately relevant to their own social lives and thus more important to them than the lawmakers' codes. If we are to appreciate the constraints of local officeholding, we must look at the latter, that is at the social factors, and other, less direct means of influence, by which officers were held back from a diligent performance. Rather than negligence, such factors reveal the frailty of authority dependent on local agents.

For local officers, the relevant moral compass was the community rather than central instructions.[50] Most frequently, conflicts arose when the officers' families were involved. In a memorial from 1708, Alexander Rigby was as resigned as he was realistic. "Either for the sake of some Consideration given, for afinity, or to help a neighbour, the people in this country" stood by each other, "never looseing a Sheepe for an half penny worth of Tarr". The people were "never failing one another, if in blood, and neighbours seldome faile neighbours, [...] their Notion being that Sanguinity and Neighbours will remember benefitts or Injuries longer then the Court that resides at so great a distance".[51] "Sanguinity", in other words, tended to trump any loyalty to institutions foreign to the social life of the communities.

But such influence was hard to prove. When John and Thomas Jordan, riding officers at Folkestone, were accused of "screening the Smugglers" in 1735, the reasoning was that both "were born in the Town and never employed out of it and [...] are related to several of the Great Smugglers". This, their accuser alleged, was why they seized little and rarely prosecuted. In the event, these allegations could not be ruled out but were hard to substantiate. The Board chose to drop the matter with a warning. The Jordans were unconcerned, making light of the matter and calling it "little Petty Stuff".[52] To the Board, it was rather more serious, and it was quick to investigate if it got wind of dodgy connections. The higher those connections were placed, the bigger the potential damage. In 1755, it was reported that the revenue of Cardiff had "suffered greatly", because the surveyor was married to the sister of a merchant trading to Bristol, who in turn has "got richer than his Neighbours in the same way of Business".[53] That such a marriage existed could hardly be denied by the collector, but it was, again, impossible to prove that this had been in any way detrimental to the revenue.

[50] Ziegler, 'Customs Officers and Local Communities'.
[51] TNA T1/105, no. 8. See also TNA T1/185, no. 63.
[52] ESRO, SAY278.
[53] TNA CUST72/1, 3 November 1755.

Occasionally, superiors turned a blind eye to such connections. In January 1720, a preventive officer on the Weymouth establishment was questioned because his son was said to be aiding the smuggling gangs. John Gregory admitted this but, remarkably, did not admit to any prejudicial effects on his duties. Even the collector confined himself to a "severe Reprimand". Could the son, running with the gang, identify any of the offenders? The possibility was explicitly mentioned by the collector but not acted upon. Neither was the fact that another officer at the same place had "contracted a very intimate acquaintance with all the smugglers of the place".[54] When the Board suggested removing Gregory, the collector doubted the wisdom of such a move. Previously, Gregory had been carried to sea by local fishermen when required for the service. But "John Gregory being related to most of the Fishermen at Lulworth and too well acquainted with the rest it will not be possible to agree with any of them to Carry the officers to sea as occasion may require, because the fellows will have a notion that such agreement will turne Gregory out of his employment".[55] As things stood, Gregory and his family remained in a station where smuggling was practised "more than at any other place", but was not considered particularly "diligent" by the collector. [56] Arguably, this should have raised doubts about his performance. Alas, it did not.

The impression of complacency is supported by similar cases: when, in June 1727, one Isabella Rice of Happisburgh claimed to have been assaulted and used "barbarously by bruising her in several places" by two riding officers, the collector at Great Yarmouth was slow to make inquiries. The officers, when charged, professed to have been attacked by Mrs. Rice first. The collector was at a loss to "thoroughly understand this affair", but was able to establish that both Isabella Rice and her husband had smuggling connections. In his final report, it is striking how the collector chose to placidly pass over the obvious implications of a family quarrel influencing the execution of office:

> There appeared such a mixture of Passions, Contradictions and private Quarrel, so vastly Different from the first Complaint that it was some time before we could form any Idea of the cause from whence such passions one to another should arise, [...] as the whole appearing to be a Quarrell founded on frivolous Occasions and on which the Revenue was no way Concerned [...]; and could not find the Least foundation of a Charge of Neglect or Fraud.[57]

---

[54] TNA CUST59/2, 30 January 1720.
[55] TNA CUST59/2, 25 May 1720.
[56] TNA CUST59/2, 30 January 1720.
[57] TNA CUST97/5, 6 March 1728; see also 26 June and 13 July 1727.

Social familiarity was both dangerous and necessary, and the contradiction was never entirely resolved. Familiarity was the work of time. But it was also indispensable for enforcement. That which made officers effective at enforcement was prone to make them unreliable. Hence central authorities were ambiguous as to how much social familiarity was to be allowed. Officers with local connections were prone to run into trouble; but so were the ones without: when, in June 1719, one Joshua Nicholson was appointed preventive officer, "the country people adjacent to Ellenfoot" (today's Maryport) were no sooner informed of this, than "they immediately altered their behaviour to him, being very sensible of his great diligence". People were apprehensive that a foreigner's diligence "would for the future debar them of some privileges they had before enjoyed".[58] Such privileges were obviously illegal ones. Deprived of these, local people were intent on making Nicholson's life difficult. A similar instance was reported in September 1759. John Hamper, a riding officer recently appointed to the port, had received "crude usage" from the inhabitants because they suspected him of being instrumental in the removal of three officers from the port and also "with design to intimidate those we sent in lieu of them from doing their duty in the manner they ought to do."[59] Such instances show that officers were prone to develop an arrangement with local people that was not necessarily advantageous to the revenue.

"A piece of Humour to intimidate officers from serving the Revenue"

It was common for preventive officers to be obstructed or attacked by the smugglers. But there were also less violent, less open and more efficient ways of intimidating preventive officers that belonged to the arsenal of the community rather than the armed smuggler.

Beyond the implicit threat of social punishments by friends, family, and relations, there were more proactive ways of intimidating the officers. Some feared that members of the local community would resort to burning their houses and attacking their families. This was not an unwarranted fear.[60] In Folkestone, in March 1744, a smuggling gang was "enquiring after the behaviour of the officers, swearing that if they were bad officers, that they would cure them".[61] Even when not performing their duty, officers often lived in "Fear of bodily harm to himself or Family" and were consequently

---

[58] TNA CUST82/1, 3 June 1719.
[59] TNA CUST82/9, 21 September 1759.
[60] WSRO, Goodwood 155, H16; TNA CUST148/12, pp. 215, 325, 449, 497, 565; GCA CE60/1/1, 30 January 1750.
[61] Cit. Winslow, 'Sussex Smugglers', p. 133.

discouraged in performing their duty.⁶² In Sussex, in the early 1740s, the situation was such that officers were told not to ride by night "which so intimidates the Officers that they cannot doe their duty as they ought for fear."⁶³ The community, presenting the mere possibility of such punishments, was thus able to elicit tacit consent.⁶⁴

Local inhabitants unsympathetic to the Customs also made use of the law to force the officers into conforming to local sentiments. Both officers, but also country people willing to aid the smugglers, were regularly served with legal processes to make them desist.⁶⁵ Such suits, born from "malice" and typically called "vexatious suits", were intended to "ruin" the officers. These were, in a collector's words, pieces "of Humour to intimidate the officers from serving the Revenue".⁶⁶ Such attempts to "harass" the officers clearly carried some support among the wider social spectrum in many local communities, for there was never a shortage of witnesses against the officers.⁶⁷ More directly threatening to the livelihood of the particular officer were the frequent attempts to discredit individual officers by reporting them to the Board for alleged breaches of duty. Any number of accusations – and often a fair number of witnesses – were used in such cases to throw seemingly diligent officers out of their employment and thus out of the way of the contraband traders.⁶⁸

Finally, local communities could exert significant pressure on the officers when it came to their lodgings. Walter Devereux had already remarked in the 1690s that it was imperfect to have officers take lodgings in public houses and thus be in the public eye, where the necessary secrecy of their dealings, such as the procuring of intelligence, was entirely lost.⁶⁹ But even in more mundane respects, such as securing a home for the officer's family or living in the vicinity of the appointed station, officers were dependent on suitable quarters. If local communities proved unwilling, however, the "want of lodging and necessary accommodation" could pose problems.⁷⁰ An officer in Southwold, for instance, was unable to procure lodgings for

---

62 TNA CUST82/5, 18 June 1746.
63 TNA CUST148/12, pp. 365–366.
64 NRS CE87/1/6, 30 June 1779; CE87/1/2, 29 June 1744; TNA CUST59/2, 16 October 1719.
65 TNA CUST59/1, 29 October 1718.
66 NRS CE87/1/2, 29 June 1744; CE87/1/3, 14 August 1753; TNA CUST59/2, 16 October 1719.
67 TNA CUST97/9, 2 February 1736, 7 May 1736.
68 TNA CUST97/11, 25 November 1740, 29 November 1740, 27 June 1741.
69 TNA T1/60, no. 12.
70 TNA CUST61/17, 25 June 1804; NRS CE51/1/7, December 1802, 12 March 1803, 17 March 1803; CUST82/1, 6 March 1719; CUST97/5, 27 July 1727.

himself due to the hostility of the local community.[71] Similarly, in the notorious Ellenfoot, the majority of local people made sure that over the course of a year, the preventive officer stationed at the port was unable to reside there, "not being able to obtain any sort of convenience" at Ellenfoot.[72]

These threats of violence and legal processes, the withholding of hospitality and general hostility may seem relatively innocent. They were not illegal, after all. But in the face of such communal pressures, combined with the pressures exacted by families and relations, officers found it easier to comply with local exigencies than with central demands. They thought twice before exposing themselves to "the Odium of whole Countrey".[73] The contemporary suggestion that Customs officers "by their Conversaccion and Example" held great influence in Customs matters and beyond in local communities, was at least partly delusional.[74]

Adversarial Rhetoric and Socially Accepted Crime

To maintain that officers were entangled locally and that their shortcomings often had social reasons rather than being solely the outcome of force or greed, results in a more sophisticated answer as to why local officeholders were negligent or corrupt. Applying such qualifications, however, still adheres to the lawmakers' rhetoric and ignores that such behaviour was grounded in positive justifying notions that were regularly stronger than central demands. "Negligence" on the part of the officers cannot be explained simply in terms of "personal inadequacy". Rather, it "derived ultimately from the strains of their mediating position between their communities and the law".[75] Next to the legal code, there was a local moral code regularly more instructive for officers' conduct. Smuggling was, to a certain extent, a socially accepted crime and this is visible in how local people thought about smuggling and in interactions between the Customs men and the smugglers. Appreciating this is key if we are to understand the enforcement of authority in coastal regions because it helps to get rid of two idealized assumptions. The expectation that the enforcement of authority was a top-down process is misleading. Nor is it convincing to assume the outright failure of enforcement due to corruption and negligence. Some objectives of central authorities were clearly met. The appreciation of the plurality of

---

[71] TNA CUST97/23, 13 August 1778.
[72] TNA CUST82/1, 3 June 1719, 27 August 1720.
[73] NRS CE87/1/5.
[74] See TNA T1/89, no. 135.
[75] Wrightson, 'Two Concepts of Order', p. 31.

codes of conduct paves the way to understanding the oscillations between the legal code and the moral code as negotiations of authority. In the context of coastal policing, the key concept is the idea of collusion. Neither outright corrupt nor strictly compliant, collusion denotes a locally made pact between the officers and the offenders beyond the reach of authorities that successfully steered a middle course between local interests and the Crown's benefit. As such, it represented a particular form of "moral economy" regarding the enforcement of Customs regulations.[76]

"The Ruin of this Kingdom"

Central authorities rejected smuggling. But the grounds on which they did so were subject to changes dependent on the political context. Condemnations ranged from brandishing smuggling as a property crime to denouncing it as treason. Similarly, whereas the smuggler was regarded as a mere thief in some quarters, he was abominated as a murderer, traitor and beast in others. Parliamentary inquiries into smuggling tended to be most even-handed, being primarily focused on criminal and fiscal concerns. They lamented the "Greatness of the Loss to the Revenue" or the "Destruction of the Revenue".[77] Regarding the perpetrators, they were categorised into two groups: firstly, merchants engaging in fraud, innocently denounced as "unfair traders".[78] Their actions were described as "artful contrivances".[79] Secondly, for those who evaded Customs laws and committed such deeds in "a violent and outrageous manner", the name of smuggler was reserved, carrying connotations of beastly violence.[80] What they engaged in was commonly denounced as either "infamous" or "pernicious" practices.[81] Next to bidding "defiance to the Revenue Officers", the organised manner of these crimes "under the open Guard and Protection of armed Troops of Men" rendered the officers "quiet Spectators of the Proceedings" and justified calling this type of smuggling an "open and avowed Profession", a

---

[76] E. P. Thompson, *Customs in Common* (London, 1991), pp. 97–184, 184–258.
[77] *The Report of the Committee appointed to inquire into the Frauds and Abuses in the Customs, to the Prejudice of Trade, and Diminution of the Revenue*. Reported on the Seventh of June 1733 by Sir John Cope, printed in *Reports from the Committees of the House of Commons*. Reprinted by Order of the House. Vol. I, Miscellaneous Subjects: 1715–1735 (1803), pp. 601–654, at p. 603; 'First Report', p. 25.
[78] *The Report of the Committee appointed to inquire into the Frauds*, p. 607.
[79] Ibid., p. 606.
[80] Ibid., p. 610.
[81] Ibid., p. 610; JHC 25, pp. 101–110; Stephen Janssen, *Smuggling Laid Open, in all its Extensive and Destructive Branches*, London 1767; Anon., *Advice to the Unwary: Or, An Abstract of Certain Penal Laws Now in Force Against Smuggling in General*, London 1780.

"mixed system of War and Trade" and a "System of Force".[82] In their glaring frauds against the revenue "the Smugglers will one time or other, if not prevented, be the Ruin of this Kingdom".[83]

Whereas parliamentary committees and merchant commentators tended to focus on the fiscal damage, in other ways, government circles regarded smuggling as much more dangerous. Both the large numbers and the armed manner made smuggling a threat to the public peace. It amounted to "a sort of open rebellion highly inconsistent with, and greatly reproachful, to civil government".[84] It was "opposite to all Principles of Government".[85] Because it was carried on with "the most open and daring Violence", and because the exertions of the officers and soldiers regularly proved futile, government concluded that "Enormities of such Violence and Extent amount to a partial State of Anarchy and rebellion; and have a tendency to weaken and impair every Idea of a regular Government, and all due Submission to the Laws of the Land."[86] In some cases, this attitude was paired with an English arrogance vis-à-vis other, supposedly less civilised parts of Britain. It was no surprise to the Edinburgh Board, for instance, that the laws were so difficult to impose on the Isle of Arran, for the people there "speake none of our Language".[87] Similarly, the Irish west coast was inhabited by people still "unreduced and uncivilized".[88] Smuggling, in those parts as well as in the coastal counties of England, was corrupting the "morals of the People, and an Interruption of all good Government."[89] It was a threat to "publick Safety", "subversive both of Law and Government".[90] It "calls aloud for the Interposition of Government".[91] And, as one official argued, if the smugglers "cannot be broke, shutt up Westminster Hall, and disband all your officers of Justice as an expensive but useless incumbrance on the Nation."[92]

---

[82] 'First Report', pp. 4, 8, 6, 5; *Second report from the committee, appointed to enquire into the illicit practices used in defrauding the revenue*, p. 3.
[83] JHC 25, p. 103.
[84] Anon., *Advice to the Unwary*, p. 4.
[85] Janssen, *Smuggling Laid Open*, preface.
[86] 'First Report', p. 6.
[87] GCA CE60/1/3, 12 September 1764.
[88] TNA T1/361, no. 21.
[89] 'First Report', p. 25; See also *Eighteenth Century Documents*, p. 290: "it substantially affects the Morals of the People, and even the Police of the Kingdom".
[90] *Eighteenth Century Documents*, pp. 239, 308.
[91] *Eighteenth Century Documents*, p. 290.
[92] TNA CUST148/12, p. 681.

In the context of episodes of war, smuggling was depicted in even darker colours and "pregnant with Evils" of "fatal Consequences".[93] Smugglers, it was believed, "serve as spies and intelligence carriers to their [the French] fleets and armies, *when, where,* and *how* to strike the fatal blow".[94] The parliamentary committee inquiring into smuggling in 1745 received credible reports to such effect.[95] This made smugglers worse than criminals: they were traitors. Smugglers, Admiral Vernon contended, were "Traitors to their Country" on two counts. First, by continuing trade with the enemy and exporting provisions and second, because they worked as "daily Spies, to give the Enemy Intelligence of all our Proceedings".[96] In exchange for such information, he claimed, the French ports allowed the smugglers to continue their commerce. Smuggling, in this view, was of more than fiscal concern and also more than a threat to public peace. It had, Vernon argued, "converted those employed in it, first from honest industrious fishermen, to lazy, drunken, and profligate Smugglers, and now, to dangerous Spies on all our Proceedings, for the Enemy's daily Information."[97]

Aside from security considerations, it was periods such as the "crime wave" of the 1740s that prompted stark warnings of the dangers of smuggling. Observers feared that any sense "of the guilt in a Violation of the Laws" was lost in the light of the potential advantages.[98] This was particularly so when the influx of decommissioned seamen and soldiers, along with the economic disruptions of the war, seriously exacerbated the economic distress in small coastal communities.[99] In such circumstances, smuggling was seen as a corrupter of the morals of the people and a facilitator for more serious offences. Richmond concluded that smuggling was not only "highly injurious to trade, a violation of the laws, and the disturber of the peace and quiet of all the maritime counties of the kingdom". It was also a "nursery of all sorts of vice and wickedness; a temptation to commit offences at first unthought of; an encouragement to perpetrate the blackest of crimes without provocation or remorse; and is in general productive of cruelty, robbery and murder."[100] In such an interpretation, the smuggler was

---

[93] Janssen, *Smuggling Laid Open*, preface.
[94] Anon., *Advice to the Unwary*, p. 6.
[95] JHC 25, pp. 102, 105.
[96] [Edward Vernon], *Some Seasonable Advice from an Honest Sailor, to whom it might have Concerned, for the Service of the Crown and Country* (London, 1746), p. 110.
[97] [Vernon], *Advice*, p. 110.
[98] *Eighteenth Century Documents*, p. 308.
[99] Nicholas Rogers, *Mayhem: Post-War Crime and Violence in Britain, 1748–53* (New Haven/London, 2012).
[100] *A Full and Genuine History*, p. 60.

a base creature, engaged in an immoral sin that corrupted the soul.[101] This changing trajectory of how smuggling was seen by the authorities is confirmed by proceedings of the Old Bailey. Here, too, smuggling was seen as a crime conducive to all sorts of vices. It bred "contempt" for the king and the law; it threatened the "common Peace of the Kingdom"; it was a "Terror of the Public" and a "Terror of the Subject"; it was a "kind of rebellion".[102] It was, in short, "a Sin of deep Dye", entirely deserving of the "Resentment of every Man, who pretends to any Share of moral Honesty".[103]

These images of smuggling in public discourse underline the "adversarial model" of law enforcement. Obviously, even in the highest circles, there was a realisation that those on the side of enforcement were not always as reliable as one would have ideally liked them to be. But they still served as a neat contrast to the smuggler. Coast officers, it was contended, were "generally well recommended, and Men of probity" "as just as other Men".[104] The law, the government, its agents, the army and the good and honest common people were set into stark contrast to all those choosing to act against decency. The smugglers were vilified as the enemies of economic prosperity, of the public peace, and of any sense of morality, lawfulness, and government. The smuggler acted beyond these laws, beyond the nation, beyond decency, and sometimes even beyond humanity. The conflict, as seen by this rhetoric, was between the state and the smuggler.

"They would have a law of their own"

Local sentiments were different. There was a powerful, justifying notion regarding smuggling that operated on various levels. To a wide social spectrum, smuggling was a "socially accepted crime".[105] This idea was, firstly, rooted in custom, contending that free trade had been the people's

---

[101] John Wesley, *A Word to a Smuggler* (London, 1783).
[102] Old Bailey Proceedings Online, t17480115-28; t17470604-13; t17470909-36; t17471209-52. See also t17470225-19; NRS CE87/1/2, 17 December 1742; TNA CUST59/1, 5 April 1718.
[103] Old Bailey Proceedings Online, Ordinary of Newgate's Account, OA17470729 (29 July 1747).
[104] George Bridges, *A Whip for the Smugglers: Or, a Curb to France. Shewing the only way to Prevent Wool-Smuggling* (London, 1742), pp. 6, 15.
[105] Winslow, 'Sussex Smugglers'; Muskett, 'English Smuggling'. See also John Rule, 'Social Crime in the Rural South in the Eighteenth and Early Nineteenth Centuries', in John Rule/Roger Wells (eds), *Crime, Protest, and Popular Politics in Southern England, 1740–1850* (London, 1997), pp. 153–168; J. A. Sharpe, *Crime in Early Modern England 1550–1750* (London, 1984), pp. 121–142; Bruce P. Smith, 'English Criminal Justice Administration, 1650–1850: A Historiographic Essay', *Law and History Review*, 25/3 (2007), 593–634.

prerogative in coastal communities for ages past.[106] Increasingly over the course of the century, there emerged a second notion which contended that what smugglers performed was an otherwise faultless form of business complete with its own labours and transaction costs, but one that happened – for arbitrary reasons – to be prohibited by the state. Perhaps most basic and often underlying the above ideas was the notion, thirdly, that smuggling was a vital form of subsistence for coastal communities often visited by considerable economic distress, resulting from decisions about warfare, imperial policies, and monopolies made in Whitehall. Smuggling, in this view, was local economic self-defence in the face of an abusive and arbitrary state. All three notions combined to lend local support to such activities, provided they remained within certain limits.[107]

Many offenders claimed to have no distinct notion that smuggling was a crime at all. Others expressed surprise that smuggling should be a capital offence. Some even had, according to their testimony, "not the least Notion" of any laws against smuggling; others were similarly "ignorant" of what the legal consequences might entail and entirely unaware they "had done any thing amiss by following the bad Practices of Smuggling".[108] After all, it was "so common a Practice, and a Thing so publickly done".[109] One offender claimed that smuggling was "the general Practice of his Neighbours" and so he "ventured among them, and got Money by it, as his Neighbours did."[110] According to these testimonies, smuggling was an occupation like any other: "It was so commonly practiced all over the Country, that he looked upon the bare Act of Smuggling as a Calling, which a Man might exercise himself in without Danger of Life, as well as any other Business".[111] Additionally, many considered smuggling their business, accusing Customs

---

[106] See Philip Payton, Alston Kennerley, Helen Doe (eds), *The Maritime History of Cornwall* (Exeter, 2014). See also John G. Rule, 'The Labouring Miner in Cornwall, c.1740–1870. A Study in Social History' (Diss. University of Warwick, 1971), 332–347.
[107] Andy Wood, *Riot, Rebellion and Popular Politics in Early Modern England* (Basingstoke, 2002); Robert B. Shoemaker, *The London Mob: Violence and Disorder in Eighteenth-Century England* (London, 2004).
[108] Old Bailey Proceedings Online, Ordinary of Newgate's Account, OA17470729 (29 July 1747); OA17480318 (18 March 1748); OA17490426 (26 April 1749). See also OA17480511 (11 May 1748).
[109] Old Bailey Proceedings Online, Ordinary of Newgate's Account, OA17471116 (16 November 1747).
[110] Old Bailey Proceedings Online, Ordinary of Newgate's Account, OA17511023 (23 October 1751).
[111] Old Bailey Proceedings Online, Ordinary of Newgate's Account, OA17511023 (23 October 1751).

men of trying to "rob a man of his property".[112] From Scotland, it was said in 1715 that local people treated the officers "as if they were Thieves".[113] As the smugglers "had ventured their lives for them already", they would "rather lose their lives before they would lose their goods."[114] If many were ignorant of the law, others chose their own, such as when a group of smugglers professed that "they did not care any thing for the law, they would have a law of their own, or else another law".[115] Even outside smuggling communities, this notion was accepted as common sense. One merchant reasonable argued in the 1746 parliamentary hearing that "if the Smuggler finds it his Interest to smuggle, he will do it."[116] In formulating the law, "some Regard should be had [...] to the Passions of Mankind." The monetary profits were too tempting and the smugglers hardly to blame.[117]

This notion was shared by a wide local spectrum. The Duke of Richmond was aware that it was a "great truth" that "the common people of this country have no notion that smugling is a crime".[118] Proceedings at the Old Bailey suggest a similar picture. One Richard Ashcroft entertained "great Hopes of Mercy", because he considered his crimes trivial. The Ordinary of Newgate lamented that these smugglers believed that the crime "was not so heinous in the Sight of God, as the Punishment was severe by the Laws of Men". And not these "unhappy Criminals" alone believed this, "but many well-meaning though unthinking Men labour under this fatal Mistake." In fact, "the common People of England in general fancy that there is nothing in it." They believed what smugglers gained "by their Dexterity" was an "honest Gain, to be enjoyed as the Fruits of their Industry and Labour".[119] Regardless of whether it was "from their habits of life, whether from their connexions with these people, or whether from the fear they have of them", many people actively supported the smugglers.[120] Who exactly these people were is often unclear, as the accounts are usually written by the authorities.

[112] Old Bailey Proceedings Online, t17760911-42.
[113] TNA T1/185, no. 63.
[114] Old Bailey Proceedings Online, t18000528-6.
[115] Old Bailey Proceedings Online, t180000115-89.
[116] JHC 25, p. 109.
[117] Anon., *A Free Apology in Behalf of the Smugglers, so far as their Case affects the Constitution. By an Enemy to all Oppression, whether by Tyranny, or Law* (London, 1749), p. 9.
[118] WSRO, Goodwood 155, H96.
[119] Old Bailey Proceedings Online, Ordinary of Newgate's Account, OA17470729 (29 July 1747). More context for the Ordinary's account in Peter Linebaugh, 'The Ordinary of Newgate and His *Account*', in J. S. Cockburn (ed.), *Crime in England 1550–1800* (London, 1977), pp. 246–269.
[120] Old Bailey Proceedings Online, t18000528-6. Other instances t17880901-138; t17910608-41; t18111030-50.

But even in their eyes, this went beyond individual members of local communities and beyond those actively engaged in smuggling. "The generality of the People on the Coast", it was claimed in 1746, "are better Friends to the Smugglers than to the Custom-house Officers."[121]

Many reports from the outports confirm this impression. Often stopping short of active participation, local communities were frequently instrumental as auxiliaries, lending logistical assistance or protection. Most commonly, these were local fishermen.[122] Given their precarious situation, this was hardly surprising. In the 1770s in Norfolk, they were devoid of "comfortable subsistance", finding employment in the fisheries five months per year, making them "destitute of any employment" for the rest of the time and ultimately rendering them "extremely poor".[123] To aid in smuggling provided an alternative form of subsistence as it resulted in rewards and favourable deals.[124] Such support took the form of either lending direct physical assistance in the loading of goods or by signals and intelligence warning of the approach of Customs men.[125] At times, there was "a perfect Fair at the Waterside" with "an army of people" assembled.[126] Public houses, too, were of particular concern to administrators, as patrons were often found to shelter smugglers or their goods.[127] In other cases, local administrators simply reported vaguely that smugglers received "all the assistance & Encouragement the Country can give them".[128] Occasionally, people assembled in "Tumultuous and Riotous proceedings", often described by Customs men as "mobs".[129]

There was also support from a more elite background. Local gentry did profit from the noticeably cheaper contraband goods to no inconsiderable

---

[121] JHC 25, p. 104. A similar sentiment in NRS CE51/1/5, 16 August 1791: "the whole Inhabitants of the Country are friendly to the Smugglers rather than to the Revenue officers."

[122] 'Third Report', p. 8.

[123] TNA CUST97/20, 10 June 1772.

[124] TNA CUST97/8, 24 June 1734; CUST97/9, 13 August 1735.

[125] JHC 25, p. 104; TNA CUST82/1, 24 September 1718.

[126] TNA CUST59/2, 16 October 1719.

[127] TNA CUST59/5, 13 October 1739, CUST59/72, 19 September 1739; CUST148/12, pp. 327–328. On the social significance of public houses Beat Kümin, *Drinking Matters: Public Houses and Social Exchange in Early Modern Central Europe* (Basingstoke, 2007); Romain Grancher, 'Fishermen Taverns: Public Houses and Maritime Labour in an Early Modern French Fishing Community', *International Journal of Maritime History*, 28 (2016), 671–685.

[128] TNA CUST97/8, 24 June 1734; CUST98/5, 9 June 1716; CUST59/1, 4 March 1718, 18 April 1719; CUST59/2, 16 October 1719; NRS CE51/1/7, 19 July 1802.

[129] TNA CUST59/2, 9 June 1719, 16 October 1719; NRS CE87/1/2, 29 June 1744; CE87/1/6, 30 June 1779; Old Bailey Proceedings Online, t17850511-79.

degree. Even Walpole was said to buy contraband.[130] Local gentry themselves also had grievances vis-à-vis national legislation and the Customs administration. In many areas, for instance, manor lords retained the right to claim wreckages that washed up on their land. Thus there was a continuous stream of legal disputes and violent encounters between Customs men and local lords.[131] This provided ample grounds for opposition to national legislation and the government's administrative arm aiming to enforce such legislation. In the case of Cornwall specifically, such resistance to central legislation could easily mix and blend with the support for smuggling and other local concerns.[132] Finally, local gentry were also reputed to turn a blind eye due to parliamentary interest. In Sussex, John Collier acted as an agent for the Duke of Newcastle in election matters and there is more than one instance where this parliamentary interest seemed to trump revenue concerns.[133] Even Richmond believed that there were those who favoured smuggling "to support their interest in the country".[134] This did not mean that local gentry approved of the practice, but it certainly speaks to a certain toleration on their part.

Some of these ideas also pervaded the ranks of the Customs service. Alongside bloody encounters, there was often a friendly communion between the officers and the smugglers, with some officers admitting to drinking with smugglers "in a friendly manner".[135] It is telling to look at how officers spoke about offenders. Often the attitude was compassionate. Occasionally, Customs men even supported the smugglers' pleas for mercy.[136] Such compassion also came from the magistrates. In 1748, Sir Cecil Bishopp, a local baronet, pleaded with Richmond to show mercy on Thomas Lilywhite, who was "seduced" at the age of seventeen. Richmond was outraged and declined.[137] John Collier, too, frequently recommended

---

[130] TNA T1/18, no. 14, no. 50; PC2/74, pp. 383, 396, 408, 425, 428; T1/105, no. 29; T1/106, no. 60; T1/110, no. 7, no. 38; T1/240, no. 45; Winslow, 'Sussex Smugglers', pp. 147–148.

[131] See, for instance, TNA CUST89/4, 22 April 1763; CUST59/1, 5 January 1716; CUST82/6, 18 May 1750; CUST97/16, 15 August 1750; CUST72/77A, January 1713; CUST97/7, 31 May 1732.

[132] See Cathryn Pearce, *Cornish Wrecking, 1700–1860: Reality and Popular Myth* (Woodbridge, 2010), pp. 145–188.

[133] See, for instance, BL Add. MS 32688, fols 123, 139; Add. MS 32692, fols 83, 93, 102, 372, 415; Add. MS 32703, fols 73, 164, 170; Add. MS 32712, fols 129, 201, 350.

[134] WSRO, Goodwood 155, H96.

[135] Old Bailey Proceedings Online, t17910608-41. See also ESRO, SAY346.

[136] ESRO, SAY2251. The entire exchange in SAY2243–2268. Evidence on this case is also in WSRO, Goodwood 156, G57, G59.

[137] WSRO, Goodwood 155, H83, H96.

mercy.[138] Officers did so simply on the grounds of these men being "miserably poor", "very young" and typically said to be enticed by professional smugglers.[139] In such cases, it could successfully be argued that the men were forced into the practice of smuggling by economic pressures rather than criminal intentions. These were the ones "of the Civiller Sort".[140] In what is another mediation between the national code of the lawmakers and the local moral code, officers sympathised with local views about the relative innocence of smuggling. But such sympathy obviously had limits.

"No officer is so far lost", or: Collusion

Before discussing these, it is necessary to look at the most prominent area of officers' mediation between the "two concepts of order". In September 1738, senior staff at Weymouth reported that with regard to instructions received relative to the seizing of smuggling vessels along with the smuggled goods, they persuaded themselves that "no officer belonging to this Port is so far lost as thus glaringly presume to disobey the Laws".[141] Of all evaluations of local staff, this was perhaps the most fair and realistic one. It acknowledges the officers to be somewhat lost vis-à-vis their instructions, but not so far as to glaringly disobey them. Yet the Board was concerned. It had become necessary to issue explicit instructions to seize smuggling vessels – instead of the goods only – because it was common practice for Customs men not to do so.[142] Presumably, this was because prosecutions were troublesome. And yet, seizing only part of a smuggling run, or leaving the carts, horses, or vessels untroubled, was part of a practice whereby the Customs men – for their own safety, profit, or convenience – struck a deal with the smugglers. The Board called this collusion.

"By collusion is meant", according to the *Preventive Officer's Pocket-Book* of 1765, "a deceitful contract or agreement between two or more [...] covered in the shew of honesty."[143] Such contracts could be of different types: it could be an agreement to seize only part of a smuggling run in return for a reward to the officer; it could also mean bringing a false action against an offender, allowing him to conduct his illegal business under the cloak of a doomed and fabricated legal action; or it could mean a private composition

---

[138] BL Add. MS 23703, fol. 170; Winslow, 'Sussex Smugglers', p. 141; Saville, *Letters*, pp. xxxviii–xl.
[139] TNA T1/61, no. 2; T1/72, no. 43; T1/80, no. 125; T1/93, no. 36; T1/97, no. 100; T1/189, no. 42; T1/190, no. 21, no. 30; CUST97/2, 9 July 1708; CUST97/9, 21 July 1735; CUST148/12, p. 285.
[140] BL Add. MS 32711, fols 90, 167.
[141] TNA CUST59/5, 4 September 1738.
[142] TNA CUST59/71, 26 March 1737, 16 June 1737; CUST59/73, 4 September 1744.
[143] Hunter, *Pocket-Book*, p. 209.

to the benefit of officer and offender, but to the loss of the Crown. Either way, it typically involved "partnerships or private Arguments" between either a number of officers or between the officers and the smugglers.[144] Such agreements could permeate an entire port establishment.[145] There was often a "whole Business of Seizures, clandestine Compositions, Connivances, and other Practices". More importantly, "from the Infirmity of Human Nature, it is impossible to suppose that such Collusions can be totally prevented".[146] Indeed, they were notoriously difficult to police. Rather helplessly, the Board asked for "true and just" accounts of any seizure. Failure to do so prompted immediate dismissal, whereas the discovering of such failure in another officer "will be esteemed good service and the commissioners will give them suitable rewards for so doing."[147] As the pocket-book summarised it: "THE LAW ABHORS COLLUSION."[148]

Part of the motivation was greed. "The greatest part of the country", a report suggested, "are all so Comely lined together in the smuggling trade that it will be impossible to prove the Collusion on them [the officers]."[149] The frustration was widely shared among the outports. "Notwithstanding our utmost endeavours", one collector complained, it was impossible to get proof of the officers' "remissness", because it was carried on "by a combination betwixt" the smugglers and the officers that made it impossible to presume either would speak up. It was also "next to an impossibility to get it from any other, being done so secretly and the name of an informer so odious here".[150] The situation being so circumstanced against easy discovery of such practices by the Board or by superior port officials (who were often just as guilty), it is not surprising that all the evidence suggests that collusion was widespread in the regions and ports across England, Wales and Scotland.[151] The officers guilty of such connivance knew very well "how far the benefit of collusive practices might attain beneficial advantages".[152]

But money was not the only factor. In many instances, it was impossible for individual officers to seize a whole smuggling run, instead of only a

---

[144] TNA CUST29/2, 21 May 1740.
[145] Ziegler, 'Customs Officers and Local Communities'.
[146] 'Third Report', p. 13.
[147] TNA CUST59/71, 26 March 1737.
[148] Hunter, *Pocket-Book*, p. 209.
[149] TNA CUST59/2, 9 June 1719.
[150] TNA CUST82/8, 24 December 1756.
[151] NRS CE51/1/5, 3 October 1791; TNA CUST31/1, 25 May 1714; CUST29/2, 21 May 1714; CUST97/10, 10 March 1738, 4 April 1738; CUST97/4, 8 April 1723; CUST82/12, 24 May 1775; CUST62/59, 30 August 1719; CUST97/25, 28 May 1783; CUST97/10, 30 September 1736.
[152] TNA CUST97/25, 30 October 1784.

part. Considering the force they often met with, protestations such as the following ring true: "If there is a Man on Earth," one riding officer accused of collusion protested, "who can say that I have in any instance whatever been in the habit of Collusion with Smugglers, I do not fear him, relying on my own Integrity".[153] What these protestations of innocence cloak, however, are the negotiations on the ground that resulted in collusion, but also reveal the motivations and pressures involved. A 1786 incident in Wiltshire illustrates these. On 25 December, officers seized a quantity of brandy tubs. Soon after, a company of about thirty smugglers appeared, demanding the brandy. The parties started threatening each other and soon a large group of local residents assembled. Violence hung in the air. It was then that one Richard Symonds, a local farmer, entreated both parties to settle the conflict without violence. To the outnumbered officers, it was perfectly clear they could not take all the tubs, whereas Symonds pleaded with the smugglers to give up part of the brandy. "Gentlemen, here will be rioting", he suggested, so "you had better agree; you cannot blame the officers, they are in the king's business." Consequently, an agreement was struck, by which the smugglers were to give up forty tubs and all "agreed that nothing should be said of the matter, if forty were given". The court, in reviewing this scene, was interested in why this deal was struck and whether it was to the benefit of James Hiscot, one of the officers involved:

> You took away your forty tubs? – Yes.
> By agreement? – Yes.
> How came you to compound? – *We could not get the whole.*
> Did you make a bargain with these smugglers to take forty, and that they should have the rest? – *They forced us to do it.*
> So that you thought if you could not make a seizure according to your duty, the next best thing was to make a bargain with the smugglers? – *I did the best I could.*

The ambiguity here was at the heart of collusion. Hiscot's benefit in the transaction could have been money, but it was, in this case, his own safety. When asked why he agreed to it, he repeated that it would have been impossible to force a delivery of all tubs and claimed he "was liable to have my house pulled about my ears" if he refused. After the incident, he left the area, for he did not "dare live in the place with any safety". When questioned, he even admitted to having seen some of the offenders after the incident, but "did not dare to touch them" and "did not dare meddle with them". He was wise not to: William England, the only one of the smugglers to be caught, was

---

[153] TNA CUST97/27, 01 March 1788.

professed not guilty at the Old Bailey on the testimony of his neighbours, family, and friends. This included Richard Symonds who, perhaps like any wise man of the community, aimed to defend both the innocence of England, his neighbour, and the officers, "whom I knew very well". [154]

Collusion was a form of negligence, an offence. Yet looking closer at the negotiations involved, it transpires that unlike outright corruption, collusion represented a locally negotiated meeting point of the two concepts of order, of abstract legal ideas and local moral codes. As such, it was a compromise that conformed to what was locally considered fair. This was "not necessarily amoral".[155] Collusion was frequently the best that officers could possibly do when faced with mediating between government ideals and local sentiments.

Temporary Instruments of Government

Faced with such ambiguity, authorities were forced to enlist private interest in the enforcement of authority. Given the entanglements of locally recruited officers, it was those with no ties that were the best enforcers. Money and pardons alone were able to transcend local cohesion, and the most effective way of breaking community influence was from *within*. Consequently, the government relied on profiteers, racketeers, social outsiders, turncoats, snitches, and informers. "Throughout the eighteenth century, the state depended on private self-interest as its cardinal means of exerting control."[156] In the context of coastal policing, this happened in three main ways. As in the mid-seventeenth century, authorities enlisted outsiders into the service by way of monetary incentives. Secondly, authorities enlisted smugglers into the revenue service. Like officers turning to smuggling, authorities saw the value of those "personally schooled in deviant practices" to combat those practices.[157] Authorities thereby purposefully facilitated the permeability of the line between the official and the criminal. They also created, thirdly, a grey area between these extremes by encouraging informers to denounce local deviances. Such use of "temporary instruments of government" contradicts the government's adversarial

---

[154] Old Bailey Proceedings Online, t17881210-93.
[155] Muskett, 'English Smuggling', p. 142.
[156] Rock, 'Law, Order, and Power', p. 201. See also Gerald Howson, *Thief-Taker General: The Rise and Fall of Jonathan Wild* (London, 1970); Douglas Hay, Francis Snyder (eds), *Policing and Prosecution in Britain 1750–1850* (Oxford, 1989).
[157] Rock, 'Law, Order, and Power', p. 213.

rhetoric as empty and helpless.[158] It also underlines that despite all attempts at bureaucratisation, it was the traditional means of private and community policing that were paramount in the enforcement of authority in the coastal regions. Successful enforcement of authority still had to pursue ways that factored in a social element.

Private Enforcement
Throughout the eighteenth century, there is less evidence of private individuals being awarded contracts or commissions to enforce Customs regulations than during Carter's time. But these people did still exist. As none of them would be kept on any establishment or regular pay list, they typically only appear in petitions to the Treasury or the Customs. The latter in particular appears to have been more reluctant to award such commissions. Petitions of one Mr. Knox for a better system of prevention in Ireland were repeatedly rejected by the Board and it was only on the intervention of the Treasury that Knox was hired. But as with other such men, his activity for the Customs remained temporary.[159] Authorities effectively hoped that these men would pay themselves via seizures. Unfortunately, this seldom worked. The petition of John Edwards detailed his "severall services" as well as his "diligence and activeness", but contrasted such efforts with the "discouragements and oppression" he had faced.[160] At other times, things met with success for both parties. As the running of victuals into Scotland's south-west, particularly from Ireland, constituted a major problem especially before the Union, certain men of "honour and interest" had been appointed at the time and executed the brief with "fidelity and diligence" and, one must assume, to their benefit.[161]

If the Board was reluctant to pursue such a course, the Treasury was decidedly less so, especially during the Walpole years. During his premiership, the Treasury handed out a large and increasing number of commissions and funds to private persons. The Customs Board had no choice but to comply. From 1721 to 1724, one John Rogers was, for instance, empowered to apprehend and seize smugglers in Kent and Sussex and was ordered by the Treasury to be given all due "encouragement" by both the Customs and civil magistrates. The Board was reluctant every time the matter of Roger's bills – who was, after all, "no Officer of this Revenue" – was being

---
[158] Ibid.
[159] TNA T1/87, no. 79; T14/8, pp. 398, 426; NRS CE87/1/5, 30 August 1774, 30 December 1774.
[160] TNA T1/18, no. 3.
[161] TNA T1/193, no. 96; T1/127, no. 2; T1/248, no. 38.

discussed, whereas the Treasury was always supportive of the payments.[162] The Board's reluctance is understandable: Walpole was using a statute from the reign of Charles II to bypass the Customs Board in handing out these commissions.[163] Walpole seemingly trusted in the "Integrity and Ability" of such men to seize contraband. In some cases, the initiative even came from certain merchant communities, such as the East India Company.[164] Whether such men were honest contractors is hard to decide and it must have been equally hard to distinguish for administrators at the time. One Richard Bonnell had promised the "immediate Recovery" of £100,000 in Customs and an annual increase of the revenue to the same amount.[165] Shortly thereafter, however, he found himself "considerably a loser" with his attempts to dive "into the depth of this Knavery" and asked for compensation. He ultimately received £200 on the express command of the Treasury, despite admitting to decidedly dodgy practices such as accepting "of several Gratuities from the Runners".[166]

Perhaps less problematic in terms of the individuals involved and increasingly common from the mid-1720s onwards was the practice to hand out seizure commissions to shipowners. Such contracts stipulated that such vessels were legally empowered to make seizures according to Customs legislation and were to be rewarded from successful prosecutions.[167] Structurally, this was similar to the cruisers and sloops on the Customs establishment, and perhaps this was the starting point of the gradually increasing practice of waterguard commissions. This contract model in the guarding of the coastal waters was still in evidence, although much criticized, by the 1780s. The idea was, again, that a considerable part of day-to-day expenses was outsourced to private contractors, whereas the Crown was to receive its share and benefit from successful seizures. Unfortunately, such a mode of conduct was often detrimental to the finances of the contractors and it also left, as many recognised, just as many loopholes for collusion as any regular establishment in the Customs.[168] Imperfect and susceptible to collusion as the enlisting private persons into the Customs by way of monetary incentives was, such practices remain in evidence throughout the rest of the eighteenth century.[169]

[162] TNA T11/18, pp. 2–7, 22–23, 78–84, 223, 465.
[163] TNA T11/18, p. 100. The relevant statute was 14 Charles II, ch. 18.
[164] TNA T11/18, pp. 163–164.
[165] CUL, Ch(H), Political Papers, 41, nos 21, 39.
[166] TNA T11/18, p. 183.
[167] TNA T11/18, pp. 228–230; T11/19, p. 9.
[168] TNA CUST97/25, 30 October 1784; *Eighteenth Century Documents*, pp. 250–256.
[169] TNA CUST82/3, 7 February 1740; CUST82/6, 27 July 1750, 4 January 1751; CUST97/20, 24 September 1770.

The Permeability of the Line

In March 1770, Robert Baker, the collector at the port of Great Yarmouth in Norfolk, reported to London that smuggling was on the rise and his officers' attempts were frequently frustrated by illegal practices. "These circumstances induced the Collector to think that it will be necessary for the suppression of those fraudulent practices, to have a person employed that is conversant in them and well acquainted with all their artifices." As it happened, he knew someone who was willing to enter a contract with the Customs. The man was not only a smuggler, but a good one, too, as he had so far escaped conviction.[170]

The reasoning was clearly that someone "conversant" in the practices of the smugglers was best placed to combat and prevent them. Paradoxical as such a strategy may seem, it was a well-rehearsed tactic in eighteenth-century law enforcement.[171] The "contingencies of social control", as Paul Rock has observed, "forced the state to recruit the deviant as its own agent. [...] Few but those personally schooled in deviant practices were able to acquire the expertise of a competent enforcement agent." This, as Rock goes on, resulted in these men exercising "equivocal roles" in enforcement, however.[172] Essentially, it meant accepting "Informations of the worst of Crimes, from the worst of Criminals".[173] But the Board was also aware that relying on its own officers was, at times, just as ambiguous, because the transition from official to criminal was easy, even for superior staff.[174] Given the odds of enforcing national legislation via their own officeholders and the resistance that permeated local communities and officers alike, therefore, enlisting smugglers was as sure a means of obtaining results as relying on Customs officers frequently held back by social ties.

Accepting smugglers into the revenue service was an extreme solution, however, and there were several preliminary stages to such measures. Under Walpole in particular, there was a notable rise in official

---

[170] TNA, CUST97/20, 1 March 1770.
[171] E.P. Thompson, *Whigs and Hunters: The Origin of the Black Act* (London, 1975), p. 218; Howson, *Thief-Taker General*; Ruth Paley, 'Thief-Takers in London in the Age of the McDaniel Gang, c.1745–1754', in Douglas Hay, Francis Snyder (eds), *Policing and Prosecution in Britain 1750–1850* (Oxford, 1989), pp. 301–342; Ruth Paley, '"An Imperfect, Inadequate and Wretched System"? Policing London before Peel', *Criminal Justice History*, 10 (1989), 95–130. See also F. F. Nicholls, *Honest Thieves. The Violent Heyday of English Smuggling* (London, 1973), p. 59; Muskett, 'English Smuggling', pp. 169–176.
[172] Rock, 'Law, Order, and Power', p. 213.
[173] See Daniel Defoe, *The True and Genuine Account of the Life and Actions of the Late Jonathan Wild* (London, 1725), p. 17.
[174] TNA CUST89/4, December 1773; CUST59/5, 4 September 1738; Ziegler, 'Customs Officers and Local Communities'.

compositions, whereby merchants caught at defrauding the revenue were allowed to pay a fine before their case went to court.[175] A second strategy was to offer pardons in exchange for information on logistics and accomplices. The Smuggling Acts of 1736 and 1746 explicitly incorporated such a strategy. Parliamentary committees and proceedings at the Old Bailey, in particular, relied, to no small extent, on the expertise obtained from former smugglers, especially when it came to their logistics.[176] The committees, however, also relied on the offenders in the recurring question as to what legal remedies were best suited to combat the smuggling trade. Unlike in the business of compositions, what stood out as immediate gains for the authorities was the knowledge of the smugglers, relating either to a specific crime or the criminal business as a whole. To break the silence cloaking a particular smuggling gang, an insider was best suited to inform.[177]

The most drastic form was to enlist the smuggler in preventive tasks. On recommending a former smuggler for a post in the preventive guard on the Cumbria coast, the Whitehaven collector remarked that "it will be for the service of the revenue and a greater discouragement to the smugglers than anything they hitherto met with."[178] The person in question was "well acquainted with all their [the smugglers'] Haunts and byplaces".[179] In such cases, the Board was willing to let the acquired insider knowledge trump the risks involved in such a strategy.[180] The case of Richard Upton is particularly instructive. During the 1680s, Upton, originally of Plymouth, was an informer on the local smuggling trade and its entanglement with the Customs service. Yet he had himself been an accomplished protagonist in the smuggling trade, admitting having "constantly Run all such goods from time to time without Entry or Payment of Customs" and that he "did what he pleased" in the illicit trade.[181] What marked him out was his readiness to report on the crimes of others. Eventually, he was taken into service, as he was "a known and approved Seaman and sober Person" and a "Person extreemly well qualified".[182] Upton was in this position well into the next century, cruising the coast of Cornwall on a smack stationed at Falmouth

---

[175] TNA T11/18–22, *passim*.
[176] *The Report of the Committee appointed to inquire into the Frauds and Abuses in the Customs*; JHC 25, pp. 101–110. See also CUST97/9, 12 May 1736, 7 June 1736; CUST82/3, 7 April 1736; CUST82/2, 18 January 1732.
[177] See, for instance, TNA CUST82/3, 7 April 1736.
[178] TNA CUST82/6, 27 July 1750.
[179] TNA CUST82/6, 27 July 1750, 4 January 1751.
[180] TNA T161/, no. 33.
[181] TNA T64/140, fols 86, 89.
[182] TNA T64/140, fol. 80.

against smuggling and protecting the local fisheries against French privateers.[183] The success of his service was such that inhabitants from Penzance and Mounts Bay petitioned for his continued service.[184] In the repeated reviews of his contract, there was never any suggestion of foul play and he was continued until at least 1704; by 1716, he was collector at St Ives.[185]

A more ambiguous case is Gabriel Tomkins. He is illustrative of the potential benefits but also the pitfalls of this strategy. Tomkins was a member of a smuggling gang at Mayfield in the early 1720s.[186] In 1722, he was suspected to be involved in the murder of Gerard Reeves, a Customs man, and later sentenced to transportation for his involvement in a smuggling run.[187] He came back to England illegally and continued his smuggling career before being caught. He later gained a pardon for giving evidence to John Cope's smuggling inquiry in 1733.[188] He was then commissioned to perform government service, especially the apprehension of smugglers, and it was in this role that he was concerned in the murder of a contraband trader.[189] This, however, did not cut short his career in the Customs either. In 1737, he appears as a supervisor of riding officers at Dartford.[190] In that year, the Treasury also received information that Tomkins was supplementing his income with smuggling activities. In fact, there was "no dispute" amongst the smugglers that Tomkins had been concerned in running contraband for nearly three years. He was "allways, as most people know, a villain when a Smugler and likewise Officer".[191] He was also involved in highway robbery. Around 1741, he was in contact with the notorious Hawkhurst gang. Eventually, in 1750, he was hanged at Hockcliffe for highway robbery.[192] Perhaps disillusioned by cases such as these, the Board issued an order in August 1788, that in future admissions to a Customs post, "enquiry is to be made of the course of Life he has followed and whether he has been known or suspected to be concerned in Smugling, or to have obstructed any Officer

---

[183] TNA T11/14, pp. 203, 298, 320; T1/80, no. 106; T1/81, no. 25; T1/87, no. 61; T1/90, no. 3, no. 17, no. 51.
[184] TNA T1/87, no. 146.
[185] Stephens, *Customs Service*, p. 26.
[186] TNA T11/18, p. 4.
[187] ESRO SAY252–259, in particular SAY256; TNA T11/18, pp. 359–360.
[188] *The Report of the Committee appointed to inquire into the Frauds and Abuses in the Customs*, p. 610. See also his petition in SP36/30/402, fol. 403.
[189] TNA T11/21, p. 199; ESRO, SAY339; TNA CUST148/12, pp. 57–68, p. 161; CUST148/12, p. 161; CUST41/42.
[190] Nicholls, *Honest Thieves*, p. 59; TNA T11/22, p. 137.
[191] Cited after Nicholls, *Honest Thieves*, p. 59.
[192] Muskett, 'English Smuggling', pp. 171, 388; TNA CUST59/73, 1 September 1746.

in the execution of his duty."[193] Before, however, the Board was comfortable blurring the line between official and criminal to the higher purpose of enhanced enforcement.

"A Society of Creeps and Informers"

Enforcement was also at the heart of common informing. As Thompson has noted: "In the state papers we seem to meet a society of creeps and informers".[194] And Goldie has remarked that "the realization of any political, religious, or moral program in early modern England could scarcely be achieved without informers."[195] For the context of smuggling, moreover, Muskett found that "the importance of the informant to the business of law enforcement is hard to exaggerate."[196] Based on common law, informing was indeed a formidable if controversial measure of law enforcement.[197] Lured by rewards, citizens were encouraged to enforce statutes irrelevant to their personal lives. As such people could more easily break local social cohesion than any official could ever hope to, this was seen as perhaps the most promising measure to enforce authority in areas where it could not otherwise be achieved. There was an entirely warranted fear, however, that such transfer of sovereign authority to greedy individuals was "the

---

[193] TNA CUST29/5, 19 August 1788.
[194] Edward P. Thompson, 'The Crime of Anonymity', in Douglas Hay, Peter Linebaugh, John G. Rule, E.P. Thompson, Cal Winslow (eds), *Albion's Fatal Tree: Crime and Society in Eighteenth-Century England* (New York, 1975), pp. 255–344, at p. 272.
[195] Mark Goldie, 'The Hilton Gang and the Purge of London in the 1680s', in Howard Nenner (ed.), *Politics and the Political Imagination in Later Stuart Britain: Essays Presented to Lois Green Schwoerer* (New York, 1997), pp. 43–73, at p. 67.
[196] Muskett, 'English Smuggling', p. 27.
[197] Geoffrey Elton, 'Informing for Profit: A Sidelight on Tudor Methods of Law-Enforcement', *The Cambridge Historical Journal*, 11 (1954), 149–167; Maurice Beresford, 'The Common Informer, the Penal Statutes and Economic Regulation', *The Economic History Review*, 10 (1957), 221–238; D. R. Lidington, 'Parliament and the Enforcement of the Penal Statutes: the History of the Act "In Restraint of Common Informers" (18 Eliz. I ch. 5)', *Parliamentary History*, 8 (1989), 309–328; Joseph A. Limprecht, 'Common Informers and Law Enforcement in England, 1603–1640' (Diss. Berkeley, 1975); Joanna Innes, 'The Protestant Carpenter – William Payne of Bell Yard (c.1718–82): the Life and Times of a London Informing Constable', in Joanna Innes, *Inferior Politics: Social Problems and Social Politics in Eighteenth-Century Britain* (Oxford, 2009), pp. 279–341; Margaret Gay Davies, *The Enforcement of English Apprenticeship: A Study in Applied Mercantilism* (Cambridge/Mass., 1956); Jessica Warner, Frank Ivis, 'Informers and Their Social Networks in Eighteenth-Century London: A Comparison of Two Communities', *Social Science History*, 25 (2001), 563–587.

Corruption of the Body Politique".[198] It was as dangerous to "commit the Sword of Justice" to "any Subject", Edward Coke had argued.[199] Yet "to make lawes and not enforce them", Nicholas Bacon had maintained, "is to breede a contempt of lawes".[200]

As it stood, penal statutes could hardly be enforced without informers, especially where such laws were held in contempt by local society. At the same time, gains of authority thereby made could easily be tarnished by a loss of sovereignty. Such ambiguity was mirrored on the side of the subjects who, individually, could see much gain in the act of informing, but who were judged as traitors to their social cosmos. As informing was understood to be a conversion from the moral code of the community – especially in the context of socially accepted crimes – to the logic of national legal codes, local sentiment was thoroughly against the informer. "Informers, they ought to be hanged. It is no sin to kill them", a mob in Chatham proclaimed in 1751.[201] This was no idle threat.[202]

Given that smuggling was popular and accepted, and given the flaws in enforcement that the Customs administration faced, informing became one of the most formidable means of alternative enforcement of Customs regulations. This was despite the much-used adversarial rhetoric.[203] The depiction of enforcement as a clash between the official and the criminal was in fact heavily contradicted by the creation of a grey zone in which

---

[198] Anon., *The Character of an Informer Wherein his Mischievous nature, and Leud Practises are Detected* (s.l., 1675), p. 1. See also Edward Stephens, *Phinehas, or, the Common Duty of All Men, and the Special Duty of Magistrates, to be Zealous and Active in the Execution of Laws Against Scandalous Sins and Debauchers: And of That in Particular Against prophane Cursing and Swearing* (London, 1695); Anon., Philagathus, *The Informer's Doom: Or, an Amazing and Seasonable Letter from Utopia, Directed from the Man on the Moon* (London, 1683); Anon., *The Informer's Looking-Glass, in Which he may see himself while he is Maliciously Prosecuting Dissenting Protestants* (s.l., 1682); Anon., *A Rebuke to the Informers: With a Plea for the Ministers of the Gospels, Called Nonconformists, and their Meetings* (London, 1675).

[199] *The Reports of Sir Edward Coke, late Lord Chief Justice of England of Divers Resolutions and Judgements given upon solemn Arguments, and with great Deliberation* [...]. (2nd ed. London, 1680), p. 480. From the legal literature see J. Randy Beck, 'The False Claims Act and the English Eradication of Qui Tam Legislation', *North Carolina Law Review*, 78 (2000), 539–642; Leon Radzinowicz, *A History of English Criminal Law and its Administration from 1750*, vol. 2: *The Clash between Private Initiative and Public Interest in the Enforcement of the Law* (London, 1956).

[200] Cit. Lidington, 'Parliament', p. 326.

[201] Cit. Winslow, 'Sussex Smugglers', p. 145.

[202] Jessica Warner, Frank Ivis, '"Damn You, You Informing Bitch". Vox Populi and the Unmaking of the Gin Act of 1736', *Journal of Social History*, 33 (1999), 299–330.

[203] Ziegler, 'Customs Officers and Local Communities'.

the informer operated. A representative neither of the law properly, nor an agent of his own community, the informer was a shadow creature, operating exclusively for his own cause. Appreciating this, as well as the extent to which authorities relied on this particular social figure of law enforcement, is key to understanding the dynamics of law enforcement in the context of coastal policing.

Contrary to recent depictions, informing was systematically used in the Customs in the eighteenth century. In August 1711, collectors received instructions that for prosecutions, notice should always be given on what "Personal Informations" such seizures were based. This was meant to increase the chance of success in court but was also done with a view to rewards for such informers.[204] Collectors were also instructed to advise preventive officers that they were to "give all reasonable encouragement to any Person who shall Discover" smuggling or fraud. Such encouragement should amount to "no less than one third of the Officers share of the appraised sale of the forfeiture". Significantly, the Board was aware that giving such information would provide difficulties for the informers, which is why it instructed each officer "to be faithful to his trust in concealing the name of his Informer".[205]

Both provisions were important: informations were much more likely if informers could hope to remain anonymous for as long as possible, so as not to come under attack in their local community. Similarly, speedy rewards were considered the main incentive for such informers to come forward and their importance was repeatedly stressed. Unfortunately, it seems to have been common practice for such rewards to be slow or entirely withheld. A parliamentary committee commented in March 1784 that rewards should be paid "within a limited Time" and that "the Deductions and Delays attending the present System, are great Discouragements" to the informers.[206] Others thought, too, that measures such as these were "of more Consequence than at first Sight it may appear". It was important to a system such as this to secure the informer his or her fair share of the reward with all due speed and order.[207]

To gain a better understanding of the local mechanics of informing, it is instructive to differentiate between types of informers. Based on the

---

[204] TNA CUST98/1, 4 August 1711; CUST97/74a, 4 August 1711.
[205] TNA CUST59/1, 20 November 1717; CUST73/62, 20 November 1717; CUST97/74a, 20 November 1717; CUST98/1, 20 November 1717. See also TNA CUST29/1, 'Informations and Informers'. The giving away of an informer's identity was punished, see CUST82/1, 23 June 1718.
[206] 'Third Report', pp. 12–13.
[207] *Eighteenth Century Documents*, p. 293.

evidence, one can distinguish informing by the keen informant, by the anonymous whistle-blower, by the knowledgeable enforcer, by the profiteering sneak, and by the rueful turncoat.

Throughout the outport letters, we find local people sending informations to the port officials or directly to cruiser captains and riding officers. The aim of informing in this manner – typically by nameable applicants – was to become eligible for rewards in seizure cases. This was the most straightforward way of informing, as it closely followed established Customs procedure and was in line with what the Board intended. It was keen to have such informations followed up and, if successful, to have informants duly rewarded.[208] In a second type, often directly to the Board, the informers were anonymous. This was more problematic to handle, because it often entailed the denouncing of particular officers for negligence and corruption. Such accusations could be malicious and were usually carefully checked by investigations conducted by superior outport officials. The Board often rightly suspected that such informations were intended to discredit particularly vigilant officers.[209] Anonymous informations were also used by smugglers in a similarly malicious way, namely, to lure the officers away from the area of a planned smuggling run. Here, too, careful circumspection was required to distinguish the malign informer from the keen informant of the first type. The Board issued specific orders for preventive officers not to go and "scour the Country" after every information "in quest of Seizures upon the bare rumour" and without first checking their reliability.[210] Valuable as the identification of a negligent officer by informers may seem, the Board was advised to treat such informations with caution. Outport officials, in particular, resented such interference in the running of their district. "It is with much concern", the Whitehaven collector wrote in 1746, that "we reflect on the great and unnecessary trouble given your honours by such dark and malicious anonymous writers".[211]

There was, thirdly, a class of informer who, rather than claiming to be instrumental in a seizure and thus due a reward, were intent on obtaining lasting favours from the Board. Their informations accordingly often read like petitions. These men either claimed to have performed services for the revenue or promised to do so because of a particular skill or knowledge.

---

[208] TNA CUST59/9, 29 September 1756; CUST97/5, 28 April 1727; CUST64/6, 29 October 1766; CUST59/71, 16 March 1738; CUST97/20, 24 September 1770.
[209] TNA CUST82/1, 23 June 1718; CUST97/11, 25 November 1740, 29 November 1740, 27 June 1741; CUST97/5, 12 October 1725, 26 August 1726, 17 February 1726; CUST82/3, 3 August 1736; NRS CE87/1/6, 14 February 1778.
[210] NRS CE87/1/7, 4 May 1785; TNA CUST29/1, "Informations and Informers"; CUST82/3, 7 February 1740.
[211] TNA CUST82/5, 21 May 1746.

Joseph Coyn, of Bowness, promised to be able to make ample seizures if provided with a commission by the Board and even produced a "scheme for suppressing without doubt to a very large degree if not totally the smuggling trade".[212] The Board was always happy to receive and peruse such proposals and sometimes, if not always, willing to engage the informer on a contract or trial basis.[213] A similar case is that of John Stainton of Workington, who provided informations to the preventive officers over the course of several years and repeatedly petitioned to be employed by the Board.[214] He received express praise by several outport officials for his skill, his "zeal", and his "good Intention".[215] The Board's minutes provide ample evidence of similar cases in which the helpful informant who was able to paint himself as a knowledgeable enforcer was indeed taken on as a regular officer.[216] Frequently, such informers had a more or less direct background in smuggling, as Stainton did.

A fourth type of informer was the sneak. Often privy to underworld dealings himself, and almost always of a disreputable character, he was of particular value to the authorities due to his easy access to criminal information. A good example is Thomas Pettet. In an often hardly intelligible prose strongly reminiscent of his French mother tongue, he was a regular informer of John Collier's in the 1730s and 40s. We know little of his background. His activity, however, consisted of snooping about the Sussex smuggling haunts in search of information. Sometimes, he simply provided the movements of certain gangs; at other times, he wrote descriptions and even witness accounts. Several times, he was ready – on Collier's instructions – to testify against individual smugglers in court. In all his letters, Pettet was constantly asking for money.[217] And he was also constantly reminding Collier that his service brought him into personal danger of being attacked, even killed, by the smugglers. "I meay louck to be mourdeared", he wrote, "I am threpned of my life", and: "theay will mack a hole for the Soun to shine through me".[218] Pettet was valuable for Collier and, by extension, for the Board. Only in terms of his appearance in court, he was difficult. He needed money for new clothes, he insisted, "before I

---

[212] TNA CUST82/6, 4 January 1751.
[213] TNA CUST97/13, 24 January 1744, 23 February 1744, 27 March 1745; CUST59/1, 5 October 1717; CUST97/20, 24 September 1770.
[214] TNA CUST82/3, 7 February 1740.
[215] TNA CUST82/6, 27 July 1750, 4 August 1750. On Stainton see Frances Wilkins, *The Isle of Man in Smuggling History* (Kidderminster, 1992), pp. 92–98.
[216] TNA CUST29/1, "Informations and Informers".
[217] CUST148/12, pp. 5, 9, 13, 45, 55, 63, 73, 107; ESRO, SAY286.
[218] TNA CUST148/12, pp. 9, 111–112.

shall befitting to coum to the sises [Assizes] for i culd apeare as Genteale as poussable for it is Best for an Evidence to apeare cleane and gentele".[219] This was a clever ruse. He knew, as did Collier, that people of mean character were little use in court. The "Bad Character of the Informer" was one of the main obstacles to the successful conviction of offenders at the Assizes.[220] It speaks to the mutually beneficial nature of this particular relationship, however, that Pettet continued his services for Collier for several years.

A similar symbiosis can also be observed with regard to the fifth type of informer, that is the turncoat. Next to former smugglers aiming to be employed in the revenue service, many of them decided to turn informer. For most, the immediate benefit was not monetary gain, but the securing of a pardon for past offences. Typically, therefore, it was against their own associates that such men informed. Matthew Jenkins, a notorious Norfolk smuggler, was convinced to give evidence on his gang in September 1736 and received protection by the Customs administration accordingly.[221] Earlier that year, the collector at Great Yarmouth had reported about similar prisoners at Norwich Gaol who were "very inclined to do all the Service" they can and were "very hearty in giving evidence". One of the men was so familiar with the smugglers that "no one is better acquainted with their Practices than he is".[222] The only trouble was to protect the witnesses "from being spirited away by the smugglers", thereby "to Stop the Mouths of the Kings Evidence".[223] In a similar vein, two known smugglers applied to the collector in November 1769 to have the process against them stayed in exchange for information. They would, they proclaimed, "for the future be always ready and willing to make any further Discoveries in their Power for the Benefit of the Revenue". As these men were poor fishing men from Cromer, the proposal was accepted and we find the same men again in the role of informers the year after.[224] "We believe they may depended on", the collector concluded.[225]

---

[219] TNA CUST148/12, p. 107. Similar in ESRO, SAY286.
[220] TNA CUST59/71, 16 March 1738. See also CUST82/2, 6 September 1732; CUST148/12, pp. 67–68.
[221] TNA CUST97/10, 30 September 1736, 9 February 1736, 14 March 1737. See for an application by a former smuggler turned informer for a Customs post CUST148/12, p. 145.
[222] TNA CUST97/9, 12 May 1736.
[223] TNA CUST97/9, 12 May 1736, 7 June 1736.
[224] TNA CUST97/20, 7 November 1769, 11 November 1769, 1 December 1769, 4 December 1769, 24 September 1770.
[225] TNA CUST97/20, 27 September 1770.

Such informing for the revenue came at a price. Informers were attacked, sometimes physically, and therefore needed protection. To be able to receive future informations, but also in order to successfully proceed at court, authorities needed to make sure that informers were protected. Pettet's desperate pleas for protection are as indicative of this as the concern that the smugglers could succeed at stopping "the Mouths of the King's Evidence."

After an information by two former smugglers at Whitehaven, they complained that no one in the town was now willing to employ them. Informing had made them social outcasts.[226] The name of an informer was "so odious", that it was easy to discredit them socially. [227] As social credit was also at the heart of court business, this was not only a matter for the informers, but also pertained to the chances of success at the Assizes. "Not only the Relations and Friends of the Persons in Gaol" the Whitehaven collector wrote in 1732, "but also the encouragers of the smuggling trade" were now "very industrious in lessening the reputations of the said informers".[228] Frequently, this extended beyond the mere threat of violence. At Annan, one William Irvine was "upbraided and abused [...] before a number of People for giving an information as to smuggled goods". He, as well as another informer were called "Informers and Villains to their Country for pursuing such practices."[229] Other informers feared that their life was under threat.[230] Others again were mobbed, abused, and beaten in public by local people involved with the illicit business.[231]

The importance of the informer to coastal enforcement can hardly be exaggerated. To obtain knowledge of the logistics, the whereabouts of individual gangs, of the ships and cargoes, as well as descriptions of individual men, the Customs could not do without them. For the officers, mistrusted as they were as Crown officials and locally entangled as they were as members of the social communities, such information was either too difficult to obtain or too dangerous to pass on. Similarly, because the Crown required reliable evidence for prosecutions, it needed the socially knowledgeable local men to come forward. For these things and others, the sneak, the turncoat, the entrepreneur, and the whistle-blower were indispensable. As

---

[226] TNA CUST82/3, 7 April 1736. Similar cases in Ziegler, 'Customs Officers and Local Communities'.
[227] TNA CUST82/8, 24 December 1756.
[228] TNA CUST82/2, 26 April 1732.
[229] NRS CE51/1/3, January/February 1761.
[230] TNA CUST58/13, 27 October 1784.
[231] TNA CUST97/9, 15 March 1765; CUST97/8, 23 September 1734; WSRO, Goodwood 155, H16.

far on the wrong side of the law as these people may themselves have been, authorities were quite willing to ignore this in return for specific services. The importance of this was such that, even in cases of doubt, the Board was willing to support the informer. When one Thomas Key, from Great Yarmouth, petitioned the collector for some consideration in return for his informations and as a reward for "being abused and threatened by the people", the collector was inclined to grant it. This was despite Key being "Shatterd in his understanding" and his informations being "without any foundation". In "his Disorders", the collector observed, he went to the alehouses and "Quarreld with the people [...] and then charges the usage he received in Turn from the Informations he has given, tho entirely false". In short, "we can't find one word of truth, his Disorder and unsettled mind makes him fancy things that are not True". However, as the man was poor and as his heart was in the right place regarding the business of informing, it was best to encourage him with some money.[232] Key's mental state and loose character notwithstanding, the collector thought it best not to give the impression that informing did go unrewarded. If, as this chapter contends, the most effective and often the only way of breaking the locally accepting sentiments towards smuggling and of undermining the solidarity of local communities was by relying on the members of these very same communities, then authorities needed to develop ways to make these individuals come forward as informers.

The Duke of Richmond and the "Exertion of the Country"

The Richmond campaign is a principal example of adversarial rhetoric used by the authorities. Richmond himself was one of its main proponents. "Cruelty", he wrote, "was the ruling Principle among the whole Body of Smugglers."[233] And "of all the monstrous Wickedness with which the Age abounds," he went on, "nothing, I will be bold to say, can parallel the Scenes of Villainy that are laid open in the following Pages."[234] The monstrosity of the smuggler is placed in square opposition to the honesty of the enforcer. It was this rhetoric that has prompted many modern commentators to embrace this logic of a neat opposition between the enforcers and the criminals. But this obscures the real intentions of Richmond's campaign. In light of the above, it is possible to retell the story of Richmond's campaign. Only

---

[232] TNA CUST97/8, 23 September 1734.
[233] *A Full and Genuine History*, p. 18.
[234] 1090 *Ibid.*, p. iv.

superficially, the argument goes, was this campaign about the enforcement of authority and the punishment of criminals. Rather, the main thrust of the campaign was to change the sentiment of the "country" in favour of the authorities in a way that ensured that the right incentives were in place for local communities to support the authorities and to encourage informers to come forward. The rhetoric and the actions of exemplary justice displayed by Richmond were part of this. They were intended to move the deeds of the Hawkhurst gang beyond the line of what was acceptable to local communities in their tacit support for the smugglers. As such, it was meant to counter the concurrent efforts of the smugglers to maintain their local influence by intimidation. The narrative of a direct clash between the authorities and the offenders was a fiction. Instead, both sides were aiming to influence local sentiment and gain control of the grey areas of law enforcement.

In early October 1747, a gang of smugglers had broken into the Customhouse at Poole to rescue a large seizure.[235] During their return from the venture, they had made a show of their success and were seen by many. One of the onlookers, Daniel Chater, a shoemaker, who had worked with John Diamond, one of the smugglers, in the past, was given a parcel of tea by him. This was publicly noted and Chater was subsequently questioned by the Customs men as to any information regarding the gang. In February 1748, Chater, along with William Galley, a riding officer from Southampton, set out to Chichester, where Chater was to testify before a JP as an informer. On the way, they chanced on some of the gang in a public house. When the purpose of their journey transpired, they were captured, tortured, and finally murdered. Later that year, the Customs received anonymous information as to the whereabouts of the bodies, and it was then that the Duke of Richmond took an active interest. He moved the London administration and local magistrates to a pursuit of the involved smugglers. He obtained a Special Commission of Oyer and Terminer to be held in Sussex for the trial of these men via his influence with the Duke of Newcastle and Henry Pelham. At the same time, magistrates, soldiers, and Customs men were sent in pursuit of the felons, of whom many were eventually caught. In January 1749, altogether seven of the men were tried, found guilty, and hanged. But Richmond did not stop here: his vendetta against the smugglers lasted

---

[235] The story is frequently retold: Winslow, 'Sussex Smugglers', McLynn, *Crime and Punishment*, pp. 172–201; McCooey, *Smuggling on the South Coast*; Rule, 'Social Crime'.

until his death in 1750. By then, 35 smugglers had been executed for various offences and eight had died in gaol.[236]

Public outrage and Richmond's personal indignation centred on the fact that Galley was an officer of the Customs and his murder an attack on the authority of both king and parliament as well as a threat to public authority in the counties. Yet it was more significant to the entire campaign that the murdered Chater was an informer.

The Duke of Richmond did not, to begin with, have an extraordinary appreciation of informers. Nobody did, who was ever a target of informing. And Richmond did have his own brush with informers. In February 1748, the duke received letters from the collector at Southampton with allegations that implicated some of his own servants in the dealings of the smuggling gang that had robbed the Poole Customhouse.[237] This was deeply embarrassing. Although he was able to clear the names of his servants before the Board, there was now an anxiety to have the offenders quickly punished.[238] Richmond was also, at this stage, very uncomfortable with the business of informing. He complained several times to the Board about not knowing the name of the informer. Of his servants, he wrote: "I know the men." But, he went on, I "do not know their accuser".[239]

There was a notable change in this sentiment throughout 1748. Chater, he observed, was the true victim of the affair, having only done "his Duty to his Country" in trying to bring the smugglers to justice.[240] He was singled out not because of any injury done, but "because Chater dared to give information against a Smugler, and to do his Duty in assisting to bring a notorious and desperate Offender to Justice".[241] Richmond was in fact convinced that Chater's murder was done in so cruel a manner "as a Terror to all such informing Rogues (as they term'd it) for the future."[242] Ultimately, to the smugglers, the killing of an informer was no crime, as they were deemed traitors.[243] For the government, however, there was an entirely different question at stake. "What avail the Laws of Society," Richmond lamented, "where no Man dares to carry them into Execution?"[244] It was this that made Richmond celebrate Chater's attempted service to

---

[236] WSRO, Goodwood 154, fol. 37.
[237] WSRO, Goodwood 155, H4, H7, H8.
[238] WSRO, Goodwood 155, H10, H11.
[239] WSRO, Goodwood 155, H10.
[240] *A Full and Genuine History*, p. 31.
[241] *Ibid.*, p. 78.
[242] *Ibid.*, p. 21.
[243] *Ibid.*, pp. 91, 167.
[244] *Ibid.*, p. 78.

the country. Consequently, throughout his writings, he continued to heap praise on the system of informing as an expression of public duty.

In this, Richmond perhaps consciously misrepresented the act of informing. Public duty was seldom the motivation for it. Rewards, or a pardon, were the most common incentives. It also dangerously bordered on a perversion of justice. According to an anonymous answer to Richmond's pamphlet, informing was an instrument of "oppression". The rewards made it open to abuse. "If excited by the Lucre of Gain, here is a strong Temptation to Perjury; if excited by Revenge, here is a strong Temptation to gratify it". As evidence was admitted long after the facts, defences against such informations were difficult to substantiate, unless a defendant "has the Foresight, or can afford to keep a Journal of all his Hours or Days". This meant that "it will always be in the Power of an Informer to swear away any Person's Life".[245] This fear was not without foundation and Richmond knew this. But his outlook on the system had changed.

The fact is that informing served his interests. It was a sure means, and perhaps the only one, of bringing the perpetrators of the Poole robbery and the subsequent murders to justice. In fact, the entire campaign rested crucially on informing. After the disappearance of Chater and Galley in February 1748, it was by way of informations that their bodies were discovered.[246] This was no coincidence. Richmond paid several agents for this very business. It was their job to roam the country in search of informers. There are vivid accounts of such searches by one of these agents, William Fletcher.[247] Richmond also pressured Whitehall into offering pardons and rewards in exchange for informations and was even willing to disburse private funds.[248] "I am very certain", he wrote in December 1748, "that it is the only way to bring these wicked villains to justice". Informers were the only way to break "into all confidence they may have with one another", and the apprehension of the murderers of Chater and Galley, he reported, "has been entirely owing to their being betrayed by their companions."[249] There was indeed no shortage of informers.[250] To Richmond, the punishment of this crime was "of the utmost Importance to the publick Justice of the Nation."

---

[245] Anon., *A Free Apology in Behalf of the Smugglers, so far as their Case affects the Constitution. By an Enemy to all Oppression, whether by Tyranny, or Law* (London, 1749), pp. 12–14.
[246] Ibid., pp. 34–41.
[247] WSRO, Goodwood 156, G24. See also G42, G72 and Goodwood 155, H71, H73.
[248] WSRO, Goodwood 155, H17, H18, H19, H24, H32, H33, H37, H97, H114.
[249] WSRO, Goodwood 155, H33.
[250] WSRO, Goodwood 155, H16, H27, H74; Goodwood 156, G17, G31, G42; ESRO, SAY307, SAY313, SAY314; SAY317, SAY2318.

If offences such as these went unpunished, "the Consequence would be, that no Crime could be punished".[251] The punishment of the offenders was meant, in part, to be a form of exemplary justice, less about individual punishment. It was designed as a lesson to the offender, a deterrence, but also as a message to the "country" meant to convey that informing was safe.[252]

Why did Richmond think such a message necessary? Why was this the only means to apprehend and convict the smugglers? In an undated memorandum designed for Henry Pelham, Richmond reported the case of one Mr. Wakefield of Hampshire, who had lately been attacked by "a set of these desperate villains". The scandal, as Richmond perceived it, was less the deed itself than the fact that Wakefield was "afraid to move towards Justice least a greater evil should fall upon him and [he] dares not complain of it even to his neighbours". JPs were afraid to act against such offences, too. What would things come to if such deeds went "unenquired into"? The problem was that "the country" was unwilling to act against smuggling. Henry Foxcroft, another landowner harassed by the smugglers, similarly complained that such "mischief" was "very much in fashion" in his neighbourhood in Hampshire and that there was nobody who dared "meddle" with the smugglers.[253] What was needed, according to Richmond, was "an active zeal in the Government manifested by publick acts". People were simply too afraid to act for the public good.[254] Richmond cited the case of Mr. Wakefield by way of example, but he was convinced that this was not an isolated case.

He was not wrong. The smugglers firmly held the country in their sway. The Hawkhurst gang in particular, operating mainly in Kent, but also through the Sussex coasts, and various similar associations of felons held great influence in the maritime counties during the 1740s. Not only were officers intimidated and threatened with murder,[255] their power was deeply felt throughout the communities. Entire communities were unwilling to report locally committed offences, to inform on known smugglers, to support the Customs men and thus do their part in establishing public order. According to government sources, such influence was almost always negative: intimidation and fear were at the heart of it. The smugglers, it seems, knew how to use this to best effect. In March 1743, one gang rode through Lydd in great show "at twelve of Clock in the day time".[256] Half a year earlier,

---

[251] *A Full and Genuine History*, pp. 90–91.
[252] *Ibid.*, p. 138.
[253] BL Add. MS 32718, fol. 312. Richmond supported Foxcroft's representation to Newcastle and the prosecution of the respective felon; see *ibid.*, fol. 309.
[254] WSRO, Goodwood 155, H24.
[255] TNA CUST148/12, pp. 365–366, 449, 529.
[256] TNA CUST148/12, p. 453.

they had "misused several Private People in the road making them Kneel down in the mud and beg their Pardons".[257] "Not a Soul in the Town" of Lydd would give any assistance to government efforts.[258] At other places, they held entire towns in their sway, taking care to always make a mighty "show to the Inhabitants, that they were such fellows as dare bid Defiance to all Laws and Government."[259] In July 1744, it was reported that the gangs controlled Dymchurch, Hythe and Sandgate, and "so insolent and impudent they are grown to be, that they fired their Pistols several times as they rode through Hythe to the Terror of the Inhabitants".[260]

In 1748, Richmond was convinced that "the whole Country" was "intimidated" and unwilling to support the government's efforts.[261] People were "terrified" at the horrible acts of revenge against anybody who dared to act against the smugglers, and against informers, so that "scarce any Body durst look at them as they pass'd through Towns and Villages in large Bodies in open Day-light". The "whole Country were afraid of them" and the "Terror of this Act of Cruelty [Chater's murder] had spread through the Country, [and] stopt every Person's Mouth, who had it in their Power to give any information".[262] It was this that needed to change.

Richmond had the intention of changing the dynamics of enforcement in coastal communities vis-à-vis smuggling. Almost every strategy observable in Richmond's campaign was, on closer inspection, not designed to punish individuals, but to win over "the Country".

The greatest effort was put into inciting the country against the smugglers and thereby to counter any sympathetic sentiments. The principal means to achieving this was rhetoric. Both Richmond's pamphlet and Old Bailey proceedings portray the deeds in the blackest of lights.[263] The murders were portrayed as a logical conclusion to smuggling. The deeds were "the most cruel Torments that Malice itself could invent" and "not the least Grain of Humanity could remain in the Breasts of these harden'd Villains."[264] Having once "wrought himself into a firm Persuasion" that smuggling was no crime, "the Transition is easy to the Belief, that it is no Sin to plunder or destroy his Neighbour".[265] Smuggling was a "Nursery of all Sorts of Vice

---

[257] TNA CUST148/12, p. 497.
[258] TNA CUST148/12, p. 492.
[259] TNA CUST148/12, pp. 517–518. See also ESRO, SAY369.
[260] TNA CUST148/12, p. 639.
[261] WSRO, Goodwood 155, H24.
[262] *A Full and Genuine History*, pp. 41–42, 43–44, 45, 95.
[263] Old Bailey Proceedings Online, t17480116-1.
[264] *A Full and Genuine History*, pp. iv, 11.
[265] *Ibid.*, p. 44.

and Wickedness", "an Encouragement to perpetrate the blackest of Crimes", "productive of Cruelty, Robbery, and Murder".[266] According to Richmond, it was important to "Alarm the Nation, and open the Eyes of all People" to the depravity of the smuggler and the blackness of his offence, which, Richmond insisted, was conducive to this "unheard-of Pitch of Wickedness".[267]

The purpose of such rhetoric was to drive home the point that the alleged innocence of smuggling as a crime against the revenue was a fiction, that it was the highest of offences. More importantly, everyone was called on to do his or her part in combatting such wickedness. This was to "shew how dangerous to their Neighbours, and to the Country in general, those Persons are, who are concerned in Smugling, and how much it concerns every Man to use his utmost Endeavours to suppress, and bring them to Justice."[268] Such words were meant to move what the smugglers did beyond what was locally acceptable. To this end, Richmond also attacked the gentry for protecting smugglers to further parliamentary interests.[269]

A related strategy was the mobilisation of the "country". In light of fearful magistrates and a complacent local gentry, it was important to incite popular actions against the smugglers. This had worked before. To combat the excesses of the Hawkhurst gang, the government had authorized "all his Majestys Subjects, both Civil and Military, Magistrates, Officers, and private Persons" to seize or apprehend any persons they found assembled and armed for the purpose of smuggling in June 1747. The advertisement was also published in *The London Gazette*.[270] Not soon after, the Board of Customs was informed that at Goudhurst, Cranbrook and Flishinghurst, associations of local men had formed a militia, ready to arm themselves and fight off the gang when they encountered them.[271] In one case, fighting was indeed reported.[272] Such measures raised legal concerns and the Board

---

[266] *Ibid.*, pp. 72–73.
[267] *Ibid.*, pp. 168–169.
[268] *Ibid.*, p. 138.
[269] Pelham was anxious not to be called an encourager of the smugglers, see ESRO, SAY 423–424. There were, however, suggestions of his abetting smuggling to favour elections, see BL Add. MS 32711, fols 211, 455. Collier, on the other hand, was so deeply involved with local elections that the suspicion that he was protecting smugglers is not unwarranted. See Winslow, 'Sussex Smugglers', p. 156; BL Add. MS 32688, fols 123, 139; Add. MS 32692, fols 83, 93, 102, 372, 415; Add. MS 32703, fols 73, 164, 170; Add. MS 32712, fols 129, 201, 350. Newcastle was certainly aware that there was a connection between smuggling and voting; see BL Add. MS 32709, fol. 274.
[270] ESRO, SAY 295, SAY 296, SAY 297.
[271] ESRO, SAY 298.
[272] *Gentleman's Magazine* 17 (1747), p. 198.

strictly inquired into the "conduct and behaviour" of these associations.[273] By all appearances, these were short-lived efforts. But it was this sort of local action that Richmond was after. He made sure to bolster local sentiment with the necessary legal protection, public calls for surrender, as well as contingents of soldiers.[274]

Most importantly, Richmond's efforts centred on informing. He encouraged informers at every turn, often by paying rewards out of his personal coffers. He also made sure that informers were protected, both from their former associates and from being prosecuted themselves.[275] Richmond also lobbied government to offer rewards and pardons in return for informations.[276] For past offenders or those complicit, it was felt that only pardons opened them up.[277] For other informers, money was key and here, too, Richmond was pressing for rewards.[278] What most endangered the entire business was when either rewards or pardons were not forthcoming. "I hope all promises made by boards to these people will always be punctually complied for otherwise the Justice of the Peace who acts in it must appear in the Worst of lights."[279] In December 1749, Richmond wrote an angry letter to the Board of Customs, complaining of a delay in payment of a reward. It had not only disappointed himself, but "all the gentlemen that act with me in this county". There was a danger that such delays would produce a "coolness" in those acting for the government, which would make further activities very difficult. As this was of "very bad consequences", Richmond hoped that the Board would "refresh the good will that I assure you began to appear very strongly some time ago (tho it fleas now)" by a speedy payment of the rewards.[280] The Board quickly complied and suggested that this was money well invested: "The more you have for your money, the better is the Bargain."[281]

Of similar importance was the question of pardons. But here there were scruples. The Attorney General was less forthcoming with pardons than Richmond would have liked.[282] And local men were equally reluctant. "Considering", one of Richmond's agents wrote about one of the gang, "he

[273] ESRO, SAY300, SAY301.
[274] Winslow, 'Sussex Smugglers', pp. 160–161; WSRO, Goodwood 155, H17, H18.
[275] WSRO, Goodwood 155, H16, H73, H74; Goodwood 156, G17, G31, G42.
[276] WSRO, Goodwood 155, H24.
[277] TNA CUST148/12, p. 617.
[278] WSRO, Goodwood 155, H32; see also *A Full and Genuine History*, p. 45.
[279] WSRO, Goodwood 156, G6.
[280] WSRO, Goodwood 155, H32.
[281] WSRO, Goodwood 155, H37, H114.
[282] WSRO, Goodwood 155, H33.

was owing himself a murderer, and taking away the lives of his Bosom-friends att the same time", it was unfortunate that "their should be a necessity to pardon such a vile wretch."[283] In these matters, however, Richmond was willing to forgive even the blackest of crimes in return for a chance to convict others. To him it was seemingly of little consequence who went to the gallows, as long as there was a public show. Accordingly, he was particularly infuriated if any informer was charged with crimes, because this would inevitably destroy the evidence of the prosecution in other cases.[284] Even after the conclusion of the Chichester trials, Richmond was at pains to protect the informers. He thought the informer should be deemed exculpated not only from the guilt of the crime he was informing on, but also from past offences. If such men were to be prosecuted, then "I should give over all expectation of future Informations".[285] In this matter, Richmond knew himself in agreement with Henry Pelham, who, in February 1749, assured Richmond that any promised pardons "will be fully made good". It was impossible, he concurred, to convict such offenders, "without some of the accomplices in the wickedness being partners in the discovery".[286]

All this went a long way to turn the sentiment of the country in favour of enforcement. But the crowning act was always intended to be the trials. The special assizes, Richmond claimed, would "strike a terror upon all evil minds".[287] They were intended as a public show of strength, visible to the public, reinforcing the message that authority was enforced in the county. This, he thought, would instil the right attitude in local people by making "publick Examples of such horrible Offenders, and to terrify others from committing the same".[288] The trials were also an encouragement to informers, lessening their "Fear of exposing themselves to the Resentment or Revenge of their Companions".[289] To accomplish this, moreover, it was quite irrelevant who exactly was punished. Whereas the indictment of the seven on trial in January 1749 did make a distinction between the principals of the murders and the accessories, the court equally reserved capital punishment for both. This, Richmond thought, "did more service than the execution even of the principals", for it was known that local people tended to entertain the notion that assisting in a crime was not liable to the same

---

[283] WSRO, Goodwood 155, H75.
[284] WSRO, Goodwood 155, H43.
[285] WSRO, Goodwood 156, G59.
[286] WSRO, Goodwood 155, H97.
[287] WSRO, Goodwood 155, H32.
[288] *A Full and Genuine History*, p. 46.
[289] *Ibid.*, p. 91, see also p. 138.

punishments as having principally committed it.[290] The entire trial, then, was a formidable piece of exemplary justice.[291] Whereas informers went away with a pardon, others who were nothing more than accessories went to the gallows. To Richmond, it was irrelevant who went which way. Pleas for mercy were stubbornly blocked by him personally.[292] Informers, on the other hand, went free. And this was exactly the message that the entire campaign was about.

Seen in this light, the Richmond campaign is the story of the conversion of a country utterly intimidated to a righteous and law-abiding country by way of the single act of the trials. When the Customs Board congratulated Richmond on the success of his efforts, the crucial bit was not the punishment of the offenders. "The best endeavours" to enforce authority in the maritime communities, the Board thought, "must fall short, unless they are seconded and supported by the spirit and exertion of the Country".[293] It was this that Richmond's campaign had, even if only for a short time, achieved. If it certainly was exceptional in its determination, the same realisation about the dynamics of the enforcement authority can be observed elsewhere. The Aberdeen collector reported in 1742 that smuggling was not only a crime in itself, but was "Destructive of the Interest of the Country".[294] Elsewhere, it was the "humour and situation of that country", that "occasioned perpetual discouragements".[295] Measures at Great Yarmouth taken in the early 1730s were similarly directed "to encourage the Country" to assist the enforcement of authority.[296] Because the "Country People" at Weymouth were largely "concerned" with the smugglers, measures were discussed to encourage the "Country" to oppose the smugglers.[297] In Ireland, finally, and in particular among the Old Irish of its western parts, plans were devised in 1755 to station a military force. This was not based on the calculation that such a force would stop smuggling, but rather that the mere show of force would both "encourage the few Protestants of those parts to become Informers" and "strike such a terror" into the minds of the

---

[290] WSRO, Goodwood 155, H96.
[291] Douglas Hay, 'Property, Authority and the Criminal Law', in Douglas Hay, Peter Linebaugh, John G. Rule, E.P. Thompson, Cal Winslow (eds), *Albion's Fatal Tree: Crime and Society in Eighteenth-Century England* (London, 1975), pp. 17–63.
[292] WSRO, Goodwood 155, H83, H96; Winslow, 'Sussex Smugglers', p. 141.
[293] WSRO, Goodwood 155, H111.
[294] NRS CE87/1/2, 17 December 1742.
[295] TNA T1/113, no. 44.
[296] TNA CUST97/8, 27 February 1733, 24 June 1734.
[297] TNA CUST59/1, 29 October 1718, 4 March 1719; CUST59/2, 9 June 1719, 16 October 1719.

offenders that the practice would stop.[298] The problem, as it looked to the authorities on closer inspection, was not the smugglers. It was the people. As elsewhere in the enforcement of the law in the eighteenth century, public support and private initiative were crucial.[299] "Though government make laws", a commentator on coastal law enforcement wrote in 1780, "the execution of them must lay in the people, and without an exertion in the latter, the intention of the former must be altogether ineffectual."[300]

Conclusions

This chapter has aimed to show the intricacy of coastal law enforcement and bring it into line with recent research on criminal law enforcement and officeholding more widely. The increase of state activity at the coastal margins of the kingdoms, it has shown, did not result in a straightforward top-down enforcement of authority. Nor were the lines between the officers and the offenders neatly drawn. Instead, coastal law enforcement was – as elsewhere – a complex equilibrium between local sentiments and central directives, in which officers and offenders had to constantly negotiate their positions. Central to this picture were those figures that operated between the official and the criminal, such as the common informer. Both central administration as well as local criminal confederacies constantly aimed to tip the balance of local sentiments in their own favour and thus encourage non-aligned agents to act on their behalf. It is hardly surprising that the result of these negotiations, as the chapter has shown, was hardly ever either a straightforward imposition of authority or downright lawbreaking. Rather, the intricate microcosm of coastal enforcement tended towards a negotiated compromise, i.e. collusion.

---

[298] TNA T1/361, no. 21.
[299] Philip Rawlings, 'Policing before the Police', in Tim Newburn (ed.), *Handbook of Policing* (London, 2008), pp. 47–71; John Styles, 'Print and Policing: Crime Advertising in Eighteenth-Century Provincial England', Douglas Hay, Francis Snyder (eds), *Policing and Prosecution in Britain 1750–1850* (Oxford, 1989), pp. 55–112; David Philips, 'Good Men to Associate and bad Men to Conspire: Associations for the Prosecution of Felons in England, 1760–1860', in Douglas Hay, Francis Snyder (eds), *Policing and Prosecution in Britain 1750–1850* (Oxford, 1989), pp. 113–170; Peter King, 'Decision-Makers and Decision-Making in the English Criminal Law 1750–1850', *HJ*, 27/1 (1984), 25–58; Francis M. Dodsworth, '"Civic" Police and the Condition of Liberty: The Rationality of Governance in Eighteenth-Century England', *Social History*, 29/2 (2004), 199–216.
[300] Anon., *Advice to the Unwary*, p. 22.

5
Reform, State-Building, and the Birth of the Coastguard (1784–1822)

Coastal policing – firmly focused on the idea of 'prevention' – was a set of institutions and actors designed to deal with contingencies, that is to say, incidences and potential events beyond the immediate grasp of central authorities, such as smuggling or military invasion. This, however, is not to say that these incidences were not to some extent directly or indirectly influenced by policies implemented by these same authorities. In terms of imperial policies (both within the British archipelago and beyond) and relative to the politics of warfare, many effects materially – though often unintentionally – interfered with regular arrangements of coastal policing. Trade politics and tariff systems directly affected Customs business in the ports of Ireland, Scotland and England. Underneath these fiscal concerns, these policies also impacted on the forms and patterns of Customs activity. Imperial trading routes, the channelling of goods by mercantilist policies, and the micro-logistics of their transport (both lawful and clandestine) and their warehousing affected both the spatial organization and the practical requirements of Customs policing and control in technical and procedural terms.[1] This is also true for the repercussions of wartime arrangements throughout the period. Concerns over coastal defences in particular reordered government priorities vis-à-vis the coast to the disadvantage of the regular peacetime functions and arrangements of the Customs. At the same time, preventive officers became themselves part of the war machinery for the purposes of anti-espionage provisions, the works of the press gangs, or – in the case of the cruisers conscripted by the Admiralty – naval

---

[1] See, for instance, Spike Sweeting, 'Policing the Ports: The Regional Dimensions of Eighteenth-Century Customs Activity in England and Wales', *Bulletin of the German Historical Institute London*, 40 (2018), 32–67; W. Farrell, 'Smuggling Silks into Eighteenth-Century Britain: Geography, Perpetrators, and Consumers', *JBS*, 55 (2016), 268–294.

combat.[2] Such pressures, moreover, did not necessarily relent after the signing of peace treaties, because the incoming tide of disbanded soldiers regularly swelled the registers of property crimes and flooded coastal areas with large bands of armed smugglers.[3] On a more abstract level, therefore, such policies of empire and warfare – especially when viewed against the backdrop of the ostensibly domestic priorities of coastal policing – point to the inherent tensions of conceiving the British state at the time: imperial aspirations were clearly at odds with ideas of territorial integrity.

That the Customs administration and its preventive service were ill-equipped to deal with their explicitly stated tasks was keenly felt by central administrators at numerous moments throughout the period. Regarding the control of coastal mobility, the coherence of the bureaucratic apparatus, the social mechanics of enforcement, and the repercussions of imperial policies, the administration was frequently found lacking. Indeed, reports in newspapers or in parliamentary inquiries seem to speak to an increasing and, at times, dramatic deterioration of conditions in coastal areas, both in terms of fiscal efficiency and social order, over the course of the century. At the same time, this palpable uneasiness over the failures of coastal policing was not necessarily mirrored in the structures and mechanics of coastal policing in situ. Regardless of wartime interruptions and changes in the legislation, coastal arrangements remained remarkably constant until the final decade of the 18th century. As such interference was as recurrent as it was predictable, this growing unease must therefore, at least partly, be attributed not to a tangible deterioration of the situation in the localities, but to changing sensitivities in the centre. Major shifts in political sensitivities, such as the waning of the politics of patronage and 'old corruption', mounting financial pressures on the revenue departments, new ideas

---

[2] See Nicholas Rogers, *Crowds, Culture, and Politics in Georgian Britain* (Oxford, 1998), pp. 85–121; Ian Gilmour, *Riot, Rising and Revolution. Governance and Violence in Eighteenth-Century England* (London, 1992), pp. 184–192; Nicholas Rogers, *The Press Gang: Naval Impressment and its Opponents in Georgian Britain* (London, 2007); Denver Brunsman, *The Evil Necessity: British Naval Impressment in the Eighteenth-Century Atlantic World* (Charlottesville, 2013).

[3] See, for instance, Stephen Conway, *War, State, and Society in Mid-Eighteenth Century Britain and Ireland* (Oxford, 2006); Nicholas Rogers, *Mayhem: Post-War Crime and Violence in Britain, 1748–53* (New Haven/London, 2012); Nicholas Rogers, 'Confronting the Crime Wave: The Debate over Social Reform and Regulation, 1749–1753', in Lee Davison, Tim Hitchcock, Tim Keirn, Robert B. Shoemaker (eds), *Stilling the Grumbling Hive: The Response to Social and Economic Problems in England, 1689–1750* (New York, 1992), pp. 77–98; Douglas Hay, 'War, Dearth and Theft in the Eighteenth Century: The Record of the English Courts', *Past and Present*, 95 (1982), 117–160.

about bureaucratic efficiency, as well as new concepts of policing, criminal justice, and domestic security, all contributed to a vision of the British state in which the Customs administration was inevitably and increasingly regarded as outdated, imperfect and inadequate. Rather than unavoidable idiosyncrasies of an ancient institution, central features of the Customs increasingly came to be seen as failings of and embarrassments to the state.

In mapping these changes in political sensitivities and the changing views of the Customs and coastal policing throughout the period, this chapter aims to chart the long history of abortive or failed attempts to reform, correct, and improve the preventive service. Whether in the form of parliamentary committees, legislative efforts, bureaucratic restructurings, or indeed in the myriad reports and schemes and suggestions from interested parties, these attempts, and how and why they failed, directly speak to the limits of state-building in the period. The chapter proceeds to show that what ultimately provided itself as the only solution to the conundrum was to ease up on the relentless push for higher tariffs and thus ease the pressures of the imperial fiscal system on the domestic shores. In adopting this perspective, in the mid-1780s, it briefly looked as if the preventive service was to become redundant. Were it not for the return of the security concerns vis-à-vis France in the last quarter of the century, this might well have happened. In the event, the French threat revived old debates about strengthening coastal defences and underscored, yet again, the sinister implications of cross-channel smuggling. The subsequent changes and modifications to the coastal preventive service resulted, around 1820, in a newly made coastguard, which – nominally, functionally, and bureaucratically – more closely resembled the administrative institution familiar to modern eyes. And yet, the 'new' ideas had already been practised in the Customs for nearly a hundred years. Given this, it is perhaps little surprise that the new coastguard was not as novel as it may seem. Its structure, its organization, and its core principles were – the rhetoric of change and reform notwithstanding – still essentially the same. Perhaps paradoxically, a system that appeared out-of-date for much of the eighteenth century suddenly carried the marks of modernity. Just as the beginnings of the preventive service allowed for a re-evaluation of fiscal-military narratives of state-building, its end questions any simple narrative of bureaucratization and modernization.

The Riddle of the Coast

When Elizabeth Hoon evaluated the eighteenth-century Customs administration, she concluded that "the chief responsibility for whatever deficiencies there were in the eighteenth-century customs service rests with the system rather than with its administrators."[4] Given the results of the preceding chapter, this evaluation seems a fair one. And yet, what does that mean exactly? Hoon also remarked that until at least the mid-1770s, there was "no concerted attempt at the badly needed reform of the system". Partly, she notes, this was because of antiquated ideas about bureaucratic efficiency and partly because the public did not demand reform.[5] At the same time, she was aware that there were *some* attempts at reforming the system. In this, she undoubtedly understated matters. Improving the Customs and its coastal branch was the subject of countless texts and discussions in the period. Certainly, what was lacking was a wholesale resolve on the part of central administration to change the system in any fundamental way. But even in the absence of this, it is still instructive to review these reform ideas. It may not always be entirely clear what their exact motivations were and why most ideas were never acted upon, but they remain immensely revelatory regarding the limits of state authority and state-formation in the period. As a reservoir of reform potential, they illustrate alternative ways of dealing with existing problems and, as such, allow for a firmer grasp on the efficiency, the pressures and the pitfalls of both the paths taken and those not taken by central administration.

Most reform proposals fall into four categories, being either regulatory, administrative, penal, or fiscal in nature. Depending on which problem and which cause were identified, the proposed solutions varied, and targeted different aspects of coastal enforcement. What emerges as an overall picture is that there was never a real consensus as to what the best solution was, because there was never a consensus as to what the main problem was. Proposals for new trade regulations acknowledged the merchants as the main problem; new administrative measures tended to see the Customs bureaucracy as the main culprit; and penal sanctions operated on the assumption that civilization had not reached certain social strata in the coastal counties.

"A Distressing Dilemma"

Throughout the entire century, there was a good case for arguing that the biggest threat to Customs enforcement was the ingenuity of the mercantile classes. On scales both big and small, frauds at import and export constituted one of the main drains on Customs revenue.[6] Three areas of

---

[4] Hoon, *Organization*, p. 44.
[5] Hoon, *Organization*, p. 78.
[6] Evan T. Jones, *Inside the Illicit Economy: Reconstructing the Smugglers' Trade of Sixteenth Century Bristol* (London, 2012); Leanna T. Parker, 'Southampton's

Customs business in particular provided opportunities for fraud: coastwise shipping, the re-export of colonial goods, and the circumvention of trade bans such as on French goods or wool. In the first two of these cases, the Customs required the merchants to enter into specific bonds and deliver securities to ensure compliance with the regulations. Coastwise shipping, which was, with few exceptions, free of the payment of duties as well as relatively insignificant in the overall volume of British trade, required merchants to procure a coast cocket in return for a bond, which was to ensure that the goods did arrive at their domestic destination. False cockets and declarations, however, provided easy opportunities to tamper with the system.[7] Similarly, the re-export of colonial goods was liable to abuse. As the navigation laws required enumerated goods such as tobacco to be landed in England before being shipped elsewhere, the Customs allowed merchants to receive so-called drawbacks. Once the goods had entered England upon the full payment of duty, a certificate for re-export could be procured that allowed the merchant to receive a certain amount or, in some cases, the total of the original duties paid on importation. Such a system was naturally open to abuse, as was the case with tobacco and, in the context of the East India Company, tea.[8] Next to a prosperous continental smuggling trade, this also affected the trade between Ireland and Britain.[9] Finally, the prohibition of French goods during certain periods of the seventeenth and eighteenth centuries, as well as the wool export ban, sparked great ingenuities on the part of the merchants, such as false declarations of goods or the fraudulent use of coast cockets.[10] An additional problem was the disparity

---

Sixteenth-Century Illicit Trade: An Examination of the 1565 Port Survey', *International Journal of Maritime History*, 27 (2015), 268–284; Ashworth, *Customs*, ch. 11. See for contemporary reports and records of merchants' illicit transactions William Mackay (ed.), *The Letter-Book of Bailie John Steuart of Inverness, 1715–1752* (Edinburgh, 1915); Rupert Jarvis (ed.), *Customs Letter-Books of the Port of Liverpool 1711–1813* (Manchester, 1954).

[7] For contemporary reports on such frauds, see CUL, Ch(H), Political Papers 41, no. 42, no. 56. For regulations to combat such frauds, see GCA CE59/2/1, 28 June 1803.

[8] R. C. Nash, 'The English and Scottish Tobacco Trades in the Seventeenth and Eighteenth Centuries: Legal and Illegal Trade', *Economic History Review*, 35 (1982), 354–372; Huw Bowen, '"So Alarming an Evil:" Smuggling, Pilfering and the English East India Company, 1750–1810', *International Journal of Maritime History*, 14 (2002), 1–31; Huw Bowen, 'Privilege and Profit: Commanders of East Indiamen as Private Traders, Entrepreneurs and Smugglers, 1760–1813', *International Journal for Maritime History*, 19 (2007), 43–88. See also the reports on drawback frauds in CUL, Ch(H), Political Papers 41, no. 18.

[9] L. M. Cullen, *Anglo-Irish Trade 1660–1800* (Manchester, 1968), pp. 139–154.

[10] On the Customs procedures at importation and exportation, the drawback system, coastwise shipping, as well as the pitfalls of these procedures, see Hoon,

of certain weights and measures that could be used to tamper with the calculation of duties.[11] As it stands, in addition to clandestine importation of goods, that is outright smuggling, and the corruption of the Customs administration, such as bribery and pilfering, the Customs system provided many opportunities for merchants to defraud the public revenue.

That this was imperfect was, by the early eighteenth century, long recognized. Already in 1679 it was openly acknowledged by the Treasury that the use of "ill securities", "fraudulent certificates, false affidavits, uncertain returning of bonds and other miscarriages" endangered the revenue.[12] At the time, orders were given to be more careful in the keeping of coast bonds, as the duty-free coastwise trade was frequently used to carry goods abroad that would have been liable to duties. The only means, it was stressed, to prevent such evils was a due comparison of the imports with the exports. The issuing and cancelling of bonds was also to be handled with strict care and supervision.[13] As the immediate problem was conceived to be fraudulent paperwork, additional checks and regulations presented themselves as the likeliest remedy.

Given the continued prevalence of such frauds well after 1679, it was in this direction that many reform proposals aimed to extend the control of the Customs over coastal activities. Such proposals varied depending on which article of trade and on which trading route they focused on. Coal, because of its special status in the coasting trade, was of particular concern, but so were tea, tobacco, brandy, lead, wine, soap, and wool.[14] Sometimes the continental trade was addressed, at other times the Irish Sea, the trade between North and South Britain, or even particular stretches of domestic coast.[15] What unites these proposals is a focus on regulatory measures. Sent

---

Organization, pp. 243–269; William B. Stephens, *The Seventeenth-Century Customs Service Surveyed: William Culliford's Investigation of the Western Ports, 1682–84* (Farnham, 2012), pp. 15–26; T. S. Willan, *The English Coasting Trade, 1600–1750* (Manchester, 1976), ch. 1; D. Hussey, *Coastal and River Trade in Pre-Industrial England: Bristol and its Region* (Exeter, 2000). On how Customs business worked on an everyday basis, see Ashworth, *Customs*, ch. 9.

[11] CUL, Ch(H), Political Papers 41, no. 48.
[12] CTB VI, p. 137.
[13] CTB VI, pp. 457–458, 756. On methods of comparison CUL, Ch(H), Political Papers 41, no. 32. By this method, losses to the revenue could be calculated; see Political Papers, 41, no. 46.
[14] See, for instance, CUL, Ch(H), Political Papers 44, no. 12 (brandy); Political Papers 41, no. 2 (corn), no. 5 and no. 6 (lead), no. 18 (tobacco, wine), no. 36 (brandy), no. 38 (tobacco), no. 40 (soap), no. 43 (brandy), no. 51 (tobacco), no. 53 (wine), no. 61 (malt).
[15] See, for instance, CUL, Ch(H), Political Papers 44, no. 19 (Scotland); Political Papers 41, no. 1 (to/from France), no. 2 (Norfolk), no. 7 (Irish Sea), no. 29, no. 30 (Jersey,

directly to the hands of Walpole, one proposal provides a typical example. Robert Bonnell, its author, addressed both potential frauds at importation and exportation, as well as the coasting trade; he also gave particular attention to the importation of tobacco and the wool ban. "A true inventory" of goods at importation, accurately checked by the Customs, explicit bonds at exportation "not to reland" the goods, but to "really and truly Export the same", as well as proper bonds for the coasting trade, were crucial to prevent frauds. More important, however, was that masters were to present certificates of their journey, duly certifying the landing of the goods at their destination. These "Regulations before mentioned", Bonnell believed, "will put the Navigation of these Kingdoms into such a Method of being looked after, that it will be impossible for any body to defraud the Customs in any considerable degree without being detected".[16] On paper, the system was faultless. But relying on the honesty of the merchants to ensure the honesty of the merchants does also speak to a certain naiveté. How compliance was to be enforced was anyone's guess. Detecting frauds via the Customs accounts was theoretically possible in this way, but it required an accuracy of the books and a central oversight of the records that did not exist.[17]

Regulatory means only covered a certain aspect of smuggling, namely merchants' fraud, and neglected other problems such as the corruption of Customs' men and the illicit compacts between merchants and officers. But in this regard, too, there were many suggestions for new regulations.[18] The ultimate judge on the introduction of new measures remained the Board of Customs. It frequently agreed that further regulatory measures were required and, with the approval of the Treasury, moved to implement additional checks in the routine business of the Customs.[19] Such responses can

---

Guernsey), no. 34 (Dunkirk), no. 35 (Boulogne), no. 37 (Ireland, Americas), no. 38 (Ireland), no. 45 (port of London), no. 49 (Flanders), no. 52 (France), no. 64 (Isle of Man).

[16] BL Add. MS 74055, fols 18–22.

[17] See 'Fifteenth Report of the Commissioners appointed to examine, take, and state, the Public Accounts of the Kingdom (1787)', in *The Reports of the Commissioners Appointed to Examine, Take, and State the Public Accounts of the Kingdom [...]*, Volume 3 (London, 1787), pp. 117–199, at p. 120: "If the London Returns were replete with Error, far more erroneous and defective were those transmitted from the Out Ports. Upon inspecting and comparing those Returns with Books and Accounts in the Office of the Customs, he discovered that few were regular, consistent, or correct. Various and numerous were their Defects."

[18] In addition to the Walpole papers, see, for instance, BL STOWE MS 865, fols 38–52.

[19] See the proposed reforms in the Scottish Customs in the 1720s in CUL, Ch(H), Political Papers 40, reports no. 15 (tobacco) and no. 16 (wine and coastwise shipping). On the introduction of various regulations to the merchants' paperwork, see the collation of general orders in TNA CUST31/1 (heading "merchants").

be seen well beyond the Customs. Walpole sought to integrate measures relating to the frauds in tobacco and wine in his Excise scheme of 1733.[20] The parliamentary inquiries of 1733, 1746, and 1783, too, painted a vivid picture of such frauds and, often being informed by the very perpetrators in such underhand dealings, proposed stricter regulations.[21] At the same time, it is also worth noting that certain groups asked for rules to be lifted or to be exempted from specific requirements that were supposedly hindering their economic success.[22] Merchants, in particular, often complained of the growing intricacy of the regulatory checks and paperwork of the Customs that made the system cumbersome to navigate.[23] They protested the "hardships and discouragement" that new regulations placed on the honest trader: "After a Merchant has learn'd his Trade, he has one thing yet more difficult to understand, viz. the manner of passing his Goods at the Custom-house", which must, according to one author, "be left as a Riddle and Mystery".[24]

Overall, the Treasury and the Board of Customs were keen on improving the paper trail of trading interactions to ascertain the veracity of individual interactions from multiple angles and by a due comparison of the books. To what extent such regulatory checks on Customs fraud were effective is a speculative question, but it is clear that whatever faith the government had in mercantile honesty, it clearly felt that it was best paired with some level of control. If the Customs thus proved a willing and competent implementer

[20] Ashworth, *Customs*, p. 171.
[21] See *The Report of the Committee appointed to inquire into the Frauds and Abuses in the Customs, to the Prejudice of Trade, and Diminution of the Revenue*. Reported on the Seventh of June 1733 by Sir John Cope, printed in *Reports from the Committees of the House of Commons*. Reprinted by Order of the House. Vol. I, Miscellaneous Subjects: 1715–1735 (1803), pp. 601–654; JHC 25, pp. 101–110; 'First Report', p. 25.
[22] See CUL, Ch(H), Political Papers 44, no. 12, no. 35; Political Papers 41, no. 2, no. 7.
[23] See GCA CE60/1/15, 27 January 1784; CE60/1/16, 24 July 1784. There was no shortage of contemporary guides to the system, see Edward Hatton, Comes Comercii: Or the Trader's Companion (London, 1723, 4th ed); Thomas Bacon, A Compleat System of the Revenue of Ireland, in its several Branches of Import, Export, and Inland Duties (Dublin, 1737); Thomas Daniel, Ductor Mercatorius: or the Young Merchants' Instructor with respect to the Customs: Being a minute and particular Detail of the Regular Method of Proceeding at Out-Port Custom-Houses, in the several Branches of Marine Commerce (Newcastle upon Tyne, 1759); James Smyth, The Practice of the Customs in the Entry, Examination, and Delivery of Goods and Merchandise, usually imported from foreign parts (…) (London, 1812); on many aspects of Customs procedures see also Crouch, Complete Guide.
[24] Anon., *A Letter to a Member of Parliament concerning Clandestine Trade. Shewing how far the Evil Practices at the Custom-house at London tend to the Encouragement of such a Trade. Written by a Fair Merchant* (London, 1700), pp. 5, 6, 10.

of the practical consequences of the Navigation Laws and the mercantilist policy of the British Empire, there were also limits as to how far the government was willing and able to go in the enforcement of coastal regulations.[25]

"An Official Self-Control seems to be practically a Contradiction"
Any attempt at ending the practice of smuggling by focusing solely on the merchants and their various fraudulent techniques was inevitably doomed. It was the complicity between merchants and officers that constituted the most serious challenge to the integrity of the Customs. Internal investigations, along with parliamentary inquiries, tended to focus on such abuses as one of the main culprits for the inefficiency of policing the coasts.[26] Thus, in addition to the integrity of the force, its general structure was frequently subject to debates. Proposals for a reform of the administration in fact tended to focus on either personal failures or systemic inadequacy as the main reasons for the perceived inefficiency.

From the 1690s until the 1820s, the preventive service of the Customs remained, at first glance, substantially unaltered: notwithstanding some fluctuations, an increase in its numbers seems to be the only material change. Below the surface, however, much did change. As chapter three has outlined, the question of the personal integrity of individual officers was a matter of constant concern at the Board, and it was tackled with a series of tools of supervision over the course of the century.[27] In a similar vein, individual removals and major purges of personnel were among the tools of the Board to increase the integrity of the service. Such changes were never free from the suspicion of serving political interests. When Walpole received a plan for a better guard of the western ports, this seemed well intended at first. Seeing that the proposal suggested the appointment of a well-salaried General Surveyor to inspect the western ports, this clearly smacks of an application for a place, rather than a reform proposal.[28] In other cases, the situation is less clear: Warren Lisle's suggestion for a better setup of the waterguard in the western ports – which included his elevation to Inspector of Sloops – does seem to have been effected for the

---

[25] The history of the failed wool register is a case in point; see Hannes Ziegler, "'This Monstrous Scheme": Die Idee eines nationalen Wollregisters im Großbritannien des 18. Jahrhunderts und die Grenzen des Merkantilismus', Vierteljahrschrift für Sozial- und Wirtschaftsgeschichte, 111 (2024), 6–34.

[26] *The Report of the Committee appointed to inquire into the Frauds and Abuses in the Customs, to the Prejudice of Trade, and Diminution of the Revenue*; JHC 25, pp. 101–110, 'Third Report', p. 13.

[27] See chapter 3.

[28] CUL, Ch(H), Political Papers 41, no. 33.

improvement of the service.[29] With larger purges of personnel, too, it is difficult to be certain of the intentions. Obviously, those left out in the cold had reason to complain of being sacrificed on the altar of political interests; and complain they did.[30] With equal justification, purges of personnel could be said to contribute to a better-run operation.[31] These fluctuations in personnel, however, were to some extent normal administrative fluctuations.

More interesting are proposals for structural changes affecting the performance of the service at its foundation. One such change concerned remuneration. In the context of the wider Customs service, perhaps the most contentious issue was the question of fees, whereby inferior officers were remunerated not by an established salary, but by gratuities received from the merchants. Despite being a practice open to abuse, it took long to address it. A realisation that fees, combined with "low Salaries and great Temptations", was "prejudicial", only prompted action in the 1780s.[32] Again, this was not an issue that applied to the fully salaried preventive service. But the rationale of such reforms did affect the cruiser establishment. Rather than let commanders of such vessels – comfortable on their salaries and allowances – slip into inaction and negligence, a long-standing rationale dictated that it was worthwhile making commanders financially interested in the performance of service. Already around 1720 a system originated in which commanders, rather than being established, were contractors of the Crown. In the early decades, vessels still tended to be the property of the Crown, whereas the commander would pay for running costs on a contractual basis that allowed his expenses to be refunded by seizure proceeds. From the 1730s, a second contract system emerged, whereby the commander would hire a vessel and crew at a monthly rental to the Crown,

---

[29] CUL, Ch(H), Political Papers 41, no. 26.
[30] An attack on Walpole's policy of removals in Anon., *The Undue Administration: Or, The Usual Management of the Customs Considered, and compared with the late pernicious Practice of Removing and Placing Officers, contrary to all former Precedents. The whole Impartially Represented, by Persons who now suffer under the Injustice and Oppression of a Quondam Minister of State, to the utter Ruin of Themselves and Families* (London, 1717).
[31] See chapter 2 (1690s) and chapter 2 (Scotland, 1710s).
[32] 'First Report', p. 10; 'Fifteenth Report'; *Fourteenth Report of the Commission for Stating the Public Accounts* (1785); William Musgrave's compilation of fees in BL Add. MS 8135. See Earl A. Reitan, *Politics, Finance, and the People: Economical Reform in England in the Age of the American Revolution, 1770–1792* (Basingstoke, 2007), pp. 206–212. Spike Sweeting, 'Capitalism, the State and Things: The Port of London, circa 1730–1800' (Diss. Univ. of Warwick, 2014), pp. 109–114; Ashworth, *Customs*, ch. 9; John R. Breihan, 'William Pitt and the Commission on Fees, 1785–1801', *HJ*, 27/1 (1984), 59–81.

once again in the hope that seizure proceeds, of which both parties would profit, would defray the charges of hiring the vessels.[33] Over the coming decades, this system gradually came to permeate the preventive service, and, due to the reduction of overhead costs and the perceived incentive for better performance on the part of the commanders, it appears to have been preferred to the established cruisers.[34]

The pinnacle of this reform of the remuneration system of the preventive service came in 1783, when William Musgrave advocated the establishment of all cruisers on a contract basis. This was a matter of incentives. Because established commanders considered their places "as pensions", contract arrangements made for "a strong incentive to activity in the Crew" to the "great benefit" of the revenue.[35] Consequently, in 1783 the Board ordered that upon vacancies in the established cruisers arising, they would be discontinued unless masters were willing to enter into a contract for such vessels.[36] This policy sparked bitter resistance. Most notably, the disagreement was what the preventive service was actually about. Captain Fisher, of the *Hunter* cutter at Great Yarmouth, viciously attacked the policy. It was beyond his power to engage in the service on those terms, he argued, for it focused a captain's attention exclusively on seizures, which was a "mere contingency" to the actual purpose of the cruisers, namely the prevention of smuggling. This would endanger the safety of his ship, on account of having to make seizures by all means possible, and it would eventually undermine the "confidence reposed in them [the captains] of not making collusive seizures or conniving at frauds". The collector, too, refuted such terms, as they would compromise the "Publick Protection by Preventing Frauds", in that captains would fare better to encourage fraud than to prevent it, in which case they would earn nothing. "Facts", he maintained, "support our sentiments".[37] Ultimately, the Board relented, perhaps because insistence would mean having no cruiser at Great Yarmouth at all.[38]

The sentiment that the contract terms risked a fundamental conflict with the cruisers' original intention, however, was more widespread. The 1783 parliamentary inquiry pointed out that the cruisers were employed upon different modes and "on Principles of Service so different, that it is

---

[33] Graham Smith, *King's Cutters: The Revenue Service and the War against Smuggling* (London, 1983), p. 36; 'Fifteenth Report', pp. 146–148.
[34] Detailed accounts and lists of those cruisers in the Musgrave papers; see BL Add. MS 8133B, fols 110–126. For an example, see TNA CUST59/71, 17 November 1734.
[35] *Eighteenth Century Documents*, pp. 255f.
[36] TNA CUST29/4, 'Cruizers', 21 February 1783, 4 September 1783.
[37] TNA CUST97/80, 15 May 1783; CUST97/25, 28 May 1783, 30 October 1784.
[38] TNA CUST29/4, 'Cruizers', 16 December 1784.

impossible to suppose that both can be right, or equally eligible."[39] In 1787, the Commissioners of Public Accounts came to a more explicit conclusion. They remarked that the contracting of cruising vessels by superior port officers was a bad practice, in that "no Interest in the Performance of a Service ought to vest in the Person whose Duty it is to control the Execution thereof". "An Official Self-Control", they went on, "seems to be practically a Contradiction".[40] The contracts, furthermore, opened the door to many abuses. Although they were supposedly not intended to influence the Board of Customs in any way, these statements found their mark. In June 1787, the employment of cruisers on contract was discontinued, and a major reorganisation of the service ensued.[41] Thus a policy originally meant to improve the efficiency of the preventive service by way of providing personal incentives to its agents was ultimately rejected on the grounds that the consideration given to private interests was too open to abuse to stand the test of an efficient and incorruptible bureaucracy in 1787.

A related concern, and one that sparked numerous proposals from both within and from without the administration, was the question of how the preventive service was best distributed geographically. Manuscript letters, printed tracts, witness statements, parliamentary inquiries, and internal reports of the different executive departments are replete with suggestions on how better to combat smuggling, counter espionage, or gain military intelligence. The design and outfit of the ships, the stationing and supervision of the riding officers, the level of involvement of army and navy, and the distribution of the forces over the coastal counties and waters are, to varying degrees and in shifting combinations, part of many of these schemes. Some are minor in their ambit, others are quite fundamental.[42] It was perfectly typical of the first category to suggest specific types of vessels and stations for the arrangements at Dover and Gravesend, as a 1727 plan suggested.[43] Equally emblematic of such proposals was a designated cordon of ships for particular stretches of the coast, such as the Irish Sea, contiguous to the Isle of Man.[44] Invariably, these proposals tended to explicitly make a case for more efficiency or a saving of expenses on adoption of their ideas.

---

[39] 'Third Report', p. 10.
[40] See 'Fifteenth Report', p. 195.
[41] TNA CUST29/4, 'Cruizers', 1 June 1787, 4 December 1787, 22 December 1787, 10 April 1788.
[42] See, for instance, WSRO, Add. MS 2610.
[43] CUL, Ch(H), Political Papers 41, no. 39/2.
[44] *The Report of the Commissioners of Inquiry for the Isle of Man* (1792), Appendix D, no. 22.

The Treasury and the Board of Customs were not insensitive to the wisdom of certain suggestions, and many small-scale reorganisations can be seen in the period.[45] It was different with more ambitious plans. In 1783, Henry Seymour Conway, then Commander-in-Chief of the Forces, submitted a proposal to Shelburne that was as novel as it was grand. Conway suggested erecting defensive towers on the southern coasts, to be manned by small contingents of soldiers who could alert the revenue men to the presence of smuggling ships, as well as form a first line of defence against enemy landings.[46] This was far-sighted, and it anticipated both the idea of the Martello Towers and the military south coast defences adopted twenty years later, but it seems to have been entirely disregarded in 1783. A different plan by one Admiral Smith, possibly Thomas Smith, printed posthumously in 1767, advised the watch of the coastlines by sixty vessels and two thousand officers.[47] Again anticipating subsequent developments, Smith envisioned these forces to be under the command of the Lord High Admiral, rather than with the Customs. Once again, however, they were too ambitious, at this time, to be acted upon. It was not until the final decade of the century that such reforms and reorganisations were to be considered more seriously.

In the meantime, the Customs Board was not averse to restructurings and redistributions of its preventive service at particular junctures. Given that a major inflation of its personnel was never an option, however, this needed to be done broadly within the limits of the existing scale. Sometimes, a reduction was actually the aim of these restructurings. Nonetheless, reform was typically their intention, and greater efficiency their aim. Looking at the pattern of such internal reviews, it was generally external impulses – such as applications by parliament or the Treasury – that prompted action. Most, in fact, appear to coincide with major debates in the executive or in parliament, which in turn regularly occurred at the conclusion of major military engagements. Internal reviews are identifiable for the late 1690s, after the Nine Years' War; around 1717, after the Spanish War of Succession; in the 1730s, in the context of Walpole's Excise scheme; in the mid-1740s, during the Austrian War of Succession, as well as after the Seven Year's War, and the American Revolutionary War. In 1717, for

---

[45] Among many others, TNA CUST148/13, pp. 18, 30, 34, 39, 41, 45, 58, 67; CUST148/12, pp. 445, 449; T1/128, no. 3; T11/15, pp. 309–314, 318.; T1/250, no. 9, report no. 2; CUST29/4, 'Cruizers', 4 December 1787, 22 December 1787.
[46] *Eighteenth Century Documents*, pp. 306–307.
[47] Stephen Janssen, *Smuggling Laid Open, in all its Extensive and Destructive Branches. With Proposals for the effectual Remedy of that most iniquitous Practice* (London, 1767, 2nd ed.), pp. 273–286.

instance, the Board ordered a general review of the preventive service for taking stock of what officers, in what districts, were performing the coastal watches, specifically asking for advice on beneficial alterations.[48]

The aims and the results, as well as the attitudes of local officers to such restructurings, are best visible in the 1783 inquiry. The initial set of questions from the Board to collectors of the outports was as clear: "Without Delay", the Board wanted all information the collectors had about smuggling in the three years past, particularly whether it had increased, and similarly of all such practices "by which the vigilance of the Administration of the Customs has been eluded and the Efforts of the Officers for the Prevention thereof defeated." Collectors were to detail all measures they had previously taken as well as their "impartial Opinion" "whether more Officers and of what description, are wanted, either occasionally or constantly, and the Places where such Officers would be more advantageously stationed". Additionally, they were to report whether any added measures, and which, needed to be taken. These reports were "very much wanted" and the collectors were "to lose no time".[49] All across England, Wales, and Scotland, collectors hurried to send in their reports, some of which arrived just days after the receipt of the order, and of which more than twenty are still traceable.[50] The degree to which the request was taken seriously, however, varied.

As for the state of smuggling, many ports, such as Stockton or Barnstaple, reported no change in its level. Others, like Sunderland, reported a decrease. Most, however, perceived a dramatic increase in the volumes of smuggling. This was the case, among others, in Newcastle, Beaumaris, Swansea, Ilfracombe, Penzance, Cowes and Portsmouth. To the second question, if and what additional Customs appointments were required,

---

[48] TNA CUST59/1, 27 May 1717; CUST62/59, 23 May 1717; CUST97/3, 7 February 1718, 28 February 1718; CUST98/1, 22 February 1718; CUST99/1, 4 July 1717.
[49] TNA CUST97/80, 11 October 1783.
[50] TNA CUST101/6, 5 November 1783 (Maldon); CUST99/11, 15 October 1783 (Harwich); CUST92/17, 7 November 1783 (Hull); CUST89/7, 23 October 1783 (Stockton); CUST85/5, 16 October 1783 (Sunderland); CUST84/19, 16 October 1783 (Newcastle upon Tyne); CUST82/13, 17 October 1783 (Whitehaven); CUST78/5, 20 October 1783 (Beaumaris); CUST73/9, 23 October 1783 (Swansea); CUST72/3, 23 October 1783 (Cardiff); CUST69/169, 20 October 1783 (Ilfracombe); CUST69/67, 18 October 1783 (Barnstaple); CUST68/12, 20 October 1783 (Penzance); CUST65/2, 23 October 1783 (Dartmouth); CUST64/9, 22 October 1783 (Exeter); CUST61/6, 23 October 1783 (Cowes); CUST60/6, 31 October 1783 (Poole); CUST59/16, 18 October 1783 (Weymouth); CUST58/12, 22 October 1783 (Portsmouth); CUST97/25, 20 October 1783 (Great Yarmouth); NRS CE87/1/6, 21 October 1783 (Aberdeen). On the basis of this report, the Board compiled a general report; see TNA T43/82.

many collectors reported a necessity of having more officers, such as at Maldon, Hull, Stockton, Newcastle, Cardiff, Dartmouth and Weymouth, among others. In other ports, such as Ilfracombe, Barnstaple, Harwich, Sunderland, or Whitehaven, the present establishment was enough, collectors believed, to counter problems that might arise. If this already points to different perceptions as to how great the challenges faced by preventive men were, other collectors discounted their efforts altogether. At Beaumaris, Swansea, Poole and Great Yarmouth, collectors insisted that no new appointments were needed, not because the present establishment was sufficient, but because it was futile. "No addition to the number of Officers would be of any material service at present", Poole reported.[51] Great Yarmouth was even more damning in its verdict: an increase of officers was "not necessary", because it would achieve nothing. In fact, "double or treble their number would only increase the Expence to Government, which their best endeavours would not repay."[52]

What these collectors wanted was assistance of a military or naval kind. Penzance, Dartmouth, Hull, Great Yarmouth, Stockton, and Poole all declared themselves to be powerless without a stationing of soldiers to their assistance. This was, as the Stockton collector put it, "at present preferable to appointing more officers".[53] At Whitehaven, Ilfracombe, Barnstaple, Exeter, or Cowes, what was required was naval assistance by sea. Additionally, some of the collectors did have further ideas on how to alleviate the present state of things. The Cardiff collector suggested, for instance, that government purchase the rights to the island of Lundy, as it operated as a principal entrepôt in his area. The collector at Cowes, in the meantime, thought that the present hovering limits should be extended from two to three leagues, so as to complicate the smugglers' business. The same was advocated from Great Yarmouth, with the difference that the extension should go to six leagues instead of just three. Additionally, the Great Yarmouth collector thought, the present duties were simply too high, affording too many incentives to the smugglers. As a general remedy, the duties needed to be lowered.

What ultimately emerges is inconsistency. No clear indications of a policy or reform emerge from the variety of voices that, each based on individual perceptions and knowledge, suggested wildly different things. These were things, moreover, that the Board of Customs had trialled, in various forms and disguises, for nearly the past hundred years. At the height of the

---

[51] TNA CUST60/6, 31 October 1783.
[52] TNA CUST97/25, 20 October 1783.
[53] TNA CUST89/7, 23 October 1783.

so-called "Age of Reform", the executive was none the wiser as to how an administrative reform could make the preventive service fit its purpose of controlling coastal activity.

"The Great and Infallible Remedy"

What is considered an adequate answer to a specific problem depends on personal views. To some extent, attempts at reform are also situated in specific political climates, and their shape is determined by what courses of action are considered acceptable or desirable. To speak of Walpolean reform attempts as if they were grounded in the same ideas that dominated Pitt's agenda is therefore misleading. The fact that the imposition of stricter trade checks and the administrative improvement of the Customs do seem to meet with the same dilemmas across the whole period has warranted the summary perspective on these reform attempts. But it is true that even here, different priorities reigned. The talk of stricter regulations imposed on the merchants notwithstanding, it is noteworthy that during Walpole's time as prime minister, the communication of the Treasury to the Customs chronicles an astounding rise in compositions in cases of merchant fraud.[54] This suggests that the Treasury, at this time, prioritized the short-term income of such compositions over a serious clamping-down on frauds and thus reflected a more lenient stance towards mercantile interests. This cavalier attitude to merchant fraud was paired, under Walpole, with extra-administrative means of enforcement via private contractors and the general view that, given the right people, the system could somehow be made to work. Purges of personnel were thus given preference to structural reforms.[55]

Later governments did take different views. With Shelburne, the younger Pitt, William Musgrave, and indeed most proponents of economic reform from the late 1770s onwards, the idea was rather that there were indeed faults with the system as such, and that any attempts at reform – regarding remuneration or administrative setup – needed to be structural. Regardless of the people in the respective posts, a change in administrative supervision and accountability could make the system function better. Arguably, this was too narrow a view, in that it exclusively focused on fiscal efficiency and failed to consider the fiscal bureaucracy and its duties in their entirety.[56] A chronology of these changes would have to consider the moments when reform ideas surfaced. As stated earlier, this is typically in times of acute

---

[54] The rise of compositions is discernible in the Treasury out-letters to the Customs in the Walpole years, for instance in TNA T11/19, T11/23.
[55] See chapter 1 (1690s) and chapter 2 (Scotland, 1710s and Ireland, 1730s).
[56] Reitan, *Politics*, pp. 206–212; Sweeting, 'Capitalism', pp. 109–114.

fiscal crises, in the aftermath of major wars, with the influx of disbanded soldiers swelling the registers of property crimes.[57] The answers to these crises, and the standards of fiscal reform, clearly differed between the Williamite restructurings, the fiscal projects of Walpole, the Townshend revenue reforms, and Shelburne's and Pitt's inquiries into the economy and the public accounts.[58]

If those differences are noteworthy, they remain relatively minor when compared with the most significant change in attitudes towards smuggling and its prevention. Until 1746, the main argument was that the degeneracy of coastal populations was to blame for the extent of smuggling and associated evils. The 1746 Smuggling Act imposed severe punitive sanctions on smuggling and all offences indicative of an intention to run contraband.[59] In line with the Waltham Black Act and the Bloody Code, numerous offences were made capital by these acts. Of course, the system still knew leniency and the convictions were regularly less severe than the Acts suggest.[60] This attitude, however, still contrasts with the monetary penalties on Customs fraud for merchants during the same period. Whereas those in the upper places of the smuggling chain could expect to get away with fines, it was the ones carrying the brunt of the work that also carried the greatest risk of

---

[57] For the impact of disbanded regiments, TNA CUST84/19, 16 October 1783. More generally, Conway, *War*, ch. 6.

[58] For the Williamite reforms chapter 1. On Walpole, Townshend, and the 'Age of Reform' Paul Langford, *The Excise Crisis: Society and Politics in the Age of Walpole* (Oxford, 1975); Harry T. Dickinson, *Walpole and the Whig Supremacy* (London, 1973), pp. 93–112; Norris Brisco, *The Economic Policy of Robert Walpole* (New York, 1907); Patrick Griffin, *The Townshend Moment: The Making of Empire and Revolution in the Eighteenth Century* (New Haven, 2017); Martyn J. Powell, *Britain and Ireland in the Eighteenth-Century Crisis of Empire* (Basingstoke, 2003); Thomas Bartlett, 'Viscount Townshend and the Irish Revenue Board, 1767–1773', *Proceedings of the Royal Irish Academy*, 79 (1979), 153–175; Thomas Barrow, *Trade and Empire: The British Customs Service in Colonial America, 1660–1775* (Cambridge/Mass., 1967), pp. 160–185; Michael J. Turner, *The Age of Unease: Government and Reform in Britain, 1782–1832* (Stroud, 2000); Arthur Burns, Joanna Innes (eds), *Rethinking the Age of Reform: Britain 1780–1850* (Cambridge, 2003); Philip Harling, *The Waning of 'Old Corruption': The Politics of Economical Reform in Britain, 1779–1846* (Oxford, 1996); Earl A. Reitan, *Politics*, pp. 206–212; J. E. D. Binney, *British Public Finance and Administration 1774–1792* (Oxford, 1958).

[59] See, for instance, CUL, Ch(H), Political Papers 44, no. 69/1.

[60] The Smuggling Acts included pardons for past offences on certain conditions. See 9 George II, c.35. On the function of discretion Douglas Hay, 'Property, Authority and the Criminal Law', in Douglas Hay, Peter Linebaugh, John G. Rule, E.P. Thompson, Cal Winslow (eds), *Albion's Fatal Tree: Crime and Society in Eighteenth-Century England* (London, 1975), pp. 17–63. See also Gilmour, *Riot, Rising and Revolution*, pp. 147–183.

criminal convictions. The contempt that parliament displayed towards the latter can be seen in the texts of the statutes as well as prints and pamphlets in support of sanctions. The 1736 and 1746 statutes called smugglers "dissolute", and "desperate", "evil minded" and "wicked" characters, spreading "terror" across the country.[61] Smugglers, the Duke of Richmond claimed, were capable of "all sorts of vice and wickedness", prone to "the blackest of crimes".[62] Smuggling was a "Sin of deep Dye", and its practitioners "the most profligate Wretches". To run with the smugglers, a man needed to prove that his conscience was resistant "against all Checks of Morality, Religion or Law". Their name was synonymous with "Barbarity", and lacking any "moral Honesty";[63] sinners before God, they were too.[64]

This attitude dominated official parlance despite indications to the contrary. Smugglers' petitions, as well as affidavits and statements, often amount to a recounting of an offender's life story. What they reveal is that the decision to engage in smuggling was almost always a rational economic choice on the part of these individuals. The slip of the local men into illicit dealings was often gradual; it was incentivised by the large sums potentially to be made, and it was accelerated by the meagre economic alternatives at hand.[65] Official language, in the meantime, did not change a great deal in the coming decades, as the post-war crises of 1748 and 1763 seemingly underscored the approved notion.

What finally changed this were the economic ideas formulated by Adam Smith. His attack on the mercantile system and the negative effect of protective tariffs also touched upon the subject of smuggling and its prevention. Smuggling, according to Smith, was the result of the high duties imposed on many imported goods. To address this problem, Smith saw two possible ways, "either by diminishing the temptation to smuggle, or by increasing the difficulty of smuggling". The former could only be achieved by lowering the import duties, whereas the latter was a matter of "establishing that system of administration which is most proper for preventing it".

---

[61] See 9 George II, ch. 35; 19 George II, ch. 34.
[62] Anon. ['Gentleman of Chichester'], *A Full and Genuine History of the Inhuman and Unparrallell'd Murders of Mr. William Galley, A Custom-House Officer at the Port of Southampton and Mr. Daniel Chater, a Shoemaker, at Fordingbridge in Hampshire, by Fourteen Notorious Smugglers* [...] (London, 1749), p. 60.
[63] Old Bailey Proceedings Online, Ordinary of Newgate's Account, OA17470729 (29 July 1747). See also 'First Report', pp. 6, 25; *Eighteenth Century Documents*, p. 290: "it substantially affects the Morals of the People, and even the Police of the Kingdom".
[64] John Wesley, *A Word to a Smuggler* (London, 1783).
[65] See, for instance, TNA T1/61, no. 2; T1/72, no. 43; T1/80, no. 125; T1/93, no. 86; T1/97, no. 100; CUST97/2, 9 July 1708; CUST97/9, 21 July 1735; CUST148/12, 285.

In this respect, his verdict on the Customs administration was not favourable. Indeed, he preferred the system of the Excise. What he promoted was a scheme of warehousing that provided better control on the movement of goods and diminished merchant frauds such as drawbacks and false bonds.[66] Unfortunately, even the Board of Trade thought that a system of warehousing was impossible.[67] What remained was to lower the duties, whereby, Smith argued, the revenue could be increased.

Smith's ideas were grounded in the Scottish enlightenment's preoccupation with human nature.[68] Economic activity was evaluated in terms of its rationality. This changed the view on what the smugglers were engaging in. Smith thought that smugglers were indeed "blamable for violating the laws of his country", but "frequently incapable of violating those of natural justice". They "would have been in every respect an excellent citizen had not the laws of his country made that a crime which nature never meant to be so".[69] This was echoed in other publications, claiming that smugglers, given the proper incentives, "would otherwise become fishermen, and useful members of the Community, thereby greatly enriching the sea coasts."[70] "There is no such thing as preventing Smuggling," one pamphlet held in 1749, "but by reducing the Duties upon the Commodities smuggled". The temptations were simply too great, and the social effects of such a policy simply too harsh. It was not, moreover, a moral judgement on any person if they engaged in smuggling. Human nature was such that it was weakened by temptations:

> Certain it is, that high Duties will eternally tempt Men, in whatever Climate they are found, to engage in an illicit Commerce, however hazardous, for the Sake of the large Profits accruing. The grasping Nature of Man is such, he's fond of growing rich on a sudden. Those who live on our Sea-coasts, think they can't obtain that End sooner than by Smuggling, which they carry on by their Money, and the Assistance of a great Number of People of the poorer and most ignorant Sort.[71]

---

[66] Adam Smith, *An Inquiry into the Nature and Causes of the Wealth of Nations*, 2 Volumes (Oxford, 1976), vol. II, p. 884.
[67] JHC 21 (1727–1732), p. 833 (6 March 1732); Brisco, *Economic Policy*, p. 119.
[68] Andrew S. Skinner, 'Economic Theory', in Alexander Broadie (ed.), *The Cambridge Companion to the Scottish Enlightenment* (Cambridge, 2003), pp. 178–204.
[69] Smith, *Wealth of Nations*, vol. II, p. 898.
[70] Anon., *Advice to the Unwary*, p. 3.
[71] Anon., *A Free Apology*, pp. 26, 21–22.

Smith's ideas quickly gained traction in parliament.[72] The Younger Pitt was, it was reported, well educated "in the school of Adam Smith."[73] The 1783 parliamentary committee, too, echoed some of these thoughts closely when they concluded their third report with an appeal to a more humane view of those that violated the laws of the Customs:

> It is the Part of Wisdom as well as of Humanity, to avoid driving to extreme Distress, or voluntary Banishment, a Multitude of Individuals, who, however combined against the Laws of their Country, are, by their Talents, Spirit, and Activity, peculiarly capable of becoming useful Members of Society.[74]

Behind this evaluation stood the same economic rationales that Smith had advocated. All the remedies against Customs fraud they suggested were, admittedly, not able to offer "permanent Relief". Neither the "Destruction of the Instruments of Mischief", nor the "Severities exercised against Individuals who use those Instruments" would solve the problem. As long as "the Necessities of the Country require the present System of Taxation", smuggling would continue. "The great and infallible Remedy", therefore, was the reduction of duties, as the "Increase of Smuggling should bear a Proportion to the Temptation".[75] This made sense. Yet it was not the first time it had been suggested. Already in 1733, it had been noted that the principal cause of smuggling was the "great Inducement and Temptation" afforded by the high duties.[76] In the 1740s, tea duties had indeed been reduced for a brief period, but this reduction did not withstand fiscal pressures for long.[77] William Pitt, too, when he introduced a bill to replace the high duties on tea with a window tax, faced initial opposition in parliament before his bill carried the day.[78]

---

[72] Kirk Willis, 'The Role in Parliament of the Economic Ideas of Adam Smith, 1776–1800', *History of Political Economy*, 11.4 (1979), 505–544.
[73] Cit. Harling, *Waning*, p. 43.
[74] 'Third Report', p. 36.
[75] 'Third Report', pp. 17, 35.
[76] *The Report of the Committee appointed to inquire into the Frauds and Abuses in the Customs, to the Prejudice of Trade, and Diminution of the Revenue*, p. 609. See also Brisco, *Economic Policy*, pp. 94–95.
[77] Hoh-Cheung Mui, Lorna H. Mui, 'Trends in Eighteenth Century Smuggling Reconsidered', *The Economic History Review*, 28 (1975), 28–63, at 29.
[78] Reitan, *Politics*, pp. 170–178; Hoh-Cheung Mui, Lorna H Mui, 'Smuggling and the British Tea Trade before 1784', *The American Historical Review*, 74 (1968), 44–73; Hoh-Cheung Mui, Lorna H. Mui, 'William Pitt and the Enforcement of the Commutation Act, 1784–1788', *HER*, 76 (1961), 447–465.

The 1784 Commutation Act was a success. Not only was the expected shortfall in duties recompensed by the window tax, but the revenue, too, profited. Lower duties also removed much of the "temptation" of smuggling and made it "no longer adequate to the Risk."[79] Was this the solution to the coastal problem? Smuggling, it was reported, suffered a rapid decline. With this, the case for expanding the preventive service was put to rest. Not incidentally, the assessment of the preventive service was at a low point. The Eden committee reported that the revenue boards thought that "their Inland Establishment is utterly unfit to suppress these Proceedings".[80] The effort "seldom goes beyond a Principle of Duty, and often falls far short of that Principle".[81] Several collectors thought it useless to appoint more officers.[82] William Musgrave objected to an expansion of the preventive service, maintaining that the only increase in their numbers that would effect anything at all was if "one half of the Inhabitants could be hired to watch the other". Ultimately, they were of "very little Service tho' a great Burden to the Revenue".[83] Given the reduction of duties had effected such a success against the contraband trade, they looked expendable. But the reforms of the Customs service as envisioned by Musgrave and Pitt were not as quickly undertaken as they would have wished. When the Commission for Public Accounts finished their inquiries in the late 1780s, Pitt seemed to have lost his taste for economic reform. It was left to the Finance Committee of 1797 and 1798 to pick up the pieces of the abandoned reforms of the 1780s.[84] In the meantime, an external situation had evolved that lent a renewed urgency to coastal matters. Similar to the 1690s, it was the French threat, revolutionary and Napoleonic, that put the preventive service back into the minds of the executive.

Napoleon and the Birth of the Coastguard

In the last decade of the seventeenth century, the preventive service first entered the scene. With it came a heightened political consciousness of the coast. Over the next hundred years, the basic setup of the administration remained relatively unchanged. It was not until the last decade of

[79] 'Third Report', p. 11.
[80] 'First Report', p. 5.
[81] 'Third Report', p. 36.
[82] TNA CUST97/25, 20 October 1783; CUST60/6, 31 October 1783; CUST73/9, 23 October 1783; CUST78/5, 20 October 1783.
[83] *Eighteenth Century Documents*, p. 255.
[84] Reitan, *Politics*, pp. 206–212, 226; Harling, *Waning*, pp. 56–88.

the eighteenth century that profound changes came under way. As a century earlier, the menace of a French invasion led to a nervous scramble to improve control of the seacoasts. On the face of it, these attempts at better control appear haphazard: several different forces – military, naval, fiscal – were created, often with competing aims. Moreover, military defences built on the coast began to change coastal space itself at the same time as central departments such as the recently created Home Office improved their attempts at counter-espionage and the control of aliens. In such a situation, the preventive service had the potential to be either pivotal to the efforts of coastal prevention or redundant in the course of a general overhaul. Which of these possibilities was the more likely course remained unclear while the war lasted. Several fundamental changes to the preventive service during these years, as well as a repeated back and forth of these forces between the fiscal domain of the Customs and the military domain of the Admiralty, speak to the general uncertainty as to whether it was better placed as a fiscal bureaucracy or a military force. The end of the war, finally, ultimately spelled the end of the preventive service. The coastguard, an amalgamation of several wartime institutions, was the result.

The British Coast through the French Wars

From 1793 to 1815, Britain was engulfed in a sustained war effort, only briefly interrupted by the Peace of Amiens from 1802 to 1803.[85] Britain was intensely shaped by the impact of the French developments and the French war. Unlike much of the campaigning of the eighteenth century carried on in European and colonial theatres of war, the wars from 1793 struck much closer to home. The danger was twofold: revolutionaries' sentiments fell on fertile ground in Britain and imposed sustained pressures on domestic peace.[86] And the sometimes capricious fortunes of the British war effort frequently meant that the domestic setting was faced with the, at times, very real scenario of invasion. This was the case from 1794 to 1797 and from 1803 to 1805. Minor contingents in fact landed in Wales and Ireland during

---

[85] See Roger Knight, *Britain Against Napoleon: The Organization of Victory 1793–1815* (London, 2013); Clive Emsley, *British Society and the French Wars, 1793–1815* (Totowa, 1979).

[86] Harry T. Dickinson, *British Radicalism and the French Revolution, 1789–1815* (Oxford, 1985); Harry T. Dickinson (ed.), *Britain and the French Revolution, 1789–1815* (London, 1989); John Dinwiddy, 'Conceptions of Revolution in the English Radicalism of the 1790s', in Eckhart Hellmuth (ed.), *The Transformation of Political Culture. England and Germany in the Late Eighteenth Century* (Oxford, 1990), pp. 535–560.

1797 and 1798, heightening invasion scares.[87] Turner's sketch at the beginning of this study is one of the products of this cultural climate.[88] For a period of twenty years, these threats were continuously kept alive.

The war with France revived British interest in the coast and coastal defences. Some of the ideas dominating the period from 1793 were already circulating in the 1780s. In 1786, the 4th Duke of Richmond, master-general of the Board of Ordnance, advocated a plan for a comprehensive fortification of the English south coast in anticipation of a potential French war. Despite his careful surveys, the resulting reports and several parliamentary bills to that purpose, however, the fortification plan was dropped.[89] During the 1790s, such concerns began to agitate a much wider part of parliament and the executive. What fuelled this interest in the coast was, however, not the invasion threat alone. Fortification plans were predominantly focused on the ability to stave off any attempt of landing French forces, either on English soil or in the more vulnerable Irish theatre. But as in the 1690s, there were several other factors that affected this interest in the coast, namely the combined problems of smuggling and intelligence.

Despite the 1784 Commutation Act, smuggling remained pervasive during the French wars. But there were several factors that limited its magnitude under wartime conditions. At the same time, wartime limitations on commercial exchange between Britain and France also added new incentives.[90] Smuggling, in its economic impact, certainly posed a problem to both France and Britain when both countries suffered immense economic pressures.[91] Both parties therefore relied on smuggling as an economic tool of war. Even if relatively small in scale, smuggling could afford economic relief in certain areas. Napoleon, for instance, used the services of the British smuggling communities in a concerted effort to drain Britain of

---

[87] Knight, *Britain against Napoleon*, pp. 81–91, 251–284; Emsley, *British Society*, pp. 56–64, 99, 112–113.

[88] Christiana Payne, 'Our English Coasts: Defence and National Identity in Nineteenth-Century Britain', in Tricia Cusack (ed.), *Art and Identity at the Water's Edge* (Farnham, 2012), pp. 21–36, at pp. 23–27.

[89] Knight, *Britain against Napoleon*, pp. 43–44.

[90] Gavin Daly, 'English Smugglers, the Channel, and the Napoleonic Wars, 1800–1814', *JBS*, 46 (2007), 30–46. See also Renaud Morieux, *The Channel. England, France and the Construction of a Maritime Border in the Eighteenth Century* (Cambridge, 2016), pp. 248–282.

[91] Patrick O'Brien, 'The Triumph and Denouement of the British Fiscal State: Taxation for the Wars against Revolutionary and Napoleonic France, 1793–1815', in Christopher Storrs (ed.), *The Fiscal-Military State in Eighteenth-Century Europe* (Farnham, 2009), pp. 167–200. See also 'A sketch of the presant state of Smuggling, c.1800', in BL Stowe MS 865, fols 38–52.

bullion, aiming to heighten the British currency crisis.[92] On Elba in 1814, Napoleon famously claimed that the smugglers had done "great mischief" to the British economy.[93] But this was only a minor factor in the appraisal of smuggling as inherently dangerous.

During the French wars, Napoleon also stressed that "all the information I received from England" during the wars was by smugglers. They brought him, he claimed, newspaper articles and dispatches, they took over French spies and housed them, and they assisted French prisoners in escaping the island.[94] If the extent of the harm done by these practices was exaggerated, they are well documented. Both sides used smugglers to gather and convey intelligence via informal channels. The French in particular relied on British smugglers.[95] Such leakages of potentially classified information, furthermore, were not simply an intelligence issue, but also played into military considerations. The clandestine escape of French prisoners of war, often effected by British smuggling vessels, was possibly a minor annoyance in this regard.[96] But the carrying of information as to the stationing of British forces, as well as coastal defences, was of serious concern. The relative inefficiency of the control of cross-channel mobility and coastal prevention thus not only fuelled the old concerns regarding the financial drawbacks of uncontrolled smuggling but also played into fears of weakening the situation of Britain through espionage and the secret communications between French revolutionaries and English Jacobins.

Given the perceived nature of these threats, the answers to these problems were coastal in nature. Plans for countering a possible invasion, in particular, were aimed at coastal defences, but so were schemes for better control of illicit coastal mobility. For the latter, Britain relied on a growing bureaucracy of intelligence gathering, as well as a new insistence on the registration of cross-channel mobility. In Whitehall, several institutions ran intelligence operations. These were based at the Foreign Office, the Home Office, and the Admiralty, in addition to the Secret Office of the

---

[92] Gavin Daly, 'Napoleon and the "City of Smugglers", 1810–1814', *HJ*, 50 (2007), 333–352.
[93] William Webb, *Coastguard: An Official History of H. M. Coastguard* (London, 1976). p. 4.
[94] Ibid.
[95] Daly, 'English Smugglers'.
[96] Gavin Daly, 'Napoleon's Lost Legions: French Prisoners of War in Britain, 1803–1814', *History*, 89 (2004), 361–380. See also Renaud Morieux, *The Society of Prisoners. Anglo-French Wars and Incarceration in the Eighteenth Century* (Oxford, 2019). For the British use of smugglers in the war, see Knight, *Britain against Napoleon*, pp. 290, 408–409.

Post Office. The first two of these were recent creations, as the Secretaries of State for the Northern and the Southern Departments had only in 1782 been renamed the Foreign and Home Office. With some exceptions with regard to the Admiralty, these institutions relied on the packet boat services for the gathering and transmitting of information across Europe and beyond.[97] In addition to the development of intelligence networks and the control of information distribution via the packet service, the beginning of the war also saw the creation of the Alien Office. Founded in 1793 as a sub-administration to the Home Office, it was responsible for the registration of passengers arriving in Britain, with the aim of greater surveillance of potential spies and traitors. The immediate background of this was the British fear of domestic revolution via an influx of ideas and people from France. Set into law with the Aliens Act (1793) and the Traitorous Correspondence Acts (1793, extended 1798), this policy also helped as a measure of counter-espionage. The Home Office bureaucracy installed a registration system on the coast that targeted, for the first time systematically, people. This new system was carried out, to some degree, by the Customs and its preventive service.[98] In the operational hands of the Alien Office and the Customs, it was, by contemporary opinion, "the most powerful means of Observation & Information (…) ever placed in the Hands of a Free Government".[99] It was, moreover, "the best and truest key to our Security".[100]

Improved intelligence and communication were also at the heart of other measures. With the outbreak of hostilities in 1793, the Admiralty pursued plans to connect the commanders-in-chief on the south coast directly with London via the use of optical shutter telegraphs. By early 1796, some stations were operational, and the Admiralty was able to convey complex messages to Portsmouth within fifteen minutes and communicate with the Channel squadrons blockading the French ports. Over the next years, the lines were continuously extended and also connected Plymouth (in 1806) and Great Yarmouth (in 1808) to London.[101] Even before the telegraph system, the Admiralty had, in 1794, begun to connect the ports of the southern and eastern coasts via signal stations. This system was more

[97] On intelligence operations in general, the various departments involved, as well as the packet service Knight, *Britain against Napoleon*, pp. 122–152, 285–312.
[98] Morieux, *Channel*, p. 297; Kimberley Berryman, 'Great Britain and the French Refugees 1789–1802' (Diss. Australian National University, 1980), p. 161. One the administration of the Alien Act more broadly, see *ibid.*, pp. 112–167; E. Sparrow, 'The Alien Office, 1792–1806', *HJ*, 33 (1990), 361–384; Ronald Nelson, *The Home Office, 1782–1801* (Durham, 1969), pp. 123–130.
[99] Cit. Nelson, *Home Office*, p. 130.
[100] Cit. Knight, *Britain against Napoleon*, p. 126.
[101] Knight, *Britain against Napoleon*, pp. 137–140.

comprehensive than the telegraphs, but it was also more basic. The hoisting of certain flags was mainly intended to warn of enemy ships in the Channel.[102] For the use of directing the militia and volunteer forces, a system of fire beacons was erected in Kent, Sussex, and Essex from 1803, with later extensions to the north and west. As an early warning system, it had its deficiencies, as false alarms more than once led to panics.[103] But it served as another communication system for coastal surveillance against military threats and invasion.

In case such threats materialised, the country was in dire need of better defences on the southern and eastern coasts facing the continent. Plymouth and Portsmouth, strategic assets in the Channel warfare, were themselves reasonably well defended, but there was little that guarded against invasion proper. The existing forts on the south coast dated back to Tudor times, and London and its dockyards were equally badly defended. Despite some surveys during the revolutionary wars and the building of occasional field fortifications, this situation changed little before 1803. With the renewal of the war, however, serious defence planning started, not least because of the considerable Napoleonic force amassed on the French Channel coast from 1803 to 1805. Detailed surveys produced "over-elaborate plans" and not all of these could be implemented.[104] What they did establish were reasonable estimations as to where Napoleon could credibly be believed to attempt an invasion and where, accordingly, additional defences were necessary. Next to London and the Thames, Kent was perceived as particularly vulnerable, particularly its westernmost foreland, Dungeness, or the flatlands and beaches around Romney Marsh.[105] Under the leadership of Henry Addington, domestic military forces were increased considerably, and plans for fortifications and artillery batteries got properly underway from 1803.[106]

---

[102] Knight, *Britain against Napoleon*, pp. 140–141, 299–302; Frank Kitchen, 'Napoleonic War Coastal Signal Stations', *Mariner's Mirror*, 76 (1990), 337–344.

[103] Peter B. Boyden, "'A System of Communication Through Each County". Fire-Beacons and their Role in the Defence of the Realm, 1803–1811', in Alan J. Guy (ed.), *The Road to Waterloo. The British Army and the Struggle against Revolutionary and Napoleonic France, 1793–1815* (Stroud, 1990), pp. 126–131.

[104] Knight, *Britain against Napoleon*, p. 256.

[105] See 'Lord Keith's Answer, Monarch, off Broadstairs, 21 October 1803', printed in Richard Glover, *Britain at Bay. Defence against Bonaparte, 1803–1814* (London, 1973), pp. 152–158.

[106] See Knight, *Britain against Napoleon*, pp. 251–284; Charles John Fedorak, 'In Defence of Great Britain: Henry Addington, the Duke of York and Military Preparations against Invasion by Napoleonic France, 1803–1804', in Mark Philp (ed.), *Resisting Napoleon. The British Response to the Threat of Invasion, 1797–1815* (Aldershot, 2006), pp. 91–110; Glover, *Britain at Bay*, pp. 103–124.

Next to the considerable planning that went into the stationing of the available forces, the coastline itself became the focus of much of this planning. The government settled on the tactic of quartering forces at inland points able to quickly respond to a landing, while the defence of the beaches was left to artillery batteries able to fire on incoming ships as soon as they came in range. As these batteries were vulnerable to enemy takeover, it was suggested, as early as 1798, that they be placed in brickwork towers. "The points of the coast", Captain Reynolds, the first to suggest this new design, remarked in 1798, "which require defence are so many", that a fortified solution was needed. What he devised was a cordon of stout, fortified, brick towers, manned by small forces and heavy ordnance.[107] In 1798, this was considered too expensive and also irrelevant, given the subsiding invasion threat. It was not until 1804 that the design was finally approved. The building of Martello towers, whose very model and name were adapted from Mediterranean examples, started in 1805 and was completed in 1810, with altogether seventy-four towers gracing the English southern coastline, and another twenty-nine towers erected in Essex and Suffolk. Around Dublin and in Scotland, Martello towers were erected in the years after 1805.[108] An additional measure was the plan for a deliberate flooding of Romney Marsh to stall the advance of a possible invasion force. This plan was ultimately dropped in favour of the Royal Military Canal, at the back of Romney Marsh, as an additional defensive line.[109]

To support the war effort and the defence of Britain, the Home Office directed the grand-scale enlistment of volunteers. In addition to the army and the militia, the volunteer movements led to tens of thousands of men standing ready for the defence of Britain against invasion, both during the revolutionary wars and, on a grander scale, during the Napoleonic War. This system had its distinct problems and it is questionable whether the volunteers would have been an effective measure against an invading force.[110] Lesser known are the Admiralty's own force of volunteers, the sea

---

[107] 'Report of Captain Reynolds, 7 April 1798', printed in Glover, *Britain at Bay*, pp. 192–193.
[108] Glover, *Britain at Bay*, pp. 114–119; W. H. Clements, *Towers of Strength. Martello Towers Worldwide* (Barnsley, 1999).
[109] Glover, *Britain at Bay*, pp. 119–122.
[110] Nelson, *Home Office*, pp. 139–141; Austin Gee, *The British Volunteer Movement 1794–1814* (Oxford, 2003); Jon Newman, '"An Insurrection of Loyalty": The London Volunteer Regiments' Response to the Invasion Threat', in Mark Philp (ed.), *Resisting Napoleon. The British Response to the Threat of Invasion, 1797–1815* (Aldershot, 2006), pp. 75–90; J. E. Cookson, *The British Armed Nation 1793–1815* (Oxford, 1997); Linda Colley, 'The Reach of the State, the Appeal of the Nation: Mass Arming and

fencibles.[111] They were an idea of Sir Home Riggs Popham, a captain of the Royal Navy, who had trialled the system in 1793. It was officially adopted by the Admiralty in 1798. The force was small, but not insignificant. By February 1804, roughly 25,000 men had been enlisted.[112] Initially, the south and east coasts were divided into districts headed by captains to organise the fencible corps. After 1803, almost forty districts covered all of Britain, with additionally over twenty districts on the Irish establishment.[113]

The task of the fencibles was to man the Martello towers and patrol the beaches against enemy invasion. The posts were publicly advertised and the men were drawn from "all fishermen and other persons occupied in the ports and on the coast, who, from their occupations are not liable to be impressed".[114] This was not a perfect system. Fishermen joined specifically for the purpose of eluding impressment;[115] others used the cover of the fencible certificates to engage in smuggling, behaving "as having a kind of prescriptive right to defraud the revenue".[116] When Vice-Admiral Hugh Phillip inspected the system in 1803 in the coastal counties, he reported all sorts of mischief.[117] Admiral George Berkeley, his successor on the inspection, went so far as to describe the fencibles as "useless and expensive".[118] Especially as a strategy for mobilising local fishing folk for the defence of Britain, the system was a failure, encouraging them rather to evade formal military duties and often joining for the very purpose of doing mischief. Joining the fencibles, Rogers has concluded, was not a "high form of patriotic endeavour". Rather it was, for many, "a perfect scam".[119] Customs collectors

---

Political Culture in the Napoleonic Wars', in Lawrence Stone (ed.), *An Imperial State at War: Britain 1689–1815* (London, 1994), pp. 165–184.

[111] Nicholas Rogers, 'The Sea Fencibles, Loyalism and the Reach of the State', in Mark Philp (ed.), *Resisting Napoleon. The British Response to the Threat of Invasion, 1797–1815* (Aldershot, 2006), pp. 41–60; Daly, 'English Smugglers', p. 44; Knight, *Britain against Napoleon*, pp. 266–267.

[112] Fedorak, 'Defence of Great Britain', p. 100. For a list of officers and districts, see TNA ADM28/145. Numbers for Kent, Sussex and Essex in NMM ADL/K/1. A more detailed breakdown with the ages and capacities of the men at Folkestone in NMM PLT/76.

[113] Letter books of the commanders at Leith in NMM MLN/17 and Sussex in NMM PGE/7.

[114] Cit. Knight, *Britain against Napoleon*, p. 266. Adverts and blank forms in NMM MRK/105/7/1–14.

[115] Rogers, 'Sea Fencibles'; NMM WYN/109/8, 7 January 1804.

[116] Cit. Knight, *Britain against Napoleon*, p. 267.

[117] Rogers, 'Sea Fencibles', pp. 46–48.

[118] Cit. Rogers, 'Sea Fencibles', p. 48.

[119] Rogers, 'Sea Fencibles', p. 51.

concurred. From Cowes, it was heard that the "Sea Fencible System tends much to promote it [smuggling], as every Smugler holds a Sea Fencible Certificate".[120] Smugglers actively used the certificates as a protection from the revenue men.[121] These difficulties notwithstanding, the corps remained in place until 1810.

The Admiralty was also responsible for the most comprehensive programme for coastal prevention of the period: the coast blockade. During the war, the Admiralty had lent protection to the domestic scene when possible.[122] With the end of the war, the navy erected, from 1817, a blockade of the coasts of Kent and Sussex.[123] The idea came from William McCulloch, commander of the revenue ship HMS *Ganymede*, cruising against smugglers on Admiralty orders in 1816. From this station, he supplied the Admiralty with a line of proposals to increase the efficiency of the fight against smuggling. His frustration resulted from the preventive arrangements then in place, which could not "be more inefficient".[124] By 1824, six divisions from Sheerness to Chichester, stretching over 200 miles and comprising over 1,200 officers, comprised the extent of the growing coast blockade still operating under McCulloch. The supposedly greater discipline and firepower of the blockade also came with a higher cost when compared to the Customs service; instructions, in the meantime, were surprisingly similar to what preventive men had done for decades.[125] After his death in 1825, the blockade operated for another six years on the Kent and Sussex coast before it was disbanded in 1831.[126]

From Preventive Guard to Coastguard

The coast had returned as a strategic concern to the minds of the executive in the last decade of the eighteenth century. Protection and prevention

---

[120] TNA CUST61/17, 11 April 1804.
[121] TNA CUST61/17, 25 June 1804.
[122] N. A. M. Rodger, *The Command of the Ocean. A Naval History of Britain 1649–1815* (London, 2004), pp. 528–574.
[123] Roy Philp, *The Coast Blockade. The Royal Navy's War on Smuggling 1817–1831* (Horsham, 2002); Geoffrey Hufton, Elaine Baird, *The Scarecrow's Legion, or Smuggling in the South East* (Sittingbourne, 1983), pp. 56–78.
[124] Cit. Philp, *Coast Blockade*, p. 31. For the setup, see TNA CUST29/7, 'Coast Blockade', 20 August 1816 (original order), 28 September 1818 (extension); 'Smuggling', 20 August 1820 (extension). For letters book of a naval captain on blockade service, see BL Add. MS 47108, Add. MS 47109 and TNA ADM7/49. See also for McCulloch's services BL Add. MS 36368, fol. 55.
[125] See TNA ADM7/225.
[126] The letter books of McCulloch and subsequent commanders, including the correspondence with the Admiralty, in TNA ADM106/3475–3509.

in a space regarded as intensely vulnerable was of high importance in Whitehall during the revolutionary and Napoleonic Wars. Some of the measures adopted, moreover, followed aims that closely resembled the preventive service. These systems competed for the very same tasks with similar means. Rivalries were inevitable, and they riddled the cooperation of coastal forces throughout this period. What did this mean for the preventive service of the Customs? Given the traditional brief of the preventive service, this branch of the executive had the potential to be either crucial to the efforts of prevention – or indeed redundant, given the concurrent efforts of other parts of the executive. The situation in the decades around 1800 also highlighted the fundamental ambiguity of the preventive service as to whether it was to be understood as part of the fiscal bureaucracy or rather to be seen and used as an auxiliary force in the war effort. It was these tensions that determined the rather changeable fortunes of the preventive service until 1822, and beyond.

The Customs records after 1793 reveal, at first glance, little change. But there were new demands in the context of the war effort. With the arrival of the Aliens Act, in January 1793, officers were instructed to inspect incoming passengers.[127] Customs cruisers, moreover, were to guard against enemy privateers.[128] This was not universally welcomed. At Great Yarmouth, the captain of the *Hunter* did not conceive "it to be the Duty of a Revenue Officer to cruise against the Enemy's Ships of War and wantonly expose the Lives and Liberty of His Crew". Unlike warships, revenue vessels had no provision for their mariners in case they were wounded or taken prisoner.[129] In reaction to such complaints, the cruisers were supplied with medicine chests.[130] Some cruisers were also drafted for combat, such as in Nelson's 1801 failed attack on Boulogne.[131] Riding officers, too, were instructed to watch out for enemy movement on the coast.[132] In 1795, supervisors and ordinary riding officers were instructed to observe amicable cooperation with the Admiralty vessels and share intelligence.[133] The artillery batteries

[127] TNA CUST97/29, 12 January 1793; GCA CE82/2/5, 12 January 1793, 9 February 1793; CE59/2/1, 22 January 1805. Customs officers were directly answerable to the Home Office; see TNA CUST29/7, 'Aliens', 30 August 1814, 5 September 1814.
[128] TNA CUST29/6, 30 October 1793; TNA CUST66/2, 17 April 1800.
[129] TNA CUST97/30, 28 January 1797.
[130] TNA CUST29/6, 30 October 1793.
[131] Smith, *King's Cutters*, p. 97.
[132] TNA CUST97/30, 7 May 1798.
[133] TNA CUST143/16, p. 117. In 1807, moreover, strict cooperation between the Customs and the navy was also enforced with a view to preventing smuggling. See, for instance, GCA CE59/2/1, 30 September 1807, 26 November 1807; CE73/2/6, 30 September 1807.

on the coast also received strict orders to report any sightings to the revenue vessels.[134] Another form of support to the war effort was the Customs' help with the impressment business. Already in 1793, the preventive officers had received letters of protection from impressment, but were, at the same time, made to assist naval impressment.[135] With the 1805 smuggling act, this was put on a more formal footing in that the crews of the revenue vessels were given monetary rewards by the Admiralty for the greatest number of captured smugglers impressed into the navy.[136]

There were also other signs of change. Across the southern and western ports, collectors requested more ships, "either Revenue or Admiralty", and more officers.[137] This, together with drastic descriptions of the state of smuggling, reinforced the impression that the way things were being dealt with was insufficient. The most direct attempt at a more efficient method of coastal prevention during the first phase of the French wars came in 1797, with the fourth report of the Select Committee on Finance.[138] It was to establish which reforms passed since 1782 had been implemented and to recommend further reductions. The Customs was no easy case, as its purpose was not the raising of revenue alone, but also the enforcement of the navigation and quarantine laws, which incurred enormous expenses without tangible returns. "They are establishments executing other services besides that of merely collecting the public money".[139] The report only suggested abolishing fees, suppressing sinecures, and improving accounting. But it also looked at the revenue cruiser establishment and lauded the general reduction in the number of cruisers since 1782.[140] In addition, it welcomed that a number of preventive offices had either had their salaries decreased in the period until 1797, or been abolished altogether.[141]

The report directly affected the rank and file of the preventive service. With explicit reference to the report, the Treasury ordered the Board to have "a special and particular regard to the conduct of the several efficient

---

[134] TNA CUST143/16, p. 146.
[135] TNA CUST143/16, p. 114.
[136] George III, ch. 121. See also TNA CUST143/16, p. 145; CUST66/5, 26 October 1805; CUST29/6, 'Cruisers', 28 July 1813.
[137] TNA CUST54/13, 3 December 1800; CUST54/21, 10 November 1807; CUST54/25, 1 July 1811; CUST61/17, 31 December 1804; CUST66/1, 22 July 1799, CUST66/2, 5 November 1801; CUST66/4, 22 December 1804. See also Philp, *Coast Blockade*, p. 14.
[138] 'Fourth Report from the Select Committee on Finance. Collection of the Public Revenue. Customs. (19 July 1797)', in *Reports from Committees of the House of Commons, Vol. XII: Finance Reports, I to XXII, 1797–1798* (London, 1803), pp. 53–106.
[139] 'Fourth Report', p. 54.
[140] 'Fourth Report', pp. 58, 83, 91.
[141] 'Fourth Report', pp. 87–90.

Officers in their Department". Riding officers were subjected to an extra level of supervision in that their seizure performance was entered into a general abstract. Cruiser captains, too, had their services entered into such general abstracts, with the explicit purpose of "shewing the comparative Zeal" in their stations. Finally, in 1812 the system of general outport surveys was put on a more regular footing.[142] The new spirit of efficiency and proper accounting also introduced the first reliable statistics as to the numbers of officers employed in the respective services, their cost, as well as a comparison with their returns in terms of seizures. In other words, the general feeling of inefficiency, vaguely grasped at the executive level since William Musgrave had first drawn up proper accounts in the early 1780s, was now cast into hard numbers that could be acted upon with a clear fiscal rationale.

It was soon carried into action. The first key date in the overhaul of the preventive service was 1809. The Treasury had ordered a comprehensive survey of the coast with a view to rendering the prevention of smuggling more effective.[143] Upon completion of the survey, a "New Preventive Waterguard System"[144] was adopted. It divided the coasts of England into three districts: from London to the Land's End, from Land's End to Carlisle, and from London to Berwick. The first district comprised 23 cruisers and 42 preventive boats, the second 10 cruisers and 13 boats, and the third 9 cruisers and 13 boats. The districts, moreover, were to be supervised by three inspecting commanders. Pay and victualling allowances were increased, but supervision was more stringent. In a clear echo of former instructions, the standing orders condemned "negligence" and stated that "vigilance", on the other hand, would not be "deprived of fair and due Reward".[145] Supervision was further strengthened by enjoining the outport collectors to a strict control of activities and journals of the cruisers.[146] All this was done "with a view to the more effectual Inspection and Control of the Officers".[147] At the same time that the waterguard underwent this reform, the establishment of riding officers was significantly reduced, from 272 officers to 127.[148]

---

[142] TNA CUST29/6, 'Officers', 28 September 1797; 'Riding Officers', 1 December 1796; 'Cruisers', 12 April 1806; 'Surveys General', 19 June 1812.
[143] TNA CUST32/1, pp. 100–102, 110–111, 195–214.
[144] TNA CUST143/16, p. 153. See also Edward Carson, *The Ancient and Rightful Customs: A History of the English Customs Service* (London, 1972), pp. 162–163.
[145] TNA CUST143/16, p. 150. In March 1815, the districts were altered; see pp. 165–168.
[146] TNA CUST143/16, pp. 153–156.
[147] TNA CUST143/16, p. 149.
[148] *Copies of the Eleventh and Twelfth Reports, and also of the Special Report, made by the Commissioners appointed to Inquire into the Departments of the Customs and Excise* (London, 1822), p. 61.

The establishment in Scotland, too, underwent changes in 1812.[149] For the moment, the service remained under the supervision of the Customs Board.

But this was soon to change. In 1814, as Napoleon stood defeated by the Sixth Coalition, an intense debate began over what the expected peace would mean for the severely damaged British economy and the contraband trade. In May 1814, the Customs Board received word that an "establishment for smuggling from Cherbourg in France, to England, is already adopted". Several smuggling merchants from Alderney were reportedly involved. In June 1814, it had word that "a large Company of People belonging to Guernsey" was intending to run contraband into Cornwall.[150] Monthly reports from Glasgow suggested similar trends.[151] Government, too, was alarmed at the prospect of peace. George Rose, the economic liberal who had served under Pitt, warned Lord Liverpool in December 1814 that peace would inevitably mean a steep rise in smuggling and that something out of the ordinary needed to be done. Somewhat counterintuitively for a man who had once devised the low tariff reforms of Pitt during the 1780s, he thought that a lowering of duties would not solve the problem. Rather, he advised defending the high tariff system "by active and immediate exertions by naval and military arrangements".[152]

> The State of our Finances however renders that [the lowering of duties] utterly impracticable without at least every possible Endeavour to maintain the Rates at their present amount. A partial lowering would have the effect of lessening the Produce of the Revenue, without affording the remotest Hope of preventing the alarming Evil. It is not a Point therefore that will admit even of Deliberations. The expedient so successfully resorted to after the American War would be ruinous now; such a lowering of the Duties on the two articles as would materially check Smuggling would at once strike off from the revenue five or six Millions a year at the least.[153]

A year later, Rose, in conjunction with one Captain Hammond, an experienced anti-smuggling commander, followed this up with a concrete proposal. Hammond advised that "nothing but a numerous, vigilant & active chain of cruisers [...] assisted by the military in small bodies at land, can

---

[149] TNA CUST143/16, p. 159.
[150] TNA CUST143/16, p. 162.
[151] GCA CE59/1/2, 13 June 1814, 19 August 1814, 5 September 1814, 6 October 1814, 2 December 1814, 5 January 1815.
[152] BL Add. MS 42774B, Rose to Liverpool, 30 December 1814, fols 331–332.
[153] BL Add. MS 38262, fol. 187.

possibly prevent or even keep down smuggling." These forces should be assigned to districts and communicate intelligence via signals.[154] The service, furthermore, needed to be placed under the Admiralty. "Revenue Vessels are objectionable both from their great expence to the Public, and being placed under Boards unacquainted with Sea affairs".[155]

Rose concurred. The present waterguard system "calls loudly for material alterations." Having preventive forces under two different revenue boards was prone to abuse and "needless expence", let alone the fact that the Board of Customs was "incompetent to that Service". The service needed to be placed under command of the Admiralty by dividing the coast into districts supervised by naval officers, and the current ships be replaced with more suitable vessels and military assistance. This "complete and entirely new arrangement of the Water Guard", once placed under the Admiralty, "could not fail to be better performed" at an expense "infinitely" less than the current one. Strict economic rationales – from the calculation of the effect of duties to the cost-value rationale of setting up a new prevention system – guided these proposals.[156]

Liverpool ultimately followed this idea. In 1816, orders were given to effect sweeping changes in the preventive service. The transfer of authority to the Admiralty, however, met with heavy criticism by the revenue boards. The Customs Board expressed "serious apprehensions" that the proposal would interfere with their duties as "guardians of the laws of revenue and navigation". The cruisers had many more duties than preventing smuggling: they attended to incoming and outgoing shipping, they enforced quarantine regulations, and they controlled the East India ships. Without them, these tasks could not be performed. To vest the right to seizure in a body of men unacquainted with the revenue laws, moreover, was ineffective and dangerous. The preventive boats, too, had an important function in the revenue, in that they provided a means of communication between different preventive branches and had a variety of functions that would cease with their placement under the Admiralty.[157] Most doubts were shared by the Scottish Board of Customs, except that they stressed that the coasts of

---

[154] An example of such a signal book from a revenue cutter on the Irish station in NMM SIG/B/54.
[155] BL Add. MS 38262, fols 184–186.
[156] BL Add. MS 38262, fols 187–196.
[157] English Board of Customs to Treasury, 30 January 1816, in *Copies of all Letters from the Chairman of the Revenue Boards to the Board of Treasury, relative to the Revenue Cutters, in the Month of January 1816* (London, 1816), pp. 1–5.

Scotland were "infinitely more difficult to guard" than the English coasts.[158] The Scottish Excise Board, too, expressed reservations. "In England, near the seat of Government, and of the Admiralty, the proposed plan may not have some inconveniencies", but in Scotland it would, the coast being of a different nature and requiring close familiarity to be properly policed.[159]

Most damning was the English Excise Board. The changing of a system, "the several parts of which are closely dependent upon each other", would have grim consequences. The transfer of a bureaucratic body concerned with the enforcement of revenue laws from a branch of the executive solely concerned with the revenue, to another to which revenue concerns were "of secondary interest and inferior importance", could not but diminish the efficiency of the system. Not only would the revenue only receive an "average share of attention", but it would affect the "character and constitution of that force itself". Preventive officers had a "keenness of feeling arising from a specific opposition of character, and an habitual hostility between the revenue officer and smuggler". This was not to be found in naval men, nor could one expect the same level of cooperation between the landguard and the waterguard if these were part of different branches of the executive. Similar to the Customs, the Excise Board also doubted the wisdom of vesting powers to seize in military officers, as it would be "pregnant with mischief", and "impossible to subject them to account". Local knowledge, too, was too valuable an asset to be thrown away by appointing naval officers to stations foreign to them. On the whole, the operation was not a military operation and required different means: "Smuggling is a system which does not contemplate warfare, but is the exercise of cunning against vigilance."[160]

These counterarguments did not carry the day. In its decision, the Treasury highlighted the increase of smuggling at the conclusion of the war and the great influx of free labour into the contraband market. The abolishment of the high duties, it ultimately concurred with Rose, was not economically viable. In the absence of means of reducing the temptation to smuggle, the Treasury chose rather to increase the difficulty of smuggling. To establish such a system, the cruiser establishment of Customs and Excise, the preventive waterguard, and an extended system of preventive boats were put under the Lords of the Admiralty. New districts and stations were devised, and small military detachments deployed on land, some housed in

---

[158] Scottish Board of Customs to Treasury, 5 February 1816, in *Copies of all Letters*, pp. 5–10.
[159] Scottish Board of Excise to Treasury, 28 January 1816, in *Copies of all Letters*, pp. 13–15.
[160] English Board of Excise to Treasury, 25 January 1816, in *Copies of all Letters*, pp. 11–13.

guardhouses, to help the running of the system.[161] The new forces were put under naval supervision, with naval pay rates and regulations. A captain of the navy – initially, Captain John Martin Hanchett – was appointed Controller General of the new establishment.[162] The cost of the establishment, however, was still borne by the revenue boards, as was the responsibility for boat repairs and accounting.[163] Some of the larger cutters were either transferred or paid off; riding officers, still on the Customs establishment, also underwent a reduction.[164] At the same time, plans for designated coastal watch houses came under way and the first were built in 1821.[165]

Whereas the changes in February 1816 originally only affected England, Wales, and Scotland, the new system was soon extended. In November 1820, the new model was adopted, in the same fashion, in Ireland. In December 1821, the Isle of Man also received a designated preventive establishment of this kind.[166] In 1817, meanwhile, the districts in Kent and Sussex were removed from the preventive waterguard system and placed under the coast blockade superintended by Captain McCullock.[167]

The system worked well. Seizure accounts looked promising.[168] But it worked at the considerable expense of £520,000 annually.[169] The coexistence of the preventive waterguard, naval warships, the former Customs cruisers additionally operated by the Admiralty, and the coast blockade also meant that there was a confusing array of concurrent efforts to achieve a single aim. This did not escape the attention of the 1821 commission of inquiry into the revenue departments. The subject of coastal prevention, the commission stated, was "inferior to none". It listed, however, no less than six administrative arrangements set up to deal with the problem. Of

---

[161] *A Copy of any Treasury Minutes, or Correspondence between the Treasury and the Revenue Boards; relating to the Revenue Cutters; since the 1st January 1815* (London, 1816).
[162] TNA CUST29/7, 'Preventive Waterguard', 5 August 1816, 3 May 1819. Instructions and regulations under the Admiralty in CUST143/16, pp. 197–198, 205, as well as ADM7/226 and ADM106/3124. A list of persons appointed to the service until 1819 in CUST143/16, pp. 211–226. See also BL Add. MS 38368, fols 50–54. The correspondence between Hanchett and his successor from 1816 to 1820 in TNA T28/40.
[163] TNA CUST29/7, 'Cruisers', 22 February, 5 April, 20 May, 7 June, 3 July 1816; CUST143/16, pp. 200–201.
[164] TNA CUST29/7, 'Cruisers', 18 December 1816, 31 January 1818, 19 September 1821; 'Riding officers', 21 August 1819.
[165] TNA CUST29/7, 'Preventive Waterguard', 19 July 1819, 18 September 1821.
[166] TNA CUST29/7, 'Preventive Waterguard', 6 November 1820, 17 December 1821. See for the new Irish arrangements also TNA T28/40.
[167] *Historical Notes on the Coastguard Service* (London, 1907), p. 9. A full copy in TNA CUST143/17, pp. 690–733; extracts in NRS CE7/12.
[168] See *Smuggling Prevention, Returns* (London, 1821).
[169] *Copies of the Eleventh and Twelfth Reports*, p. 56.

these, the commission argued, only the preventive waterguard and the coast blockade were effective. The waterguard was "best calculated for the purpose", only it lacked "concert" with the other coastal forces. This was the result of the 1816 reforms and the fact that these forces did not operate under a single command. If the preventive guard were returned to the Customs, this would not only establish a single command over these forces but also enable a decrease in cruisers and riding officers. Ultimately, this would make for a "greater degree of efficiency". A committee was to attend to preventive measures and half-yearly reports to the Treasury were to satisfy the Treasury's need for accountability. Riding officers could be dispensed with, as their service did not repay the expense of their salaries. Under the name of a mounted guard, a few should be retained for "keeping up the communication". These changes would save £15,000. The original revenue cruisers, now under Admiralty commands, could be reduced and reverted to the Customs. The preventive waterguard as a principal force, and the riding officers and cruisers as auxiliaries would then form what the commission first named the "coast guard". As for the coast blockade, it was best left in place. With these suggestions, the purpose of coastal prevention would be "more effectually as well as economically answered".[170]

Table 7: Preventive Establishments in England and Scotland, 1821.

	Numbers of Persons	**Salaries and Pay (£)**
Riding officers	157	19,507
Preventive Waterguard	1,250	92,003
His Majesty's Ships	2,375	154,399
Revenue Cruisers (Admiralty)	1,553	158,089
Revenue Cruisers (Revenue Boards)	97	7,373
Coast Blockade	1,276	89,152
	6,708	520,525

[170] *Copies of the Eleventh and Twelfth Reports*, pp. 54–60. Another report in TNA CUST143/18, pp. 111–137.

Table 8: Preventive Establishments in England, Ireland, Scotland, 1820–1844.

	1820	1833	1844
England/Wales			
Preventive/Coastguard	1105	3894	3170
Cruisers	47	35	43
Scotland			
Preventive/Coastguard	146	407	201
Cruisers	12	4	5
Ireland			
Preventive/Coastguard	488	1882	1515
Cruisers	11	10	18

The Treasury welcomed the proposals: "My Lords entirely concur with the Commissioners of Inquiry."[171] On 19 February 1822 the coastguard was officially born, and the above forces consolidated under Customs command and under the controllership of the naval officer William Bowles.[172] With this, there now existed, as the Customs Board was quick to state, "one united force for the important object of prevention".[173] The riding officer, once the mainstay of coastal prevention, virtually vanished, whereas prevention by small vessels under supervision was now considered the more efficient and economic choice. In 1831, the coast blockade was dissolved and amalgamated into the coastguard.[174]

The early 1820s saw important changes in Scotland and Ireland, too. The revenue boards of Ireland, Scotland and England were consolidated into one body in 1824. And there was a general reform of port establishments, including the establishment of a warehousing system.[175] An 1823 inquiry into the Scottish outport system concluded that the coastguard in Scotland could be dispensed with because the cost of the establishments exceeded the returns.[176] The commission was in fact rather "struck with the

---

[171] *Copies of the Eleventh and Twelfth Reports*, p. 67.
[172] TNA CUST29/7, 'Preventive Waterguard', 19 February 1822, 6 July 1822. Details of the new arrangement in TNA CUST147/1/1 and CUST147/1/2.
[173] Customs Board, General Letter, 22 February 1822, TNA CUST143/16, p. 264.
[174] TNA CUST143/17, p. 456. See also TNA CUST147/1/1.
[175] George IV, ch. 23.
[176] *Sixth Report of the Commissioners of Inquiry into the Collection and Management of the Revenue arising in Ireland, Scotland, etc. Out-Ports of Scotland* (London, 1823), p. 3. For the implementation of the new regulations in Scotland see GCA CE60/4/10, pp. 67ff.

magnitude" of the expenses for the coastguard. It proceeded to show that smuggling was inconsiderable and the coastguard ill-adapted to the geography. Instead of this system, which "should be wholly discontinued", an establishment of a few smaller boats would both save money and be more efficient.[177] These suggestions ran directly counter to the evidence of Captain George Knight, the inspector general of the Scottish coastguard, who by no means concurred that smuggling was not a problem in Scotland. In fact, he recommended an increase of the coastal watches.[178] The Scottish coasts were admittedly more difficult to guard, but economically the situation of Scotland neither warranted nor repaid big investments in coastal watches.

In the following year, the commission also inquired into the Irish situation.[179] Again the commission noted the "magnitude of the expenses" of the coastguard relative to the overall expenses at the outports. But unlike in Scotland, the commission concluded that Ireland did warrant such a force, especially with a view to the clandestine trade in tobacco. "Foreign Smuggling actually prevails on these Coasts, to a degree which requires the maintenance of an extraordinary force for its prevention". Such a force had already, in 1820, been introduced, when the preventive waterguard after the English model was adopted in Ireland. Returning to the old system, as in Scotland, would be "wholly inadequate". Next to minor administrative changes, therefore, the commission advocated the continuance of prevention in Ireland "on its present footing", with the exception that the authority over these forces should, after the British model, be vested in the Board of Customs, and the preventive forces be understood as a "united force" under the name of coastguard.[180]

A New Departure?

Administrative control over a unified force of coastal prevention in the entire United Kingdom now rested, for the first time, in one single executive body. If one follows traditional accounts of the history of the coastguard, this is the final conclusion to be drawn from the experience of the French wars: as a redemption from over a hundred years of inefficiency, disorganization, and corruption, the coastguard is characteristically seen as a new

---

[177] *Sixth Report of the Commissioners*, p. 19.
[178] *Sixth Report of the Commissioners*, Appendices 20, 21.
[179] *Tenth Report of the Commissioners of Inquiry into the Collection and Management of the Revenue arising in Ireland, Scotland, etc. Ports of Ireland, Preventive Coast Guard, Quarantine, etc.* (London, 1824).
[180] *Tenth Report of the Commissioners of Inquiry*, pp. 20–24.

departure: into the nineteenth century, into a new idea of bureaucracy, into modern Britain.[181] Certainly, to some extent, the preventive idea of coastal policing had won the day.[182] Put under heavy administrative competition from a number of departments and institutions during the French wars, it was the preventive service that remained, and that swallowed these competing forces in the course of the post-war period. If George Rose claimed that coastal prevention had "hardly been out of my mind" during the Napoleonic wars, this reflects a wider political anxiety directed towards the seacoasts.[183] The seacoasts, during the course of these wars, were invested with ever greater cultural and ideological importance.[184] If the preventive service did not fall into redundancy, however, it can hardly be said to have escaped the reforms untouched. Important parts of its eighteenth-century structure disappeared, whereas others gained in importance. Likewise, the bureaucratic reforms made an impact on the way it operated. With a view to these reforms and changes, the question remains to what extent the establishment of the coastguard had put to rest the old tensions inherent in the coastal service. To what extent, in structural terms, was the coastguard a new departure? To what extent did it solve the ambiguities and contradictions that had pervaded the preventive service?

The discussions about coastal policing during the French wars consistently show that the questions of economic viability not only remained a central concern but even gained in importance with the introduction of proper statistics. The debate turned into a numbers game. Commissions and reports weighed the costs of coastal establishments against their profitability in terms of seizure returns. The third, and perhaps the crucial variable in this numbers game, however, remained as elusive as ever, namely to what extent smuggling had been prevented. As something that did not happen could not possibly enter the account books in any direct way, the original purpose and ultimate success of coastal prevention was and remained a matter of conjecture. Much as the commissioners of inquiry asked Captain Roger Knight for evidence as to his claim that smuggling was considerable, all they could get from him in their inquiry into the Scottish Customs was the reference to sundry reports received from sundry officers.[185] Anec-

---

[181] See Webb, *Coastguard*; Bernhard Scarlett, *Shipminder: The Story of Her Majesty's Coastguard* (London, 1971).
[182] Hannes Ziegler, 'The Preventive Idea of Coastal Policing. Vigilance and Enforcement in the Eighteenth-Century British Customs', *Storia della Storiografia*, 74 (2018), 75–98.
[183] BL Add. MS 38262, fol. 190.
[184] Payne, 'Our English Coasts'.
[185] *Sixth Report of the Commissioners*, Appendix 20.

dotal evidence of this kind clearly frustrated the government, but it was frequently what it was left with. What it could calculate, in the meantime, was that a reduction of the high tariffs was likely to solve the extent of the coastal problems. As this road remained closed in the immediate post-war climate, the cost-value rationale applied to coastal prevention continued to be riddled with miscalculations.

Nothing underscores this better than the administrative back and forth of the executive with a view to the preventive forces from 1809 to 1822, and the fluctuations in the numbers of the preventive forces during the period from 1797. While the government was able to form an idea of what constituted proper economic efficiency in coastal prevention, it lacked the numbers to realize this idea administratively. Every inquiry, having obtained an understanding of the Customs administration, ultimately faced the "peculiar circumstances" that a large share of its duties could not be framed in terms of revenue calculations. As in the preceding century and especially with a view to the coastal service, "it is impossible to separate the charges applicable to regulations of trade and navigation, from those which are incurred for the exclusive purposes of revenue."[186] In a sense, therefore, the professionalization of economic thinking and fiscal rationalities in the executive made the solving of the inherent tensions of the Customs not less of a problem, but more so. The question, regularly put to local officers in these years, "whether the preventive waterguard can be more economically managed", remained as elusive as ever.[187] By 1823, the seizure proceeds from the coastguards of Scotland, Ireland, and England still fell far short of their respective expenses.[188]

Throughout the eighteenth century, the traditional way of dealing with uncertainties regarding the fiscal performance of the service had been to ensure proper superintendence, accountability, and control. Given the continued ambiguity in this respect, this was also the fallback option from 1809. These reforms introduced strict age caps for certain offices and aimed to ensure proper qualification, as well as training and promotion of the officers.[189] Much ink was also spilled over the question of rewards, the distribution of seizures, and adequate salaries to instil activity and vigilance and remove incentives for corruption and fraud.[190] Elaborate supervisory

---

[186] 'Fourth Report', p. 54.
[187] *Tenth Report of the Commissioners of Inquiry*, p. 332.
[188] TNA CUST143/17, p. 372.
[189] See TNA CUST29/7, 'Ages of Admission', 21 July 1819; 'Preventive Waterguard', 10 February 1817.
[190] See, for instance, TNA CUST143/16, pp. 143, 145, 147, 151, 161, 164, 197–198, 208, 266; CUST29/7, 'Preventive Waterguard', *passim*.

structures, reciprocal control between port officials and superior officers of the coastguard, and extensive authority for punishments supplemented this.[191] On the initiative of the commission of inquiry in 1822, it was ordered that officers should, under no circumstances, be employed at or near places where they were locally connected. Additionally, it was suggested that they were made removable between stations.[192] After the consolidation of the Customs boards of Ireland, Scotland, and England, officers were informed that a deputation from the Board meant they could be removed to stations anywhere in the United Kingdom.[193] At the same time, and to facilitate preventive operations, Exchequer prosecutions were sped up, and the hovering limits, which had previously stood at four leagues, were extended to one hundred leagues, removing an acknowledged obstacle to successful seizures.[194]

Superficially, this looked like a new departure. Looking back at the preventive service, however, these were remedies that had repeatedly been tested for the past century. As ever, the question was not whether there was an intention to remove corruption and negligence, but to what extent this was actually achieved in practice. There is no indication that the problems pervading the bureaucratic structure of the preventive service during the eighteenth century ceased to be a problem between 1809 and 1822. There was corruption. There was collusion.[195] And there was negligence. By 1821, it was still necessary to remind riding officers that "the state of the Moon or Weather" was "no excuse for Riding Officers less alert on duty".[196] The extension of legal powers, moreover, often led to additional problems. In all seriousness, the question had to be asked whether the extension of the hovering limits meant that the British Customs could now legally seize suspected smuggling vessels within the limits of the French and Dutch ports.[197] On yet another level, the new accountability measures were also incapable of removing traditional sources of inefficiency: due to their different executive supervision and rationales, the services were rife with competition, conflict, and a "want of cordiality".[198]

---

[191] TNA CUST143/16, pp. 153–156, 167–168; CUST29/7, 'Preventive Waterguard', 11 March 1817.
[192] *Copies of the Eleventh and Twelfth Reports*, p. 54.
[193] TNA CUST143/17, p. 375.
[194] George III, ch. 121.
[195] Philp, *Coast Blockade*, pp. 52, 171; McCooey, *Smuggling on the South Coast*, pp. 172–186; *Copies of the Eleventh and Twelfth Reports*, p. 60.
[196] TNA CUST29/7, 'Riding Officers', 5 May 1821.
[197] TNA CUST143/16, p. 163.
[198] TNA CUST143/17, p. 456. See also *Copies of the Eleventh and Twelfth Reports*, pp. 56–57; TNA CUST29/7, 'Coast Blockade', 4 February 1819; English Board of Excise to Treasury, 25 January 1816, in *Copies of all Letters*, pp. 11–13.

Another tension resulted from the idea that the preventive service was best understood as a naval affair. George Rose thought the Customs Board was "incompetent" to supervise the service, being "unacquainted with Sea affairs".[199] This rationale also informed the changes made in 1816, with the Treasury arguing that the performance of the service called for "naval watchfulness and discipline".[200] To some extent, this corresponded to feelings among the officers. In terms of armament, vessel outfit, pay, and rewards, the captains of the revenue vessels consistently pushed for an adaptation to naval standards during the period of the French wars.[201] Patriotism and social mobility were clearly relevant factors in this. Civilians serving under the Customs Board developed considerable pride for serving in a force that more closely than ever before resembled, especially under wartime conditions, a naval command.[202] Not all of this was welcomed by either the Treasury or the Admiralty. When captains of the Customs cruisers requested, in June 1804, new uniforms that included silver epaulettes, this was denied, "lest the same should interfere with H.M.s Naval Service".[203] From 1816 onwards, however, the assimilation in pay rates and terms of service was well under way. Naval officers already commanded preventive forces in the coast blockade, and when the force returned to the Customs in 1822, many naval men remained in the superior posts. In 1831, the Admiralty was even granted the right to conduct the appointments in the coastguard, which was, in all other respects, supervised by the Customs Board.[204] The rationale was that naval men were persons "who, from habit and long experience, are better calculated to increase its [the coastguard's] efficiency than Civilians." As an additional incentive for the men, the ranks and promotions in the coastguard were adapted to naval service. Ultimately, this would also serve the additional purpose of protecting the coasts "against any hostile disembarkation".[205]

Although the Customs Board did protest against the changes at this time, the apparent tension over whether the coastguard constituted a revenue affair or a naval affair was a structural ambiguity in the service from around 1816. It is also reminiscent of the older question of what the purpose of the

---

[199] BL Add. MS 38262, fols 184–196.
[200] *A Copy of any Treasury Minutes, or Correspondence between the Treasury and the Revenue Boards; relating to the Revenue Cutters; since the 1st January 1815* (London, 1816).
[201] TNA CUST143/16, pp. 203–204. See also Smith, *King's Cutters*, pp. 125–144.
[202] Smith, *King's Cutters*, pp. 89–90.
[203] TNA CUST143/16, p. 140.
[204] TNA CUST143/17, p. 455.
[205] TNA CUST143/17, p. 719.

preventive service actually was and how this purpose was best served. This could be framed as a question of competence on the part of the officers, proper supervision, and knowledge. Proponents of naval appointments stressed the "high professional character" of these men and the superior measures of supervision, discipline, and control. But proponents of revenue appointments dismissed such notions. Revenue men needed local knowledge, local connections, as well as the "particular habits of life" from which these sprang. Their opposition to the smugglers was a question of "character" and habit that naval officers did not possess.[206]

> In this view the officer of the Navy is not so well qualified as the one who has been employed by the Revenue, as the former, or local knowledge, is only to be obtained by long and hardly-gained experience, and the latter only to be carried into execution by persons with whom *gain*, not *high professional character*, is the ruling principle. It will take some time to give the newly appointed officers local experience; it would perhaps not be practicable to make them so far descend from the distinction of naval officers, as to induce them to become effectual spies upon actions of the Smugglers, and their associates, or to enter into the necessary correspondence with persons on shore.[207]

In a succinct way, this passage captures the rationales of preventive policing upon the old system, in which individual gain, rather than professionalism, reigned supreme. Much as the executive wanted the latter to be the ruling principle, there was much to be said about the former still being the surer road to success. As far as the system as a whole was concerned, moreover, and beyond the characteristics of the individual officers, the debate could also be cast into the traditional argument of the purpose of coastal policing. The revenue men insisted that it was "a system which does not contemplate warfare, but is the exercise of cunning against vigilance".[208] It was a wider and more complex system than the Admiralty or the Treasury was willing to acknowledge. The prevention of smuggling was but one purpose of the service and while this could, theoretically, be just as well performed by the navy, other things could not. Next to revenue duties, the coastguard enforced the Public Health Acts and Alien Acts, the Contagious Diseases Acts and Post Office Acts, the Merchant Shipping Acts and The Navigation

---

[206] English Board of Excise to Treasury, 25 January 1816, in *Copies of all Letters*, pp. 11–13.
[207] Scottish Board of Excise to Treasury, 28 January 1816, in *Copies of all Letters*, p. 14.
[208] English Board of Excise to Treasury, 25 January 1816, in *Copies of all Letters*, p. 12.

Laws.[209] To portray them exclusively as an anti-smuggling force, and to supplement this service with officers unfamiliar with any of these duties, was to misunderstand what the coastguard was about. With this debate, and the tensions described above, there is a distinct feeling that rather than constituting a new departure, the creation of the coastguard had, in many structural respects, come full circle. The rebranding of the coastal administration as "coastguard" ultimately did little to solve the structural ambiguities of coastal enforcement.

Conclusions

The present chapter was an attempt to chart the long history of abortive and failed attempts to reform, correct, and improve the preventive service throughout the eighteenth century. Whether in the form of parliamentary committees, legislative efforts, bureaucratic restructurings, or indeed in the myriad reports and schemes and suggestions from interested parties, these attempts, and how and why they failed, directly speak to the limits of state-building in the period. Often guided mainly by fiscal concerns, the preventive service could not be made productive in a fiscal perspective, because that was not its only and, in certain respects, not even its main function. What ultimately proved itself as the best solution to the conundrum was to ease up on the relentless push for higher tariffs and thus ease the pressures of the imperial fiscal system on the domestic shores. In adopting this perspective, in the mid-1780s, it briefly looked as if the preventive service was to become redundant and the coastal riddle thereby solved.

In the event, however, the French threat that began to manifest around 1790 quickly revived old debates about strengthening coastal defences and underscored, yet again, the sinister implications of cross-channel smuggling. The subsequent changes and modifications to the coastal preventive service resulted, around 1820, in a newly made coastguard, which – nominally, functionally, and bureaucratically – more closely resembled the administrative institution familiar to modern eyes. Yet this is not, the chapter concludes, a story of an inefficient and obscure premodern bureaucracy that suddenly came to be saved via professionalization through modern bureaucratic tools and ideas. A new name did not make for a new institution. After all, the 'new' ideas had already been practiced in the Customs for nearly a hundred years. Thus it is little surprising that the new coastguard was not as novel as it may seem. Its structure, its organization, and its core principles were – the

---

[209] TNA CUST143/17, p. 678.

rhetoric of change and reform notwithstanding – still essentially the same. Perhaps paradoxically, a system that appeared out-of-date for much of the eighteenth century suddenly carried the marks of modernity, despite being, at its core, unchanged. Ultimately, therefore, the story told here questions any simple narrative of bureaucratization and modernization. Just as a century earlier, coastal enforcement remained a riddle.

Conclusion

To end the story with 1822 is, to some extent, an arbitrary decision. In many ways, the history told here continues rather seamlessly. The shifting of coastal responsibilities between the Customs administration and the Admiralty, for instance, features quite prominently in the post-1822 history of the preventive service, or rather, the coastguard. Neither is the administrative rupture as stark as modern histories of the coastguard will have us believe. Its nineteenth-century history, moreover, is almost as neglected as the one that has been the subject of this study.[1] At the same time, there are certain factors that change the shape of that history. Some of these are external. The ultimate dominance of the Royal Navy over European waters finally achieved the aspiration of a blue-water defence of the domestic scene and greatly facilitated naval operations against coastal threats.[2] The firm integration of Ireland, in 1800, ultimately also removed many of the loopholes afforded by the previous indirect means of domination.[3] And the demise of mercantilist protectionism, perhaps best exemplified, in the present context, with the end of the wool ban in 1824, obliterated many of the incentives previously afforded to the illicit trader.[4] A more professional intelligence service, both abroad and at home, and the relative professionalization of dealing with aliens in the context of the Home Office bureaucracy eliminated another matter that had previously lent urgency to the preventive efforts of the Customs. Some of these things, in fact, had already happened by the 1780s and 1790s, and only the Revolutionary and Napoleonic Wars had kept the old rationales alive.

---

[1] Exceptions are William Webb, *Coastguard: An Official History of H. M. Coastguard* (London, 1976), and Bernhard Scarlett, *Shipminder: The Story of Her Majesty's Coastguard* (London, 1971).

[2] N. A. M. Rodger, *The Command of the Ocean. A Naval History of Britain 1649–1815* (London, 2004), pp. 563–574.

[3] R. B. McDowell, *Ireland in the Age of Imperialism and Revolution, 1760–1801* (Oxford, 1991), pp. 678–704.

[4] Martin Daunton, *Trusting Leviathan: The Politics of Taxation in Britain, 1799–1914* (Cambridge, 2001). See also Philip Harling, Peter Mandler, 'From "Fiscal-Military" State to Laissez-faire State, 1760–1850', *JBS*, 32 (1993), 44–70.

Internal circumstances add to the sense of a fundamentally altered scene. In the late 1810s, lifesaving entered the list of duties of the coastguard for the first time and would, over the coming decades, become a dominant feature of the service. This, among other things, changed the very meaning of what prevention, on the seacoasts, signified.[5] The naval element, too, continued to change the shape of the bureaucracy.[6] And finally, new modes and techniques of communication, such as the optical telegraph system that connected the Kentish coast to London as early as 1796 and that was further developed in the 1810s, meant that the response time to any particular incident on the coast was significantly reduced, and the nature of coastal surveillance altered.[7] This made the constant presence of designated officers somewhat redundant, and thus removed another previously important feature of the preventive service. The sands were irretrievably shifting.

Nonetheless, to mark the end of the study with the rather convenient date of 1822 runs the risk of lending credibility to the suggestion that the coastguard, as it was established in that year, bears the marks of a 'modern' institution with little resemblance to what went before. The policing of Customs fraud and Customs related crime, too, could easily be conceived as being dealt with by a professionalized bureaucracy that conveniently appeared on the national scene just a few years prior to the Metropolitan Police of 1829. If the latter was, until recently, being credited with "a revolution in traditional methods of law enforcement", is not the assumption warranted that the coastguard, to the extent that it was also a unit concerned with policing of specific crimes, was part of that same revolution and consequently did away with "traditional methods" to the same extent?[8] If only to dispel such notions, a brief look at the coastguard after 1822 will show that the forms and methods of old regime policing did not, through the act of renaming the preventive service, disappear in the nineteenth century, at least not initially. Such a brief view of the nineteenth-century developments also helps render the results of this study more precise.

[5] TNA CUST143/16, p. 209. The introduction of designated mortars for lifesaving purposes occurred in 1819 and gradually became more important. See *Tenth Report of the Commissioners of Inquiry into the Collection and Management of the Revenue arising in Ireland, Scotland, etc. Ports of Ireland, Preventive Coast Guard, Quarantine, etc.* (London, 1824), p. 22.

[6] Webb, *Coastguard*, pp. 31–37.

[7] See Daniel R. Headrick, *When Information Came of Age: Technologies of Knowledge in the Age of Reason and Revolution, 1700–1850* (Oxford, 2000), pp. 181–215; Roland Wenzlhuemer, *Connecting the Nineteenth-Century World: The Telegraph and Globalization* (Cambridge, 2012).

[8] J. L. Lyman, 'The Metropolitan Police Act of 1829', *Journal of Criminal Law and Criminology*, 55/1 (1964), 141–154, at p. 141.

"A Measure of False Economy"

The coastguard remained largely unaltered, compared to its 1822 setup, under the authority of the Board of Customs until 1856. During that time, approximation to naval rationales became more powerful: in 1831, all staff were to be appointed by the Admiralty. In 1845, moreover, coastguard staff were made to sign written agreements to serve on ships of the navy when required. This happened, for the first time on a larger scale, in 1854, when around 3,000 coastguards were drafted into the navy in the context of the Crimean War. Increasingly, the coastguard came to be seen as a naval reserve. During the same time, the building of designated coastguard stations continued, providing, again for the first time, a visible physical architecture of coastal prevention. In some cases, new coastguard stations were erected; in others, the converted Martello towers were used for such purposes. The same period also saw a change in emphasis in coastal prevention in that lifesaving became a more important purpose. The 1829 instructions still regarded the prevention of smuggling as paramount, but by 1841 the focus was increasingly leaning towards lifesaving. Reports from 1839 and 1849 suggested, if tenuously, that the coastguard was slowly getting the better of the smugglers; in some cases, the forces were reduced, especially the larger vessels formerly maintained. In the meantime, the experience of the usefulness of coastguard men as a trained naval reserve in the Crimean War led to the request at the Admiralty to get the coastguard, once again, under its command structure. By an Act of Parliament of 1856, this change was effected. In the new situation, the coastguard was even more confidently used as a naval reserve, with smuggling prevention and rescue operations increasingly taking second place. The statute in fact explicitly stated the aims of the coastguard to act, firstly, as coastal defence and secondly as naval reserve, whereas the protection of the revenue was awarded merely third place.[9] Rescue operations, in the meantime, were gradually being taken over by designated volunteer brigades, later developing into the lifeboat service. After the First World War, in 1923, growing dissatisfaction with the services of the coastguard finally led to the definite withdrawal of the coastguard from the Admiralty command and a reestablishment under the Board of Trade, where it ultimately remained until the 1990s.[10]

---

[9] 19/20 Victoria, ch. 83.
[10] This is based on Webb, *Coastguard*, pp. 21–80; Smith, Graham, *King's Cutters: The Revenue Service and the War against Smuggling* (London, 1983), pp. 162–167; Edward Carson, *The Ancient and Rightful Customs: A History of the English Customs Service* (London, 1972), pp. 690–733; TNA CUST143/17, pp. 690–733.

Despite what may seem a rather seamless and smooth progression towards the twentieth century, the coastguard remained, in its everyday practices, subject to the same administrative problems that had dominated its earlier history. Old regime policing, in the policing of revenue crimes as elsewhere, was not, in the first half of the nineteenth century, a thing of the past.[11] Without wanting to give an elaborate analysis here, even a superficial glance at the available records and literature shows that, among other things, bribery and collusion were widespread in the service.[12] "Instead of being done by violence and meeting on the coast", the solicitor of the Customs reported in 1844, smuggling was now done by concealment and "a good deal by bribes".[13] Of a particular mode of smuggling tobacco in Ireland, a Liverpool merchant was asked, "Your belief is that such a transaction can take place only by connivance?" His answer was brief: "Only by connivance."[14] When two superior coastguard officers in England were questioned, in 1844, about the conduct of inferior officers and possible collusive practices, they were asked, "Do you know of any of them [the inferior officers] being tempted? – We hear reports of it. – Whom are they tempted by? – The smugglers."[15] James Combrain, in the meantime, the inspector general of the coastguard in Ireland, was asked, also in 1844, about the rolling procedure implemented in 1822: "Have you generally, in practice, allowed the chief boatmen and the men to remain at one place for a number of years? – Yes, frequently." As it turned out, this was even the case when the officers had married locally or when they had formed local social connections.[16] In other words, the bureaucratic reforms of the 1820s had not, after all, achieved a more professional bureaucracy, partly because they were, once again, not strictly implemented. Negligence, too, was still an issue: in 1833, a coastguard report held that there had recently been several instances of superior officers "making entries in their journals of the duty performed by themselves and of the conference said to have been held with their crews on their guard during the night which, on examination, have been proved to be false."[17] Despite the express orders

---

[11] See David Churchill, 'Rethinking the state monopolisation thesis: the historiography of policing and criminal justice in nineteenth century England', *Crime, History and Societies*, 18 (2014), 131–152.
[12] Webb, *Coastguard*, p. 29.
[13] TNA CUST143/17, p. 517.
[14] TNA CUST143/17, p. 521.
[15] TNA CUST143/17, p. 525.
[16] TNA CUST143/17, p. 539.
[17] Cit. Webb, *Coastguard*, p. 26.

to the contrary, coastguard officers also still meddled in local politics.[18] In the meantime, new modes of smuggling and concealment of contraband continued to be devised and practised, often very successfully.[19] The extent and amount of such smuggling, however, remained guesswork, often frustratingly conducted by interviewing local officers, who were able to provide impressionistic views at best.[20]

This latter problem was still tied, to a large extent, to the attempts at economising the administration, which, by 1851, still cost upwards of £500,000.[21] Here too, however, the old conundrums remained. Without the political will to reduce certain important duties, especially on tobacco, which in Ireland and parts of Great Britain remained an important staple of illicit trade, it was simply not feasible to reduce the establishment of the coastguard. Protectionism inevitably put pressure on the seacoasts, as it consistently had during the eighteenth century. While an 1851 committee inquiring into the public expenses of the Customs administration was perfectly willing to reduce the establishment so as to save expenses, it expressed considerable caution at doing so. "The mere reduction of expense, irrespective of sufficient protection to the revenue, would be a measure of false economy." Much as it wanted to do away with the last remaining relict of the old preventive service, namely the riding officers, or mounted guard, it could not, in good conscience, recommend this.[22] It later transpired, in fact, that the ordered reduction of the riding officers in 1822, when the coastguard was founded, had not even been carried out.[23] For all the declarations of a new mode of guarding the coasts, the core elements of the preventive service were slow to disappear as long as the old fiscal rationales remained in place. The geographic setup of the service, too, remained largely unchanged when compared to eighteenth-century preferences.[24] To put it in the words of an official writing in 1907:

> The history of the Coastguard from 1822 to 1856 is mainly a record of administrative changes and staff fluctuations, for although different branches of the force were from time to time either suppressed or amalgamated, no material alterations were made in the methods adopted for the prevention of smuggling.[25]

[18] TNA CUST143/17, pp. 492–496.
[19] TNA CUST143/17, pp. 500–501, 515, 517.
[20] For example TNA CUST143/17, pp. 541–542.
[21] TNA CUST143/17, p. 577.
[22] TNA CUST143/17, p. 578.
[23] TNA CUST143/17, p. 707.
[24] See, for instance, TNA ADM175/2, ADM175/5, ADM175/7.
[25] TNA CUST143/17, p. 713. Appointments did change, with a more elaborate method of nominations; see TNA ADM175/74, ADM175/75.

Something similar can be said with a view to the purpose of coastal policing. The same 1851 report also reiterated the by then commonly held opinion that for maintaining the coastguard's efficiency "at its highest possible degree", naval officers were to fill the commanding posts in the coastguard.[26] Whereas this was entirely uncontroversial at this point, with the coastguard essentially being regarded as a naval reserve, the question of the general oversight over the coastguard services was not. The removal of the coastguard from the Customs to the Admiralty in 1856, in particular, reignited the familiar debate over the aims and purposes of coastal policing. Just days before the Coastguard Act passed into law in July 1856, the Board of Customs directed a strongly worded letter to the Treasury regarding the proposed transfer. With reference to the 1821 commission of inquiry, which had strongly alleged widespread corruption in the Admiralty-led coast blockade in Kent and Sussex, the Customs Commissioners reported that the communication about these frauds between Admiralty and Customs had not always been "in a friendly spirit" and that it had been nearly impossible to resolve these disputes to the benefit of the revenue. After the amalgamation in 1831, things had run much better. Removing the coastguard from Customs authority at this stage would, the Board argued in 1856, recreate that "jealousy and distrust" between the branches of the service and thus endanger the "security of the revenue". Naval men, often appointed for short periods, were also unable to acquire the local knowledge required for the service and could not be depended upon. The duties of the coastguard, after all, were "entirely of a fiscal character" and if that character be changed "as to become a naval defence of the coast", the object of revenue protection, inclusive of many other duties, would certainly be neglected.[27]

The change was made regardless of this protest. The tension expressed in this exchange regarding the purposes of coastal policing, however, was to remain with the service for quite some time. When T. Freeman, Chairman of the Customs Board, was interviewed by the Select Committee on Inland Revenue and Customs Establishments in 1862, this particular issue was discussed at length. The coastguard under Admiralty commands, he said, could not properly be called a fiscal administration, because "it is now a guard of the coast as against the possibility of invasion". The Board of Customs, in fact, was still required to retain additional preventive officers to combat smuggling. Freeman admitted that this constituted, again, "a double service". With a view to the Admiralty vessels, they similarly, and perhaps predominantly, performed naval purposes. If the prevention of smuggling were to be the singular object of the coastguard, it would, Freeman said,

---

[26] TNA CUST143/17, p. 583.
[27] TNA CUST143/17, pp. 732–733.

have to be done in a different manner. But if the coastguard were again to be made a revenue service, it would enable the Board to have them perform important duties not in the purview of the present force. "There is no doubt that they could receive lights, that they could rummage ships, and attend to wrecks and do many things which our officers now do." Given this situation of double duties on the part of the Customs and the Admiralty, the question was whether the purposes of the coastguard were actually performed efficiently. Evidently, they were not. When Freeman was asked whether the coastguard, under the present establishment, was effective at preventing smuggling, he answered, "I hardly think that it does prevent smuggling to any very great extent".[28]

As this brief outlook into the nineteenth century demonstrates, the old ambiguities and problems were, by the middle of the century, still in place and slow to change. The advent of lifesaving and rescue operations, the evolving of the coastguard into a naval reserve and, not least, the arrival of the steamship in the coastal and foreign trade as well as the coastguard, were all factors that can be said to have had an effect on the terms and practicalities of the service. But the ambiguities and problems in coastal space were still guided by policies that had no direct concern with the coast but affected this space on an everyday basis.

General Conclusions

Looking ahead at the history of the coastguard in the nineteenth century shows that the overall scene was permanently altered. Since the early history of the preventive service in the second half of the seventeenth century, things had changed quite drastically in some respect. In others, however, they had not. A number of conclusions can be drawn from this. The contrast between coastal arrangements in the eighteenth and the mid-nineteenth century demonstrates that the preventive service, such as it existed during the eighteenth century, was the product of rather specific circumstances that, in various ways, transformed the coast into a decidedly sensitive political space. Economic demands resulting from both imperial and mercantilist projects and doctrines, as well as the fiscal, military, and political pressures triggered by the Anglo-French antagonism, the Jacobite/Jacobin threat, and more broadly, Britain's continental commitment, ensured that the coast became, and remained, a space perceived as both important and fragile. None of these pressures alone were consistent and urgent enough

[28] TNA CUST143/17, pp. 659–665, 715.

to warrant the continuance of an administrative effort that was seen by many as rather dysfunctional. Rather, as the situations of the 1690s and 1790s underscore, it was the conflation of seemingly unconnected threats that, each in their own way, pointed to the seacoast as a space of vulnerability that kept the minds and the attention of central administrators fixed on the shore. As the study has shown in several places, such conflations were most frequently the result of war, usually with France. Perhaps unsurprisingly, war must be considered the main driver of both actual bureaucratic changes and political discussions about the necessity of such changes. Ultimately, this was also why the preventive service was kept alive throughout the period, despite its alleged and obvious failures. Frequently ignored when such pressures relented, the coastal service reliably resurfaced in the debates of central bodies when they felt, in times of crisis (i.e., war), that something – anything – needed to be done with regard to the coast.

Ironically, the service almost constantly disappointed. In administrative terms, coastal policing could not be made efficient. It was not, as many observers pointed out, productive in fiscal terms. It failed to live up to the expectation of quelling the strong tide of smuggling and other property crimes in coastal areas. And it certainly was no serious military agent either. In some way, such disappointments were a result of two political misunderstandings that were as obvious as they were persistent. At the moment of its creation, during the 1690s, the exact aim of the administrative structure was far from clear. It was designed as an answer not to one, but to several problems, whose only connection was the space in which they originated. Subsequent developments in the eighteenth century never resolved that tension. In adapting a measure of efficiency that focused exclusively on either fiscal demands, criminal prevention, or military support, the service could only be found wanting, simply because it was not designed to perform any of these exclusively, but rather all at once. Narrow criteria of efficiency, as several chapters of the study have illustrated, were bound to be misleading. The seacoasts were never a space of exclusively fiscal, criminal, or military activity.

That the main reason for this was never sufficiently understood represents the second misjudgement regarding coastal policing, namely the assumption that both the origin and the solution of coastal problems lay at the coast. This was not at all the case. But it was only to a limited extent that executive departments appreciated this. Smuggling, for instance, was not a result of coastal deviance but an indirect offspring of economic policies that were created at the centre. Consistently, it was mercantilist protectionism and the imperial aspirations of the Whitehall administrations that increased the pressures on coastal enforcement. The expectations regarding the performance of an ill-designed preventive service were particularly far-fetched given the consistent failure to understand, at central level, that the answer to coastal problems was not necessarily an executive clampdown but a fundamental reconsideration of centrally devised economic and political policies. No matter how much effort and rhetoric were poured into the punishment of smugglers during the 1740s, for instance, only a reassessment of fiscal policies during the 1780s achieved, for a short period, measurable successes. Ultimately, it was by far too little appreciated that the imperial policies of subsequent British governments during the eighteenth century directly and indirectly worked against any insular idea of the domestic scene, much as economic and political thought seemed to favour such an idea. In the face of imperial and global ambitions, the dependence on domestic policies that relied on the aspiration of complete control of coastal space was – and still is – an ambivalent and frail course of action.

The study has also aimed to illustrate why this was so. Bureaucratically speaking, there is much to dispute older assumptions about a relative inefficiency of the Customs bureaucracy when compared to other structures, such as the Excise. Many of the reform ideas that made the latter an example of bureaucratic innovation during the eighteenth century were, in fact, also applied in the Customs. That there was little consistency in the application of such bureaucratic tools is true. But it is also true for the Excise. What has made the historiographic difference in assessing the relative successes of these institutions was their fiscal performance, in turn usually discussed in the grand scheme of the fiscal-military narrative. At this point, however, it should be sufficiently clear that it is grossly misleading to apply this narrative to the entire structure of the Customs administrations and to lump its various parts together as if fiscal rationales were, at any point, the leading rationale. This was not true in the context of the port administrations, and it certainly was not true in the wider context of coastal policing. The preventive service, it has been argued, is better understood as an agent for the enforcement of authority in a much wider sense than merely in fiscal terms. The allegedly wicked effects of smuggling in terms of the erosion of deference, order, and political authority in the coastal counties repeatedly and necessarily transformed the preventive service, in the eyes of central authorities, into a policing operation or, as an 1831 report summarised the situation, into an "internal Police".[29] At the local level, too, most contemporaries were acutely aware that in the policing of the seacoasts, the authority of the central state was fundamentally at stake – and fundamentally threatened.

---

[29] TNA CUST147/1/1, p. 11.

It makes better sense for understanding these arrangements, as the study has shown, to follow this wider contemporary view. The ambiguities of enforcing political authority in the coastal counties cannot be fully appreciated if the Customs bureaucracy is exclusively seen as a fiscal agent. Only when viewed in its wider contemporary context can the successes and the shortcomings of the administration be fully understood. In this view, the social implications of coastal enforcement illustrate that much of what past research in the field of criminal history has shown regarding the negotiation of authority beyond Whitehall applies, to much the same extent, in the administrative context of the Customs. The near impossibility for local officers to conform to central expectations of efficiency, the deep ambivalence of local officeholding, the permeability of the line between officer and offender, and the necessity for central authorities to rely, their own avowals notwithstanding, on the offender, the common informer, and other temporary instruments of government for the enforcement of authority is very much in line with what past research has shown to be the case in the parishes. If anything, there was even more at stake in the coastal counties, as the recurring debates about smuggling persistently illustrate. Lost revenue was certainly an important concern to the central bodies, but it was the universal loss of deference and authority, the ever-lurking threat of invasion and foreign infiltration, and the perceived impossibility of controlling illicit mobility at the vulnerable margins of the several kingdoms that occupied the minds of central administrators. Even contemporaries had to admit that, in the final analysis, coastal enforcement presented a political and social problem as much as an economic one. The historiographic reduction of these problems to themes such as Customs borders and tax evasion does not begin to embrace the full extent of coastal ambiguities.

In these respects, the study ultimately also adds, in several ways, to the ongoing debate on state-building in eighteenth-century Britain. Coastal policing, as the introduction has shown, sits rather oddly at the very meeting point of two different narratives of state-building, namely the fiscal-military account and the idea of the state as a domestic regulator of paternalism. To both narratives, the study of coastal surveillance and prevention, seemingly marginal in a double sense, adds important insights. The fiscal-military interpretation of eighteenth-century Britain, several chapters have shown, can be grossly misleading even in an arena at first glance directly concerned with both military and fiscal concerns. Its narrow criteria fail to appreciate the full extent of an administration to which both fiscal and military matters were inherently relevant but which is inadequately studied by applying either one of these, or even both, exclusively. To put it simply: one of the two main contributors of government revenue in the eighteenth century is not adequately understood as a revenue collecting body. This realisation is important because it affects both the structural interpretations of the eighteenth-century British state as well as its potential for the explanation of major turning points and changes, as the re-evaluation of the 1690s has illustrated. At the very least, this should help introduce caution into attempts at reading the British state in the eighteenth century in too narrow a fiscal-military interpretation. To adopt such a narrow view is, the study has illustrated, prone to an ultimately premature dismissal of bureaucratic structures as inefficient that must, on second glance, simply be viewed with a different set of heuristic tools to understand how they fit into the machinery of the eighteenth-century British state. Accordingly, to adopt such narrow views is also prone to miss the opportunity to study the wider political significance of eighteenth-century bureaucratic structures at the very core of the British state. As an agency of criminal enforcement, as an economic regulator in the widest sense, as a controller of coastal mobility, and as a tool for the negotiation of political authority, the preventive service of the Customs is better understood in the broader sense of state-building, i.e. as a socio-political tool in the context of the "patriarchal state". In adopting this perspective, moreover, the case of coastal policing illustrates similar limits to state authority that have been shown to operate in other settings. Exacerbated by its location at the geographical margins of the realm, the negotiation of state authority and the limits to state authority imposed by local populations are as evident as elsewhere in Britain. Rather than a straightforward story of either successful or unsuccessful tax extraction, this was a story of continuous conflict and inherent contradictions.

The focus on such conflicts and contradictions also underscores another important result of this study. Against the grain of what historiography in the vein of the new coastal history and its earlier predecessors have consistently argued, the story of the discovery of the coast in the eighteenth century and its emphatic appraisal as a space of leisure is quite evidently only a part of the history of the coast in the eighteenth century. The overall picture is more ambiguous than that. From its first discovery as an object of deep-seated political anxieties in the second half of the seventeenth century, the coast gradually acquired the status of a politically distinct space over the course of the eighteenth century. Designated coastal legislation, administrative measures of surveillance and control, and the manifold attempts at regulating coastal mobility of people and goods are all indicative of a space both vulnerable and important. That this story of the coast should have happened concurrent with its discovery as an emphatically positive space of leisure and recreation is in itself rather striking. But it is not surprising. The coast, as many scholars have suggested, is a space riddled with contradictions, and this evidently extends to its representation in historiographic narratives. The present study of the political attempts at controlling coastal space, however, has also highlighted the existence of these contradictions and ambiguities in the arena of state activity. No measure of bureaucratic expenses was enough to achieve control of coastal space, because the more central bodies – driven by ideological policies – imagined the coast as a linear edge that could be effectively sealed off, the more the geographical and social realities of coastal life were to undermine such idealized assumptions. This ambiguity in the understanding of coastal space is directly tied to more abstract political ideas of the time: the insular understanding of the British state on which these policies of coastal control rested were deeply and fundamentally at odds with the imperial ambitions, the mercantilist protectionism, and the continental commitments of Great Britain during the eighteenth century. In other words, the political difficulties of coastal administration that frustrated the British state during the eighteenth century were *made* by the British state during the eighteenth century. This particular finding evidently goes well beyond the thematic scope of this study. The overall change of political circumstances over the nineteenth and twentieth centuries, as well as technological and bureaucratic developments notwithstanding, many of the contradictions and ambivalences encountered first in the eighteenth century remain the same. As in the eighteenth century, moreover, the problem is less the inherently permeable space of the seacoast but rather the imposition of political agendas onto coastal space that operate with idealized expectations of surveillance and control.

By way of a final conclusion, it is, at this point, perhaps appropriate to return to Turner's coastal sketch for one last time. Turner's vision of the English south coast in 1808 is dominated by the natural conditions of the seacoast itself: the rugged shoreline and the vast cliffs, the storm clouds, and the wind, and the water. Equally prominent are the material artefacts of coastal defence, such as the Martello towers. In what is clearly the least imposing aspect of this view, however, Turner has placed the people and their means of transport. The figures are struggling, the boat is broken. This rather implicit hierarchy of the things of coastal space and, in particular, the evident frailty of the human element underscores one final result of this study, and it is a theme that has come to the fore throughout all the chapters. Any political attempt at creating a system of coastal surveillance and control that does not take into account the will of the local people to follow and enforce its rules and its spirit will be, as the eighteenth-century history of coastal policing has shown time and again, "altogether ineffectual". Imperial and expansionist policies aimed at both global influence *and* isolation, moreover, were evidently bound to come back haunting the domestic scene. Rather than insularity being the source of Britain's natural rise to imperial ambitions, as older assumptions will have us believe, it was Britain's imperial ambitions that persistently thwarted ideological assumptions of the islands' splendid isolation. Whether, in the face of this conundrum, it was wiser to rethink the underlying policies devised by central government or whether it was more effective to throw increasingly elaborate efforts at preventing their effects was, as the reform movement of the 1780s has shown, a matter of intense debate. It evidently still is. But, as one of the commentators on this particular problem aptly wrote in 1749, it is never too late to appreciate that "in the framing all Laws, some Regard should be had […] to the Passions of Mankind."[30]

[30] Anon., *A Free Apology in Behalf of the Smugglers, so far as their Case affects the Constitution. By an Enemy to all Oppression, whether by Tyranny, or Law* (London, 1749), p. 9.

Bibliography

Primary Sources (Manuscripts)

British Library, London (BL)
Add. MS 4761, 18903, 23703, 28157, 28879, 30229, 33924, 42586, 42774B, 47108, 47109, 74055 (Various)
Add. MS 8133A, 8133B, 8133C, 8134, 8135 (Musgrave Papers)
Add. MS 32688, 32692, 32702–3, 32706, 32709, 32711–12, 32718 (Newcastle Papers)
Add. MS 38262, 38368, 38462, 38463 (Liverpool Papers)
Add. MS 61546, 61596, 61603, 61607–9, 61614 (Blenheim Papers)
Add. MS 70047, 70048 (Harley Papers)
Add. MS 72569, 72570 (Trumbull Papers)
Lansdowne MS 707/3
Stowe MS 865

Cambridge University Library, Cambridge (CUL)
Ch(H), Political Papers 40: Nos 6, 7, 15, 16
Ch(H), Political Papers 41: Nos 2–7, 18, 21, 23, 25, 26, 29, 32–36, 38–43, 46, 48, 51, 53–56, 59, 61–64
Ch(H), Political Papers 44: Nos 9, 12, 14, 16, 19, 35, 55, 69

East Sussex Record Office, Brighton (ESRO)
SAY252–59, SAY260–267, SAY278, SAY279–283, SAY286, SAY288–294
    SAY295, SAY296, SAY297, SAY298, SAY300, SAY301, SAY307, SAY313,
    SAY314, SAY317, SAY339, SAY346, SAY369, SAY423, SAY424, SAY2245,
    SAY2251, SAY2243–68, SAY2318

Glasgow City Archive, Glasgow (GCA)
CE59 (Glasgow Outport) 1/2, 2/1
CE60 (Greenock/Glasgow Port Outport) 1/1–1/4, 1/15, 1/16, 1/37, 4/10
CE73 (Rothesay Outport) 1/1, 1/2, 2/6
CE74 (Tobermory Outport) 2/6
CE82 (Campbeltown Outport) 1/1, 1/2, 1/11, 2/5

Hampshire Archive and Local Studies, Winchester
MS 25A03

National Maritime Museum, Greenwich (NMM)
ADL/K/1, MLN/17, MRK/105/7/1–14, PGE/7, PLT/76, SIG/B/54, WYN/109/8

National Records of Scotland, Edinburgh (NRS)
CE3 (Scottish Establishment Lists) 1, 2, 8, 11, 14, 17
CE7 (Miscellanea) 12
CE14 (General Orders) 1–3
CE51 (Dumfries Outport) 1/3, 1/5, 1/7
CE87 (Aberdeen Outport) 1/2, 1/3, 1/5–1/8

The National Archives, Kew (TNA)
Admiralty (ADM)
    1/3865, 1/3866, 1/3867, 1/4283, 7/49, 7/225, 7/226, 28/145, 106/3124, 106/3475–3509, 175/2, 175/5, 175/7, 175/74, 175/75
Board of Trade (CO)
    CO388/7
Customs (CUST)
    CUST18 (Establishment Lists) 12, 25, 40, 49, 51, 59, 77, 105, 115, 213
    CUST20 (Irish Establishment Lists) 56, 58, 69, 81, 110, 149
    CUST29 (Board Minutes Extracts) 1–7
    CUST51 (Sandwich Outport) 25
    CUST54 (Dover Outport) 1, 13, 21, 25, 147
    CUST58 (Portsmouth Outport) 12, 13, 75
    CUST59 (Weymouth Outport) 1–5, 8, 9, 10, 16, 69–77
    CUST60 (Poole Outport) 6
    CUST61 (Cowes Outport) 6, 17
    CUST62 (Southampton Outport) 59
    CUST64 (Exeter Outport) 6, 9
    CUST65 (Dartmouth Outport) 2
    CUST66 (Plymouth Outport) 1, 2, 4, 5
    CUST68 (Penzance Outport) 12
    CUST69 (Barnstaple Outport) 59, 67
    CUST69 (Ilfracombe Outport) 169
    CUST72 (Cardiff Outport) 1, 3, 77A
    CUST73 (Swansea Outport) 1, 3, 7, 9, 62
    CUST78 (Beaumaris Outport) 1, 2, 3, 5
    CUST82 (Whitehaven Outport) 1–13
    CUST84 (Newcastle Outport) 19
    CUST85 (Sunderland Outport) 5
    CUST89 (Stockton Outport) 1, 4, 6, 7
    CUST92 (Hull Outport) 11, 17

CUST97 (Great Yarmouth Outport) 1–16, 19, 20–28, 30, 73, 74a, 74b, 75–77, 80
CUST98 (Ipswich Outport) 1, 5
CUST99 (Harwich Outport) 1, 11, 67
CUST101 (Maldon Outport) 1, 6
CUST143 (Parry Collection) 16, 17, 18
CUST148 (Collier Records) 11, 12, 13
Various (CUST)
   CUST31/1, CUST32/1, CUST37/2, CUST41/42, CUST141/4, CUST147/1/1, CUST147/1/2
Privy Council (PC)
   1/1/171, 1/3,50, 1/5/111
   2/72, 2/73, 2/74, 2/75, 2/76, 2/77
Treasury (T)
   T1 (Treasury In-Letters)
   4, 6, 8, 11, 13, 14, 18, 22, 24, 30, 33, 34, 38, 41, 43, 45, 47, 51, 54–58, 60, 61, 63, 64, 66, 69, 70, 72, 74, 76, 80–90, 93, 96, 97, 100–103, 105–108, 110, 113, 114, 116, 117, 121–123, 126, 127, 128, 131–133, 137, 138, 141, 145, 146, 147, 149, 151, 157, 159, 173, 185, 189, 190, 193, 202, 224, 240, 243, 248, 250, 252, 342, 361, 388, 392, 402, 434, 437, 514
   T11 (Customs Out-Letters)
   12–23
   T14 (Ireland Out-Letters)
   8
   T17 (Scotland Out-Letters)
   1–4, 6, 7
Various (T)
   T28/40, T29/11, T48/82, T64/139, T64/140, T64/143, T64/144, T64/153, T64/238, T64/240
Various
   AO3/1101/1, SP34/2/23, SP36/30/402
War Office (WO)
   1/827, 1/875, 1/876, 1/877, 4/125, 5/32, 5/33, 5/40, 5/41, 5/42

West Sussex Record Office, Chichester (WSRO)
Add. MS 2610
Goodwood 154
Goodwood 155
   H4, H7, H8, H10, H11, H16, H17, H18, H19, H24, H32, H33, H37, H42, H43, H47, H71, H73, H74, H75, H83, H96, H97, H111, H114
Goodwood 156
   G6, G17, G24, G31, G42, G57, G59, G72

Primary Sources (Printed)

Contemporary Books and Articles

Anon. ['Gentleman of Chichester'], *A Full and Genuine History of the Inhuman and Unparrallell'd Murders of Mr. William Galley, A Custom-House Officer at the Port of Southampton and Mr. Daniel Chater, a Shoemaker, at Fordingbridge in Hampshire, by Fourteen Notorious Smugglers* [...] (London, 1749).

Anon., *A Free Apology on Behalf of the Smugglers, so far as their Case affects the Constitution. By an Enemy to all Oppression, whether by Tyranny, or Law* (London, 1749).

Anon., *A Letter to a Member of Parliament concerning Clandestine Trade. Shewing how far the Evil Practices at the Custom-house at London tend to the Encouragement of such a Trade. Written by a Fair Merchant* (London, 1700).

Anon., *A Rebuke to the Informers: With a Plea for the Ministers of the Gospels, Called Nonconformists, and their Meetings* (London, 1675).

Anon., *Advice to the Unwary: Or, An Abstract of Certain Penal Laws Now in Force Against Smuggling in General* (London, 1780).

Anon., *Philagathus, The Informer's Doom: Or, an Amazing and Seasonable Letter from Utopia, Directed from the Man on the Moon* (London, 1683).

Anon., *Reasons humbly offered for Regulating the Importation of Tobacco into this Kingdom, for the Preservation of the Revenue, and the better Carrying on of the said Trade* (s.l., 1722).

Anon., *The Case of the Merchants Trading in Tobacco, at Whitehaven, in the County of Cumberland* (s.l., 1715).

Anon., *The Character of an Informer Wherein his Mischievous nature, and Leud Practises are Detected* (s.l., 1675).

Anon., *The Deplorable Case of the Chief and other Agents or Officers that have been deputed...* (s.l., s.d.).

Anon., *The Informer's Looking-Glass, in which he may see himself while he is Maliciously Prosecuting Dissenting Protestants* (s.l., 1682).

Anon., *The Rules of the Water-Side: Or, the General Practice of the Customs* (London, 1714).

Anon., *The Undue Administration: Or, The Usual Management of the Customs Considered, and compared with the late pernicious Practice of Removing and Placing Officers, contrary to all former Precedents. The whole Impartially Represented, by Persons who now suffer under the Injustice and Oppression of a Quondam Minister of State, to the utter Ruin of Themselves and Families* (London, 1717).

Bacon, Thomas, *A Compleat System of the Revenue of Ireland, in its several Branches of Import, Export, and Inland Duties* (Dublin, 1737).

Bridges, George, *A Whip for the Smugglers: Or, a Curb to France. Shewing the only way to Prevent Wool-Smuggling* (London, 1742).

Bridges, George, *Plain Dealing: Or the Whole Method of Wool-Smuggling Clearly Discovere'd, And the Weakness of the Laws in Force, put in a clear Light* (London, 1744).

[Carter, William], *England's Interest Asserted in the Improvement of its Native Commodities; and more especially the Manufacture of Wool* (London, 1669).

[Carter, William], *The Proverb Crossed, or A new Paradox Maintained* (London, 1677).

Carter, William, *An Abstract of the Proceedings of W. Carter; Being a Plea to some Objections Urged against HIM* (London, 1694).

Carter, William, *An Abstract of the Proceedings to Prevent Exportation of Wooll Un-Manufactured* (London, 1689).

Carter, William, *The Usurpations of France upon the Trade of the Woollen Manufacture of England* (London, 1695).

Clarendon, R. V., *A Sketch of the Revenue and Finances of Ireland and of the Appropriated Funds, Loans and Debt of the Nation from their Commencement* (London and Dublin, 1791).

Coke, Edward, *The Reports of Sir Edward Coke, late Lord Chief Justice of England of Divers Resolutions and Judgements given upon solemn Arguments, and with great Deliberation [...]*. (2nd ed. London, 1680).

Coxe, William (ed.), *Private and Original Correspondence of Charles Talbot, Duke of Shrewsbury, with King William, the Leaders of the Whig Party, and other Distinguished Statesmen* (London, 1821).

Crookshanks, John, *Instructions for the Collectors and other Officers Employ'd in HER MAJESTIES Customs, etc. in the North-Part of Great-Britain* (Edinburgh, 1707).

Crouch, Henry, *A Complete Guide to the Officers of His Majesty's Customs in the Outports* (London, 1732).

Crouch, Henry, *A Complete View of the British Customs* (London, 1725).

Danby Pickering (ed.), *The Statutes at Large from Magna Charta to the End of the Eleventh Parliament of Great Britain, Anno 1761* (and continued series) (Cambridge, 1762–1807).

Daniel, Thomas, *Ductor Mercatorius: or the Young Merchants' Instructor with respect to the Customs: Being a minute and particular Detail of the Regular Method of Proceeding at Out-Port Custom-Houses, in the several Branches of Marine Commerce* (Newcastle upon Tyne, 1759).

Defoe, Daniel, *A Tour Through the Whole Island of Great Britain, Divided into Circuits or Journies* (London, 1727).

Defoe, Daniel, *The History of the Union between England and Scotland with a Collection of Original Papers Relating Thereto* (London, 1709, repr. 1786).

Defoe, Daniel, *The True and Genuine Account of the Life and Actions of the Late Jonathan Wild* (London, 1725).

Gibson, John, *The History of Glasgow, from the Earliest Accounts to the Present Time* (Glasgow, 1777).

Hatton, Edward, *Comes Comercii: Or the Trader's Companion* (London, 1723, 4th ed).
Hayes, Richard, *Rules for the Port of London: Or, the Water-side Practice* (London, 1722).
Haynes, John, *A View of the Present State of the Clothing Trade in England* (London, 1706).
Haynes, John, *Great Britain's Glory: Or, An Account of the Great Numbers of Poor Employ'd in the Woollen and Silk Manufacturies, to the Increase of Trade, the Enlargement of the Revenues of the Crown, and Augmenting our Navigation* (London, 1715).
Hunter, William, *The Tidesman's and Preventive Officer's Pocket-Book, Explaining the General Nature of Importation and Exportation, so far as concerns them in the Execution of the Water Guard Duty* (London, 1771).
Janssen, Stephen, *Smuggling Laid Open, in all its Extensive and Destructive Branches. With Proposals for the effectual Remedy of that most iniquitous Practice* (London, 1767).
Macky, John, *Memoirs of the Secret Services of John Macky, Esq. During the Reigns of King William, Queen Anne, and King George I* (London, 1733, 2nd edition).
Manley, Thomas *A Discourse shewing that the Exportation of Wooll is destructive to this Kingdom* (London, 1676).
Owen, W., *A Free Apology on Behalf of the Smugglers, So far as their Case affects the Constitution* (London, 1749).
Smith, John, *Chronicon Rusticum-Commerciale; Or, Memoirs of Wool. Being a Collection of History and Argument, concerning the Woolen Manufacture and Woolen Trade*, 2 Volumes (London, 1747).
Smyth, James, *The Practice of the Customs in the Entry, Examination, and Delivery of Goods and Merchandise, usually Imported from Foreign Parts* (London, 1812).
Stephens, Edward, *Phinehas, or, the Common Duty of All Men, and the Special Duty of Magistrates, to be Zealous and Active in the Execution of Laws Against Scandalous Sins and Debauchers: And of That in Particular Against prophane Cursing and Swearing* (London, 1695).
The Parliamentary History of England, from the Earliest Period to the Year 1803. Vol. IX, A.D: 1733–1737 (London, 1811).
[Vernon, Edward], *Some Seasonable Advice from an Honest Sailor, to whom it might have Concerned, for the Service of the Crown and Country* (London, 1746).
Wesley, John, *A Word to a Smuggler* (London, 1783).

Official Documents and Publications

Bateson, Edward (ed.), *Calendar of State Papers Domestic: William III, 1699–1700* (London, 1937).
Chadwick, Edwin, 'The Preventive Police', *London Review* (1 February 1829).

Cross, Arthur Lyon (ed.), *Eighteenth Century Documents Relating to the Royal Forests, the Sheriffs and Smuggling* (London, 1928).
Hardy, William John (ed.), *Calendar of State Papers Domestic: William and Mary, 1689–90* (London, 1895).
Hardy, William John (ed.), *Calendar of State Papers Domestic: William and Mary, 1693* (London, 1903).
Hardy, William John (ed.), *Calendar of State Papers Domestic: William and Mary, 1694–5* (London, 1906).
Hardy, William John (ed.), *Calendar of State Papers Domestic: William III, 1697* (London, 1927).
Historical Manuscripts Commission, *Eighth Report of the Royal Commission on Historical Manuscripts. Report and Appendix (Part I)* (London, 1881).
Historical Manuscripts Commission, *Report on the Manuscripts of the Late Allan George Finch Esq., of Burley-on-the-Hill, Rutland*, 5 vols (London, 1913–2004).
Historical Manuscripts Commission, *Report on the Manuscripts of the Marquess of Downshire*, vol. 1 (London, 1924).
Historical Notes on the Coastguard Service (London, 1907).
[House of Commons], *A Copy of any Treasury Minutes, or Correspondence between the Treasury and the Revenue Boards; relating to the Revenue Cutters; since the 1st January 1815* (London, 1816).
[House of Commons], *Copies of all Letters from the Chairman of the Revenue Boards to the Board of Treasury, relative to the Revenue Cutters, in the Month of January 1816* (London, 1816).
[House of Commons], *Copies of the Eleventh and Twelfth Reports, and also of the Special Report, made by the Commissioners appointed to Inquire into the Departments of the Customs and Excise* (London, 1822).
[House of Commons], *Fourteenth Report of the Commission for Stating the Public Accounts* (London, 1785).
[House of Commons], *Reports from Committees of the House of Commons, vol. XII: Finance Reports, I to XXII, 1797–1798* (London, 1803).
[House of Commons], *Sixth Report of the Commissioners of Inquiry into the Collection and Management of the Revenue arising in Ireland, Scotland, etc. Out-Ports of Scotland* (London, 1823).
[House of Commons], *Smuggling Prevention, Returns* (London, 1821).
[House of Commons], *Tenth Report of the Commissioners of Inquiry into the Collection and Management of the Revenue arising in Ireland, Scotland, etc. Ports of Ireland, Preventive Coast Guard, Quarantine, etc.* (London, 1824).
[House of Commons], *The Fifteenth Report of the Commissioners Appointed to Examine, Take, and State, the Public Accounts of the Kingdom* (London, 1787).
[House of Commons], *The Report of the Commissioners of Inquiry for the Isle of Man* (London, 1792).

Jarvis, Rupert (ed.), *Customs Letter-Books of the Port of Liverpool 1711–1813* (Manchester, 1954).
Journal of the House of Commons, vol.10, 1688–1693 (London, 1802).
Journal of the House of Commons, vol.12, 1697–1699 (London, 1803).
Journal of the House of Commons, vol.13, 1699–1702 (London, 1803).
Journal of the House of Commons, vol.25, 1745–1750 (London, 1803).
Lambert, Sheila (ed.), *House of Commons Sessional Papers of the Eighteenth Century, Volume* 19 (Wilmington, 1975).
Lambert, Sheila (ed.), *House of Commons Sessional Papers of the Eighteenth Century, Volume* 38 (Wilmington, 1975).
Mackay, William (ed.), *The Letter-Book of Bailie John Steuart of Inverness 1715–1752* (Edinburgh, 1915).
Mahaffy, R. P. (ed.), *Calendar of State Papers Domestic: Anne, 1702–1703* (London, 1916).
Saville, Richard (ed.), *The Letters of John Collier of Hastings 1731–1746* (Lewes, 2016).
Shaw, William A., F. H. Slingsby (ed.), *Calendar of Treasury Books, 1660–1718*, 32 vols (London, 1904–1962).
Smith, Adam, *An Inquiry into the Nature and Causes of the Wealth of Nations*, 2 Volumes (Oxford, 1976).
The Report of the Committee appointed to inquire into the Frauds and Abuses in the Customs, to the Prejudice of Trade, and Diminution of the Revenue. Reported on the Seventh of June 1733 by Sir John Cope, printed in *Reports from the Committees of the House of Commons.* Reprinted by Order of the House. Vol. I, Miscellaneous Subjects: 1715–1735 (1803), pp. 601–654.

Periodicals
The Gentleman's Magazine
The London Magazine and Monthly Chronologer

Online Sources
Old Bailey Proceedings Online
t17470225-19 (Trial of Edmund Henley, February 1747)
t17470604-13 (Trial of Richard Ashcroft, June 1747)
t17470909-36 (Trial of Thomas Puryour, September 1747)
t17471209-52 (Trial of Peter Ticknor and James Hodges, December 1747)
t17480115-28 (Trial of Samuel Chilvers and Robert Scott, January 1748)
t17480116-1 (Trial of Benjamin Tapner, John Cobby, et al., January 1749)
t17760911-42 (Trial of Robert Harley and Edward George, September 1776)
t17850511-79 (Trial of George Cossans, May 1785)
t17880901-138 (Trial of John Snell, September 1788)
t17881210-93 (Trial of William England, December 1788)
t17910608-41 (Trial of Anthony Balless and Stephen Edwards, June 1791)
t18000115-89 (Trial of William Blatchford, January 1800)

t18000528-6 (Trial of William Strick, May 1800)
t18111030-50 (Trial of James Mansfield, October 1811)
Old Bailey Proceedings Online, Ordinary of Newgate's Account
OA17470729 (29 July 1747)
OA17471116 (16 November 1747)
OA17480318 (18 March 1748)
OA17480511 (11 May 1748)
OA17490426 (26 April 1749)
OA17511023 (23 October 1751)

Secondary Sources

Allen, Nicholas, *Ireland, Literature and the Coast: Seatangled* (Oxford, 2021).
Allen, Nicholas, Nick Groom, Jos Smith (eds), *Coastal Works: Culture of the Atlantic Edge* (Oxford, 2017).
Allen, Nicholas, Nick Groom, Jos Smith, 'Introduction', in Allen, Groom, Smith (eds), *Coastal Works*, pp. 1–20.
Armitage, David, *The Ideological Origins of the British Empire* (Cambridge, 2000).
Asch, Ronald G., 'War and State-Building', in Frank Tallett, D. J. B. Trim (eds), *European Warfare 1350–1750* (Cambridge, 2010), pp. 322–337.
Asch, Ronald G., Dagmar Freist (eds), *Staatsbildung als kultureller Prozess: Strukturwandel und Legitimation von Herrschaft in der Frühen Neuzeit* (Köln, 2005).
Ashworth, William, *Customs and Excise: Trade, Production, and Consumption in England 1640–1845* (Oxford, 2003).
Aylmer, G. E., 'From Office-Holding to Civil Service: The Genesis of Modern Bureaucracy', *Transactions of the Royal Society*, 30 (1980), 91–108.
Barker, T. C., 'Smuggling in the Eighteenth Century. The Evidence of the Scottish Tobacco Trade', *The Virginia Magazine of History and Biography*, 62 (1954), 387–399.
Barrow, Thomas, *Trade and Empire: The British Customs Service in Colonial America, 1660–1775* (Cambridge/Mass., 1967).
Barry, Jonathan, Christopher Brooks (eds), *The Middling Sort of People: Culture, Society and Politics in England 1550–1800* (Basingstoke, 1994).
Bartlett, Thomas, 'Viscount Townshend and the Irish Revenue Board, 1767–1773', *Proceedings of the Royal Irish Academy*, 79 (1979), 153–175.
Bashford, Alison, 'Terraqueous Histories', *HJ*, 60 (2017), 253–272.
Baxter, Stephen, *The Development of the Treasury 1660–1702* (London & New York, 1957).
Beattie, J. M., *Crime and the Courts in England, 1660–1800* (Princeton, 1986).
Beattie, J. M., *Policing and Punishment in London, 1660–1750: Urban Crime and the Limits of Terror* (Oxford, 2001).

Beck, J. Randy, 'The False Claims Act and the English Eradication of Qui Tam Legislation', *North Carolina Law Review*, 78 (2000), 539–642.
Beier, A. L., *Masterless Men: The Vagrancy Problem in England, 1560–1640* (London, 1985).
Bentley, Jerry, Renate Bridenthal, Kären Wigen (eds), *Seascapes: Maritime Histories, Littoral Cultures, and Transoceanic Exchanges* (Honolulu, 2007).
Beresford, Maurice W., 'The Common Informer, the Penal Statutes and Economic Regulation', *Economic History Review*, 10/2 (1957), 221–238.
Binney, J. E. D., *British Public Finance and Administration 1774–1792* (Oxford, 1958).
Blockmans, Wim, Daniel Schläppi, André Holenstein, and Jon Mathieu (eds), *Empowering Interactions: Political Cultures and the Emergence of the State in Europe 1300–1900* (Farnham, 2009).
Borsay, Peter, *A History of Leisure: the British Experience since 1500* (Basingstoke, 2006).
Borsay, Peter, John K. Walton (eds), *Resorts and Ports. European Seaside Towns since 1700* (Bristol, 2011).
Boulton, Jeremy, 'The "Meaner Sort": Labouring People and the Poor', in Keith Wrightson (ed.), *A Social History of England 1500–1750* (Cambridge, 2017), pp. 310–329.
Bowden, J., *The Wool Trade in Tudor and Stuart England* (London, 1962).
Bowen, Huw, 'Privilege and Profit: Commanders of East Indiamen as Private Traders, Entrepreneurs and Smugglers, 1760–1813', *International Journal for Maritime History*, 19 (2007), 43–88.
— '"So Alarming an Evil:" Smuggling, Pilfering and the English East India Company, 1750–1810', *International Journal of Maritime History*, 14 (2002), 1–31.
Boyden, Peter B., '"A System of Communication Through Each County", Fire-Beacons and their Role in the Defence of the Realm, 1803–1811', in Alan J Guy (ed.), *The Road to Waterloo. The British Army and the Struggle against Revolutionary and Napoleonic France, 1793–1815* (Stroud, 1990), pp. 126–131.
Braddick, Michael, 'Administrative Performance: the Representation of Political Authority in Early Modern England', in Braddick, Walter (eds), *Negotiating Power*, pp. 166–187.
— *Parliamentary Taxation in Seventeenth-Century England* (Woodbridge, 1994).
— *State Formation in Early-Modern England, c.1550–1700* (Cambridge, 2000).
— 'The Early Modern English State and the Question of Differentiation from 1550 to 1700', *Comparative Studies in Society and History*, 38 (1996), 92–111.
— *The Nerves of State. Taxation and the Financing of the English State, 1588–1714* (Manchester & New York, 1996).
Braddick, Michael, John Walter (eds), *Negotiating Power in Early Modern Society: Order, Hierarchy and Subordination in Britain and Ireland* (Cambridge, 2001).

Bradshaw, Brendan, John Morrill (eds), *The British Problem, c.1534–1707: State Formation in the Atlantic Archipelago* (New York, 1996).
Brakensiek, Stefan, 'Akzeptanzorientierte Herrschaft: Überlegungen zur politischen Kultur der Frühen Neuzeit', in Helmut Neuhaus (ed.), *Die Frühe Neuzeit als Epoche* (Munich, 2009), pp. 395–406.
Brakensiek, Stefan, 'New Perspectives on State Building and the Implementation of Rulership in Early Modern European Monarchies', in Antje Flüchter, Susan Richter (eds), *Structures on the Move: Technologies of Governance in Transcultural Encounters* (Berlin, 2012), pp. 30–41.
Brakensiek, Stefan, Corinna von Bredow, Birgit Näther (eds), *Herrschaft und Verwaltung in der Frühen Neuzeit* (Berlin, 2014).
Brakensiek, Stefan, Heide Wunder (eds), *Ergebene Diener ihrer Herren? Herrschaftsvermittlung im alten Europa* (Köln, 2005).
Breihan, John R., 'William Pitt and the Commission on Fees, 1785–1801', *HJ*, 27/1 (1984), 59–81.
Brewer, John, 'Revisiting The Sinews of Power', in Graham, Walsh (eds), *Fiscal-Military States*, pp. 27–34
— 'Servants of the Public – Servants of the Crown: Officialdom of Eighteenth-Century English Central Government', in Brewer, Hellmuth (eds), *Rethinking Leviathan*, pp. 127–47.
— 'The Eighteenth-Century British State: Contexts and Issues', in Lawrence Stone (ed.), *An Imperial State at War: Britain from 1689–1815* (London, 1994), pp. 52–71.
— *The Sinews of Power. War, Money, and the English State, 1688–1783* (London, 1989).
Brewer, John, Eckhart Hellmuth (eds), *Rethinking Leviathan: the Eighteenth-Century State in Britain and Germany* (Oxford, 1999).
Brisco, Norris, *The Economic Policy of Robert Walpole* (New York, 1907).
Brooke, Stopford, *Notes on the Liber Studiorum of J. M. W. Turner* (London, 1885).
Brooks, Colin, 'Interest, Patronage and Professionalism: John, 1st Baron Ashburnham, Hastings and the Revenue Service', *Southern History*, 9 (1987), 51–70.
Bruce, Mark P., Katherine H. Terrell (eds), *The Anglo-Scottish Border and the Shaping of Identity, 1300–1600* (London, 2012).
Brunsman, Denver, *The Evil Necessity: British Naval Impressment in the Eighteenth-Century Atlantic World* (Charlottesville, 2013).
Burns, Arthur, Joanna Innes (eds), *Rethinking the Age of Reform: Britain 1780–1850* (Cambridge, 2003).
Carson, Edward, *The Ancient and Rightful Customs: A History of the English Customs Service* (London, 1972).
Cérino, Christophe, Aliette Geistdoerfer, Gérard Le Bouëdec, François Ploux (eds), *Entre terre et mer: Sociétés littorales et pluriactivités (XVe–XXe siècle)* (Rennes, 2004).

Bibliography

Chan Smith, David, 'Fair Trade and the Political Economy of Brandy Smuggling in Early Eighteenth-Century Britain', *Past and Present* 251 (2021), 75–111.

Chandaman, C. D., *The English Public Revenue 1660–1688* (Oxford, 1975).

Childs, John, *The British Army of William III, 1689–1702* (Manchester, 1987).

Churchill, David, 'Rethinking the State Monopolisation Thesis: the Historiography of Policing and Criminal Justice in Nineteenth-Century England', *Crime, History and Societies*, 18 (2014), 131–152.

Clark, Peter, 'Migration in England during the Late Seventeenth and Early Eighteenth Centuries', *Past and Present*, 83 (1979), 57–90.

Clark, Peter, David Souden (eds), *Migration and Society in Early Modern England* (London, 1987).

Clements, W. H., *Towers of Strength. Martello Towers Worldwide* (Barnsley, 1999).

Coats, Anne, Alan Lemmers, 'Dutch and English Dockyards and Coastal Defence, 1652–89', in: David Ormrod, Gijs Rommelse (eds), *War, Trade and the State. Anglo-Dutch Conflict, 1652–89* (Woodbridge, 2020), pp. 137–178.

Cockburn, James, *A History of English Assizes, 1558–1714* (Cambridge, 1972).

— (ed.), *Crime in England 1550–1800* (London, 1977).

Coleby, Andrew, *Central Government and the Localities: Hampshire, 1649–1689* (Cambridge, 1987).

Colley, Linda, *Britons: Forging the Nation, 1707–1837* (New Haven, 1992).

— 'The Reach of the State, the Appeal of the Nation: Mass Arming and Political Culture in the Napoleonic Wars', in Lawrence Stone (ed.), *An Imperial State at War: Britain 1689–1815* (London, 1994), pp. 165–184.

Conway, Stephen, *War, State, and Society in Mid-Eighteenth Century Britain and Ireland* (Oxford, 2006).

Cookson, J. E., *The British Armed Nation 1793–1815* (Oxford, 1997).

Corbin, Alain, *The Lure of the Sea. The Discovery of the Seaside in the Western World, 1750–1840* (Berkeley, 1994).

Cracknell, Basil B., *Outrageous Waves: Global Warming and Coastal Change in Britain through Two Thousand Years* (Chichester, 2005).

Cressy, David, *England's Islands in a Sea of Troubles* (Oxford, 2020).

Cruickshanks, Eveline (ed.), *Ideology and Conspiracy: Aspects of Jacobitism, 1689–1759* (Edinburgh, 1982).

Cullen, L. M., *Anglo-Irish Trade 1660–1800* (Manchester, 1968).

— 'H.M.S. "Spy" off the Galway Coast in the 1730s: The Politics and Economics of Wool Smuggling', *Journal of the Galway Archaeological and Historical Society*, 65 (2013), 27–47.

— 'Smugglers in the Irish Sea in the Eighteenth Century', in L. M. Cullen, *Economy, Trade and Irish Merchants at Home and Abroad, 1600–1988* (Dublin, 2012), pp. 118–136.

— 'Smuggling in the North Channel in the Eighteenth Century', *Scottish Economic and Social History*, 7 (1987), 9–26.

Cusack, Tricia (ed.), *Art and Identity at the Water's Edge* (Farnham, 2012).

Daly, Gavin, 'English Smugglers, the Channel, and the Napoleonic Wars, 1800–1814', *JBS*, 46 (2007), 30–46.
— 'Napoleon and the "City of Smugglers", 1810–1814', *HJ*, 50 (2007), 333–352.
— 'Napoleon's lost legions: French Prisoners of War in Britain, 1803–1814', *History*, 89 (2004), 361–80.
Daunton, Martin, *Trusting Leviathan: The Politics of Taxation in Britain, 1799–1914* (Cambridge, 2001).
Davies, Margaret Gay, *The Enforcement of English Apprenticeship: A Study in Applied Mercantilism* (Cambridge/Mass., 1956).
Davis, Ralph, 'The Rise of Protection in England, 1689–1786', *Economic History Review*, 19 (1966), 306–317.
Davison, Lee, Tim Hitchcock, Tim Keirn, Robert B. Shoemaker (eds), *Stilling the Grumbling Hive: The Response to Social and Economic Problems in England, 1689–1750* (Stroud, 1992).
Dening, Greg, *Beach Crossings: Voyaging Across Times, Cultures and Self* (Philadelphia, 2004).
— *Islands and Beaches: Discourse on a silent land, Marquesas, 1774–1880* (Carlton, 1980).
— 'Writing, Rewriting the Beach: An Essay', *Rethinking History*, 2 (1998), 143–172.
Devereaux, Simon, 'The Historiography of the English State during "the Long Eighteenth Century": Part I – Decentralized Perspectives', *History Compass*, 7 (2009), 742–764.
— 'The Historiography of the English State During "The Long Eighteenth Century". Part II – Fiscal-Military and Nationalist Perspectives', *History Compass*, 8 (2010), 843–865.
Dickinson, Harry T. (ed.), *Britain and the French Revolution, 1789–1815* (London, 1989).
— *British Radicalism and the French Revolution, 1789–1815* (Oxford, 1985).
— *Walpole and the Whig Supremacy* (London, 1973).
Dickinson, John R., 'The Overseas Trade of the Isle of Man, 1576–1755', *Transactions of the Historic Society of Lancashire and Cheshire*, 154 (2005), 1–30.
Dickson, David, 'Edward Thompson's Report on the Management of Customs and Excise in County Kerry in 1733', *Journal of the Kerry Archaeological and Historical Society*, 7 (1974), 12–20.
Dickson, P. G. M., *The Financial Revolution in England: A Study of the Development of Public Credit, 1688–1756* (London, 1967).
Dinwiddy, John, 'Conceptions of Revolution in the English Radicalism of the 1790s', in Eckhart Hellmuth (ed.), *The Transformation of Political Culture. England and Germany in the Late Eighteenth Century* (Oxford, 1990), pp. 535–560.
Dodsworth, Francis, 'Civic police and the condition of liberty: the rationality of governance in eighteenth-century England', *Social History*, 29 (2004), 199–216.

Eastwood, David, *Government and Community in the English Provinces, 1700–1800* (Basingstoke, 1997).
Edmond, Rod, Vanessa Smith (eds), *Islands in History and Representation* (London, 2003).
Ehrman, John, *The Navy in the War of William III 1689–1697: Its State and Direction* (Cambridge, 1953).
Elton, Geoffrey, 'Informing for Profit: A Sidelight on Tudor Methods of Law-Enforcement', *Cambridge Historical Journal*, XI/2 (1954), 149–167.
Emsley, Clive, *British Society and the French Wars, 1793–1815* (Totowa, 1979).
— (ed.), *Theories and Origins of the Modern Police* (Farnham, 2011).
Environment Agency: *The State of the Environment of England and Wales: Coasts* (London, 1999).
Eric Shanes, *Turner's Rivers, Harbours and Coasts* (London, 1981).
Ertman, Thomas, '*The Sinews of Power* and European State-Building Theory', in Lawrence Stone (ed.), *An Imperial State at War: Britain from 1689–1815* (London, 1994), pp. 33–51.
Farran, Sue, 'The Coastal Zone of Islands: Comparative Reflections from the North and South', *Island Studies Journal*, 1 (2006), 55–80.
Farrell, W., 'Smuggling Silks into Eighteenth-Century Britain: Geography, Perpetrators, and Consumers', *JBS*, 55 (2016), 268–294.
— 'The Silk Interest and the Fiscal-Military State', in Graham, Walsh (eds), *Fiscal-Military States*, pp. 113–130.
Fedorak, Charles John, 'In Defence of Great Britain: Henry Addington, the Duke of York and Military Preparations against Invasion by Napoleonic France, 1803–1804', in Mark Philp (ed.), *Resisting Napoleon. The British Response to the Threat of Invasion, 1797–1815* (Aldershot, 2006), pp. 91–110.
Fisher, Stephen, *Studies in British Privateering, Trading Enterprise and Seamen's Welfare, 1775–1900* (Exeter, 1987).
Fleming, D. A., *Politics and Provincial People: Sligo and Limerick, 1691–1761* (Manchester/New York, 2010).
Fletcher, Anthony, *A County Community in Peace and War: Sussex 1600–1660* (London, 1975)
Fletcher, Anthony, John Stevenson (eds), *Order and Disorder in Early Modern England* (Cambridge, 1985).
French, Henry, *The Middle Sort of People in Provincial England 1660–1750* (Oxford, 2007).
Fumerton, Patricia, *Unsettled: The Culture of Mobility and the Working Poor in Early Modern England* (Chicago, 2006).
Fusaro, Maria, Amélia Polónia (eds), *Maritime History as Global History* (St. John's, 2010).
Gambles, Anna, 'Free Trade and State Formation: The Political Economy of Fisheries Policy in Britain and the United Kingdom circa 1780–1850', *JBS*, 39 (2000), 288–316.

Ganev, Robin, 'Britain's Fiscal-Military State in the Eighteenth Century: Recent Trends in Historiography', *History Compass*, 22 (2024).
Gange, David, *The Frayed Atlantic Edge* (London, 2020).
Gaskill, Malcolm, *Crime and Mentalities in Early Modern England* (Cambridge, 2000).
Gauci, Perry, *The Politics of Trade: The Overseas Merchant in State and Society, 1660–1720* (Oxford, 2001).
Gawne, C. W., *The Isle of Man and Britain Controversy 1651–1895: From Smuggling to the Common Purse* (Douglas, 2009).
Gee, Austin, *The British Volunteer Movement 1794–1814* (Oxford, 2003).
Gestrich, Andreas, Michael Schaich (eds), *The Hanoverian Succession: Dynastic Politics and Monarchical Culture* (Farnham, 2015).
Gillis, John, Franziska Torma (eds), *Fluid Frontiers: New Currents in Marine Environmental History* (Cambridge, 2015).
Gillis, John, *Islands of the Mind: How the Human Imagination Created the Atlantic World* (Basingstoke, 2004).
— *The Human Shore: Seacoasts in History* (Chicago/London, 2012).
Gilmour, Ian, *Riot, Rising and Revolution. Governance and Violence in Eighteenth-Century England* (London, 1992).
Glover, Richard, *Britain at Bay. Defence against Bonaparte, 1803–1814* (London, 1973).
Godsey, William D., Petr Mat'a (eds), *The Habsburg Monarchy as a Fiscal-Military State. Contours and Perspectives 1648–1815* (Oxford, 2022).
Goldie, Mark, 'The Hilton Gang and the Purge of London in the 1680s', in Howard Nenner (ed.), *Politics and the Political Imagination in Later Stuart Britain: Essays Presented to Lois Green Schwoerer* (New York, 1997), pp. 43–73.
— 'The Unacknowledged Republic: Officeholding in Early Modern England', in Tim Harris (ed.), *The Politics of the Excluded, c.1500–1850* (Basingstoke, 2001), pp. 153–94.
Graham, Aaron, Patrick Walsh (ed.), *The British Fiscal-Military States, 1660–c.1783* (London, 2016).
Graham, Aaron, Patrick Walsh, 'Introduction', in Graham, Walsh (ed.), *Fiscal-Military States*, pp. 1–26.
Grancher, Romain, 'Fishermen Taverns: Public Houses and Maritime Labour in an Early Modern French Fishing Community', *International Journal of Maritime History*, 28 (2016), 671–685.
Griffin, Patrick, *The Townshend Moment: The Making of Empire and Revolution in the Eighteenth Century* (New Haven, 2017).
Griffiths, Paul, Adam Fox, Steve Hindle (eds), *The Experience of Authority in Early Modern England* (Basingstoke, 1996).
Griffiths, Paul, Adam Fox, Steve Hindle, 'Introduction', in Griffiths, Fox, Hindle (eds), *Experience of Authority*, pp. 1–10.

Guilfoyle, James, 'Ireland, Mercantilism, and the Navigation Acts, 1660–1686', in Douglas Kanter, Patrick Walsh (eds), *Taxation, Politics, and Protest in Ireland, 1662–2016* (Basingstoke, 2019), pp. 19–42.

Halvorson, Michael J., Karen E. Spierling (eds), *Defining Community in Early Modern Europe* (Abingdon, 2008).

Hamilton, Douglas, John McAleer (eds), *Islands and the British Empire in the Age of Sail* (Oxford, 2021).

Hanson, Gillian Mary, *Riverbank and Seashore in Nineteenth and Twentieth Century British Literature* (Jefferson, 2006).

Harling, Philip, Peter Mandler, 'From "Fiscal-Military" State to Laissez-faire State, 1760–1850', *JBS*, 32 (1993), 44–70.

Harling, Philip, *The Modern British State: An Historical Introduction* (Oxford, 2001).

— *The Waning of 'Old Corruption': The Politics of Economical Reform in Britain, 1779–1846* (Oxford, 1996).

Harris, Bob, *Politics and the Nation: Britain in the Mid-Eighteenth Century* (Oxford, 2022).

Hassan, John, *The Seaside, Health and Environment in England and Wales since 1800* (Aldershot, 2003).

Hay, Douglas, 'Property, Authority and the Criminal Law', in Hay, Linebaugh, Rule, Thompson, Winslow (eds), *Albion's Fatal Tree*, pp. 17–63.

— 'War, Dearth and Theft in the Eighteenth Century: The Record of the English Courts', *Past and Present*, 95 (1982), 117–160.

Hay, Douglas, Peter Linebaugh, John G. Rule, E. P. Thompson, Cal Winslow (eds), *Albion's Fatal Tree: Crime and Society in Eighteenth-Century England* (London, 1975).

Hay, Douglas, Francis Snyder (eds), *Policing and Prosecution in Britain 1750–1850* (Oxford, 1989).

Hay, Douglas, Francis Snyder, 'Using the Criminal Law, 1750–1850: Policing, Private Prosecution, and the State', in Hay, Snyder (eds), *Policing and Prosecution*, pp. 3–53.

Headrick, Daniel R., *When Information Came of Age: Technologies of Knowledge in the Age of Reason and Revolution, 1700–1850* (Oxford, 2000).

Heitsch, Dorothea, Jeremie C. Korta (eds), *Early Modern Visions of Space, France and Beyond* (Chapel Hill, 2021).

Hellmuth, Eckhart, 'The British State', in Harry T. Dickinson (ed.) *A Companion to Eighteenth-Century Britain* (Oxford, 2002), pp. 19–29.

Hemming, Charles, *British Painters of the Coast and Sea. A History and a Gazetteer* (London, 1988).

Hermant, Héloïse (ed.), *Le pouvoir contourné: infléchir et subvertir l'autorité à l'âge moderne* (Paris, 2016).

Herrup, Cynthia B., *The Common Peace: Participation and the Criminal Law in Seventeenth-Century England* (Cambridge, 1987).

Hindle, Steve, *On the Parish? The Micro-Politics of Poor Relief in Rural England, 1550–1750* (Oxford, 2004).
— *The State and Social Change in Early Modern England, 1550–1640* (Basingstoke, 2002).
Hitchcock, David, 'Editorial: Poverty and Mobility in England, 1600–1850', *Rural History*, 24 (2013), 1–8.
— *Vagrancy in English Culture and Society, 1650–1750* (London, 2016).
Hoon, Elizabeth, *The Organization of the English Customs System 1696–1786* (Newton Abbot, 1938, repr. 1938).
Hopkins, Paul, 'Sham Plots and Real Plots in the 1690s', in Eveline Cruickshanks (ed.), *Ideology and Conspiracy: Aspects of Jacobitism, 1689–1759* (Edinburgh, 1982), pp. 89–110.
Hoppit, Julian, *A Land of Liberty? England 1689–1727* (Oxford, 2000).
— *Britain's Political Economies: Parliament and Economic Life, 1660–1800* (Cambridge, 2017).
— 'Scotland and the Taxing Union, 1707–1815', *SHR*, 98 (2019), 45–70.
Horwitz, Henry, *Parliament, Policy and Politics in the Reign of William III* (Manchester, 1977).
Houlding, J. A., *Fit for Service: The Training of the British Army, 1715–1795* (Oxford, 1981).
Howson, Gerald, *Thief-Taker General: The Rise and Fall of Jonathan Wild* (London 1970).
Hufton, Geoffrey, Elaine Baird, *The Scarecrow's Legion, or Smuggling in the South East* (Sittingbourne, 1983).
Hunt, Margaret R., 'Wives and marital "rights" in the Court of Exchequer in the early eighteenth century', in Paul Griffiths, Mark S. R. Jenner (eds), *Londinopolis. Essays in the Cultural and Social History of Early Modern London* (Manchester, 2000), pp. 107–129.
Hunt, Margaret R., *The Middling Sort: Commerce, Gender, and the Family in England, 1680–1780* (London, 1996).
Hussey, D., *Coastal and River Trade in Pre-Industrial England: Bristol and its Region* (Exeter, 2000).
Ingleby, Matthew, Matthew P. M. Kerr (eds), *Coastal Cultures of the Long Nineteenth Century* (Edinburgh, 2018).
Innes, Joanna, *Inferior Politics: Social Problems and Social Policies in Eighteenth-Century Britain* (Oxford, 2009).
— 'Parliament and the Shaping of Eighteenth-Century Social Policy', *Transactions of the Royal Society*, 40 (1990), 63–92.
— 'The Domestic Face of the Military-Fiscal State: Government and Society in Eighteenth-Century Britain', in Lawrence Stone (ed.), *An Imperial State at War: Britain from 1689–1815* (London, 1994), pp. 96–127.
— 'The Protestant Carpenter – William Payne of Bell Yard (c.1718–82): the Life and Times of a London Informing Constable', in Innes, *Inferior Politics*, pp. 279–341.

James, F. G., 'Irish Smuggling in the Eighteenth Century', *Irish Historical Studies*, 7 (1961), 299–317.

Jarvis, Rupert C., 'Illicit Trade with the Isle of Man, 1671–1765', *Transactions of the Lancashire and Cheshire Antiquarian Society*, 58 (1947), 245–267.

— 'The Customs Cruisers of the North-West in the Eighteenth Century', *Transactions of the Historic Society of Lancashire and Cheshire*, 99 (1949), 41–61.

Jones, D. W., 'Defending the Revolution: The Economics, Logistics, and Finance of England's War Effort, 1688–1712', in Dale Hoak, Mordechai Feingold (eds), *The World of William and Mary: Anglo-Dutch Perspectives on the Revolution of 1688–89* (Stanford, 1996), pp. 59–74.

— *War and Economy in the Age of William III and Marlborough* (Oxford, 1988).

Jones, Evan T., *Inside the Illicit Economy: Reconstructing the Smugglers' Trade of Sixteenth Century Bristol* (London, 2012).

Kearney, H. F., 'The Political Background to English Mercantilism, 1695–1700', *Economic History Review*, 11/3 (1959), 484–496.

Keirn, Tim, 'Parliament, Legislation and the Regulation of English Textile Industries, 1689–1714', in Davison, Hitchcock, Keirn, Shoemaker (eds), *Stilling the Grumbling Hive*, pp. 1–24.

Kelly, Patrick, 'The Irish Woollen Export Prohibition Act of 1699: Kearney re-visited', *Irish Economic and Social History*, VII (1980), 22–43.

Kent, Joan, *The English Village Constable 1580–1642: A Social and Administrative Study* (Oxford, 1986).

— 'The English Village Constable, 1580–1642: The Nature and Dilemmas of the Office', *JBS*, 20/2 (1981), 26–49.

— 'The Centre and the Localities: State Formation and Parish Government in England, circa 1640–1740', *HJ*, 38 (1995), 363–404.

King, Peter, *Crime and Law in England, 1750–1840: Remaking Justice from the Margins* (Cambridge, 2006).

— *Crime, Justice and Discretion in England, 1740–1820* (Oxford, 2000).

— 'Decision-Makers and Decision-Making in the English Criminal Law 1750–1850', *HJ*, 27/1 (1984), 25–58.

King, Peter, Richard Ward, 'Rethinking the Bloody Code in Eighteenth-Century Britain: Capital Punishment at the Centre and on the Periphery', *Past and Present*, 228 (2015), 159–205.

Kitchen, Frank, 'Napoleonic War Coastal Signal Stations', *Mariner's Mirror*, 76 (1990), 337–344.

Knight, Roger, *Britain Against Napoleon: The Organization of Victory 1793–1815* (London, 2013).

Knights, Mark, *Representation and Misrepresentation in Later Stuart Britain. Partisanship and Political Culture* (Oxford, 2005).

— *Trust and Distrust: Corruption in Office in Britain and its Empire, 1600–1850* (Oxford, 2021).

Knutsson, Anna, Charlotte Bellamy, 'From Valet to Smuggler: A Microhistorical Study of a French Intermediary in Stockholm, 1775–1832', *Revue d'histoire nordique* 27 (2018), 115–140.

Kraus, Johannes, 'War Administration: Subjects, Local Officers, and the Contribution System in the Thirty Years War', in Martín Romera, Ziegler (eds), *Officer and the People*, pp. 251–272.

Kümin, Beat, *Drinking Matters: Public Houses and Social Exchange in Early Modern Central Europe* (Basingstoke, 2007).

— *The Communal Age in Western Europe, c.1100–1800: Towns, Villages and Parishes in Pre-Modern Society* (Basingstoke, 2013).

Laget, Frédérique, Philippe Josserand, Brice Rabot (eds), *Entre horizons terrestres et marins: Sociétés, campagnes et littoraux de l'Ouest atlantique* (Rennes, 2017).

Land, Isaac, 'Tidal Waves: The New Coastal History', *Journal of Social History*, 40 (2007), 731–743.

Langford, Paul, *The Excise Crisis: Society and Politics in the Age of Walpole* (Oxford, 1975).

Law, Alex, 'Of Navies and Navels: Britain as a Mental Island', *Geografiska Annaler*, 87 (2005), 267–277.

Le Bouëdec, Gérard, *Activités maritimes et sociétés littorales de l'Europe atlantique, 1690–1790* (Paris, 1997).

— 'La pluriactivité dans les sociétés littorales XVIIe–XIXe siècle', *Annales de Bretagne et des Pays de l'Ouest*, 109 (2002), 61–90.

Lees, Robert M., 'The Constitutional Importance of the "Commissioners of Wool" of 1689. An Administrative Experiment of the Reign of William III', *Economica* 40 (1933), 147–168 and 41 (1933), 264–274.

Lemmings, David, *Law and Government in England during the Long Eighteenth Century: From Consent to Command* (New York, 2015).

Lidington, D. R., 'Parliament and the Enforcement of the Penal Statutes: the History of the Act "In Restraint of Common Informers" (18 Eliz. I ch. 5)', *Parliamentary History*, 8 (1989), 309–328.

Lincoln, Margarette, *Representing the Royal Navy: British Sea Power, 1750–1815* (Aldershot, 2002).

Linebaugh, Peter, 'The Ordinary of Newgate and His *Account*', in Cockburn (ed.), *Crime in England*, pp. 246–269.

Lipman, Andrew, *The Saltwater Frontier: Indians and the Contest for the American Coast* (New Haven, 2015).

Lüdtke, Alf (ed.), *The History of Everyday Life: Reconstructing Historical Experiences and Ways of Life* (Princeton, 1995).

Lunn, Ken, Ann Day, 'Britain as Island. National Identity and the Sea', in Helen Brocklehurst, Robert Phillips (eds), *History, Nationhood and the Question of Britain* (Basingstoke, 2004), pp. 126–136.

Lyman, J. L., 'The Metropolitan Police Act of 1829', *Journal of Criminal Law and Criminology*, 55/1 (1964), 141–154.

282   Bibliography

Marshall, Alan, *Intelligence and Espionage in the Reign of Charles II, 1660–1685* (Cambridge, 1994).

Marshall, P. J., 'Empire and British Identity: The Maritime Dimension', in David Cannadine (ed.), *The Empire, the Sea, and Global History* (New York, 2007), pp. 41–59.

Martín Romera, María Ángeles, Hannes Ziegler (eds), *The Officer and the People: Accountability and Authority in Pre-Modern Europe* (Oxford, 2021).

Masterson, William E., *Jurisdiction in Marginal Seas with Special Reference to Smuggling* (New York, 1929).

Matar, Nabil, *Britain and Barbary, 1589–1689* (Gainesville, 2005).

Matthews, Jodie, Daniel Travers (eds), *Islands and Britishness: A Global Perspective* (Newcastle, 2012).

McCooey, Christopher, *Smuggling on the South Coast* (Stroud, 2012).

McDowell, R. B., *Ireland in the Age of Imperialism and Revolution, 1760–1801* (Oxford, 1991).

McGrath, Charles Ivar, *The Making of the Eighteenth-Century Irish Constitution: Government, Parliament and the Revenue, 1692–1714* (Dublin, 2000).

— 'Waging War: The Irish Military Establishment and the British Empire', in William Mulligan, Brendan Simms (eds), *The Primacy of Foreign Policy in British History, 1660–2000: How Strategic Concerns Shaped Modern Britain* (Basingstoke, 2010), pp. 102–118.

McLynn, Frank, *Crime and Punishment in Eighteenth-Century England* (London, 1989).

Mewett, Ryan, '"To the Very Great Prejudice of the Fair Trader": Merchants and Illicit Naval Trading in the 1730s', *Historical Research* 93 (2020), 692–714.

Mhurchadha, Maighréad Ní, *The Customs and Excise Service in Fingal, 1684–1764: Sober, Active and Bred to the Sea* (Dublin, 1999).

Miller, Jonah, *Gender and Policing in Early Modern England* (Cambridge, 2023).

— 'The Touch of the State: Stop and Search in England, c.1660–1750', *History Workshop Journal*, 87 (2019), 52–71.

Milne, Graeme J., *People, Place and Power on the Nineteenth Century Waterfront* (Basingstoke, 2016).

Monod, Paul, 'Dangerous Merchandise: Smuggling, Jacobitism, and Commercial Culture in Southeast England, 1690–1760', *JBS*, 30 (1991), 150–182.

— *Jacobitism and the English People, 1688–1788* (Cambridge, 1989).

Morieux, Renaud, *The Channel. England, France and the Construction of a Maritime Border in the Eighteenth Century* (Cambridge, 2016).

— *The Society of Prisoners. Anglo-French Wars and Incarceration in the Eighteenth Century* (Oxford, 2019).

Morley, B. M., *Henry VIII and the Development of Coastal Defence* (London, 1976).

Morley, Geoffrey, *Smuggling in Hampshire and Dorset 1700–1850* (Newbury, 1983).

— *The Smuggling War: The Government's Fight against Smuggling in the 18th and 19th Centuries* (Stroud, 1994).

Morrill, John, 'Dynasties, Realms, Peoples and State Formation, 1500–1720', in Robert v. Friedeburg, John Morrill (eds), *Monarchy Transformed. Princes and Their Elites in Early Modern Western Europe* (Cambridge, 2017), pp. 17–43.

Mui, Hoh-Cheung, Lorna H. Mui, 'Smuggling and the British Tea Trade before 1784', *The American Historical Review*, 74 (1968), 44–73.

— 'Trends in Eighteenth Century Smuggling Reconsidered', *Economic History Review*, 28 (1975), 28–63.

— 'William Pitt and the Enforcement of the Commutation Act, 1784–1788', *HER*, 76 (1961), 447–465.

Muskett, Paul, 'Military Operations against Smuggling in Kent and Sussex, 1698–1750', *Journal for the Society of Army Historical Research*, 52 (1974), 89–110.

Nash, Robert C., 'The English and Scottish Tobacco Trades in the Seventeenth and Eighteenth Centuries. Legal and Illegal Trade', *Economic History Review*, New Series 35 (1982), 354–372.

Nelson, Ronald, *The Home Office, 1782–1801* (Durham, 1969).

Newman, David, 'On Borders and Power: A Theoretical Framework', *Journal of Borderland Studies*, 18 (2003), 13–25.

Newman, Jon, '"An Insurrection of Loyalty": The London Volunteer Regiments' Response to the Invasion Threat', in Mark Philp (ed.), *Resisting Napoleon. The British Response to the Threat of Invasion, 1797–1815* (Aldershot, 2006), pp. 75–90.

Nicholls, F. F., *Honest Thieves. The Violent Heyday of English Smuggling* (London, 1973)

O'Brien, Patrick, 'The Political Economy of British Taxation, 1660–1815', *Economic History Review*, 41 (1988), 1–32.

— 'The Triumph and Denouement of the British Fiscal State: Taxation for the Wars against Revolutionary and Napoleonic France, 1793–185', in Christopher Storrs (ed.), *The Fiscal-Military State in Eighteenth-Century Europe* (Farnham, 2009), pp. 167–200.

O'Brien, Patrick, Philip A. Hunt, 'The Rise of the Fiscal State in England, 1485–1815', *Historical Research*, 66 (1993), 129–176.

O'Hara, Glen, '"The Sea is Swinging into View": Modern British Maritime History in a Globalised World', *EHR*, CXXIV (2009), 1109–1134.

Ogborn, Miles, *Spaces of Modernity: London's Geographies 1680–1780* (New York & London, 1998).

— 'The Capacities of the State: Charles Davenant and the Management of the Excise, 1683–1698', *Journal of Historical Geography*, 24 (1998), 289–312.

Paley, Ruth, '"An Imperfect, Inadequate and Wretched System"? Policing London before Peel', *Criminal Justice History*, 10 (1989), 95–130.

— 'Thief-takers in London in the Age of the McDaniel Gang, c.1745–1754', in Hay, Snyder (eds), *Policing and Prosecution*, pp. 301–342.
Parker, Leanna T., 'Southampton's Sixteenth-Century Illicit Trade: An Examination of the 1565 Port Survey', *International Journal of Maritime History*, 27 (2015), 268–284.
Pastore, Christopher L., *Between Land and Sea: The Atlantic Coast and the Transformation of New England* (Cambridge, MA, 2014).
Payne, Christiana, 'Our English Coasts: Defence and National Identity in Nineteenth-Century Britain', in Tricia Cusack (ed.), *Art and Identity at the Water's Edge* (Farnham, 2012), pp. 21–36.
— *Where the Sea Meets the Land: Artists on the Coast in Nineteenth Century Britain* (Bristol, 2007).
Payton, Philip, Alston Kennerley, Helen Doe (eds), *The Maritime History of Cornwall* (Exeter, 2014).
Pearce, Cathryn, *Cornish Wrecking, 1700–1860: Reality and Popular Myth* (Woodbridge, 2010).
Pearson, Michael N. 'Littoral Society: The Case for the Coast', *The Great Circle*, 7 (1985), 1–8.
— 'Littoral Society: The Concept and the Problems', *Journal of World History*, 17 (2006), 353–373.
— (ed.), *The World of the Indian Ocean, 1500–1800: Studies in Economic, Social and Cultural History* (Aldershot, 2005).
Philips, David, 'Good Men to Associate and Bad Men to Conspire: Associations for the Prosecution of Felons in England, 1760–1860', in Hay, Snyder (eds), *Policing and Prosecution*, pp. 113–170.
Philp, Roy, *The Coast Blockade. The Royal Navy's War on Smuggling 1817–1831* (Horsham, 2002).
Platt, Richard, *Smuggling in the British Isles: A History* (Stroud, 2011).
Plumb, J. H., *The Growth of Political Stability in England 1675–1725* (London, 1967).
Pohlig, Matthias, *Marlboroughs Geheimnis. Strukturen und Funktionen der Informationsgewinnung im Spanischen Erbfolgekrieg* (Köln/Weimar/Wien, 2016).
— 'Speed and safety. Infrastructuring the English postal service to the Low Countries during the War of the Spanish Succession', in Matthias Pohlig, Michael Schaich (eds), *The War of the Spanish Succession. New Perspectives* (Oxford, 2018), pp. 343–368.
Powell, Martyn J., *Britain and Ireland in the Eighteenth-Century Crisis of Empire* (Basingstoke, 2003).
Price, Jacob, 'Glasgow, the Tobacco Trade, and the Scottish Customs, 1707–1730: Some Commercial, Administrative and Political Implications of the Union', *SHR*, 63 (1984), 1–36.

Radzinowicz, Leon, *A History of English Criminal Law and its Administration from 1750*, vol. 2: *The Clash between Private Initiative and Public Interest in the Enforcement of the Law* (London, 1956).
Rau, Susanne, *History, Space, and Place* (London/New York, 2019).
Rawlings, Philip, `Policing before the Police`, in Tim Newburn (ed.), *Handbook of Policing* (Routledge, 2008), pp. 47–71.
Readman, Paul, Cynthia Radding, Chad Bryant (eds), *Borderlands in World History, 1700–1914* (Basingstoke, 2014).
Reitan, Earl A., 'From Revenue to Civil List, 1689–1702: The Revolution Settlement and the 'Mixed and Balanced' Constitution', *HJ*, 13 (1970), 571–588.
— *Politics, Finance, and the People: Economical Reform in England in the Age of the American Revolution, 1770–1792* (Basingstoke, 2007).
Riley, P. W. J., *The English Ministers and Scotland 1707–1727* (London, 1964).
Roberts, Clayton, 'The Constitutional Significance of the Financial Settlement of 1690', *HJ*, 20 (1977), 59–76.
Rodger, N. A. M. 'Honour and Duty at Sea, 1660–1815'. *Historical Research*, 75 (2002), 425–47.
— *The Command of the Ocean. A Naval History of Britain 1649–1815* (London, 2004).
Rogers, Nicholas, 'Confronting the Crime Wave: The Debate over Social Reform and Regulation, 1749–1753', in Davison, Hitchcock, Keirn, Shoemaker (eds), *Stilling the Grumbling Hive*, pp. 77–98.
— *Crowds, Culture, and Politics in Georgian Britain* (Oxford, 1998).
— *Mayhem: Post-War Crime and Violence in Britain, 1748–53* (New Haven/London, 2012).
— *The Press Gang: Naval Impressment and its Opponents in Georgian Britain* (London, 2007).
— 'The Sea Fencibles, Loyalism and the Reach of the State', in Mark Philp (ed.), *Resisting Napoleon. The British Response to the Threat of Invasion, 1797–1815* (Aldershot, 2006), pp. 41–60.
Rose, Craig, *England in the 1690s: Revolution, Religion and War* (Oxford, 1999).
Roseveare, Henry, *The Treasury 1660–1870: The Foundations of Control* (London, 1973).
Rössner, Philipp Robinson, *Scottish Trade in the Wake of Union (1700–1760): The Rise of a Warehouse Economy* (Stuttgart, 2008).
Rule, John, 'Social Crime in the Rural South in the Eighteenth and Early Nineteenth Centuries', in John Rule, Roger Wells (eds), *Crime, Protest, and Popular Politics in Southern England, 1740–1850* (London, 1997), pp. 153–168.
Rutz, Andreas, *Die Beschreibung des Raums. Territoriale Grenzziehungen im Heiligen Römischen Reich* (Köln/Weimar/Wien, 2018).
Scarlett, Bernhard, *Shipminder: The Story of Her Majesty's Coastguard* (London, 1971).
Scholz, Luca, *Borders and Freedom of Movement in the Holy Roman Empire* (Oxford, 2020).

Schultz, Jenna M., *National Identity and the Anglo-Scottish Borderlands, 1552–1652* (Woodbridge, 2019).
Schwoerer, Lois G., *'No Standing Armies!' The Antiarmy Ideology in Seventeenth-Century England* (Baltimore, 1974).
— 'The Role of King William III of England in the Standing Army Controversy', *JBS*, 5 (1966), 74–94.
Scott, Jonathan, *When the Waves Ruled Britannia: Geography and Political Identities, 1500–1800* (Cambridge, 2011).
Shakespeare, William, *Richard II*. Edited by Anthony B. Dawson, Paul Yachnin (Oxford, 2011).
Sharma, Yogesh (ed.), *Coastal Histories. Society and Ecology in pre-Modern India* (Delhi, 2010).
Sharpe, J. A., *Crime in Early Modern England 1550–1750* (London, 1984).
— 'Enforcing the Law in the Seventeenth-Century English Village', in V. A. C. Gatrell, Bruce Lenman, Geoffrey Parker (eds), *Crime and the Law: The Social History of Crime in Western Europe since 1500* (London, 1980), pp. 97–119.
Shaw, Keith, 'Bringing the Anglo-Scottish Border "Back in": Reassessing Cross-Border Relations in the Context of Greater Scottish Autonomy', *Journal of Borderlands Studies*, 33 (2018), 1–18.
Shepard, Alexandra, Phil Withington (eds), *Communities in Early Modern England: Networks, Place, Rhetoric* (Manchester, 2000).
Shoemaker, Robert B., *Prosecution and Punishment: Petty Crime and the Law in London and Rural Middlesex, c.1660–1725* (Cambridge, 1991)
— *The London Mob: Violence and Disorder in Eighteenth-Century England* (London, 2004).
Singer, Christoph, *Sea Change: The Shore from Shakespeare to Banville* (Leiden, 2014).
Skinner, Andrew S., 'Economic Theory', in Alexander Broadie (ed.), *The Cambridge Companion to the Scottish Enlightenment* (Cambridge, 2003), pp. 178–204.
Smith, Bruce P., 'English Criminal Justice Administration, 1650–1850: A Historiographic Essay', *Law and History Review*, 25/3 (2007), 593–634.
Smith, Graham, *King's Cutters: The Revenue Service and the War against Smuggling* (London, 1983).
— *Something to Declare: 1000 Years of Customs and Excise* (London, 1980).
Soothill, Eric, Michael J. Thomas, *The Natural History of Britain's Coasts* (London, 1987).
Sparrow, E., 'The Alien Office, 1792–1806', *HJ*, 33 (1990), 361–384.
Stephens, William B., *The Seventeenth-Century Customs Service Surveyed: William Culliford's Investigation of the Western Ports, 1682–84* (Farnham, 2012).
Stock, Paul (ed.), *The Uses of Space in Early Modern History* (London, 2015).

Stone, Lawrence (ed.), *An Imperial State at War: Britain 1689–1815* (London, 1994).
Storrs, Christopher (ed.), *The Fiscal-Military State in Eighteenth-Century Europe: Essays in Honour of P.G.M. Dickson* (Farnham, 2009).
Styles, John, 'Print and Policing: Crime Advertising in Eighteenth-Century Provincial England', in Hay, Snyder (eds), *Policing and Prosecution*, pp. 55–112.
Sweeting, Spike, 'Policing the Ports: The Regional Dimensions of Eighteenth-Century Customs Activity in England and Wales', *Bulletin of the German Historical Institute London*, 40 (2018), 32–67.
Sybill, Jack, 'Customs, Tobacco and Smuggling in South-Western Scotland', *Journal of the Sydney Society for Scottish History*, 2 (1994), 52–75.
Thompson, E. P., *Customs in Common* (London, 1991).
— 'The Crime of Anonymity', in Hay, Linebaugh, Rule, Thompson, Winslow (eds), *Albion's Fatal Tree*, p.p. 255–344.
— *Whigs and Hunters: The Origin of the Black Act* (London 1975).
Thomson, A., 'Louis XIV and the Origins of the War of the Spanish Succession', *Transactions of the Royal Historical Society*, 5th ser., 4 (1954), 111–34.
Timmons, Stephen A., 'The Customs Service in the West Country, 1671–1692', *The Mariner's Mirror*, 92 (2006), 148–167.
Turner, Michael J., *The Age of Unease: Government and Reform in Britain, 1782–1832* (Stroud, 2000).
Viles, Heather, Tom Spencer, *Coastal Problems* (London, 1995).
Waddell, Brodie, 'The Economic Crisis of the 1690s in England', *HJ*, 66 (2023), 281–302
— 'The Politics of Economic Distress in the Aftermath of the Glorious Revolution, 1689–1702', *HER*, 130 (2015), 318–351.
Waddell, Brodie, Jason Peacey (eds), *The Power of Petitioning in Early Modern Britain* (London, 2024).
Wallace, Valerie, 'Presbyterian Moral Economy. The Covenanting Tradition and Popular Protest in Lowland Scotland, 1707–c.1746', *SHR*, 89 (2010), 54–72.
Walsh, Patrick, 'Enforcing the Fiscal State: The Army, the Revenue and the Irish Experience of the Fiscal-Military State, 1690–1769', in Graham, Walsh (eds), *Fiscal-Military States*, pp. 131–158.
— 'Patterns of Taxation in Eighteenth-Century Ireland', in Douglas Kanter, Patrick Walsh (eds), *Taxation, Politics, and Protest in Ireland, 1662–2016* (Cham, 2019), pp. 89–119.
— 'The Fiscal State in Ireland, 1691–1769', *HJ*, 56/3 (2013), 629–656.
— *The Making of the Irish Protestant Ascendancy: The Life of William Conolly, 1662–1729* (Woodbridge, 2010).
— 'The Sin of With-Holding Tribute, Contemporary Pamphlets and the Professionalisation of the Irish Revenue Service in the Early Eighteenth Century', *Eighteenth Century Ireland*, 21 (2006), 48–65.

Walter, John, '"Law-Mindedness": Crowds, Courts and Popular Knowledge of the Law in Early Modern England', in Michael Lobban, Joanne Begatio, Adrian Green (eds), *Law, Lawyers and Litigants in Early Modern England. Essay in memory of Christopher W. Brooks* (Cambridge, 2019), pp. 164–184.

Walton, John K., *The English Seaside Resort: A Social History 1750–1914* (Leicester, 1983).

— 'Coastal resorts and cultural Exchange in Europe, 1780–1870', in Peter Borsay, Jan Hein Furnée (eds), *Leisure Cultures in Urban Europa, c.1700–1870. A Transnational Perspective* (Manchester, 2016), pp. 260–277.

Ward, W. R., 'Some Eighteenth Century Civil Servants: The English Revenue Commissioners, 1754–98', *EHR*, 70/274 (1955), 25–54.

Warner, Jessica, Frank Ivis, '"Damn You, You Informing Bitch". Vox Populi and the Unmaking of the Gin Act of 1736', *Journal of Social History*, 33 (1999), 299–330.

Warner, Jessica, Frank Ivis, 'Informers and Their Social Networks in Eighteenth-Century London: A Comparison of Two Communities', *Social Science History*, 25 (2001), 563–587.

Waugh, Mary, *Smuggling in Kent and Sussex 1700–1840* (Newbury, 1985).

Webb, William, *Coastguard: An Official History of H. M. Coastguard* (London, 1976).

Weil, Rachel, *A Plague of Informers: Conspiracy and Political Trust in William III's England* (New Haven & London, 2013).

Wenzlhuemer, Roland, *Connecting the Nineteenth-Century World: The Telegraph and Globalization* (Cambridge, 2012).

Whatley, C. A., 'Economic Causes and Consequences of the Union of 1707', *SHR*, 68 (1989), 150–181.

— *Scottish Society 1707–1830: Beyond Jacobitism, towards Industrialisation* (Manchester and New York, 2000).

Wilkins, Frances, *The Isle of Man in Smuggling History* (Kidderminster, 1992).

Willan, T. S., *The English Coasting Trade, 1600–1750* (Manchester, 1976).

Williams, Fiona (ed.), *Locating Agency: Space, Power and Popular Politics* (Newcastle-upon-Tyne, 2010).

Williams, Neville, *Contraband Cargoes: Seven Centuries of Smuggling* (London, 1959).

Willis, Kirk, 'The Role in Parliament of the Economic Ideas of Adam Smith, 1776–1800', *History of Political Economy*, 11.4 (1979), 505–544.

Wilson, Charles, *England's Apprenticeship 1603–1763* (London, 1965).

Wilson, Kathleen, *The Island Race. Englishness, Empire and Gender in the Eighteenth Century* (London, 2003).

Wilson, Thomas H., Hastings Donnan (eds), *A Companion to Border Studies* (London, 2012).

Winslow, Cal, 'Sussex Smugglers', in Hay, Linebaugh, Rule, Thompson, Winslow (eds), *Albion's Fatal* Tree, pp. 119–66.

Withington, Phil, *The Politics of Commonwealth: Citizens and Freemen in Early Modern England* (Cambridge, 2005).

Wood, Andy, *Riot, Rebellion and Popular Politics in Early Modern England* (Basingstoke, 2002).
Worthington, David, 'Ferries in the Firthlands: Communications, Society and Culture along a Northern Scottish Rural Coast, c. 1600 to c. 1809', *Rural History*, 27 (2016), 129–148.
— 'Introducing the New Coastal History: Cultural and Environmental Perspectives from Scotland and Beyond', in Worthington (ed.), *New Coastal History*, pp. 3–30.
— (ed.), *The New Coastal History: Cultural and Environmental Perspectives from Scotland and Beyond* (London, 2017).
Wrightson, Keith, *English Society 1580–1680* (London, 1982).
— 'The Politics of the Parish in Early Modern England', in Griffiths, Fox, Hindle (eds), *The Experience of Authority*, pp. 10–46.
— 'Two Concepts of Order: Justices, Constables and Jurymen in Seventeenth-Century England', in John Brewer and John Styles (eds), *An Ungovernable People: The English and their Law in the Seventeenth and Eighteenth Centuries* (New Brunswick, NJ, 1980), pp. 21–46.
Ziegler, Hannes, 'Competition in Coastal Water: Customs Sloops and Admiralty Cruisers in Eighteenth-Century Britain', *Journal for Maritime Research*, 23/1 (2021), 1–17.
— 'Cultures of the Edge? The Place of the Coast in Maritime Historiographies of Britain', *German Historical Institute London Bulletin*, 40 (2018), 68–90.
— 'Customs Officers and Local Communities: Informing in Late Seventeenth-Century England', in Martín Romera, Ziegler (eds), *Officer and the People*, pp. 325–348.
— 'Smuggling and the Customs Administration in Post-Union Scotland, c.1707–1724', SHR, 103 (2024), 436–458.
— 'The Preventive Idea of Coastal Policing. Vigilance and Enforcement in the Eighteenth-Century British Customs', *Storia della Storiografia*, 74 (2018), 75–98.
— '"This Monstrous Scheme": Die Idee eines nationalen Wollregisters im Großbritannien des 18. Jahrhunderts und die Grenzen des Merkantilismus', *Vierteljahrschrift für Sozial- und Wirtschaftsgeschichte*, 111 (2024), 6–34.
— '"Very Prejudicial to the Service of the Revenue": The British Army on Coastal Duty in Eighteenth-Century East Anglia', *British Journal for Military History*, 7/1 (2021), 46–63.

Unpublished Theses

Appleby, John C., 'English Privateering during the Spanish and French Wars, 1625–1630' (Diss. University of Hull, 1983).
Berryman, Kimberley, 'Great Britain and the French Refugees 1789–1802' (Diss. Australian National University, 1980).

Egan, Seán, 'Finance and the Government of Ireland, 1660–1685' (Diss. University of Dublin, 1983).
Ferguson, Catherine, 'Law and Order on the Anglo-Scottish Border 1603–1707' (Diss. St Andrews, 1981).
Hattendorf, John B., 'England in the War of the Spanish Succession' (Diss. University of Oxford, 1979).
Hopkins, Paul, 'Aspects of Jacobite Conspiracy in England in the Reign of William III' (Diss. Cambridge, 1981).
Limprecht, Joseph A., 'Common Informers and Law Enforcement in England, 1603–1640' (Diss. Berkeley, 1975).
McGrath, Charles Ivar, 'The Irish Revenue System: Government and Administration, 1689–1702' (Diss. University of London, 1997).
Muskett, Paul, 'English Smuggling in the Eighteenth Century' (Diss. Open University, 1996).
Rule, John G., 'The Labouring Miner in Cornwall, c.1740–1870. A Study in Social History' (Diss. University of Warwick, 1971).
Sweeting, Spike, 'Capitalism, the State and Things: The Port of London, circa 1730–1800' (Diss. Univ. of Warwick, 2014).

Index

Aberdeen 68 n.88, 69, 94, 138, 153, 202, 217 n.50
Admiralty 36, 44, 45, 67, 75, 101–2, 141–3, 227–47, 252–6
Alderney 87, 236
Alien Office 228
American Revolutionary War 216
Annan 92, 192
Arran, Isle of 87, 170
Assizes 146, 191, 192
Austrian War of Succession 216

Baker, Henry 39–40, 42, 44–5, 50, 62, 76, 114, 117, 120, 122, 150, 163
Bank of England 29
Beachy Head 32
Beaumaris 43, 63, 83, 87, 138 n.246, 217
Belfast 77, 78
Bentick, William, 1st Earl of Portland 35, 37
Berwick 62, 66, 71, 235
Bishopp, Cecil 176
Board of Ordnance 226
Board of Trade 40, 44, 75, 222, 252
Boulogne 210 n.15, 233
brandy 51, 54, 57, 78, 179, 209
Brent, Humphrey 69
Bridlington 43, 63
Bristol 92, 151, 164
Bute, Isle of 87
Butler, James 2nd Duke of Ormond 75

Canterbury 42
Cardiff 86, 93, 164, 218
Carlisle 43, 62–3, 71, 93, 235
Carter, William 22–7, 33–4, 37, 43, 44, 47, 181
Channel 7, 8, 32, 85, 227, 229
Charles II of Spain 45
Charles II 22, 27, 54, 182
Cherbourg 236
Cheshire 64, 82
Chester 63
Chichester 62, 163, 194, 201, 232
Christ's Hospital, London 25
Churchill, John, 1st Duke of Marlborough 105
Clarkesse, Charles 120
Coast Blockade 232, 239–41, 246, 255
coastguard 206, 232–48, 250–6
Collier, John 121–2, 163, 176, 190–1
collusion 44, 95, 116, 149, 169, 177–80, 182, 245
Connaught 77, 78
constable 134, 138–9
Conway, Henry Seymour 216
Cork 77
Cornwall 56, 64, 82, 106, 141, 176, 184, 235
corruption 11, 42–3, 66–8, 111–12, 159, 189, 209–10, 224–5
Cowes 58, 59, 132, 217, 218, 232
Crimean War 252
Cromer 56, 191
Culliford, William 163
Cumberland 64, 82, 88
Cumbria 184

Deal 62, 109
Declaration of Rights 28, 30
deputations 46, 68, 104, 115

292 Index

deserter   110 n.59
Devereux, Walter   42–3, 44 n.175, 118, 167
Devon   43, 56, 63, 64, 141
Dorset   63, 64, 92, 110, 134, 139, 141
Dover   28, 29, 36, 37, 62, 107, 109, 110, 215
dual officeholding   72–3, 104
Dublin   77, 78, 230
Dukes of Atholl   81, 85–6
Dumfries   69, 71, 83, 86, 90, 93, 138, 140
Dungeness   37, 229
Dunkirk   210 n.15

Earls of Derby   81, 85
East Anglia   45
East India Company   182, 208
Edinburgh   69, 71, 94
elections, parliamentary   105, 176
Elizabeth I   7
embargo   38, 102, 106–7
Essex   32, 64, 141, 229, 230
Exchequer   11, 24, 130–2, 145 n.300, 147, 150, 151
Excise   17–19, 29, 41, 44, 62, 66, 72, 73, 98, 100, 117, 148, 154, 211, 216, 222, 238, 258
Exeter   63, 87, 150, 218

Falmouth   63, 184
fees   103, 213–14, 234
Finch, Daniel, 2nd Earl of Nottingham   34, 35, 36, 37, 39
First Wold War   252
Firth of Clyde   66, 69
Firth of Forth   66, 69
Fitzmaurice, William Petty, 1st Marquess of Lansdowne, Earl of Shelburne   216, 219, 220
Flamborough Head   56, 142
Flanders   210 n.15
Folkestone   109, 164, 166
Foreign Office   227

George I   54, 56
Glasgow   69, 70, 236
Glorious Revolution   30
Godolphin, Sidney, 1st Earl of Godolphin   38–9, 41, 47, 64, 68
Gravesend   35, 62, 63, 215
Great Yarmouth   58, 60, 61, 91, 103, 107, 114, 121, 123, 127, 136, 146, 165, 183, 191, 193, 202, 214, 218, 233
Greenwich Hospital   102
Guernsey   55, 87, 236

Hampshire   63, 64, 141, 197
Happisburgh   165
Harley, Robert, 1st Earl of Oxford   68
Haynes, John   46–8
Henry V   81
Henry VIII   7
Home Office   225, 227, 228, 230, 250
Huguenots   40
Hunter, William   133

informer/informing   186–93
Inverness   66, 68, 69, 70
Irish Revenue Board   75, 100
Irish Sea   75, 78, 81, 209, 215
Isle of Man   54, 61, 64, 81–8, 91, 215, 239
Isle of Portland   95
Isle of Sheppey   62
Isle of Skye   66
Isle of Wight   62, 63

Jacobitism   28, 32–40, 45
James II   20–1, 27, 32, 43, 45
Jersey   55, 87, 209 n.15
Justice of the Peace   36, 55, 57, 58, 67, 107, 130, 135, 139, 194, 197

Kent   24, 25, 28, 32, 36, 39, 40, 43–5, 51, 55, 58, 62–4, 104, 105, 113, 118–21, 141, 144, 161, 163, 181, 197, 229, 232, 239, 255

Index

Kingston, Richard   34–7, 39, 41
Knox, Thomas   75–6, 181

Lancaster   63, 64
land tax   29
Land's End   235
Lennox, Charles, 2nd Duke of Richmond   155–7, 171, 174, 176, 193–203, 221
Lincolnshire   63
Lisle, Warren   150, 163, 212
Liverpool   151, 253
Lizard Point   56
Locke, John   75
Lutwidge, Charles   82, 86
Lydd   197, 198

Macky, John   37
Martello Towers   216, 230, 231, 252, 261
Mary II   17, 30, 53
Maryport (=Ellenfoot)   139, 166, 168
McCulloch, William   232, 239
Medcalfe, George   150
Metropolitan Police   251
Milford   43
militia   36, 147 n.315, 199, 229, 230
Moray Firth   93, 94
Munster   77, 78
Musgrave, William   111–12, 121, 214, 219, 224, 235

Napoleon Bonaparte   226–7, 229, 236
Navigation Acts   14, 38, 71, 73, 101, 208, 212, 234, 247
Newcastle   43, 63, 71, 109, 217, 218
Nine Years' War   20, 26, 32, 73, 74, 216
Norfolk   56, 60, 63, 64, 106, 109, 134, 140, 141, 175, 183, 191
Northumberland   64
Norwich   62, 135, 161, 191

Old Bailey   172, 174, 180, 184, 198
Ordinary of Newgate   174

packet service   37, 102, 110, 228
patronage   11, 41, 66 n.123, 101, 104–6, 111, 205
Pelham, Henry   194, 197, 201
Pelham, Henry, Duke of Newcastle   176, 194, 197 n.253, 199 n.269
Penzance   63, 185, 217, 218
Peterhead   70, 94, 124 n.170
Pitt, William   219, 220, 223, 224, 236
Plymouth   63, 92, 124, 184, 228, 229
Poole   92, 95, 155, 194, 196, 218
Portsmouth   62, 90, 217, 228, 229
post office   38, 228
Prawle Point   56
press gangs/impressment   38, 102, 110, 143 n.284, 204, 231, 234
Prestonpans   68
preventive service
   dismissal   43, 123, 129, 178
   journals   119–29
   oaths   112, 115
   origin   17–52
   qualifications   112–16
   rolling procedure   117–19
   salaries   44, 123, 162–3, 213, 244
   seizure   129–53
   sureties   112, 115, 161
   writs of assistance   134
Privy Council   27, 33, 36, 46, 55, 101, 102, 106, 107, 141
prosecutions   61, 66, 105, 130–7, 145–50, 177, 182, 192, 201
prosecutions, malicious/vexatious   129, 135–7, 139, 167
public houses   62, 118, 167, 175

quarantine   38, 102, 106–7, 234, 237
Quarter Sessions   135

Restoration   20, 55, 71, 73

Rigby, Alexander   67, 164
Romney Marsh   55, 62, 109, 229, 230
Rose, George   236–7, 243, 246
Royal Military Canal   230
Royal Navy   69, 84, 105, 110, 141–3, 148, 231–4, 247, 250, 252
Rye   109
Ryswick, Peace of   45, 48

Sandgate   42, 198
Saxby, John   144
Scarborough   109
Scilly, Isles of   87
Scottish Borders   43, 45, 47–8, 51, 55, 62, 119
sea fencibles   230–1
shipwrecks   102, 106, 176, 256
sinecures   11, 100, 101, 103, 104, 234
Smith, Adam   221–3
Solway Firth   66, 85, 92, 93
Southampton   54, 62, 95, 126, 194, 195
Southwold   167
Spanish War of Succession   51, 216
Stiles, William   59
Stock, Abraham   36–7
Stockton   145, 217, 218
Suffolk   66, 109, 141, 230
Sussex   24, 25, 28, 32, 39, 43, 33, 45, 48, 51, 55, 58, 62–4, 105, 118, 118–20, 141, 144, 163, 167, 176, 181, 190, 194, 197, 229, 232, 239, 255

Talbot, Charles, 1st Duke of Shrewsbury   35, 39

tea   51, 54, 57, 78, 132, 194, 208, 223
Thames   99, 229
tobacco   51, 54, 69–70, 78, 208, 209, 210, 242, 253, 254
Tomkins, Gabriel   185–6
Trenchard, John   35
Trumbull, William   35, 37, 39, 48

Ulster   77–8
Union of 1707   64–7, 70, 71, 119, 181
Upton, Richard   184–5

vagrancy   54, 55, 57
Vernon, Edward   143, 171

Walpole, Robert   69, 108, 132, 176, 181–2, 183, 210, 212, 216, 219, 220
War Office   101, 141–2, 144
West Country   26, 46
Weymouth   63, 92, 95, 114, 121, 134, 138, 140, 150, 165, 177, 202, 218
Whitehaven   63, 64, 69, 82, 83, 84, 85, 87, 93, 110, 128, 136, 184, 189, 192, 218
Whitstable   42, 62
William III   17, 19, 28, 30–3, 35, 36, 38–40
Wiltshire   179
wool register   55, 212 n.25
wrecking   2, 8

Yorkshire   56, 64

Studies in the Eighteenth Century
ISSN: 2398-9904

This major series from Boydell & Brewer, published in association with the British Society for Eighteenth-Century Studies, aims to bring into fruitful dialogue the different disciplines involved in all aspects of the study of the long eighteenth century (c.1660–1820). It publishes innovative volumes, singly or co-authored, on any topic in history, science, music, literature and the visual arts in any area of the world in the long eighteenth century and particularly encourages proposals that explore links among the disciplines, and which aim to develop new cross-disciplinary fields of enquiry.

Series editors: Ros Ballaster, University of Oxford, UK; Helen Berry, University of Exeter, UK; Matthew Grenby, Newcastle University, UK; Mark Knights, University of Warwick, UK

Previously published

Material Enlightenment: Women Writers and the Science of Mind, 1770–1830, Joanna Wharton, 2018

Celebrity Culture and the Myth of Oceania in Britain, 1770–1823, Ruth Scobie, 2019

British Sociability in the Long Eighteenth Century: Challenging the Anglo-French Connection, edited by Valérie Capdeville and Alain Kerhervé, 2019

Things that Didn't Happen: Writing, Politics and the Counterhistorical, 1678–1743, John McTague, 2019

Converting Britannia: Evangelicals and British Public Life, 1770–1840, Gareth Atkins, 2019

British Catholic Merchants in the Commercial Age, 1670–1714, Giada Pizzoni, 2020

Lessons of Travel in Eighteenth-Century France: From Grand Tour to School Trips, Gábor Gelléri, 2020

Political Journalism in London, 1695–1720: Defoe, Swift, Steele and their Contemporaries, Ashley Marshall, 2020

Fictions of Presence: Theatre and Novel in Eighteenth-Century Britain, Ros Ballaster, 2020

Ephemeral Print Culture in Early Modern England, Tim Somers, 2021

The Geographies of Enlightenment Edinburgh, Phil Dodds, 2022

Changing Pedagogies for Children in Eighteenth-Century England, Michèle Cohen, 2023

Transnational Women Writers in the Wilmot Coterie, 1798–1840: Beyond Borders and Boundaries, Alexis Wolf, 2024

Administrative Reform in Late Eighteenth-Century Britain and its Empire: A System of Economy, Sebastian Meurer, 2025

Printed in the United States
by Baker & Taylor Publisher Services